CAPTURING THE COMPLEXITY OF CONFLICT

CAPTURING THE COMPLEXITY OF CONFLICT

Dealing with Violent Ethnic Conflicts of the Post-Cold War Era

DENNIS J. D. SANDOLE

Foreword by Christopher R. Mitchell

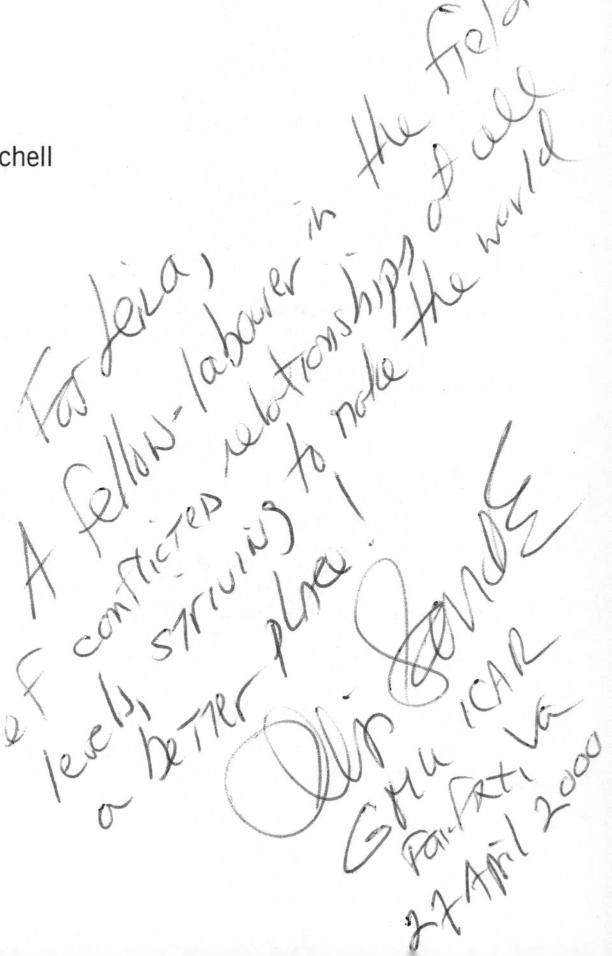
A fellow-labourer in the field
of conflicted relationships at all
levels, striving to make the world
a better place!
GMU ICAR
Fairfax VA
27 April 2000

PINTER

London and New York

PINTER
A Cassell imprint
Wellington House, 125 Strand, London WC2R 0BB
370 Lexington Avenue, New York, NY 10017-6550

First published 1999

British Library Cataloguing-in-Publication Data
A catalogue record for this book is available from the British Library.

ISBN 1-85567-618-4 (hardback)
1-85567-619-2 (paperback)

Library of Congress Cataloging-in-Publication Data
Sandole, Dennis J. D., 1941–
Capturing the complexity of conflict: dealing with violent ethnic conflicts in the post-Cold War era / by Dennis J. D. Sandole; foreword by Christopher R. Mitchell.
p. cm.
Includes bibliographical references (p.) and index.
ISBN 1–85567–618–4 (Hardback). — ISBN 1–85567–619–2 (Paperback)
1. Social conflict. 2. Social conflict—Simulation methods. 3. Conflict management. 4. Pacific settlement of international disputes. 5. Ethnic relations. 6. War. I. Title.
HM136.S245 1999
303.6—dc21 99–11397
CIP

Typeset by York House Typographic Ltd, London
Printed and bound in Great Britain by Biddles Ltd, Guildford & King's Lynn

Contents

List of Tables

Foreword

The Institute for Conflict Analysis and Resolution (ICAR) was originally established as an academic center at George Mason University in Virginia, but the intentions of its founders were rather different from those underlying the setting up of many other university research institutions. Quite deliberately, one of the stated tasks of the Institute was to develop theories about the origins, dynamics and ending of conflicts, but to ensure that this would be relevant and usable theory, so that the actual practice of conflict resolution – by ICAR members and others – could be informed by the latest ideas about how conflicts developed and how they might best be resolved. In the words of one of the pioneers of our field, Kurt Lewin, the conception was to produce useful intellectual tools for "practical theorists."

My colleague, Dennis Sandole, was one of the first scholars to be appointed to the faculty of the Institute, and *Capturing the Complexity of Conflict* is the third book he has published under its auspices. As such, it is an admirable fulfillment of the wishes of the founders of the Institute, in that it combines broad and formidable scholarship with a consideration of some of the practical implications of its findings and a number of recommendations for future action, especially as regards the growing number of violent and intractable intra-society conflicts that have, in the past decade, emerged from a latent condition to make a mockery of any ideas about the ending of history. *Capturing the Complexity of Conflict* is thus as much about the Bosnias, the Northern Irelands, the Somalias and the Nagorno Karabakhs of this world as it is about the Kuwaits, the Falklands/Malvinas or the Peru/Ecuador border dispute.

One of the great strengths of the book is the way in which the author uses a variety of approaches ("triangulation," in the fashionable phrase) to throw light on the reasons for wars – and other forms of large-scale and violent conflicts – starting, escalating and continuing for long periods of time. (The latter is a particularly important aspect of this work, as Sandole helps to illuminate the psycho-social dynamics which operate to ensure that conflicts persist over generations, and how they can be revived from a dormant condition by leaders who – for their own reasons – know how to manipulate the right signs, symbols and historical memories.) Sandole surveys the disparate literature on wars, both empirical and theoretical, in developing a three-level taxonomy of types of explanation for the onset and continuation of wars and civil strife – decision-making, societal and trans-societal levels. The taxonomy draws upon but elaborates and improves Kenneth Waltz's familiar three images of the origins of war, but it includes much of the recent work by scholars such as, for example, Volkan and Kelman on the psychodynamics of conflict, and it enables the author to develop a 23-variable model of key influences on large-scale human conflict.

Sandole then recounts and analyzes data from a series of simulations based upon the somewhat misleadingly named *Prisoners' Dilemma Simulation* (itself an elaboration of such large-scale role-playing simulations as Guetzkow's *Inter-nation Simulation* and Smoker's *International Process Simulation*), mounting en route a vigorous and convincing defense of the use of simulation to incorporate empirically based theories of conflict into increasingly complex models; and to provide an alternative and additional check on the relevance and validity of those theories. He then matches the findings from the simulation series with empirical data available from comparative studies of wars from that of Quincy Wright (1942) onward, and highlights areas of strong agreement between and within both sets of evidence.

In this part of the work, some of the most interesting findings have to do with the way in which different variables come into play (and have a major impact) at different developmental stages of conflicts, with the implication that we need alternative theories (and hence remedies) for understanding the dynamics of conflicts depending upon whether we are dealing with the escalatory or continuity stages of a dispute. Another interesting and counter-intuitive argument put forward by Sandole, but supported by his data and much other evidence, is the relatively low influence of decision-making variables once the conflict has become protracted and developed dynamics of its own that resist efforts to ameliorate, manage or resolve it. This contrast between "conflict as start up" and "conflict as process" is one which has been hinted at in much of the literature, but Sandole's discussion of the difference is both thorough and persuasive.

For practitioners, however, the most interesting part of *Capturing the Complexity of Conflict* will be the concluding chapters, in which Sandole takes his theoretical findings back into the real world of the 1990s – mainly Europe of the 1990s – and investigates how our best theories about the dynamics of protracted conflicts might be used in order to remove the causes of such conflict while they remain in their dormant state ("provention" rather than prevention in a term he has borrowed from John Burton). He carries out a thorough survey of the origins and development of the Organization for Security and Co-operation in Europe (OSCE), with its emphasis on "confidence- and security-building measures," and argues for the strengthening of its conflict resolution capacities, especially in a pre-emptive mode. Perhaps this is the least persuasive part of the book, knowing the speed with which most intergovernmental institutions adapt themselves, and the OSCE's record to date in places such as the former Yugoslavia is not impressive. However, Sandole is realist enough (with a small "r") to acknowledge the OSCE's shortcomings and to argue for a more complex approach to conflict resolution. This involves the coordinated use of an array of institutions and processes tailored to the need to deal with an equally complex array of factors that ensure the continuation of violent conflicts. What he calls a New European Peace and Security System (NEPSS) involves efforts by governments, international governmental organizations (such as OSCE, an expanded NATO and the Council of Europe), development and aid agencies, unofficial "Track 2" interveners and human rights organizations to work in a coordinated manner – "integrated systems of conflict resolution networks" – in order to deal with the complex of psychological, social, political and economic variables that move a conflict from a dormant to a manifest stage and continue to drive it once the "conflict as start up" stage is passed. There is a great deal here that is worth practical consideration, but the great strength of Sandole's argument is that it is based in the "best findings" of his – and many others' – theoretical answers to the question: why do wars start up and why do they persist and protract over time?

In summary, *Capturing the Complexity of Conflict* is a work combining an impressive grasp of a wide range of literature concerned with the phenomenon of large-scale human conflict with some practical ideas for how research findings might be used to do something to mitigate conflict's worst excesses and – in the best of circumstances – prevent overt conflicts developing at all. It is one of those rare things, a hopeful book about war and the human propensity to engage in this activity, besides being scholarly, comprehensive and practical. The work fully deserves to be widely read by audiences within – but more importantly outside – academia, and I am delighted to have been asked to provide its Foreword.

C. R. Mitchell
French-Cumbie Professor of International Conflict Analysis and Resolution
Institute for Conflict Analysis and Resolution
George Mason University
Fairfax, Virginia

Preface

The study reported here – the *Genesis of War* project – began some years ago as a simulation-based study of the causes of war, leading to, among other things, a doctoral dissertation (Sandole, 1979a). A veritable research odyssey, it has evolved over the years to include the development and application of a *generic theory* of violent conflict and war to more effectively understand and deal with the violent ethnic warfare of the post-Cold War world, e.g. the wars in former Yugoslavia. It was, and remains, a reaction to an overwhelming tendency, particularly (but not only) in quantitative international relations, to study complex conflicts in terms of bivariate bits and pieces.

Rather than yield to one ("fashionable") reaction to this state of affairs, and throw the "positivist baby" out with the bathwater, this study has attempted to capture the *complexity* of complex conflicts by, among other things, identifying multidisciplinary variables at various levels; studying their impact on conflict at successive stages within dynamic behavioral systems generated by gaming-simulation; subjecting the models of complex conflicts generated by simulation to comprehensive real-world (and other lab/sim) *validation* assessments; and, in general, reflecting agreement with Michael Nicholson (1996, p. 3) that:

> We desperately need answers to questions such as why there are wars. However, if we cannot recognize an answer when we see one, or doubt we can have such an answer even in principle, then we are in serious trouble.

Since this research journey began some time ago, when it was more fashionable to employ gaming-simulation as a methodological tool in the field of international relations, it refers to sources published at different times throughout that period. Hence, as befits a research odyssey, there is a co-mingling of "older" and "newer" references. However, in contrast to the otherwise "post-modern" style of storytelling employed here (about an essentially "modernist" project), these combine with other elements of the study to produce a coherent narrative: one which may auger well for a renaissance in the use of gaming-simulation in the analysis and resolution of complex conflict processes.

The study is not intended to be exhaustive, in terms of either covering all disciplines or covering all variables that any one discipline might have to offer in mapping, modelling, and responding to the etiology of violent conflict and war. More importantly than "covering it all," which would have added considerably to an already lengthy tome, this study is a potential theoretical/methodological exemplar – a *research paradigm* – of how complex conflicts, particularly in the post-Cold War world, might be analyzed as a necessary precondition to doing something about them.

Since the launching of this project, the very phenomenon which gave rise to it – the ideological *jihad* of the Cold War, with its specter of thermonuclear annihilation – has come to an end: the Berlin Wall, the Warsaw Pact, the Soviet Union, and Communism in Eastern Europe and in the former Soviet Union have all been relegated to history, leaving a reunified Germany and multiple aspiring democracies in their wake. Nevertheless, many wars and other violent conflicts have come and some have even gone, with few if any appropriate institutions for dealing with them, all against the background of the continuing threat of thermonuclear war and other massive assaults to the global "commons." Among the wars of the post-Cold War period, those in former Yugoslavia stand out for a number of reasons, e.g. as a metaphor for the return of war and genocide to Europe and as a model of wars yet to come.

Over the course of time that I have worked on the project, I have endeavored to examine the "fit" between my experimental data and the real world of violent conflict and war. It has only been during the wars of the post-Cold War era, however, that I felt compelled to contribute meaningfully to theory development, on the causes, conditions and perpetuation of violent conflict and war, not as an abstract exercise, but as a basis for dealing with the ethnic warfare in former Yugoslavia and elsewhere: to design a peace and security system that could prevent "future Yugoslavias."

I leave it to the reader to determine the "goodness-of-fit" between the theory developed here and the violent ethnic conflict and warfare of the post-Cold War world.

Dennis J. D. Sandole
Institute for Conflict Analysis and Resolution
George Mason University
Fairfax, Virginia

Acknowledgments

Since 1993, I have been fortunate to spend up to four weeks each year at the Austrian Study Center for Peace and Conflict Resolution (ASPR) and European University Center for Peace Studies (EPU), at Stadtschlaining, Austria. I also enjoyed a six-month sabbatical there during January–August 1996. These visits helped considerably in completing this volume, not only because I was teaching courses relevant to it (e.g. ethnic conflict and conflict resolution in former Yugoslavia), sometimes to students from the conflict areas themselves, but also because of the proximity to the "front" not just of the two world wars of this century but also of the ethnic warfare still occurring, or threatening to occur, in parts of post-Cold War Europe.

More importantly, perhaps, Stadtschlaining provided me with blocks of time to work for sustained periods and to "whip the manuscript into shape," a process which came close to reaching culmination during the closing days of the sabbatical. For this, I am grateful to ASPR and EPU at Stadtschlaining – to Dr Gerald and Frau Gertrude Mader, Dr Josef Binter, Arno Truger, Dr James M. Skelly, Wolfgang Sützl, Frau Jutta Kronar, Frau Dagmar Maitz, their colleagues and staffs, and the townspeople of Stadtschlaining – and to my wife Ingrid and son Tim who did without me during those periods, including, to an extent, during the sabbatical when, at least, they were with me in Stadtschlaining.

I also took advantage of blocks of time to complete the volume provided by overseas flights, lengthy waits in airport lounges, and stays in hotels. It is perhaps appropriate that I initiated the final fine-tuning of the volume during a trip – taken as part of my institute's U.S. Institute of Peace-supported Transcaucasian Project (see Sandole, 1997a, b) – to Turkey, Armenia and Azerbaijan: countries whose relationships reflect the violent conflict and war with which this volume deals, and two of which (Armenia and Azerbaijan) were, at the time, on the brink of a breakthrough in their conflict over Nagorno-Karabakh, which, thus far, has failed to materialize.

I want to acknowledge the efforts of Jarle Crocker, a former research assistant, who liaised with Ann Bonanno and Sandra Slater of George Mason University's Computing and Information Systems Support Center to get parts of the manuscript converted to *WordPerfect 5.1*. Jarle also word-processed an initial draft of the bibliography. Ilana Shapiro, another former assistant, helped keep alive the "drive to finish" by printing and sending copies of chapters I had sent to her on diskette during my sabbatical in Stadtschlaining. Landon Hancock, my current assistant, read through the volume in its entirety, suggesting areas for further fine-tuning and other improvements. He also assisted in responding to queries which emerged from copy-editing, read through the page proofs, and worked with me in preparing the index. Ingrid, my life partner, also read through the page proofs.

I also wish to thank John Taylor who did a fine job of copy-editing the book. And at Cassell in London, I am indebted to commissioning editor Petra Recter for taking on this project and to Colin Hutchens and Sandra Margolies for seeing it through to completion.

Finally, I am grateful to Christopher R. Mitchell for taking the time from an otherwise impossible schedule to write the Foreword.

Dedicated to all those who
have tried to make a difference
in the complex conflict environment
of the post-Cold War world.

1 Violent Conflict and War: Old Problems (Still!) in Need of Solution

Introduction

Some thirty years ago, David Edwards (1969, p. 179) wrote:

> War has attracted more attention than any other aspect of international relations. There have been numerous studies of particular wars, many studies of war as a general phenomenon, many theories, partial theories, or pretheories of war. . . . Since [the publication in 1942 of Quincy Wright's *A Study of War*] several hundred more wars have erupted, and several thousand more books and articles on them have been published.[1]

The question arises: thirty years after Edwards's comment, is there a need for yet another book on war? Clearly, I must think so, and for two reasons: war is still a problem in need of solution and there is no adequate theory to explain or to guide efforts to prevent or otherwise deal with it.

Implicit here is that war is a *research* as well as a *practical* (political) problem. As a practical problem, war continues to occur and to exact great costs among its participants and others. Solving war as a practical problem means, among other things, "taking . . . knowledge (assuming it exists) and attempting to influence decisionmakers who preside over the political process at various levels" (Sandole, 1993b, p. 282). If it is not clear what the causes and conditions of war are, or how war can be prevented or otherwise dealt with, then war is a research problem as well. The study reported here deals with both: war as a continuing high-cost human tragedy (practical problem) which requires an appropriate theory for understanding and dealing with it (research problem).

To facilitate developing that theory, I distinguish between war "writ small" and war "writ large." War "writ small" includes war in the traditional interstate sense as well as war within states. War "writ large" comprises acts of physical, biological, psychological, social, cultural and other destruction at *all levels*, e.g. intrapsychic, interpersonal, intergroup, interorganizational, and international. War "writ large," therefore, which includes war "writ small," is concerned with violent conflict in a *generic* sense.

One assumption underlying this study is that, apparent differences notwithstanding, there are significant similarities between violent conflicts occurring at the various levels, such that a *generic theory* could be developed to capture them.

A related assumption is that any attempt to understand and deal with violent conflict at any particular level (e.g. war "writ small") would be enhanced by locating that effort within a generic theoretical framework, such that knowledge usually associated with one level may be seen to have relevance to other levels as well. This study is an attempt to explore to what extent the development of such a theory is possible. But first, war "writ small" as a practical problem.

Wars and Rumors of War

Although war "writ small" is not the only analytical component of war "writ large," it is the dominant element. War in this sense is, like conflict in general, as old as human history itself. For instance, Thucydides' *History of the Peloponnesian War*, one of the earliest accounts of war, dates back to the fifth century BC. More recently, there have been, among others, the Iran–Iraq, U.S. Gulf, Armenian–Azerbaijani, Yugoslavian, Somalian, Rwandan, and Russian–Chechen wars. The Iran–Iraq war, for example, "lasted eight years, cost half a million lives, destroyed whole cities, devastated great swaths of Iran and Iraq, yet in the end settled little" (Bulloch and Morris, 1989, p. x). By contrast, the relatively "lower-tech" Rwandan civil war, which began in early April 1994, also resulted in casualties of half a million lives, but in *less than one month* (Abdulai, 1994, p. 38). By July 1994, "genocide had claimed an estimated one million lives" (Vassall-Adams, 1994, p. 4; also see Keane, 1996). War "writ small," therefore, not only continues to be a major problem, including *still* in Rwanda (see Buckley, 1997), but appears to be shifting in character as well.

According to figures compiled by William Eckhardt for Ruth Leger Sivard (1987, pp. 28–31), there were 471 wars between 1700 and 1987.[2] Total fatalities produced by these wars have been estimated at 101,550,000, over 90 percent of which occurred during the twentieth century. The number of civilian deaths as a proportion of total fatalities is increasing: 52 percent during the 1960s, 73 percent during the 1970s and 85 percent during the 1980s, up to 1987. For wars which began between 1988 and 1990, Eckhardt reports civilian deaths of 74,000 and military fatalities of 7000, with the civilian proportion of total deaths for this period reaching 92 percent (see Sivard, 1991, pp. 22–5; *State of World Conflict Report 1991–1992*, pp. 86–90).

Apropos wars which began between 1990 and 1992, Sivard (1993, pp. 20, 21) reports that

> The global number of conflicts, which had decreased between 1987 and 1990, rose rapidly in 1991 and 1992, setting an all-time record of 29 major wars underway in a single year. . . . War deaths were the highest in 17 years, extending a pattern of growing violence and human suffering in *local* wars (emphasis added).

For much of the past 300 years, Europe has been the main battleground. Since the end of World War II, however, the overwhelming majority of wars (often with great power involvement) has occurred in the Third World: "From 1945 through 1992 over 92 percent of all conflicts were in [the developing] countries" (*ibid.*, p. 20). Most of these have been civil wars, which have increased dramatically during the twentieth century. Civil wars are currently the dominant form of warfare.

The Third World hold on wars remains a continuing fact, despite the resurrection of ethnic conflict and warfare in parts of Europe following the end of the Cold War. That violent ethnic conflict and warfare in Europe have been occurring primarily at the intrastate level strengthens the basic observation that civil wars continue to be the dominant mode of warfare worldwide. Indeed, the number of *intra*state *major armed conflicts*[3] is not only vastly larger than the number of *inter*state major armed conflicts, but, relative to the latter, has been increasing (see Lindgren, 1991; Lindgren *et al.*, 1990; Heldt, 1992; *State of World Conflict Report 1991–1992*, pp. 16–18; Wallensteen and Axell, 1993). As this shift in character continues, with war becoming more "local," more subnational and more like the wars of medieval Europe, "any fine distinctions ... between armies on the one hand and peoples on the other [are] bound to break down. Engulfed by war, civilians [will suffer] terrible atrocities" (van Creveld, 1991, p. 51).

Among current trends in warfare, therefore, are: (a) increases in ferocity; (b) increases in the civilian proportion of total fatalities; (c) increases in the civil war proportion of total wars; and (d) increases in the Third World proportion of total wars. Why the Third World? Sivard (1987, pp. 26–7) has determined that, in 1960, 26 percent of the independent states in the Third World were ruled by military governments. In 1987, that proportion climbed to 52 percent, or 59 out of 113 countries. By 1992, the number of developing countries under military control increased to 61 (out of 112), "with a corresponding increase in the record of human rights violations" (Sivard, 1993, p. 22). In 58 of these countries,

> the most extreme forms of repression, including torture, brutality, disappearances, and political killings, were used by the authorities. ... In more than half of the countries terror tactics were so frequent as to appear to be institutionalized (*ibid.*).

Although other data suggest that, overall, the "community of democratic states" is expanding (see Kegley and Hermann, 1995, pp. 5–6), Sivard observes that a "look back over the years in which [she] has reviewed human rights violations ... gives little cause for optimism" (Sivard, 1993, p. 22). Hence, paralleling the growing trend of civil wars and civilian casualties in the Third World has been an expanding trend of military governments and governmental repression in the Third World; perhaps a complex relationship between governmental repression and civil wars in the Third World which, assuming further democratization worldwide, may diminish in the future.

Current trends also indicate that Europe, in the post-Cold War period, has re-emerged as a venue for brutal warfare.[4] The Yugoslav wars between Serbs, Croats, and Muslims, for example, are among those with the most significant implications for international peace and security: either by exacerbating existing or encouraging new conflicts elsewhere or by stimulating external intervention, these wars could develop into wider conflicts. Hence, Robert Hunter's (1989) prophetic observation, prior to the dissolution of former Yugoslavia, that "we have more chance of [a European] war now than we had during the last thirty years."

Beyond Yugoslavia, ethnic conflict and warfare have occurred in Azerbaijan (Nagorno-Karabakh), Georgia (Abkhazia, South Ossetia), Moldova (Trans-Dniester), Russia (Chechnya), and elsewhere in the former Soviet Union, suggesting trends in conflict and warfare across a broader front: *Balkanization* seems to be at work in the former Soviet Union as well as in Eastern Europe. While "history" may be in the process of, in some sense, "ending" for East–West relations (Fukuyama, 1989), it is clearly being revived, or is otherwise alive and well, among parts of the East. There are security implications here for the West which, in any case, has its own problems, lest we forget, among others: Greece and Turkey on the Cyprus question; the reappearance of xenophobic violence in Austria, Britain, France, Germany,[5] and elsewhere; and the emergence of the U.S.A. as the most violent ("democratic") nation in the industrialized world (see Reiss and Roth, 1993), where, according to the Centers for Disease Control and Prevention, "Nearly three-quarters of all the murders of children in the industrialized world occur" (Havemann, 1997, p. A1).[6]

These trends in violent conflict and war can be seen against the background of other aspects of the *Global Problematique*: the continued militarization of space; the global proliferation of nuclear as well as chemical, biological, and conventional weapons, plus the means for delivering them; increases in global warming; depletion of the ozone layer; and revival of the Malthusian population nightmare. One possible consequence of the combination of, and *interaction* among, some of these and/or other components of the *Problematique* is facilitated movement of the international system toward Morton Kaplan's (1957) *unit veto* state: a highly volatile condition where all actors have the capability to destroy everyone else. Without having to make the point further, it would seem that violent conflict and war are alive and well: *practical* problems (still!) in need of solution.

Five years before the publication of David Edwards' comment, which appears at the start of this chapter, Karl Deutsch (1964, p. xii) issued a Cold War era clarion call which still has relevance:

> In the age of nuclear weapons, if we do not abolish war, war is likely to abolish most of us. In our own time, research on the causes of war and ways to contain, control, and finally abolish all-out war has become an expression of mankind's will to live.

Reinforcing further the idea that *research* problem-solving may be a necessary (but not sufficient) condition of *practical* problem-solving, Deutsch continued: "War, to be abolished, must be understood. To be understood, it must be studied" (*ibid.*). In order to prevent or otherwise deal with violent conflict and war, we must know something about the underlying factors: their identities, sequences, relative weights, combination, and interaction. We require, in other words, theory which would enable us to explain these processes, not only as an otherwise noteworthy academic objective, but as a prerequisite to attempting to manage, control, prevent, or otherwise deal with them.

I have, thus far, argued or otherwise implied that theory in this sense is deficient, and that this volume is a response to that deficiency. But what *is* the state of theory on the causes and conditions of war "writ small"?

Studies of War: The State of the Art (Science?)

Bruce Bueno de Mesquita (1989, p. 53) characterizes theory in the study of international conflict, simply and dramatically: the field "has languished without appreciable evidence of scientific progress for more than two millennia." An assessment by the Deutsche Forschungsgemeinschaft (the German Research Society) put it this way (*AFB-INFO 1/91*, p. 9):

> Basic research still lacks both a concrete theoretical definition of peace as a dynamic interactive pattern and a theory of violent international conflicts – their etiology, their structure, their causes, and their course of development. Existing quantitative analyses (e.g., Singer/Small) do not suffice to allow accurate insights in the root causes and development of such conflicts and hence of suitable transformational strategies. The traditional theory of realism (Waltz), which derives the use of force in international politics one-dimensionally from the structure of the international system, must be considered obsolete. But even neo-realism (Nye/Keohane), so far more a model than a theory, is in need of substantial improvements and refinements before it becomes suitable for the analysis of conflicts and for concepts of transformation. . . .
>
> Science is therefore far away from a quasi theory of peace and war. Research is not yet capable of explaining conclusively "how wars come about" (Ruloff).

John Vasquez's (1976) major assessment of quantitative international relations research, including research on international conflict, provides empirical substantiation for these sentiments. On international relations research in general, Vasquez reports (*ibid.*, p. 181):

> Of . . . 7,678 independent variable clusters, 92.38% (7,093) produce findings which are statistically insignificant and/or have measures of association less than .501. Only 2.35% (181) of the . . . clusters produce findings [with measures of association equal to, or greater than 0.72].

Specifically regarding research on international conflict, Vasquez writes (*ibid.*, p. 194): "what is most disappointing is that the considerable amount of effort placed on inter-nation conflict has had little payoff; only 30 hypotheses out of 4,289 (0.70%) have measures of association greater than .50."[7] Vasquez concludes, therefore, that research in international relations, inclusive of international conflict, has been far less than successful.

In a more recent assessment of studies of war, especially those of a quantitative nature, K. J. Holsti (1989a, p. 4) has put the question "Is there a need for another book on war?" as follows:

> At what point does the proliferation of "hunches" add confusion or avoid critical issues in the field? Does yet another study that finds some statistically significant relationship between ecological [i.e. attribute and relational] variables and the incidence or some other characteristic of war help develop theory?

In his own attempt to answer these questions, Holsti (*ibid.*, pp. 1–2) has observed that an impressive literature exists on *descriptive* relations between attribute/relational variables and the incidence of war, and that an equally impressive literature exists on the incidence, location, and severity of war.[8] Where the literature is weak, however, is in that area which has preoccupied international relations scholars for centuries, *explanation*: "For the most part, the causes of war . . . remain as obscure as ever. Modern research has left a trail of uncertainty, partial clues, contradiction, and continued mystery."

Included in Holsti's review (also see Holsti, 1991, Chapter 1) are the findings of studies associated with the most enduring quantitative project to date on the causes of war, the Correlates-of-War (COW) project, launched by J. David Singer in 1963. Singer (1981) himself has not been too sanguine about the explanatory power of his own or anyone else's studies: *Though we have come a long way, we still do not know, or if we do, we cannot convince others that we know what causes war (or for that matter, peace)* (also see Nicholson, 1996, pp. 1–2).

John Vasquez (1987), who has conducted one of the most thoroughgoing evaluations of COW, is in broad agreement with both Singer and Holsti. The past thirty or so years *have* seen an increase in statistical data on the correlates of war, such findings constituting "a new body of evidence and insight separate from those provided by history, traditional discourse, and political philosophy."[9] However:

> The scientific study of war began with the hope and promise that the collection of reproducible evidence and its systematic analysis would result in a major breakthrough in our understanding of general factors associated with war and peace. That breakthrough has not yet occurred (*ibid.*, p. 108).[10]

To complicate matters further, "Many of the studies [of war] employing modern social scientific techniques have emerged with . . . findings that contradict those of other studies" (Holsti, 1989a, p. 2). Hence, not only do we not know much, if anything, about the sources of influence on decisions to go to war, but what we think we know could be challenged by other (contradictory) findings. To borrow Singer's characterization of the level of knowledge in international relations in general, still valid after nearly 40 years, we seem to have a "potpourri of discrete, disparate, noncomparable, and isolated bits" (Singer, 1961, p. 92), most of which are comprised of independent variables operative at either the international systemic or national level, with few addressing the decision-making level: the "human dimension."

Why this overall state of affairs? For Holsti (1989a), a major reason is that the "quantifiers" tend to ignore and therefore do not appear to deal effectively with some important variables, e.g. the "meaning of war" for participants and (following Mansbach and Vasquez, 1981) the issues that motivate them. Holsti also observes that, although most researchers accept in theory the arguments of Kenneth Waltz (1959) and others that variables operative at multiple levels must be examined to account for war, in practice "a significant proportion of the studies continue to employ single independent variables" (Holsti, 1989a, p. 4). Apparently, nothing much has changed since Hans Morgenthau (1946, p. 95) wrote some fifty years ago:

> The age is forever searching for the philosopher's stone, the magic formula, which, mechanically applied, will produce the desired result and thus substitute for the uncertainties and risks of political action the certitude of rational calculation. Since, however, what the seekers after the magic formula want is simple, rational, mechanical, and what they have to deal with is complicated, irrational, incalculable, they are compelled . . . to simplify the reality of international politics and to develop what one might call the "method of the single cause."

Even before the end of the Cold War and the generation of further "anomalies," Vasquez (1983) argued that the basic reason for the fragmented state of affairs in international relations was the dominance of the *realist paradigm* in theory construction, data making, and research. Realism's portrayal of reality is fundamentally flawed; hence, the theory, data, and research which flow from realism are also flawed. Vasquez's sense of the realist paradigm, which he derives from Morgenthau's *Politics among Nations* (1973), comprises three fundamental assumptions (corresponding to dimensions of Kuhn's, 1970, prototypic model of *paradigm*[11]):

> (1) Nation states (and their decisionmakers) are the most important actors in (and for understanding) international relations (*units of analysis*);
> (2) Domestic and international politics are distinct (e.g., law and order versus anarchy) (*theory*); and
> (3) "International relations is the struggle for power and peace." Explaining and controlling that struggle are the major (and only) objectives of the field (*problems* in need of solution). (Vasquez, 1983, p. 18)

The realist paradigm for Vasquez does not include a specific research methods component: realists can be either quantitative (*behavioralist*) or qualitative (*traditionalist*). Vasquez's realist paradigm also does not include what could be viewed as the hallmark of *classical realism*: a generally bleak view of human nature (see Dougherty and Pfaltzgraff, 1990, p. 120). In this regard, he distinguishes between the *realist paradigm* and the *power politics* school (or *realism*), arguing that the paradigm refers only to the three fundamental assumptions mentioned above (Vasquez, 1983, p. 30). It does not share with power politics (*realism*) its "conceptual baggage or . . . explanations" (e.g. the generally bleak view of human nature). This more "primordial" sense of realism, which I refer to as the *Realpolitik* paradigm, comprises the following (see Sandole, 1993a, p. 4):

1. *Descriptive realism.* The world is always a potential, and often an actual, battlefield (*subject matter*).

2. *Explanatory realism.* The reason for this state of affairs is twofold: (a) negative biological determinism – humans are basically evil and they are born that way; and (b) there are few if any mechanisms for preventing wars (*theory*).
3. *Prescriptive realism.* If 2(a) and (b) are the reasons for 1, then decision-makers have no choice but to do anything and everything they can to advance and protect their interests, the most basic of which are individual and group survival (*problems* in need of solution).

Whether one defines political realism technically as the *realist paradigm* (Vasquez's three assumptions) or primordially as *power politics* or *realism* ("Morgenthau's own specific conceptual framework and theoretical explanations": Vasquez, 1983, pp. 35, 39) or as the *Realpolitik* paradigm, it appears to have dominated the study and practice of international relations, with problematic consequences in each case. For example, to the extent that the realist paradigm is a flawed picture of the real world, e.g. in its nearly theological distinction between domestic and international politics,[12] it may be, as Vasquez has argued, responsible, to some extent, for the fragmented state of affairs in international relations theory.

But far more interesting, for me, at least, is realism's hold on the practice of international relations. In this regard, Vasquez (1983, p. 52) has observed that:

> Even with [some] exceptions, policy analysis [has been] dominated by a *power politics* [primordial realism] perspective which employed the national interest concept to analyze substantive foreign policy questions. This is true not only of intellectuals like Morgenthau who have affected policy indirectly, but also of those intellectuals like Kennan, Kissinger, and Brzezinski who have held government positions. (Emphasis added; also see Brady, 1997)

Vasquez comments on the implications of this dominance in his more recent work (1993, p. 86):

> *Power politics* behaviour is a series of steps to war, not to peace. It is one of the great contradictions of the history of the modern global system that while the *theory* of power politics has been offered as the only realistic path to attain and secure peace, the *practices* of power politics have been associated with the outbreak of war. (Emphasis added)

Accordingly, while political realism in Vasquez's technical sense may no longer be viable as the paradigm influencing the study of international relations, including international conflict, primordial realism's influence on the practice of international relations appears to be dangerously counterproductive. A major implication here is that our conflict theories should include primordial realism as itself a source of influence on violent conflict and war.

Political realism's apparent failure to produce comprehensive, coherent explanations of, and solutions to, war "writ small" and its apparent role in the genesis of war has contributed to the development of an ongoing "Kuhnean crisis" among international relations scholars: "a period of pronounced professional insecurity ... generated by the persistent failure of the puzzles of [paradigm-based] normal science to come out as they should [resulting in] a search for new [rules]" (Kuhn, 1970, pp. 67–8). Over 25 years ago, for example, Charles McClelland (1972, p. 15) commented that "issues have been raised which call into question a number of long-established orientations to the field," thereby producing "conceptual disturbance." Similarly, for James Rosenau (1973, p. 15), "What was yesterday's secure knowledge ... has become today's pervasive doubt ... Confidence has given way to uncertainty." More recently, the collapse of the Berlin Wall, the Warsaw Pact, Communist regimes, the Soviet Union itself and, indeed, of the Cold War and its bipolar international system, all suggest and reinforce the need for alternatives to technical and primordial realism as *primary* approaches to studying and dealing with the world.[13]

These alternatives should, among other things, confront and "nip in the bud" the tendency of quantitative international relations (and other) researchers to fragment their subject matter into bivariate bits and pieces.

Parsimony: The Illusion of (Bivariate) Complexity Management

Quantitative researchers in international relations tend toward bivariate fragmentation, in part, because of their emulation of (their perception of) the natural sciences' analytical tradition: the segmenting of complex wholes into individual bits and pieces in order to facilitate the experimental and/or statistical exploration of specific cause-and-effect relationships and other associations. Ideally, when relationships between all or many of the bits and pieces have been analyzed, the fragments should be reassembled to explore the impact of any one variable on another after the others have explained all that they could. This tends not to happen, however, in part because not all the bits are studied by any one researcher or research group (e.g. the omission in COW of the role of decision-making factors in the genesis of war). But even if they were, the fragments might still not feature in a subsequent reassembly because of an adherence to a narrow conception of what is probably more an aesthetic than a methodological or theoretical norm, *parsimony*: accounting for a phenomenon in terms of as small a number of independent variables as possible (see Singer, 1961, p. 79; Singer and Small, 1968, p. 248; Keohane, 1986b, pp. 21, 25–6, n. 7).

Complementing the appeal of aesthetic parsimony is that of practical parsimony, or complexity management: reducing as much as possible the overwhelming complexity of one's subject matter by attempting (and hoping) to identify the one right variable in terms of which war or any other phenomenon can be adequately explained. This is the compelling attractiveness of what Morgenthau (1946, p. 95) has bemoaned as the "method of the single cause":

The abolition of war is obviously the fundamental problem confronting

> international thought. ... Were it possible to reduce all [the] multiple causes to a single one capable of rational formulation, the solution of the problem of war and peace would no longer seem to be impossible.

The power of the appeal of complexity management is such that it can lead ironically to scholars refraining, in their empirical work, from using multilevel frameworks that have themselves been developed to facilitate complexity management. Snyder *et al.*'s (1962) grand model, for example, was designed to account for the complex of factors involved in decision-making processes. As such, it specifies variables on: (a) decision-making processes; (b) internal settings of decision-making/social structures and behaviors of decision-making states; and (c) external settings of decision-making. Perception plays a major role in the model, as do subjective and objective influences on perception. The model constitutes a radical departure from studies which ignore multiple levels of influence on behavior, ignore perception, and assume that states are homogeneous actors. However, despite its conceptual range and apparent verisimilitudinous relationships with the realities of decision-making, few attempts have been made to employ it in empirical research because of, paradoxically, its own "complexity."[14] According to Trevor Taylor (1978, p. 11):

> Hypotheses or models which incorporate a very large number of variables have ... significant disadvantages. They become difficult to understand and utilize, especially if the relevant variables are not carefully weighted and their interrelationship specifically analyzed.

McClosky (1956), in his critique of the scheme, has said that "no single researcher could deal with all the variables ... and expect to complete more than a very few comparative studies in his lifetime" (cited in Singer, 1961, p. 79). It is little wonder, then, that Michael Sullivan (1976, p. 320), in his comprehensive assessment of scholarship in international relations has commented that "There are, quite simply, few systematic, empirical studies attempting to test complex models using multiple variables."[15]

Clearly, "The superficial virtue of the single-cause explanation is that it permits a simple, neat solution" (Waltz, 1959, p. 146). This is also the virtue of stereotyping: the all-pervasive human tendency to simplify reality (which in one of its more brutal forms, plays a role in the phenomenon we have come to call "ethnic cleansing"). And like stereotypes in general, single-factor accounts of war provide not only partial (see Allison, 1971, Chapter 7) but usually distorted pictures of reality: "in any real situation behavior will be the result of factors from *all* levels" (Scott, 1958, p. 2; emphasis added). Consequently, there is a need to "put Humpty Dumpty back together again," to reflect and act on "the view that no single factor generates conflict among nations, [instead] conflict is the result of a *complex network of causes*" (Choucri and North, 1975, p. 164; emphasis added). As Jack Levy (1996, p. 4) puts it: "It is logically possible, and in fact often desirable, to combine variables from different levels of analysis in causal explanations."

Kenneth Waltz (1959) was one of the first to recognize this: he looked at the causes of war (and conditions of peace) in terms of a multilevel framework comprised of three dimensions – (a) the *individual* level (image I), (b) the *societal* level (image II), and (c) the *international* level (image III) – commenting that "Some combination of [the] three images, rather than any one of them, may be required for an accurate understanding of [war]":

> The partial quality of each image sets up a tension that drives one toward inclusion of the others. . . . Men make states, *and* states make men; but . . . states are shaped by the international environment as are men by both the national and international environments. (*ibid.*, pp. 14 and 230)

In addition to arguing the multilevel thesis, therefore, Waltz also indicated how the three levels might be interrelated: "the *immediate* [or *efficient*] causes of every war must be either the acts of individuals or the acts of states [but] the *permissive* [or *underlying*] cause is the fact that there is nothing to prevent state[s] from undertaking the risks of war" (*ibid.*, pp. 232, 234; emphasis added):

> The third image describes the framework of world politics, but without the first and second images there can be no knowledge of the forces that determine policy; the first and second images describe the forces in world politics, but without the third image it is impossible to assess their importance or predict their results. (*ibid.*, p. 238)

Using Waltz's analysis as a basis for ranking these three levels in terms of their relative explanatory potencies, the international level would appear to be primary in influencing decisions to go to war. The individual and societal levels would either tie for second place or move back and forth between second and third place, depending upon other factors.[16] The hypothesis of third-image primacy, which has not gone unchallenged,[17] is more clearly articulated in Waltz's later work (1979) on *structural realism* (or *neorealism*), in which he "attempt[ed] to systematize political realism into a rigorous [parsimonious], deductive *systemic* theory of international politics" (Keohane, 1986b, p. 15; emphasis added; also see Waltz, 1989; Dougherty and Pfaltzgraff, 1990, pp. 119–23).[18]

Since Waltz (1959) looked primarily at what political philosophers (and to some extent, behavioral scientists) had to say about the causes of war and conditions of peace, his work is largely philosophical and theoretical in nature: it is, therefore, one side of the theoretical–empirical coin. Arguably, a need has existed for some time – and, as suggested by Jack Levy's (1996) multilevel review of "contending theories of international conflict," *still exists* – to do empirical versions of Waltz. Given Singer's multilevel, developmental model of world politics and scheme for guiding COW (Singer, 1969; Singer and Small, 1968), it would appear that COW was meant to do this, but, as already noted, thus far has not: "The *comparative* explanatory weights of ecological and decision-making/organizational/psychological [variables have] not yet been investigated" (Holsti, 1989a, p. 8; emphasis added). COW has concentrated exclusively on variables operative at the national and international levels – the "ecological" variables – at the expense of variables operative at the individual level.[19]

Interestingly enough, the "multilevel promise" of Waltz (1959) was not realized in Waltz's (1979) neorealist statement of the primacy of the international level. According to one critic:

> [In contrast to] Waltz [who] accepts the separation of international and domestic political theory ... [s]ome of us seek eventually to build an *integrated* theory of world politics, *linking* the domestic and international levels of analysis, rather than being content with unit-level and system-level theories that are inconsistent with one another. (Keohane, 1986b, pp. 23–4; emphasis added)

The study reported in this volume is an attempt to develop, in part on the basis of empirical data, such a multilevel theory of violent conflict and war.[20] As such, the study involves not only a *multilevel framework*, but:

1. A *pretheory* for identifying concepts operative at each level, and for explaining how the concepts relate to violent conflict and war.
2. A *methodology* for (a) generating data, (b) translating concepts into variables, (c) systematically exploring relationships between variables, and (d) testing competing explanations.
3. Overall, an *integrative design* that facilitates the development of a *generic theory* applicable to understanding and dealing with the complex ethnic conflicts and warfare of post-Cold War Europe.

Translating this design into a chapter outline, we have in Chapter 2 a multilevel framework and pretheory of violent conflict and war (*theory*); in Chapter 3 an examination of experimentation and simulation in general, plus discussion of the particular simulation selected to generate data for analysis, the *Prisoners' Dilemma Simulation* (PDS) (*research design*); in Chapters 4 and 5 the PDS findings, plus the extent to which they appear to have been validated by corresponding real-world and other laboratory/simulation studies (*research design continued* and *findings*); in Chapter 6 a prototypic generic theory of violent conflict and war, based on an integration of (validated) PDS findings, the pretheory and a revisiting of the literature (*theory revisited*); in Chapter 7 the generic theory as a basis for explaining and dealing with violent ethnic conflict and warfare in post-Cold War Europe; and finally, in Chapter 8, further steps for theory, research, and practice.

Conclusion

Holsti (1989a) has commented that, since "Studies linking variables from different levels ... are few, ... Any model of explanation that emphasizes dynamics and the interplay of variables at different ... levels over time is a distinct step forward" (pp. 8, 9, 10). This promises to be such a study. Reflecting Holsti's concerns and comments, Most and Starr (1989) have suggested that the reasons for the "Kuhnean crisis" reflect all three pillars of the "research triad": method, theory, and logic. The ways in which international relations scholars have dealt with these, they argue, have pushed the field, including those who study war "writ small," into the direction of *additive cumulation* of descriptive data on *static* systemic and actor attributes, at the expense of data on *dynamic* decision-making processes. To deal effectively with war "writ small" as a research problem, scholars should also aim for *integrative cumulation* of multilevel theory of dynamic processes (also see Zinnes, 1976; Bremer and Cusack, 1995). This study is a push toward "integrative cumulation": it reflects more the *theory–research design–findings–theory* process associated with integrative cumulation than it does the *theory–findings–theory* process associated with additive cumulation (see Most and Starr, 1989, p. 9).

Needless to say, we will leave it to Chapter 8 to assess to what extent the study has actually achieved integrative cumulation. In the meantime, we continue our journey toward that end, turning now to Chapter 2 and our multilevel framework and pretheory.

Notes

1. Among the more prominent works on war, in addition to Wright (1942/1964), are Lewis Richardson (1960a, b), J. David Singer (1979a, b, 1980) and Pitirim Sorokin (1937). Recent contributions, including extensive bibliographies, can be found in Midlarsky (1989), Vasquez (1993), and Bremer and Cusack (1995).
2. War, for Eckhardt (1987), covers "any armed conflict which includes one or more governments, and causes deaths of 1,000 or more people per year."
3. A "major armed conflict" involves more than 1000 deaths during the course of the conflict (see Wallensteen and Axell, 1993).
4. This development has coincided, perhaps ironically, with the fiftieth anniversary of Hitler's attack on Poland and the commencement of World War II in Europe (1989).
5. Concerning Germany's vulnerabilities to post-Cold War developments, Chancellor Helmut Kohl has said that, if Germany failed to complete its own unification and European integration in the next few years, "we will experience the same evil spirits that have re-emerged in Yugoslavia and Central Europe. We are not invulnerable to nationalism, chauvinism and xenophobia, to all the evils that have found their way here often enough" (cited in Marc Fisher, 1993, p. 6).
6. Also, the U.S.A. has "the highest rates of childhood ... suicide and firearms-related deaths of any of the world's 26 richest nations. The suicide rate alone for children age 14 and younger [is] double that of the rest of the industrialized world" (Havemann, 1997, p. A1).
7. One measure of (bivariate) association, Pearson's *product-moment correlation coefficient* (r), varies between 0 and + or − 1.00. It can be squared, resulting in the *coefficient of determination* (r^2), which can "be interpreted as the proportion of the total variation in the one variable explained by the other" (Blalock, 1960, p. 298). Hence, an r of 0.50, one of Vasquez's threshold values, would mean that 25 percent of the variation in the behavior of one variable was accounted for by the behavior of the other.
8. See Cioffi-Revilla (1990) for a survey of some of "the most scientifically accurate, reliable, and potentially valuable" data-sets on international crises and war.
9. This view is in sharp contrast to Hedley Bull's (1966) earlier, classic critique of the value of quantitative methods in international relations research.
10. Because COW researchers have not synthesized "the major findings into a coherent scientific explanation of war," Vasquez has endeavored to "piece existing clues together and build upon various theoretical suggestions within the [COW] project in order to construct a scientific explanation of war" (Vasquez, 1987, pp. 109, 116, fn. 20),

a project which he has continued and further developed in Vasquez (1993). (See Chapter 5 for an examination of Vasquez's "steps to war.")

11. A "paradigm" for Kuhn (1970) is basically a collective belief-value system – a worldview (*Weltanschauung*) – which defines for some community of practitioners the legitimate parameters of their activities, such as:

    (a) *Metaphysical.* The nature of the subject matter, including actors (units of analysis) and concepts/variables in terms of which actors are observed to behave.
    (b) *Theoretical.* Theory(ies) for explaining actors' behavior.
    (c) *Instrumental.* Techniques for conducting research on actors.
    (d) *Methodological.* Problems in need of solution and criteria for determining what constitutes valid solutions (see Kuhn, 1970, Chapter IV).

12. For a *poststructuralist* critique of this distinction and other aspects of the *modernist* conception of international relations, see Ashley (1989).
13. For some sense of what directions the study of international relations has been moving in during this period, see, among others, Waltz (1979), Mansbach and Vasquez (1981), Maghroori and Ramberg (1982), Banks (1984), Keohane (1986a), Biersteker (1989), Czempiel and Rosenau (1989), Der Derian and Shapiro (1989), George (1989), Holsti (1989b), Lapid (1989), Most and Starr (1989), Ashley and Walker (1990), Burton (1990a, b), Rosenau (1990), Tickner (1992), Baldwin (1993a), Buzan *et al.* (1993), Holm and Sorensen (1993), Sylvester (1994), Stern and Druckman (1994/5), Bremer and Cusack (1995), Lapid and Kratochwil (1995), Neufeld (1995), Crocker *et al.* (1996), Nicholson (1996), Smith *et al.* (1996), Brady (1997), Doyle and Ikenberry (1997), and Holsti (1998).
14. One study that has employed the model is Glenn Paige's (1968) analysis of the U.S. decision to enter the Korean War.
15. The avoidance of "complex, multivariate, cross-level models" seems to characterize quantitative scholars more so than nonquantitative analysts in government as well as in academia. There are, however, problems with nonquantitative, multilevel research. According to Sullivan (1976, pp. 320–1), "First, variables are not always explicitly tied into larger theoretical concerns . . . . Second, though the explanations are plausible they rarely include systematic attempts to measure the variables. Third, as presented, there is really no way to allow for nonconfirmation of the hypotheses. Finally, there is no way of assessing the strength of competing explanations" (also see O'Leary *et al.*, 1974). This is the irony of nonquantitative research: it may be empirically as well as conceptually "on target," but given the nature of its methodology, we may never know. Still, qualitative research has a very useful role to play as a source of hypotheses which can be systematically explored and tested later on (see Kelman, 1993).
16. Robert North (1990) has added a fourth level to Waltz's original scheme, the *global (ecological)* level, which could either enhance the hypothesized primacy of the international level or "bump" it from first place altogether (also see Homer-Dixon, 1991; Homer-Dixon *et al.*, 1993). In either case, the result for the genesis of war would be to leave intact the hypothesized primacy of the international level over the societal and decision-making levels.
17. Richard Ashley (1989, p. 299), for instance, has argued, "most emphatically, *not* to give explanatory priority to the 'Third Image' of the international system" (emphasis added).
18. Other critiques of Waltz's (1979) neorealism can be found in, among others, Keohane (1986a) and Buzan *et al.* (1993). Also, see Baldwin (1993a) for some sense of the debate between neorealists and neoliberals, which Baldwin (1993b, p. 24) sees as moving toward synthesis.
19. Singer (1989, p. 8) does recognize, however, that, "unless one can illuminate the decisional links between environmental conditions and the behavior of the nations

making up the system, any model of systemic effects on the incidence of war must remain less than complete." He also "strongly suspect[s] that our most powerful explanations for war – and most other eventualities in world politics – will rest on assumptions about the decision process [and that] the decisional approach may turn out to offer an efficient route to a cumulative body of knowledge" (Singer, 1995, pp. 229, 230). But that said, "The point [remains] that direct observation of the decision process is difficult in the extreme" (*ibid.*, p. 230).

20. See Geller (1990) for references to other attempts to respond to this problem, and his own effort to combine levels.

2 A Multilevel Framework and Pretheory of Violent Conflict and War

Introduction

This chapter provides definitions of violent conflict and war and indicates what kinds of conflict have been selected as *dependent* variables. It also delineates a multilevel framework and corresponding pretheory, spelling out definitions for each of the potential *independent* variables, and suggesting their possible relationships with conflict in general and with the selected dependent variables in particular.

Violent Conflict and War: Concepts and Definitions

Conflict is defined here as a dynamic phenomenon, a *manifest conflict process* (MCP), comprised of phases of initiation, escalation, controlled maintenance, abatement, and termination/resolution (Sandole, 1980b, 1986, 1993a). An MCP is a situation in which at least two actors, or their representatives (e.g. lawyers, diplomats), try to pursue their perceptions of mutually incompatible goals by undermining, directly or indirectly, the goal-seeking capability of one another.[1]

MCPs can occur in the absence of aggression: actions which, whether intentional or not, have the effect of physically damaging or destroying something; or psychologically or physically injuring, destroying, or otherwise forcibly eliminating somebody.[2] Two modes of conflict behavior come to mind as examples of MCPs that can occur in the absence of aggression: *games* and *debates* (Rapoport, 1960, 1974, pp. 181–2).

Just as an MCP can occur without aggression, so aggression can occur in the absence of an MCP, e.g. participating in the commission of euthanasia, with not only the consent, but also the active encouragement, of the "victim."[3] It is probably safe to assume, however, that most aggressive acts outside of MCPs (e.g. unprovoked attacks on unsuspecting persons) in which victims are left alive and otherwise functional would develop into some kind of conflict relationship. Even a victim prevented by internal or external constraints from exercising self-defense would be, at least cognitively, involved in an MCP with his or her attacker, especially in the event of repeated attack. And if the victim can and does exercise self-defense via aggressive means, then the conflict will have developed into an *aggressive manifest conflict process* (AMCP): a situation in which at least two actors, or their representatives (e.g. law enforcement or armed forces personnel), try to pursue their perceptions of mutually incompatible goals by physically damaging or destroying the property and high-value symbols of one another; and/or psychologically or physically injuring, destroying, or otherwise forcibly eliminating one another. Rapoport's *fights* (1960, 1974, pp. 180–1) are an example of AMCPs. It is with fights and the processes leading to them that we are primarily concerned here.

Violent Conflict and War: Dependent Variables

As one approach to getting close to AMCPs or fights in general – war "writ large" – types of conflict associated with war "writ small" were selected as dependent variables which could be observed within the context of the *Prisoners' Dilemma Simulation* (PDS). These include one domestic conflict variable, *DOMESTIC INSTABILITY*, and (originally) five foreign conflict variables: *MANIFEST DISTRUST*, *BELLICOSITY*, *CHANGE IN BELLICOSITY*, *ALLIANCES*, and *AGGRESSIVE ATTACKS*.

DOMESTIC INSTABILITY (DI), or internal challenges to incumbent political authority, can be expressed nonviolently: for instance, as low voter turnout or protest votes during elections, and as non-electoral demonstrations against governmental policies. It can be expressed violently as *turmoil* (riots, political clashes, localized rebellions), *conspiracy* or *subversion* (highly organized acts with limited popular participation such as assassinations, coups d'état, mutinies, and small-scale terrorism and guerrilla wars), and *internal war* (highly organized acts with widespread popular participation such as large-scale terrorism and guerrilla wars, and civil wars and revolutions) (see Rummel, 1963, pp. 11–12; Gurr, 1970, pp. 11, 334).

Among the foreign conflict variables, *MANIFEST DISTRUST* (MD) refers to a political actor's location in a conflict–cooperation space – its ratio of conflictful to cooperative behaviors. MD reflects the assumption that "relations among nations involve elements of both competition and cooperation" (Leng and Goodsell, 1974, p. 192):

> Just as the relevant *interests* of actors normally involve a mix of conflicting interests and common interests, a mix is also usually to be found at the *behavioral* level. A conflict system normally involves collaborative elements, and a collaborative system usually contains elements of conflict. (Scott, 1967, p. 139)[4]

BELLICOSITY (BEL) refers to a political actor's active capability to wage war, while *CHANGE IN BELLICOSITY* (%BEL) refers to the *rate of change* in BEL over time. Combining BEL with %BEL enables one to determine whether increases in BEL are occurring at *increasing* or *decreasing rates*, i.e. whether there is an accelerating or decelerating conflict spiral.

ALLIANCES (ALL) refers to a political actor's cooperative associations with other actors for the purpose of common defense. ALL refers, therefore, specifically to defense pacts and does not include neutrality/non-aggression pacts and ententes (see Singer and Small, 1968, p. 266).

AGGRESSIVE ATTACKS (ATT), the most violent of the selected foreign-conflict variables, refers to the employment by a political actor of its active capability to wage war against one or more other actors for any length of time and with any degree of environmental and human destruction.

A Multilevel Framework (Map) and Pretheory of Violent Conflict and War

The multilevel framework developed for this study (see Table 2.1) comprises the *decision-making*, *societal*, and *trans-societal* levels, corresponding to Waltz's (1959) individual, state, and international (inclusive of North's, 1990, global (ecological)) levels, as well as to Snyder *et al.*'s (1962, pp. 62–74) (a) decision-making process, (b) internal setting of decision-making/social structure and behavior of the decision-making state, and (c) external setting of decision-making.[5]

There are a total of 23 potential independent variables specified in the framework. Independent variables 1 to 10 are operative at the decision-making level. Among these, variables 1 to 8 – *DOGMATISM*, *AUTHORITARIANISM*, *POLITICAL CYNICISM*, *PERSONAL CYNICISM*, *POLITICAL EFFICACY*, *NEED FOR ACHIEVEMENT*, *NEED FOR AFFILIATION*, and *NEED FOR POWER* – are concerned with psychological dimensions of decision-making. Variables 9 and 10 – *SUB-SYSTEMIC ENVIRONMENTAL COMPLEXITY* and *TEMPORAL OVERLOAD* – are concerned with spatial–temporal aspects of decision-making.

The societal level of the framework comprises independent variables 11 to 21 (inclusive of time-lagged versions of the dependent variables): *DOMESTIC INSTABILITY*, *RELATIVE ECONOMIC STATUS*, *RELATIVE ECONOMIC DEPRIVATION*, *MANIFEST DISTRUST*, *CHANGE IN MANIFEST DISTRUST*, *BELLICOSITY*, *CHANGE IN BELLICOSITY*, *ALLIANCES*, *AGGRESSIVE ATTACKS*, *CHANGE IN AGGRESSIVE ATTACKS*, and *ATTACK VICTIM*.

DI, MD, BEL/%BEL, ALL, and ATT were built in to the study as (time-lagged) independent as well as dependent variables to allow for the possibility of *self-stimulating/self-perpetuating conflict processes*, as well as the possibility that some might be "causes" of the others, e.g. among the "steps to war."

Finally, independent variables 22 and 23 – *SYSTEMIC ENVIRONMENTAL COMPLEXITY* and *SYSTEMIC ATTACK CONTAGION* – are operative at the trans-societal level.

These particular independent variables, and not others which are also implicit in the framework, were selected because of their amenability to observation within the dynamic behavioral systems generated by the PDS, as

Table 2.1 A multilevel framework

I. Decision-making level
- A. Personal (attributes of decision-makers)
    - 1. Biological/physiological dimension
    - 2. Psychological dimension
        - 1. *Dogmatism* (DOG)
        - 2. *Authoritarianism* (AUTH)
        - 3. *Political cynicism* (POLC)
        - 4. *Personal cynicism* (PERC)
        - 5. *Political efficacy* (POLE)
        - 6. *Need for achievement* (ACH)
        - 7. *Need for affiliation* (AFF)
        - 8. *Need for power* (POW)
    - 3. Physical/material dimension
- B. Spatial/temporal (attributes of decision-making group)
    - 1. Size dimension
        - 9. *Sub-systemic environmental complexity* (SSEC)
    - 2. Structure dimension
    - 3. Stress dimension
        - 10. *Temporal overload* (TO)

II. Societal level
- A. Social
    - 1. The social system and its recent behaviors
    - 2. Social distance from other societal actors
    - 3. Social relationships with other societal actors
    - 4. Recent outgoing and incoming behaviors with respect to other societal actors
- B. Political/legal
    - 1. The political/legal systems and their recent behaviors
        - 11. *Domestic instability* (DI) — 1. DI
    - 2. Political/legal distance
    - 3. Political/legal relationships
    - 4. Recent outgoing and incoming behaviors
- C. Economic
    - 1. The economic system and its recent behaviors
    - 2. Economic distance
    - 3. Economic relationships
    - 4. Recent outgoing and incoming behaviors
        - 12. *Relative economic status* (RES)
        - 13. *Relative economic deprivation* (RED)
- D. Defense
    - 1. The defense system and its recent behaviors
    - 2. Defense distance
    - 3. Defense relationships
    - 4. Recent outgoing and incoming behaviors
        - 14. *Manifest distrust* (MD) — 2. MD
        - 15. *Change in MD* (%MD)

(table continues)

Table 2.1 *continued*

16. *Bellicosity* (BEL)	3. BEL
17. *Change in BEL* (%BEL)	4. %BEL
18. *Alliances* (ALL)	5. ALL
19. *Aggressive attacks* (ATT)	6. ATT
20. *Change in ATT* (%ATT)	
21. *Attack victim* (VICT)	
III. Trans-societal level	
A. Human-made environment	
1. Societal actors	
a. Total number and distribution by type	
22. *Systemic environmental complexity* (SEC)	
b. Types of inter-societal subsystems and systems	
c. Stability	
23. *Systemic attack contagion* (SAC)	
2. Trans-societal actors	
a. Organizations	
(1) Governmental	
(2) Nongovernmental	
b. Groups	
B. Natural environment	
1. Natural resources	
2. Climate	

well as their hypothesized relevance to the initiation and escalation of violent conflict and war. As such, they and the framework within which they are embedded are one response to Jack Levy's (1996, pp. 18–19) challenge that the daunting nature of

> Forecasting the future in [the] more complex and chaotic [post-Cold War] world . . . makes it all the more important that our attempts to understand world politics be guided by well-developed theoretical frameworks that help to illuminate and structure this complexity.

We turn now to a discussion of each of these variables, complete with derived impressions of their possible relationships with the conflict variables, rendered in more of a theoretical than an empirical mode, reserving discussion of relevant findings from corresponding empirical studies for our multivariate validation assessment in Chapter 5. Operational definitions of the variables appear in Appendix C.

Decision-making Level (Psychological Dimensions)

DOGMATISM (DOG) refers to "an authoritarian outlook, an intolerance of those with opposing beliefs, and a sufferance of those with similar beliefs" on the part of some actor (Rokeach, 1960, p. 4). A DOG-actor is characterized by:

a relatively closed cognitive organization of beliefs and disbeliefs about reality, (b) organized around a central set of beliefs about absolute authority which, in turn, (c) provides a framework for patterns of intolerance and qualified tolerance toward others. (Rokeach, 1954, p. 195)

In contrast to fascist or right-wing authoritarianism (which is defined below under *AUTHORITARIANISM*), "*general* authoritarianism or dogmatism is conceptualized as openness or closedness of belief systems. The emphasis is on structure rather than content – how a person believes rather than what he believes" (Kerlinger and Rokeach, 1966, p. 391). In effect, DOG refers to "total systems of beliefs and disbeliefs which are closed or resist change" (Rokeach and Fruchter, 1956, p. 356).

According to Rokeach and his associates, DOG develops from, and as a defense against, *anxiety*: "By overidentification with absolute authority and a cause and by succumbing to the arbitrary reinforcements arising therefrom, an attempt is made to defend the self against feelings of aloneness and isolation, self-hate and misanthropy" (Rokeach, 1960, p. 69). DOG is not, however, just one defense against anxiety; instead, it is an integrated system of defense mechanisms – e.g. repression, rationalization, denial, projection, reaction-formation – all of which can operate without the actor being aware of them, and are combined in order to enhance a person's defense against the uncomfortable emotional state associated with anxiety (*ibid.*, p. 70).[6]

The more dogmatic a person – i.e. the more closed his or her belief system – the more likely he or she will see the world as threatening (*ibid.*, p. 62). Here we have the operation of the *paradox of the defender*: the more a person defends against threatening situations, the more vulnerable she or he will be to threats and, consequently, the less secure the person will feel. This offers some explanation for the tendency of DOG-actors to define even opposing belief systems as threatening and to condemn those who hold them while "rationalizing and justifying egocentric self-righteousness" (*ibid.*, p. 69).

Defining opposing belief systems as threatening and condemning those who hold them equates with a tendency to externalize conflict, i.e. to engage in conflict with others in order to shield oneself from internal conflict. Applying this to a dogmatic group or a generally authoritarian nation would suggest the maintenance of internal peace at the price of external conflict, e.g. the more dogmatic the political decision-makers of a nation, the more likely they are to perceive aspects of their world as threatening and, therefore, the more likely they are to defend themselves through armaments and alliances.

But given the paradox of the defender, specifically John Herz's (1959) *security dilemma* at the international level, such actions may be negatively self-fulfilling and self-defeating, in that the decision-makers of other nations may perceive these actions as threatening and seek to defend themselves also through armaments and alliances. In other words, dogmatic decision-makers of different nations could, as a consequence of their respective efforts to defend their nations, generate a conflict spiral which leaves them even less secure than they were before they acted.

As dogmatic decision-makers of various nations become embroiled in counterproductive relationships – the failure of their defenses at the international level increasing the fragility of their defenses at the intrapsychic level – we can imagine further pathological consequences.[7] Heightened anxiety resulting from self-defeating international strategies could, for example, elicit from dogmatic decision-makers increasingly *competitive* (instead of *cooperative*) processes of conflict resolution (Deutsch, 1971, p. 44), including accelerating investments in national defense as well as attacks against those whom they have defined as threatening.

In general, then, there would seem to be a *positive relationship* between DOG and external or foreign conflict. Assuming either a generally authoritarian electorate or, for decision-making elites, the irresistibility of the *functions-of-conflict thesis* – i.e. that external conflict has the "function" of reducing or preventing internal conflict (see Simmel, 1955; Coser, 1956) – a positive relationship between DOG and foreign conflict could, at some point in the development of a complex conflict relationship, be accompanied by a *negative relationship* between DOG and internal or domestic conflict.[8]

AUTHORITARIANISM (AUTH) or fascism refers to an anti-democratic syndrome, which includes: rigid adherence to conventional values; a submissive attitude toward ingroup authorities; a tendency to look for, and to condemn, reject and punish violators of conventional values; a tendency to think in terms of rigid categories; a preoccupation with power and toughness and a rejection of the subjective, the imaginative, the tender-minded; and generalized hostility – the vilification of human beings (Adorno *et al.*, 1950, pp. 255–7).

As already noted, authoritarianism applies to DOG as well as to AUTH. The major difference between the two is that DOG concerns a general form while AUTH concerns a particular form of authoritarianism (Rokeach, 1960, p. 121). Specifically, as mentioned above, DOG is concerned with the *structure*, the openness or closedness of belief systems, which is relevant to left- as well as to right-wing persons. AUTH, on the other hand, is concerned with *content*, the extent to which belief systems are anti-democratic. AUTH is presumably more relevant to right-wing persons.

Given their common basis in authoritarianism, whatever characterizes DOG-actors would seem to characterize AUTH-actors or fascists as well. Put another way, all fascists are dogmatic. However, in view of the structure–content difference between the two, not all DOG-actors are fascists. That is, while DOG-actors tend to be egocentric and to condemn individuals holding opposing belief systems, fascists tend to be ethnocentric and to reject and vilify whole groups (outgroups), while glorifying their ingroup (Rokeach, 1960, p. 12; Bailes and Guller, 1970, p. 144). This is not to say that DOG-actors do not condemn whole groups, but only that fascists are more likely to jump immediately to the group level, whereas DOG-actors are more likely to begin with individuals and then, under some circumstances, to focus on the group that includes such individuals.

While DOG-actors tend to see individuals with opposing belief systems as threats, fascists tend to see groups of such individuals as deviants: as violators of important cultural norms. In this regard, although DOG-actors enter into hostile relationships with individuals or groups, they tend to do so with a *defensive* orientation, e.g. the dogmatic decision-makers of a nation may become involved in a war with another nation in order to protect their nation against the threats of the other. Fascists, on the other hand, tend to enter hostile relationships because they are looking for deviants; moreover, to punish them. The orientation of fascists, therefore, tends to be *offensive*.

The punitiveness of fascists towards deviants – who are, effectively, members of any outgroup – seems to reflect a tendency to displace onto others a repressed anti-authority hostility (Greenstein, 1969, pp. 106–7). Unable to rebel against the frustrating norms and leaders of the ingroup because of the guilt and *anxiety* and, perhaps, even external punishment that would follow in the wake of such rebellion, fascists take their aggression out on "legitimized" targets: those who have, by definition, rebelled.

It is because this *Radfahrernaturen* ("bicyclist's personality") – i.e. "Above they bow, below they kick" (Adorno, 1951, p. 291n; cited in Greenstein, 1969, p. 103) – is capable of being manifested at all levels that Adorno and his fellow authors of *The Authoritarian Personality* have defined AUTH as a disease that poses a grave "threat to our traditional values and institutions" (Adorno *et al.*, 1950, pp. 1, 974).[9]

In view of the authoritarian basis of both DOG and AUTH, the same conflict behaviors expected for DOG should be expected for AUTH: at some point in the development of a complex conflict relationship, a positive relationship with foreign conflict could be accompanied by a negative relationship with domestic conflict, with one exception: given that fascists seem to be more aggressive than DOG-actors, we would expect the magnitudes of these relationships to be greater in the case of AUTH.[10]

POLITICAL CYNICISM (POLC) refers to a contemptuous distrust of politicians and the political process: the "extent to which people hold politicians and politics in distrust, the extent to which these words symbolize something negative rather than something positive" (Agger *et al.*, 1961, p. 477).

PERSONAL CYNICISM (PERC) refers to a contemptuous distrust of people in general, a negative view of human nature (*ibid.*, p. 490).

POLITICAL EFFICACY (POLE) refers to the view that political and social change is possible; moreover, that one can participate in effecting such change (*ibid.*, p. 493).

These variables will be discussed together because, in part, they cohere with the concept of *alienation*, which, according to Seeman (1959), is comprised of five dimensions: (a) powerlessness, (b) meaninglessness, (c) normlessness, (d) isolation, and (e) self-estrangement (cited in Aberbach, 1969, p. 86). Isolation is compatible with cynicism, and powerlessness is compatible with (low) efficacy. Consequently, cynicism and (low) efficacy are both forms of alienation. Moreover, each can be characterized by two foci of alienation: political and personal (*ibid.*).

On the relationship between alienation and behavior, Aberbach (*ibid.*, p. 87), in reference to the work of William Kornhauser (1959), tells us:

> One prominent interpretation is that the alienated are quiescent under ordinary circumstances, but subject to mobilization into mass movements

> (or at least support of extremist, demagogic and/or authoritarian political leaders) when the material or psychological circumstances are proper and the right leader presents himself.
>
> Economic dislocation, social shock caused by events like defeat in war and/or social confusion accompanied by demagogic attack on the existing political system can arouse the public susceptible to mass appeals. The mass man (who suffers from "a lack of proximate attachments") lacks internalized standards and is, therefore, politically volatile. When there are no clear signals available his *anxiety* is mixed with political apathy, but spasmodic "flights into activity" are also characteristic. (Emphasis added)

Although this applies particularly to "mass man," alienation can also affect elites, including political decision-makers, who might, under some circumstances, also be susceptible to demagogic manipulation. In any case, it seems that alienated actors – those high in POLC and PERC, and low in POLE – could play a role in the incidence of conflict: alienated masses could affect the incidence of domestic conflict, while alienated elites could affect the incidence of foreign as well as domestic conflict.

A model based upon voting studies "holds that perceived powerlessness [low POLE] leads to political distrust [high POLC] which, in turn, leads to voting against the prevailing order" (Aberbach, 1969, pp. 98–9). Hence, in addition to hanging together as components of alienation, POLC, PERC, and POLE may link up coherently in an alienation-based conflict system in terms of the following sequence: (a) diminished *POLITICAL EFFICACY*, (b) increased *POLITICAL CYNICISM*, (c) increased *PERSONAL CYNICISM*, and then (d) the incidence of aggressive behavior. The system could be one of either internal or external conflict (or both), depending upon whether masses or elites are alienated.

Accordingly, whether we view POLC, PERC, and POLE as discrete components or as interrelated, sequential aspects of alienation, we have in alienation a concept which seems to figure in conflict processes.[11] We might expect, therefore, at some point in the development of a complex conflict relationship, positive relationships between POLC/PERC and foreign conflict, accompanied by negative relationships with domestic conflict; and negative relationships between POLE and conflict in general.

NEED FOR ACHIEVEMENT (ACH) refers to a predisposition to strive for success in accordance with one or more standards of excellence, such as those having to do with intelligence and leadership capacity (McClelland, 1961, pp. 40–1).

NEED FOR AFFILIATION (AFF) refers to a predisposition to establish, maintain, or restore a positive affective relationship with another person or persons (*ibid.*, p. 160).

NEED FOR POWER (POW) refers to a predisposition to control the means of influencing others (*ibid.*, p. 167).

David McClelland, who has pioneered investigating the relationships between these needs (particularly ACH) and behavior, writes that American males who are high in ACH tend to:

> come more often from the middle class than from the lower or upper class, have better memory for uncompleted tasks, are more apt to volunteer as subjects for psychological experiments, are more active in college and community activities, choose experts over friends as working partners, are more resistant to social pressure, [and] cannot give accurate reports of what their "inner concern" with achievement is. (*Ibid.*, pp. 43–4)

Choosing experts over friends as working partners is suggestive of the high-level determination of ACH-actors to do well; moreover, their resistance to social pressure suggests that they might even employ conflictful means in order to succeed, particularly in situations where losing as well as winning is possible.

Of the various forms of conflict behavior discussed by Anatol Rapoport (1960), there is one which seems compatible with high ACH: *games*. Games are situations in which the opponents attempt to outwit each other on the basis of rational analysis and in accordance with rules (Rapoport, 1974, p. 181). That ACH-actors tend to volunteer for psychological experiments, and that many such experiments involve games, suggests a connection between the two.

However, there is something which is more suggestive of this connection. ACH-actors seem to be reflective of a *neutral* affective orientation in interpersonal relationships, i.e. their main consideration in deciding whether to select a certain option tends to be not whether the option would damage or enhance human relationships, but whether it would lead to success in terms of some standard of excellence (Terhune, 1968, p. 32). Games also seem to suggest a neutral affective orientation in that rational analysis and an adherence to rules are essential ingredients of play.

Given that in games the opponent is essential and, indeed, cooperates in keeping the game going (Rapoport, 1974, pp. 181–2), we would expect that, when ACH-actors do decide on a conflictful option, it would not be of a type or intensity intended to remove "for good" the opponent (unless the game were defined as no longer worthwhile). In general, then, when ACH-actors are aggressive, we would expect their behavior to be more *cognitive* than *affective*: more planned than spontaneous, more oriented to fulfilling "rational" goals than to simply reducing internal tension; or, as Coser (1956, pp. 48–55) puts it, more into "realistic" than "nonrealistic" conflict.

With regard to *AFFILIATION*, McClelland (1961, p. 160) tells us that persons who are high in AFF "tend to be approval-seeking, to select faces rather than neutral stimuli in perceptual tasks, to be considered likely to succeed by peers, and to choose friends over experts to work with on a performance task." Consequently, we would expect them to be reflective of a *positive* affective orientation (Terhune, 1968, p. 32); indeed, to find conflict with others an undesirable experience.

Nevertheless, AFF-actors may feel that they have no choice in some situations but to enter into conflictful relationships with others. By virtue of their need, however, they might attempt to limit the type or the degree of their conflictful reaction to others. For instance, with respect to Rapoport's (1960) conflict typology, they might attempt to enter into *debates* with those who threaten them: exchanges where the objective is to persuade the opponent to see things as one sees them oneself, to convert the opponent to one's perspective (Rapoport, 1974, p. 182). If the AFF leadership of a nation feels that it has to go a bit further to make its point, it might enter into an alliance with one or more other nations. In either case, as long as the AFF-actor continues to talk with the opponent, it will be attempting to fulfill its need to establish, maintain, or restore a positive affective relationship with others.

Of course, an alliance relationship is also a fulfillment of this need. However, to go beyond debates and alliances – to arm and to declare war – would serve to offset this gain: in addition to the material and other psychological costs associated with preparing for and waging war, AFF-actors would, in the event, also experience need deprivation.

POW-actors could be characterized by pleasure in winning or anger in losing an argument; by demanding or enforcing something, giving a command, punishing someone; or by a view of the world as comprised of superior persons having control of the means for influencing subordinates (McClelland, 1961, pp. 167–8). In any case, POW-actors would seem to be characterized by a *negative* affective orientation (Terhune, 1968, p. 32). Given the presumably negative affective orientation of those who participate in Rapoport's *fights* – i.e. situations where the objective is to "harm, destroy, subdue, or drive away the opponent" (Rapoport, 1960, p. 9; 1974, pp. 180–1) – there would seem to be an affective identity between POW and fights. There would also seem to be an association between POW and AUTH, the latter also being linked to fights.

In view of the above, we could expect, at some point in the development of a complex conflict relationship, positive relationships between ACH/POW and foreign conflict, accompanied by negative relationships with domestic conflict, with the intensity of relationships being greater for POW than for ACH; and negative relationships between AFF and conflict in general.

Decision-making Level (Spatial–Temporal Dimensions)

SUB-SYSTEMIC ENVIRONMENTAL COMPLEXITY (SSEC) refers to the number of decision-makers acting on behalf of a political actor. On the relationship between group size and conflict, Kenneth Boulding (1962, p. 160) argues that:

> one of the most acute problems in the perpetuation of an organization is that of maintaining internal cohesion. The larger an organization grows, the more tendency there is for factions and dissident elements to grow within it and for the organization ultimately to split or to fall apart.

Similarly, Quincy Wright (1964, p. 250) tells us that, in groups, "policy is founded on opinions which usually differ among [the] members . . . . The larger the group, therefore, the more likely is internal conflict."

Archeologist Arthur Demarest provides an example from antiquity of the operation of this hypothesized relationship. Before AD 761, he argues, wars among the Maya in the Petexbatun region of present-day Guatemala:

> were well-orchestrated battles to seize dynastic power and procure royal captives for very public and ornate executions. But after 761, he notes, "wars led to wholesale destruction of property and people, reflecting a breakdown of social order comparable to modern Somalia." ... The reason for the abrupt change in the Maya's battleground behavior, he suspects, was that *the ruling elite had grown large enough to produce intense rivalries among its members*. Their ferocious competition, which exploded into civil war, may have been what finally triggered the society's breakdown. Similar breakdowns, he believes, happened in other areas as well. (Lemonick, 1993, p. 47; emphasis added)

The larger a group becomes, then, the more likely it is that the number of different opinions within the group will increase. The larger the number of different opinions, the greater the probability of internal conflict – conflict, perhaps, between the establishment old guard and newly arrived "Young Turks" or a less neat multiactor conflict within the *bureaucratic politics model* of decision-making (see Allison and Halperin, 1972).

Depending upon the extent to which there is a dominant group view and the extent to which new arrivals feel compelled to agree with that view, internal conflict may be short-lived and replaced by the *groupthink* syndrome (Janis, 1972). In any case, increases in the number of members/different opinions may lead to increases in the incidence of internal conflict because of *frustrations* resulting from the group's inability to develop a common position within a certain time period. Alternatively, as the number of members/opinions increases, "the greater the chance of misunderstanding, and the greater the chance of misunderstanding, the more likely is conflict to occur" (Strickland *et al.*, 1968, p. 44).

Whether we talk about decision-making units or whole societies, increases in membership have implications for external or foreign conflict as well as internal or domestic conflict. In terms of societies, for instance, Wright (1964, p. 240) suggests an internal/external or domestic/foreign conflict linkage: "as the in-group becomes larger, less homogeneous, and more in need of a scapegoat to relieve internal stresses, opposition to the out-group serving as a scapegoat becomes more intense." In relation to decision-making units, conflicts among decision-makers may eventually spill over to conflicts between corresponding factions within the larger society, in which case the same need for an external scapegoat may arise.

In view of the above, therefore, we would expect positive relationships between SSEC and conflict in general, although at some point in the development of a complex conflict relationship, perhaps with a positive relationship with foreign conflict accompanied by a negative relationship with domestic conflict.

TEMPORAL OVERLOAD (TO) refers to time limits within which decision-makers acting on behalf of a political entity have to make decisions. Decision time can be limited by reducing actual recorded time (by increasing TO) as well as by increasing task-complexity while keeping time constant (e.g. by increasing SSEC) (Hermann, 1969, p. 30; Holsti, 1972, p. 14). In either case, time will probably appear to those deprived of it as one of the most valuable resources in decision-making (Strickland *et al.*, 1968, p. 44).

Whenever decision-makers feel themselves pressured to respond to demands – either explicit ones such as ultimata or those implicit in rapid technological and cultural change – "the shorter the time period within which . . . adjustments have to be made, the greater the probability that they will prove inadequate and that violence will result" (Wright, 1964, p. 352). Given the tendency of people in general during periods of reduced decision time to rely upon stereotypes, to narrow their focus of attention, and to be impeded in their use of available information (Holsti, 1972, p. 15), they are likely to "perceive hostility in others and to choose more extreme and violent responses" (Deutsch and Senghaas, 1973, p. 300).

When the sources of these demands are external to the society as a whole, then foreign conflict may ensue. When the sources are internal, then domestic conflict can occur. Accordingly, as in the case of SSEC, we would expect positive relationships between TO and conflict in general, but at some point in the development of a complex conflict relationship, perhaps with a positive relationship with foreign conflict accompanied by a negative relationship with domestic conflict.

Societal Level

DOMESTIC INSTABILITY (DI) (see above definition of DI as a dependent variable). Here we are concerned with the relationship between DI and itself at two points in time, and also with the relationship between DI at one point in time and each of the foreign-conflict variables at later points in time.

On the relationship between DI and itself at two points in time, the expression "violence begets violence" suggests, in part, that internal or domestic conflict at one point in time can stimulate internal or domestic conflict at a later point in time. It is not difficult to imagine the operation of this relationship in dynamic conflict situations, such as in Northern Ireland, where, in action–reaction fashion, Republican paramilitary violence has often followed British Army or Unionist paramilitary violence (and vice versa) in fairly rapid succession. In the United States, it is not only the same conflict situation that can be related to itself over time (e.g. racial conflict in Los Angeles), but also different conflict situations that can be interrelated over time (e.g. rioting in Los Angeles stimulating rioting in other American cities).

Hence, when a positive relationship occurs between DI and itself in multi-conflict societies, this may be because of *cross*-conflict as well as *intra*-conflict dynamics: certain behaviors articulated by actors in one conflict situation may be seen by actors involved in other conflict situations as models to be emulated, especially if the behaviors are seen to be successful. Such *cross-conflict contagion* could apply to different societies as well as to any one society: a problem which, as we discuss further in Chapter 7, we face in the post-Cold War world.[12]

With regard to DI and foreign conflict, a good deal of theoretical speculation suggests a firm relationship, one which might be called the first phase of the *functions-of-conflict thesis*; that is, many historians, politicians, and others have argued that domestic conflict leads to foreign conflict because the latter is, or is thought to be, "functional" in the re-establishment of domestic stability. According to Georg Simmel (1955, pp. 97–8):

> the unity of a group is often lost when it has no longer any opponent. . . . Within certain groups, it may even be a piece of political wisdom to see to it that there be some enemies in order for the unity of the members to remain effective and for the group to remain conscious of this unity as its vital interest.[13]

Accordingly, political decision-makers may have to *invent an enemy* if none already exists in order to ensure, to the extent possible, the maintenance of internal stability (and epiphenomenally fulfill their need for *role defense*: see Burton, 1979, Chapter 7). Needless to say, defining an outgroup as an enemy can increase the probability that an orchestrated foreign conflict will escalate into a war. This development in less tranquil domestic circumstances may not be accidental, for even war, with all the possible costs associated with it, has been defined as functional: "war with the outside is sometimes the last chance for a state ridden with inner antagonists to overcome these antagonisms, or else to break up definitely" (Simmel, 1955, p. 93).

In general, then, the functions-of-conflict thesis holds that foreign conflict not only performs the function of promoting domestic stability but – according to Lewis Coser (1956), who has expanded upon Simmel's ideas – may also be "an essential element in the existence of any social entity." While *foreign* conflict may be conducive to domestic stability, which clearly would be suggested by a negative relationship between foreign and domestic conflict (the second phase of the functions-of-conflict thesis), what is not clear is how to conceptualize the relationship between *domestic* and foreign conflict (the first phase), which is what concerns us here.

For instance, would we expect domestic conflict to have a positive or a negative relationship with foreign conflict? Off the tops of our heads, we would probably expect a positive relationship, for that would mean, simply, that domestic conflict stimulates foreign conflict, although whether we can interpret the positive relationship in terms of the functional thesis may not be so simple, because foreign conflict may index decision-makers' reactions, not to an existing domestic conflict as such, but to external intervention, e.g. to a state which has intervened on behalf of the rebels.

However, a negative relationship could also be commensurate with the first phase of the functional thesis. That is, in addition to suggesting that domestic conflict did not stimulate foreign conflict (which, clearly, would seem to run against the grain of the functional thesis), a negative relationship between domestic and foreign conflict could also mean that, in order to ensure that a decreasing trend in the level of domestic conflict is not reversed, decision-makers have increased the level of foreign conflict. It could be argued, however, that this more properly characterizes a "third phase" of the functional thesis. That is, assuming a positive relationship between *domestic* and foreign conflict during the first phase and a negative relationship between *foreign* and domestic conflict during the second phase, a subsequent negative relationship between *domestic* and foreign conflict could mean that decision-makers have decided to reinforce the second-phase decrease in domestic conflict by continuing to engage in foreign conflict: a source of the ethnic warfare in, and beyond, former Yugoslavia?

The relationship between domestic and foreign conflict, therefore, can be a complex, *nonlinear* one, characterized by different directions of relationship at different points in time (which may account for some of the apparently contradictory findings noted in Chapter 1).[14] Also, the relationship between DI and itself at different points in time will tend to be a slightly nonlinear positive one, throughout all phases of the functions-of-conflict process.

RELATIVE ECONOMIC STATUS (RES) refers to a political actor's level of economic development relative to that of other actors. On the relationship between economic development and domestic conflict, Ivo and Rosalind Feierabend (1966/1970, p. 218) have hypothesized that "The highest and the lowest points of the modernity continuum in any given society will tend to produce maximum stability in the political order, while a medium position ... will produce maximum instability." In other words, the relationship between modernity (which is inclusive of economic development: Kean and McGowan, 1973, p. 224) and domestic conflict will tend to be nonlinear.[15] The Feierabends (1966/1970, p. 220) suggest the following reasons for their conceptualization:

> The acquisition of modern goals, although an integral aspect of modernity, is hardly synonymous with their attainment. The notion of "the revolution of rising expectations" (Lerner, 1958), also termed "the revolution of rising frustrations," points to the essentially frustrating nature of the modernization process. ... it may be postulated that the *peak discrepancy between systemic goals and their satisfaction*, and hence the *maximum frustration*, should come somewhere in the *middle of the transitional phase* between traditional society and the achievement of modernity. It is at this middle stage that awareness of modernity and exposure to modern patterns should be complete ... whereas achievement levels would still be lagging far behind. ... After the middle stage, exposure can no longer increase, since it already amounts to complete awareness, but achievement will continue to progress, thus carrying the nation eventually into the stage of modernity. (Emphasis added)

The Feierabends' explanation is suggestive of the principle of the *diminishing marginal utility of income*, i.e. "as society gets richer, the significance to the individual of additions to income presumably grows less and less" (Boulding, 1962, p. 191). Hence, according to John Kenneth Galbraith, "in the affluent society, economic conflict virtually disappears, for who can get excited about another square foot of chrome on the tail fin when all major needs are satisfied" (cited in *ibid.*).

On the relationship between economic development and foreign conflict, Maurice East and Charles Hermann (1974, pp. 276, 278) hypothesize that "Governments of economically developed nations will initiate ... a higher percentage of foreign events involving military skills and resources," because:

> A nation enjoying a relatively high standard of living under existing conditions will foster a government quick to draw upon its military resources – separately or in collaboration with others [i.e. via alliances] – to defend itself against those whom the elites within the society feel might plunder its wealth.

Specifically, East and Hermann (*ibid.*, p. 279) hypothesize that governments of economically developed nations will initiate a higher percentage of foreign conflict events because:

> development increases the number of international issues in which a government believes its nation has a stake. As a consequence, more conflicts of interests, which in turn lead to foreign conflict behavior, arise between the government of a developed nation and various external entities.

East and Hermann also "anticipate that governments ruling developed nations will initiate less cooperative behavior than those in less developed societies" (*ibid.*).

Accordingly, we might expect a positive relationship between RES and foreign conflict, and a nonlinear relationship between RES and domestic conflict, with low and high levels of RES associated with low levels of domestic conflict and intermediate levels of RES associated with high levels of domestic conflict. Since high levels of RES could be associated with high levels of foreign conflict as well as low levels of domestic conflict, the functions-of-conflict principle might be at work here.

RELATIVE ECONOMIC DEPRIVATION (RED) refers to the discrepancy between a political actor's *preferred* economic status and its *actual* economic status, relative to other actors. Whenever we talk about a *negative* disjunction between a preferred and an actual state of affairs – a situation which falls short of, rather than transcends hopes or expectations – we are talking basically about *frustration*. John Dollard and his associates (1939/1970) have defined frustration as an "interference with the occurrence of an instigated goal-response at its proper time in the behavior sequence" (*ibid.*, p. 25). Quite simply, when we wish to achieve a certain state of affairs at a certain point in time, and either we are prevented from initiating an attempt or our attempt is prevented from reaching fruition, then we will experience frustration: an uncomfortable emotional state whose intensity will depend upon, among other things, the magnitude of the difference between the desired and actual state of affairs (*ibid.*, pp. 27–8).

According to the classic formulation of the frustration–aggression hypothesis put forward by the Dollard group, "the occurrence of aggressive behavior always presupposes the existence of frustration and, contrariwise ... the existence of frustration always leads to some form of aggression" (*ibid.*, pp. 23–4). In the original formulation, therefore, frustration was both a *necessary* and a *sufficient* condition of aggression.[16] For such a "tight" causal system to work, however, aggression could not refer to anything more than feelings of hostility. That is, depending upon the level of anticipated punishment as well as the magnitude of the instigation to aggression, and the interaction between the two, frustration could be expressed as a nonovert aggressive thought or as an overt aggressive act, and in either case, directed against the perceived source of frustration or displaced on to other targets. Hence, frustration may be a necessary and/or sufficient condition of aggression, but only of aggressive *feelings*, which, depending upon other factors, may or may not be expressed as some kind of aggressive *behavior*.

Whatever aggression does flow from frustration would fall into the category of *affective aggression*. That *cognitive aggression* – aggressive behavior designed primarily to achieve goals other than tension-reduction – also occurs in human affairs reinforces the view that, in general, frustration is not a necessary condition of aggressive behavior.[17]

Other concepts implicit in RED besides John Dollard's frustration are Ted Robert Gurr's *relative deprivation* (1970, pp. 13, 24, 319) and Ivo and Rosalind Feierabend's *systemic frustration* (1970, pp. 214–15), both of which are also related to conflict, primarily domestic conflict but, through government-encouraged displacement of internal grievances on to outside targets, foreign conflict as well (*ibid.*, p. 215; Gurr, 1970, pp. 308–9).

In view of the above, we would expect a positive relationship between RED and conflict in general, but at a certain point in the development of a complex conflict relationship, with a positive relationship with foreign conflict accompanied by a negative relationship with domestic conflict.

MANIFEST DISTRUST (MD): see above definition of MD as a dependent variable.

CHANGE IN MANIFEST DISTRUST (%MD) refers to the rate of change over time in a political actor's location in a conflict–cooperation space.

As mentioned earlier, it is assumed that relations between nations are a complex mix of conflictful and cooperative elements; moreover, that at any given time, some behavioral systems will be primarily cooperative while others will be primarily conflictful. The proportions of conflictful and cooperative elements in any behavioral mix, however, will normally vary over time (Scott, 1967, p. 140). Accordingly, what is "more important than the mere presence of [for instance] conflict in a collaborative system would be . . . the ratio of conflict to collaboration and whether the ratio is changing and, if so, how" (*ibid.*).

MD and %MD are concerned with these two elements. If MD is increasing at an *increasing* rate, this could lead to increases in other forms of foreign conflict, primarily because of the rapid polarization in the relations between actors suggested by accelerating increases in the ratio of conflictful to cooperative behaviors.

On the relationship between foreign conflict in general and domestic conflict, Lewis Coser (1956, p. 92) tells us that "Internal cohesion is likely to be increased in the group which engages in outside conflict." This is, of course, part of the functions-of-conflict thesis discussed above. This does not, however, apply to groups under all conditions (*ibid.*, p. 93): "If a group is lacking in basic consensus, outside threat leads not to increased cohesion, but to general apathy, and the group is consequently threatened with disintegration."

In general, then, we might expect a positive relationship between MD (MD/%MD) and other forms of foreign conflict and, assuming internal consensus, a negative relationship between MD (MD/%MD) and domestic conflict.

BELLICOSITY (BEL) and *CHANGE IN BELLICOSITY* (%BEL): see above definitions of BEL and %BEL as dependent variables.

BELLICOSITY has something in common with *RELATIVE ECONOMIC STATUS*, in that both may be viewed as components of *national attribute theory* and *power theory*, i.e. both are national attributes in general as well as elements of national power in particular. In either case, they are possible influences on foreign policy-making processes.

There is another connection between BEL and RES, to the extent that the former is dependent upon the latter. In this regard, given East and Hermann's (1974) observation that economically developed nations tend to be the most active in foreign affairs and, in particular, the most conflictful and least cooperative, we would expect not only an overarching connection between RES and foreign conflict in general, but also connections between BEL and other forms of foreign conflict, especially *AGGRESSIVE ATTACKS* (ATT). According to Kenneth Boulding (1962, p. 145):

> the perception of conflict is frequently heightened by the existence of organizations that are specialized for conflict. The existence of weapons predisposes both animals and men to fight, the existence of specialized conflict agencies such as armed forces predisposes nations to war.

Weapons systems and specialized conflict agencies, however, are more than contributory conditions of war. In addition to predisposing states to war, they also seem to be necessary conditions of war (Levi, 1960/1971, p. 321). Quite simply, wars cannot be waged without a warfare capability. However, BEL, or even increases in BEL, is not a condition which results directly in war (*ibid.*, pp. 321–2). What may come closer to being a sufficient condition of war is increases in BEL at *increasing* rates.

Such a condition could imply what increases in BEL alone might not necessarily imply: that a distribution of power between two or more political actors has become unstable and war-prone. Instability in this sense could mean either that one actor was attempting to upset the system by bridging the distance between it and some establishment actor or that an establishment actor was responding to such threats to its position by attempting to maintain the distance between it and the revolutionary power, or both. This is essentially Organski's (1968) *power transition theory*, which holds that war is more likely to occur under conditions of power transition because:

> (1) the dissatisfied country may feel that its newfound power permits it to take on the predominant power, or
> (2) the dominant power, viewing the growing power potential of the dissatisfied nation, may decide on preemptive aggression. (Cited in Sullivan, 1976, p. 168)

If the dominant power does not respond in the short run by pre-emptive aggression, it may attempt to maintain its lead by increasing or improving its warfare capabilities, in which case the dissatisfied or revolutionary power may also continue arming, its decision-makers feeling that the time is not yet ripe for an attack on the predominant power. At some point in this "bite-and-counterbite" process, the distinction between threatener and threatened probably becomes moot, because each side would be responding to perceived threats. Hence, successive and reciprocal increases in *BELLICOSITY* at *increasing* rates (i.e. arms races) would seem to suggest a corresponding increase in tensions. Once a certain threshold in tension acceleration has been passed, e.g. the "point of no return," war could break out.

As is implied here, the paradox inherent in increasing *BELLICOSITY* at *increasing* rates is that such behavior may lead, in seemingly deterministic fashion, to the very blow-up it may have been intended to prevent. The actors could lock in to a negative self-fulfilling conflict spiral where, "if they did not stop to think", the system could explode. This, in brief, is Lewis Richardson's (1939/1960a) theory of the link between arms races and war. It is also the aforementioned "paradox of the defender" or "security dilemma."

On the other hand, the system might not explode, at least not in a linear fashion. According to Ernst Haas (1953/1961, p. 325):

> Further increases on the part of one side will always bring corresponding increases on the part of its competitors, so that in effect a rough equality of power potential will always prevail, a factor which may make for either open conflict or induce fear of refraining from hostilities, depending on circumstances. (Also cited in Sullivan, 1976, p. 165)

In other words, at certain points in an arms race, the probability of war may actually decrease because an original power relationship has been re-established in the form of a "balance of terror": a system of mutual deterrence based upon "mutual assured destruction" (MAD). However, in the absence of explicit attempts at conflict management/resolution, fear-induced inhibitions may prove to be short-lived.

In general, then, there could be a positive relationship between BEL/%BEL and war, albeit a slightly nonlinear one. There could also be positive relationships between BEL/%BEL and the remaining forms of foreign conflict (including (future) BEL/%BEL). Given the functions-of-conflict thesis, increases in BEL/%BEL might stimulate decreases in domestic conflict.

ALLIANCES (ALL): see above definition of ALL as a dependent variable. ALL is like *BELLICOSITY* in that it could facilitate the occurrence of the very phenomenon that it was designed to prevent: war. A defensive alliance, for example, could be perceived by outsiders as an offensive instrument, in which case it might actually provoke, instead of deter, pre-emptive attacks on its members.

Also, the more alliances that a nation enters, or the more nations that enter particular alliances, the more likely that "interaction opportunities" in the system will be reduced (Singer and Small, 1966/1969, p. 514), i.e. nations in the same alliance would be inhibited from competing with their allies and cooperating with outsiders (Singer and Small, 1968, p. 249). Accordingly, alliances would tend to work against previously existing pluralistic cross-pressures, creating a situation where "all members in class Blue line up with one another and against all or most of those in class Red" – in effect, a situation of a wide and deep cleavage (Deutsch and Singer, 1964/1969, p. 317). In such a polarized or polarizing situation, according to Singer and Small, the probability is increased "that some of the many inevitable international conflicts will escalate into military hostilities" (1966/1969, p. 514) – that war will increase not only in frequency, but also in magnitude or severity (1968, p. 249). By implication, alliances should also stimulate increases in other forms of foreign conflict comprising the "steps to war" (e.g. BEL).

While ALL may increase the probability of war, it might not be functional in reducing domestic conflict. Decision-makers intent on defusing explosive internal situations would probably decide on action more reflective of urgency and, therefore, more likely to ensure public perception of an outside threat. But even if decision-makers did decide to enter alliances for the purpose of decreasing domestic instability, such comparatively passive and indirect action alone might not facilitate achievement of the desired objective.

In view of the above, therefore, we would expect positive relationships between ALL and foreign conflict in general, including (future) ALL, and perhaps a negative relationship with domestic conflict.

AGGRESSIVE ATTACKS (ATT): see above definition of ATT as a dependent variable.

CHANGE IN AGGRESSIVE ATTACKS (%ATT) refers to the rate of change over time in a political actor's employment of its active capability to wage war.

A situation characterized by increases in the frequency of war at *increasing* rates would probably involve the socialization of actors into *aggressive cognitive sets* whereby they continually expected to wage war, always prepared for it, and, indeed, always found reasons for waging it. Consequently, we would expect a positive relationship between (lagged) ATT/%ATT and (future) ATT, as well as positive relationships between ATT/%ATT and other forms of foreign conflict.

Increases in ATT at *increasing* rates would probably tend to be associated with decreases in domestic conflict because of the potential internal solidifying power of this extreme form of external conflict. However, depending upon specific war outcomes, the degree of basic consensus within a war-making actor, and the internal impact over time of "more guns than butter," the relationship could be a nonlinear one.

ATTACK VICTIM (VICT) refers to a political actor coming under attack by the armed forces of one or more other actors. As already indicated in our discussion of BEL and %BEL, increases in arms levels at *increasing* rates may be a decision-making unit's response to its perception of similar behaviors undertaken by other actors. Of course, such a response may itself be an unintended provocative encouragement to those other actors to respond in kind. And so, according to the "paradox of the defender" and the "security dilemma," a conflict spiral may be born. Similarly, an aggressive attack by one actor on another may be the attacker's response to previous aggression by the victim as well as an unintended stimulus for the victim to reciprocate the aggression later on. Such is the stuff of *action–reaction theory*, which posits that outgoing behavior is a nearly automatic, mirror-image reaction to incoming behavior: "bite and counter-bite."

When aggression characterizes relations between nations for relatively long periods of time, we have, in effect, reciprocal socialization into aggressive cognitive sets, or an *international feud.* According to Quincy Wright (1964, p. 399), "these feuds grow in part . . . from the sentiment of revenge natural in a population which has been the victim of war." Such sentiments derive not only from personal experience of an assault upon one's nation but also from "dramatic accounts of the invasions and barbarities of past wars in popular histories" (*ibid.*). To explain international feuds only in terms of a quasi-mechanistic action–reaction model, therefore, would seem to conceal the operation of *learning* processes: direct or vicarious learning, not only of an act of victimization, but also of the means by which it was carried out.

Of the two types of learning, Kenneth Boulding (1956, p. 114) appears to give more weight to direct experience than to vicarious learning: "the shared experience of danger . . . more than anything else creates the national spirit. Nations are the creation not of their historians, but of their enemies." It is probably some combination of both direct and vicarious learning, however, that encourages a reaction in kind to perceived victimization.

The knowledge that one's national group has been victimized could lead to a tension associated with *frustration*: a felt discrepancy between a preferred state of affairs (not having been attacked) and an actual state of affairs (having been attacked). Given the extreme nature of VICT, a likely means for expressing and releasing this tension, and, therefore, for returning to some semblance of affective equilibrium, would be "to fight fire with fire." Such is the stuff of *balance theory* (a composite of frustration–aggression and similar theories), which posits that increased tension motivates actors to reduce it: the more extreme the tension, the more extreme the motivation (and corresponding attempt) to reduce it.

Although *balance theory*, *learning theory* and *action–reaction theory* emphasize different aspects of international feuds, together providing a fuller account of the phenomenon than does any one of them alone (see Patchen, 1970; Milstein, 1972), all three agree that a positive relationship between VICT and foreign conflict behavior is likely.

On the relationship between VICT and domestic conflict, the effect of an attack upon a group could be a strengthening of its internal unity. However, depending upon the extent to which the group enjoyed basic consensus before the attack and whether the attack was successfully fought off, VICT could also lead to increases in domestic conflict. Hence, VICT may have a nonlinear relationship with domestic conflict.

Trans-societal Level

SYSTEMIC ENVIRONMENTAL COMPLEXITY (SEC) refers to the number of other actors in a political actor's external environment. In this regard, Quincy Wright (1964, p. 122) has proposed that balance-of-power "stability will increase and the probability of war will decrease in proportion as the number of states in the system increases." Wright anticipated here Karl Deutsch and David Singer (1964/1969), who argued that, at least in the short run, there is a positive relationship between the number of independent actors in a system and the stability of that system.[18]

In the long run, however, the relationship between number of actors and stability may be negative (see *ibid.*, pp. 323–4). Wright (1964, p. 123) also proposed that an increase in system size might be destabilizing if establishment system-members were uncertain about the intentions of new members. In this regard, he seems to have anticipated Richard Rosecrance (1966/1969, pp. 329–30), who, in his critique of Deutsch and Singer (and of Waltz, 1964), put forward the following:

> a multipolar international system, while reducing the significance of any single change of alignment or military posture, inevitably compounds uncertainty. In a bipolar world, an adjustment in relative position of the two poles is important for the entire system. Changes, however, are relatively simple to predict. In a multipolar world a single alteration in alliance combination or military prowess may not be decisive for the system as a whole, but its consequences are far more difficult to calculate (see Burns, 1957). The number of tentative combinations is astronomic; military dispositions may take myriad forms. Multipolarity, then, raises the difficulty of policy-making. Results may be altogether unforeseen; choice becomes very complex. Since multipolarity raises incalculability, the system finds it more difficult to achieve stable results. War may occur, not through a failure of will, but through a failure of comprehension.

Rosecrance (1966/1969, p. 329) also argues that multipolarity increases diversity – producing a "bewildering range of claims and interests" – and, therefore, increases "the number of international conflicts, though it may possibly reduce their significance." In this regard, Rosecrance seems to have anticipated, to some extent, Daniel Frei (1974, p. 629), who has proposed that, "The greater the number of new states entering the international system, the higher the probability that consensus about norms will disintegrate."

In view of the above, we can assume: (a) that increases in SEC will be associated with a tendency for the system to move away from bipolarity toward multipolarity; (b) that increases in multipolarity will tend to be associated with increased interaction opportunities; (c) "that, in the international system of the nineteenth and twentieth centuries, such opportunities are as likely to be competitive as they are to be cooperative" (Deutsch and Singer, 1964/1969, p. 317); (d) that the *cognitive overload* associated with increases in environmental complexity may be reduced by translating some of these opportunities into indirectly competitive ones (e.g. through increases in alliance-aggregation); (e) that the uncertainty associated with change in general and the intentions of new system-members in particular may be reduced by translating some of these opportunities into directly competitive ones (e.g. through increases in *BELLICOSITY* and in *AGGRESSIVE ATTACKS*); and (f) as long as decision-makers can attempt to displace internal conflicts on to external targets through increases in *ALLIANCES*, *BELLICOSITY*, and *AGGRESSIVE ATTACKS*, that increases in SEC (the number of potential targets) would be associated with decreases in domestic conflict.

In general, then, we would expect a nonlinear positive relationship between SEC and foreign conflict, with a positive relationship with foreign conflict associated with a negative relationship with domestic conflict.

SYSTEMIC ATTACK CONTAGION (SAC) refers to the number of wars waged by others in a political actor's external environment. Our various environments provide us with opportunities for *learning* to behave aggressively in certain situations. Aggressive models are implicit in certain actions which others direct at us (e.g. *ATTACK VICTIM*), at themselves (e.g. *DOMESTIC INSTABILITY*), and at others. *SYSTEMIC ATTACK CONTAGION* is concerned with the last – with the aggressive learning opportunities implicit in our awareness of how some actors have behaved toward other actors.

George Modelski (1972, p. 290) tells us that, "under all conditions ... violence must be kept under some degree of restraint and control, because it has a tendency *to spread at an explosive rate*, by *infection* or by *demonstration effect*" (emphasis added). Although this statement may conform to conventional wisdom, the nature of the process by which awareness translates into emulation of an aggressive model may not be so clear. Modelski's discussion, however, offers some clues. A *demonstration-effect* occurs when people are exposed to a certain way of doing things – when they are confronted with a model that *demonstrates* to them a certain response to certain situations. *Infection*, on the other hand, concerns the *bandwagon-effect*, which occurs when people are exposed to the phenomenon of more and more people behaving in a certain way in certain situations. The difference between the two is one of kind as well as degree.

In terms of *kind*, the *demonstration-effect* involves becoming aware of a mode of behavior, whereas the *bandwagon-effect* involves becoming compellingly aware that more and more people are behaving in terms of that mode. In the demonstration-effect, the model is primary, whereas in the bandwagon-effect increasing numbers of others behaving in terms of the model is primary. In relation to *degree*, more people may be involved in and affected by the bandwagon- than by the demonstration-effect.

Returning to Modelski's statement, we can imagine that both demonstration- and bandwagon-effects would be involved in the explosive spread of violence. For instance, an aggressive incident somewhere in the world may have a demonstration-effect on actors who are susceptible to the implicit aggressive model. As these actors emulate the model, their behavior can have a bandwagon-effect on others, not because the latter are susceptible to the model but because of a need which may be fulfilled by doing what others are doing (see Asch, 1956; Janis, 1972). "Doing something" in this sense may involve an attempt to reduce tension which has been brought about, in part, by diffusion of the model. As Quincy Wright (1964, p. 273) points out, "threats of, or resort to, violence in any corner of the world, under modern conditions of communication ... induce a general rise in the tension level." In either case, whether one is influenced by demonstration- or bandwagon-effects, one may reflect either *homogeneous ("intra-conflict") contagion*, i.e. join in one particular (perhaps the original) violent exchange, or *heterogeneous ("cross-conflict") contagion*, i.e. replicate the model elsewhere (both of which seem to characterize the "spillover potential" inherent in the ethnic wars in former Yugoslavia).

In general, then, there would seem to be a positive relationship between SAC and foreign conflict, although probably a nonlinear one in most cases. That is, increases in SAC would probably stimulate increases in BEL at constant or *decreasing* rates when the threat of being drawn into a conflict was low, and at *increasing* rates when the threat was high. If SAC stimulated increases in BEL at constant or *decreasing* rates, it could have a negative relationship with MD. On the other hand, it could have a positive relationship with MD if SAC stimulated increases in BEL at *increasing* rates. Increases in SAC would probably also stimulate increases in ALL, but as conflict throughout the global system became more and more frequent or intense, drawing more and more actors in, alliance systems could begin to fragment into their individual parts. In contrast to these possibly nonlinear relationships, there would probably be a positive (linear) relationship between SAC and ATT, with different actors being pulled into aggressive conflict situations at different times, depending upon whether they were, among other things, susceptible to demonstration- or bandwagon-effects.

Given the functions-of-conflict thesis, whenever SAC has a positive relationship with foreign conflict, it may have a negative relationship with domestic conflict. Alternatively, increases in the number of wars being waged by others might have an internal solidifying effect on actors not involved, perhaps because of their expectation that they, too, might be drawn into one of the ongoing conflicts. Over time, however, increases in SAC could have an internal bandwagon-effect and lead to increases in domestic conflict, which might, later on, lead to increases in foreign conflict and other phases of the functions-of-conflict process. The relationship between SAC and domestic conflict, therefore, is likely to be nonlinear.

General Observations: Cross-variable Commonalities

At least five "cross-variable" themes stand out in the above discussions of the variables comprising the pretheory:

1. Most of the potential independent variables are associated with the *functions-of-conflict thesis*, e.g. hypothesized positive relationships with foreign conflict are associated with hypothesized negative relationships with domestic conflicts.
2. Some variables appear to develop from (and become *defense mechanism* responses to) *anxiety* (e.g. DOG, AUTH, POLC, and PERC). Other variables can produce anxiety (e.g. SEC and SAC). Still other variables

(e.g. SSEC, TO, RES, RED, and VICT) appear to be related to *frustration*, which itself has a connection with anxiety as well as violent conflict.

3. *Learning theory* is implicated in, among others, the functions-of-conflict thesis and in relationships involving other independent variables (e.g. VICT and SAC).
4. Observations 2 and 3 reinforce the sense that there is a dynamic, interactive link between *organism* (anxiety, frustration) and *environment* (learning), which is implicit in our multilevel framework; or as I have argued elsewhere (Sandole, 1984, p. 40): "to explain any human behavior, we must take into account (1) the *actor(s)* involved, (2) the actor's *environment*, and (3) *interaction* between the actor and *his/her* environment" (emphasis added).
5. Finally, quite a few *nonlinear* relationships have been hypothesized, many of which concern DI as the dependent variable, reinforcing the aforementioned suggestion that nonlinearity – "complexity" – may offer at least part of an explanation for the otherwise contradictory findings noted in Chapter 1.

Conclusion

In this chapter, we have presented a multilevel, multidimensional framework and corresponding pretheory linking each of 23 potential independent variables to domestic and foreign conflict. Although comprising hypothesized *bivariate* relationships, the pretheory can be characterized as an embryonic set of linked *concatenated theories*, i.e. for each of our dependent variables:

> A concatenated theory is one whose component laws [i.e. our hypothesized relationships] enter into a network of relations so as to constitute an identifiable configuration or pattern. Most typically, they converge on some central point [i.e. the dependent variable], each specifying one of the functions which plays a part in the phenomena which the theory is to explain. (Kaplan, 1964, p. 298)

Since we indicated in Chapter 1 that we would be conducting an empirical assessment of Waltz's proposition that, in the genesis of violent international conflict, variables operative at the international level are more potent than those at the societal and decision-making levels, we could, at this juncture, also hypothesize that the two trans-societal variables, SEC and SAC, would have stronger relationships with some or all of the foreign conflict variables than would any of the decision-making or societal variables.

We will explore these and the other hypotheses via simulation-based multivariate conflict models in Chapter 4 and validation assessment of simulation results in Chapter 5. We will also explore, in Chapter 6, the extent to which our pretheory, conflict models, validation results, and a revisiting of the literature combine into a *generic theory* of violent conflict and war – one which is at least a *concatenated*, if not (to some extent) a *hierarchical*, theory (see Kaplan, 1964, pp. 298–9). But first, in Chapter 3, we explore the world of simulation: the source of the data which produced the "stuff" of our multivariate conflict models.

Notes

1. The literature reveals very little consensus on the nature of conflict, defining it variously in terms of: (a) *antecedent conditions* (e.g. scarce resources or positions); (b) *affective states* (e.g. stress, tension, hostility, anxiety); (c) *cognitive states* (e.g. perceptions of awareness of conflictful situations); and (d) actual *conflictful behavior*, which may lie anywhere on a continuum bounded by passive resistance on one end and overt aggressive behavior on the other (see Pondy, 1967/1972, p. 359). The definition of conflict used here, *qua* "manifest conflict process" (MCP), is a synthesis of various definitions found in the literature. It incorporates antecedent conditions (mutually incompatible goals generated by scarcity), cognitive states (awareness of such goals), and conflictual behavior (attempts by the parties to undermine each other's goal-seeking capability). Although the definition does not make specific reference to affective states, it is assumed that all MCPs involve some degree of tension, which may or may not translate into hostility.
2. The literature also reveals very little consensus on the nature of aggression. This definition, like that of MCP, is a synthesis of various definitions found in the literature.
3. This is, of course, a complex example. The requestors and facilitators of euthanasia could be in an MCP with state authorities who prohibit such acts, with the facilitators, perhaps, experiencing an MCP with (active) aggression (e.g. prosecution followed by a severe sentence). On the other hand, by refusing to submit to the request of a person in great pain who is slowly dying to facilitate his or her death, the state, or those who comply with its prohibitions, could be viewed as perpetrators of (passive) aggression within an MCP. In Ottawa, for example, the Canadian Supreme Court:

   > ruled, 5 to 4, against a terminally ill woman who had asked for the right to a doctor-assisted suicide. . . .
   >
   > Sue Rodriguez, . . . of Victoria, B.C., has been suffering from amyotrophic lateral sclerosis or Lou Gehrig's disease, for two years. She is too disabled to take her own life, but has said she has found a doctor who was willing to help her if the court declared it legal.
   >
   > Speaking with difficulty at a news conference after the ruling, Rodriguez said, "While I may not benefit from this decision, I hope Parliament will act and allow those who are in my position" to take their own lives. (Swardson, 1993)

   In defiance of this ruling, Sue Rodriguez, with the assistance of a physician, had her wishes carried out on February 12, 1994 (see Trueheart, 1994).
4. These "complex" definitions of conflict and cooperative systems are compatible with a *complexity theory* interpretation of conflict and cooperation (see Waldrop, 1992). (Chapter 8 includes a discussion of complexity theory and its further relevance to this study.)
5. Others whose ideas are reflected here include Kelman (1965, pp. 31–3), Mack and Snyder (1957, p. 225), Midlarsky (1975, pp. 4–8), Rosenau (1966, pp. 42–3), Singer and Small (1968, pp. 247–8), and Singer (1969).
6. Rokeach and his colleagues have reported correlations between *DOGMATISM* and anxiety in the range of + 0.36 to + 0.64 (Rokeach, 1960, pp. 348, 380). Also, results of

factor analyses suggest that *DOGMATISM* and anxiety are factorially similar (*ibid.*, p. 360; Kerlinger and Rokeach, 1966).

7. According to Morton Deutsch (1971, p. 41), the "literature dealing with psychopathology suggests that intense psychic conflict is likely to have pathological consequences when it elicits anxiety, when it is unconscious, and when the individual in conflict lacks ego strength."
8. A positive relationship between two variables means that changes in the values of the variables occur in the same direction, e.g. increases in the values of one variable are accompanied by increases in the values of the other variable. A negative relationship, on the other hand, means that changes in the values of the variables occur in opposite directions, e.g. increases in one variable are accompanied by decreases in the other variable.
9. According to Greenstein (1969), however, not all fascists are pathological. In this regard, note his distinction between "ego-defensive authoritarianism" and "cognitive authoritarianism" (*ibid.*, pp. 108–11).
10. For some critiques as well as defenses of Adorno's work on authoritarianism, see Ray (1988a, b, 1990), Eckhardt (1991), Sidanius (1988), Duckitt (1989), Meloen *et al.* (1988), Jackson (1991), Smither (1993).
11. Alienation certainly plays a role in Marxist conflict theory (see McBride, 1977, p. 136; Ollman, 1971, especially Part III).
12. Some insights into these kinds of conflict processes are provided later in this chapter by our discussion of *SYSTEMIC ATTACK CONTAGION*.
13. Three centuries prior to Simmel, Jean Bodin (1955, pp. 168-9) argued: "the best way of preserving a state, and guaranteeing it against sedition, rebellion, and civil war is to keep the subjects in amity one with another, and to this end, to find an enemy against whom they can make common cause" (cited in Waltz, 1959, p. 81; Levy, 1989b, p. 259; Levy, 1996, p. 10).
14. A *linear* relationship is one whose spatial representation conforms to a straight line. A positive linear relationship would be characterized by a southwest-to-northeast directional line in a two-dimensional space. A negative linear relationship, on the other hand, would appear spatially as a line connecting northwest with southeast.

    Aspects of the real world, however, may not conform to this pattern. When conflict researchers measure their variables, they are effectively capturing – and freezing in time – *static* bits and pieces ("snapshots") of otherwise complex, *dynamic* evolving behavioral systems. Different researchers may not only be measuring the "same" variables in different ways, with different kinds of measurement error creeping in, but at different points (phases/stages) in an overall *nonlinear* conflict relationship: during part of a period under study, the relationship between two variables may be positive, but during another period, negative. The spatial representation of such a relationship would conform to some kind of curve.
15. The spatial representation of this relationship would be a curve, similar in appearance to a backwards-facing "C," drawn from north to south along the vertical (y) axis (the "modernity continuum") in a two-dimensional space.
16. A "necessary" condition is one which must be present in order for a hypothesized state of affairs to occur, but its presence does not assure the realization of that state of affairs. A "sufficient" condition, on the other hand, does assure the realization of the state of affairs.
17. Needless to say, it might be difficult to empirically distinguish an act of cognitive aggression from an act of affective aggression. In any case, for an early attempt to resolve this problem with the original formulation of the frustration–aggression hypothesis, see Miller (1941).
18. While Wright speaks of a decrease in the probability of war without specifying whether he means *frequency* or *intensity* (or both), Deutsch and Singer (1964/1969, p. 315) begin their article by stating, "as the system moves away from bipolarity towards

multipolarity, the frequency *and* intensity of war should be expected to diminish" (emphasis added). Wright does, however, make a distinction elsewhere in his *Study of War*: "If the world's population is divided into many small groups . . . oppositions are likely to be moderate, whereas if there are a few large groups they are likely to be intense. In the latter case, while conflicts will be less frequent, they will be more violent" (Wright, 1964, p. 240).

3 Accessing Violent Conflict and War: A Simulation-based Design

Introduction

As operational background to the conflict models presented in Chapter 4, we discuss, in this chapter, experimentation and simulation as methods of data generation; the particular gaming-simulation selected for use in this study, the *Prisoners' Dilemma Simulation* (PDS); and the reasons for its selection.

Experimentation

According to Abraham Kaplan (1964, pp. 9–10), the "most widely accepted reconstruction of science," the *hypothetico-deductive method*, involves:

> the scientist, by a combination of careful observation, shrewd guesses, and scientific intuition arriv[ing] at a set of postulates governing the phenomena in which he is interested; from these he deduces observable consequences; he then tests these consequences by *experiment*, and so confirms or disconfirms the postulates, replacing them where necessary, by others, and so continuing. (Emphasis added)

Without concerning ourselves here with the question of whether this exemplar of scientific method is a *prescriptive* ideal or a *descriptive* norm, or both – and for whom – we note that experiment plays a central role in it. Also, we could imagine that experiment in this context means *controlled experiment*, which involves scientists in, for instance, laboratory settings manipulating the values of one independent variable at a time while holding the values of the remaining independent variables constant, in order to determine the effect of changes in each independent variable on a given dependent variable.

For many scholars and lay-persons, experiment in this strict sense *is* the scientific method; moreover, it is a criterion by which one can determine which fields are, and which fields are not, *sciences* (and, therefore, who are, and who are not, *scientists*). Accordingly, there are those who argue that only fields concerned with the systematic study of the natural world – which, more than others, employ experiment in the strict sense – are sciences, whereas fields concerned with the study of human behavior – in which it is ethically as well as methodologically problematic to conduct experiments in the strict sense – are not!

Such arguments, which are often linked to other dimensions of academic "great debates," reflect an assumption of a simplistic binary world where scholars can, or cannot, experiment; where they are, or are not, scientific.[1] Such an assumption does metaphysical violence to some of the natural as well as to the social sciences. For instance, in addressing the question, "Is controlled experimentation a *sine qua non* for achieving warranted factual knowledge, and in particular for establishing general laws?", Ernest Nagel (1961, p. 452) points out that:

> Neither astronomy nor astrophysics is an experimental science, even if each employs many assumptions that are patently based on the experimental findings of other disciplines. Although during the eighteenth and nineteenth centuries astronomy was rightly held to be superior to all other sciences in the stability of its comprehensive theory and in the accuracy of its predictions, it certainly did not achieve this superiority by experimentally manipulating celestial bodies. Moreover, even in branches of inquiry nowhere near the theoretical level of astronomy (e.g. geology, or until relatively recently embryology), lack of opportunity for controlled experiment has not prevented scientists from arriving at well-grounded general laws.

Controlled experimentation would not, therefore, appear to be a necessary condition for the development of general laws on any (natural or social) subject matter. What does qualify for this pivotal role is what Nagel calls *controlled empirical inquiry*, which may be pursued via controlled experimentation or controlled investigation.

Whereas *controlled experimentation* involves intervening directly into a subject matter and performing operations directly on it within an operational setting reflective of various degrees of control, *controlled investigation* involves either direct or statistical intervention into a subject matter, statistical manipulation of data on the subject matter (e.g. via transformations)[2] and statistical control of data on the subject matter (e.g. via computation of *partial correlation coefficients*).[3] In effect, in controlled experimentation, we manipulate and control the subject matter *directly*, whereas in controlled investigation, we manipulate and control the subject matter *indirectly* via statistical operations on its data.

Despite these differences, controlled experimentation and controlled investigation are characterized by an "identity in logical function" (Nagel, 1961, p. 453):

> From the perspective of the logical role which empirical data play in inquiry, it is clearly immaterial whether the observed variations in the assumed determining factors for observed changes in the phenomenon are introduced by the scientist himself, or whether such variations have been produced "naturally" and are simply found by him – provided that in each case the observations have been made with equal care and that the occurrences manifesting the variations in the factors and in the phenomenon are alike in all other relevant respects. It is for this reason that

experimentation is often regarded as a limiting form of controlled investigation, and that sometimes the two provisos are not even distinguished.

Accordingly, we now have a basis for an alternative vision of scientific method, with *controlled empirical inquiry* playing the pivotal role. Such a conception would seem to qualify students of human behavior, as well as their counterparts in the natural sciences, as "scientists."

But even here (as suggested in note 1), there are those who would argue that, given the nature of the subject matter of the social sciences, the measurement of variables and statistical processing and manipulation of these constitute operations that are either impossible to perform or improper or irrelevant.[4] For these scholars, even controlled investigation is beyond the reach of social scientists; consequently, students of human behavior might be disqualified as scientists yet again. In any case, "it is less important to draw a fine line between what is 'scientific' and what is not than to cherish every opportunity for scientific growth" (Kaplan, 1964, p. 28). The significance of controlled investigation is that it constitutes such an opportunity. But this still leaves unanswered the question of whether social scientists can conduct experiments, in the strict or any other sense, as well as controlled investigations.

A literature review in the social sciences would indicate that "much empirical research ... does not even attempt to be controlled inquiry" (Nagel, 1961, p. 459); that the majority of research studies which are controlled inquiries are of the controlled investigation type (*ibid.*, p. 457); and that controlled investigations are subdivided into (a) statistical interventions, i.e. analyses of existing data (*secondary analyses*), and (b) direct interventions, where researchers generate, collect, and analyze their own data (*primary analyses*). *Controlled-investigation primary analyses* include observations of ongoing processes within actual social settings, as in *field studies*.[5] They also include data collected through survey questionnaires or interviews designed to explore actors' cognitive and evaluative systems, as in *verbal "experiments."*[6]

Although not as common as the controlled investigation variety, *controlled-experimentation primary analyses* are also conducted in the social sciences. In *field experiments*, for example, researchers intervene directly into and manipulate aspects of actual – or what appear to be actual – environmental settings, in order to explore the factors underlying actor behavior.[7] In *laboratory experiments*, researchers create, intervene directly into, and manipulate artificial settings in order to explore determinants of behavior.[8]

While verbal experiments (controlled investigations) can indicate, in *static* terms, how actors have behaved or might behave in certain situations, field and laboratory experiments (controlled experiments) can, in *dynamic* terms, reveal actors' actual behaviors or behavioral tendencies in these and similar situations. But while verbal experiments are "widespread in contemporary behavioral science" (Kaplan, 1964, p. 163), field and laboratory experiments are less so, because of the operational and ethical difficulties involved in directly manipulating and controlling aspects of actual or contrived social settings (see Nagel, 1961, p. 455).

Because they are conducted in actual, or near-actual, social settings, field experiments tend to be less widespread than laboratory experiments (*ibid.*, p. 457), i.e. it is far easier to manipulate and control variables, and achieve *internal validity*, in contrived rather than in actual settings.[9] Laboratory experimenters, however, pay a price for their comparative ease in securing "unambiguous evidence about causation" (Frankfort-Nachmias and Nachmias, 1996, p. 147), as the necessity to generalize, i.e. to validate findings in the sense of *external validity*, is greater in laboratory than in field experiments.[10]

In any case, "despite widespread claims that experimentation in the strict sense is not feasible, several types of experiments are in fact employed in the social sciences" (Nagel, 1961, p. 456). *Postmodernism* notwithstanding, social scientists do, and therefore can, conduct experiments in the strict (laboratory) or nearly strict (field) sense as well as controlled investigations. Hence, "the argument that the behavioral scientist cannot experiment because his subject matter does not lend itself to manipulation is embarrassingly superficial" (Kaplan, 1964, p. 163).

Simulation

Simulation, like laboratory experimentation, involves the creation of artificial settings in which researchers can intervene. But while laboratory experimentation involves direct intervention into a subject matter, simulation involves intervention into a *model* of a subject matter. Also, while laboratory experimentation in the social sciences always involves humans (or animals) as subjects, simulation, even when concerned with human processes (e.g. decision-making), may not employ real people at all. In such cases, attempts can be made to replicate human processes by designing appropriate subsystems and operating them via computer.

These distinctions notwithstanding, simulation and laboratory experimentation often blur into one another. For instance, in laboratory experiments involving animal subjects, where the findings are meant to be applicable to human beings, the animals may be viewed as "models" of human beings as well as a subject matter in their own right. Also, in simulations with human subjects, researchers can conduct laboratory experiments *within* the simulations. First, they can investigate the human subjects themselves in terms of their own "real properties" (e.g. beliefs and values); second, they can investigate them as the human components (e.g. "decision-makers") in models of corresponding real-world systems.

Accordingly, while controlled experimentation can include a simulation component, simulation can lend itself to controlled experimentation. Hence, the expression "lab/sims." Researchers can also use, within simulation, much of the research methodology they employ in the real world. For instance, they can conduct field studies and observe the structures and processes of simulation life, as anthropologists observe tribal subcultures. They can conduct verbal experiments by interviewing simulation actors, as political scientists and sociologists interview elites, specific groups and mass publics. They can also content-analyze simulation messages, documents (e.g. "treaties"), and actors' notes, and systematically observe video tapes of group and intergroup processes.[11]

Simulation also lends itself, therefore, to controlled investigation. In such cases, researchers can statistically manipulate and control data generated by field studies and verbal experiments in the simulate-world, as I have done in this study (see Chapter 4).

Whether simulation is used for controlled experimentation or controlled investigation, it comprises not only a *model* of some corresponding referent but also a *script* which governs the operation of the model, as well as an endogenous *agent of operation* which plays out the model in accordance with the script. Some scripts call for human players, and some do not, even, as already mentioned, in cases where the simulation has been designed to replicate human processes. And all scripts call for some degree of exogenous human operation.

According to Table 3.1,[12] simulations in a strict sense, such as the *Technological, Economic, Military and Political Evaluation Routine* (TEMPER), *Simulated International ProcessER* (SIPER), and *Generating Long-range Options by Using Simulation* (GLOBUS), involve highly structured models that are played out by computers in accordance with highly structured formats or scripts. *Scenario-games*, such as the *Political Military Exercise* (PME), on the other hand, involve relatively simple models and scripts as well as human players. Somewhere in between the model-script complexity of simulations and simplicity of scenario-games are *gaming-simulations*, such as the *Inter-Nation Simulation* (INS), *International Process Simulation* (IPS), and *World Politics Simulation* (WPS), which involve human – or some combination of human and machine – agents of operation.

The more empirically valid an existing theory and the ease with which it translates into a model for use in simulation, the more empirically valid the simulation input. And the more empirically valid the interactive dynamics of the operating model, the more empirically valid the simulation output. There is no necessary connection, however, between input validity and output validity. In cases where theory is virtually nonexistent or, if existent, inadequate for transformation into a simulation, a researcher can still, on the basis of intuition, construct and operate a simulation whose output may be, to some extent, empirically valid. Especially in a simulation with human participants, who bring into the operation "real properties" (Hermann, 1967, pp. 227–8), the starting conditions can be overtaken by the interactive dynamics of the operation, producing output that is relevant to the real world.[13]

Simulation constitutes, for human participants, an apparently effective pedagogical device (see Boocock and Schild, 1968; Taylor and Walford, 1972). And "if a procedure is sufficiently realistic to be regarded as an adequate training device, it will also be realistic enough to serve as a research device" (Nicholson, 1975, p. 2). As a research tool, simulation generates dynamic behavioral systems which are *accessible*, *controllable* and *replicable* (see Hermann, 1969, pp. 37-41). Consequently, it facilitates the exploration of "what-if" situations, the development of a predictive capability, and the generation of hypotheses. However, until simulation output is assessed against the background of the corresponding real world, it will constitute either hypotheses in

Table 3.1 A typology of simulations

Type	Model	Script	Endogenous agent of operation	Examples
Formal format (sometimes referred to, simply, as *simulation*)	All units, the multitude of variables in terms of which they behave, and interrelationships among the variables are incorporated into the model in terms of various degrees of generality (coarseness) or specificity (fineness)	A structured format governs unit behavior and outcomes of unit behavior	Computer (hence, sometimes referred to as *computer simulation*)	1. *Simple Diplomatic Game* 2. *Technological, Economic, Military and Political Evaluation Routine* (TEMPER) 3. *Simulated International ProcessER* (SIPER) 4. *Generating Long-range Options by Using Simulation* (GLOBUS)
Casual format (sometimes referred to as *scenario-exercise*)	All units and some variables are provided for in terms of various degrees of coarseness or fineness. However, the relationships among the variables are "black-boxed" (i.e. unspecified)	The behavior of the units is, within the model, not structured except to the extent that specific role categories and an initial problem or scenario are provided. Moreover the rules of the game and the outcomes of unit behavior tend to be governed by the implicit "reality" criteria of a control team	Human (hence, sometimes referred to as *manual simulation*)	*Political Military Exercise* (PME) or *Political Exercise* (PE)

Table 3.1 *(continued)*

Type	Model	Script	Endogenous agent of operation	Examples
Symbiotic format (sometimes referred to as *gaming-simulation*)	All units, and some variables and their interrelationships, are provided for in terms of various degrees of coarseness or fineness	The behavior of some units is, within the model, not structured except to the extent that role categories, behavior categories, and rules of the game are provided. The behavior of the remaining units, and their relationships to the above units, and/or the outcomes of all behavior, are governed by a structured format	Human or a mixture of human and computer (hence, sometimes referred to as *man–computer simulation*)	1. *Inter-Nation Simulation* (INS) 2. *International Process Simulation* (IPS) 3. *World Politics Simulation* (WPS) 4. *Prisoners' Dilemma Simulation* (PDS)

need of real-world testing or sources of hypotheses which have to be mined from the raw data and ultimately tested. In either case, simulation output may be heuristically but not demonstrably relevant to the real world. Consequently, if theory development is a primary objective, as it is in this study, then output validation ("external validity") must be an important facet of simulation use.[14]

If simulation output holds up relatively well in relation to aspects of the real world to which we do have access, it may also be useful for exploring those aspects to which we do not (yet) have access. While the use of simulation output in this latter sense may be methodologically problematic, it may also be practical. Given the progressively dysfunctional nature of violent *intra*- and *inter*national conflict, it may be in our best (local and global) interests to explore and exploit indirect routes rather than bemoan the absence of direct routes or the difficulties inherent in whatever direct routes we do have to the development of a generic (multilevel, multidimensional) theory of violent conflict and war.[15]

The Prisoners' Dilemma

The *Prisoners' Dilemma Simulation* (PDS) was selected to generate primary data for this study. Prisoners' Dilemma is the name given by the mathematician A. W. Tucker to the now well-known paradox in *game theory* (Axelrod, 1984, pp. 7 and 216 n2),[16] in which, according to Rapoport (1972, p. 261):

> Each of two prisoners, held in separate cells, has a choice of confessing or not confessing to a crime of which both are accused. Neither is to be told what choice the other makes but they are told that if both confess, both will be convicted but given light sentences [−5]; if neither confesses, both will be set free [+5]; if only one confesses, he will be set free and, in addition, rewarded [+10], while the other will be convicted and punished severely [−10].

The essence of this decision-making challenge can be expressed in matrix form, as indicated in Table 3.2.[17]

Finding oneself in this situation, Prisoner A may reason that she is better off confessing, *no matter what the other does*, because: (a) if she does not confess and

Table 3.2 The Prisoners' Dilemma

	Prisoner B	
Prisoner A	Don't confess	Confess
Don't confess	5, 5	−10, 10
Confess	10, −10	−5, −5

Source: From Rapoport, 1964, p. 49, 1965, p. 210.

the other does, she stands to suffer a severe loss (−10) while the other stands to gain a singular victory (+10); or (b) if she does confess and the other does not, she stands to gain (+10) and the other will lose (−10). "The trouble with this cold calculation of self-interest," Rapoport (1960, p. 174) tells us, is that *both* prisoners may reason the same way, each ending up with −5, "whereas if they trusted each other's integrity (as it is understood in the underworld), they would end up with +5 each."

The type of dilemma reflected in PD characterizes not only noncooperative interactions where the players cannot communicate to make agreements on strategy, but also cooperative situations where the actors can communicate to make such agreements. In real-world international relations, a noncooperative version of the Prisoners' Dilemma might be a situation in which it is in the *individual* interests of each of two nations, whose decision-makers do not talk to each other, to add to their respective arsenals, no matter what the other nation does, whereas it is in their *collective* interest to reduce their armaments. In the cooperative version of this situation, where representatives of the two nations have met, communicated and agreed to control and/or reduce their armaments, "it is in the interest of each to break the pact regardless of whether the other keeps it" (Rapoport and Chammah, 1965, p. 25), but in their collective interest to adhere to the agreement.

PD is an illustration of the failure of game theory as prescriptive theory (Axelrod, 1984, p. 29) in any but *zero-sum* contexts: situations of pure conflict where one actor's gain is another's loss. PD is also suggestive of a tendency, for professional as well as lay strategists, especially (but not only) within a *Realpolitik* framework, to apply a zero-sum model and its attendant behavioral norms to *nonzero-sum* situations, i.e. situations in which the actors could generate *positive-sum* (e.g. [+5] + [+5] = +10) or *negative-sum* (e.g. [−5] + [−5] = −10) as well as *zero-sum* (e.g. [+10] + [−10] = 0) outcomes. Such a tendency results in "a gross distortion of the problem under consideration" (Rapoport, 1964, p. 5), whereby the "lack of mutual trust, coupled with perfectly 'rational' considerations, leads to disaster" (Rapoport, 1960, p. 173).

A major positive outcome of attempts to employ game theory in the social sciences has been that the PD phenomenon has facilitated our becoming aware of this tendency and of the possible need for remedial action.[18] One provocative response has been Axelrod's (1984) development, within a PD framework, of a *theory of cooperation*, in which he argues that the evolution of cooperative behavior in an iterated PD context is a generic phenomenon applying to all levels, even the biological. (We will revisit Axelrod in Chapter 8.)

The Prisoners' Dilemma Simulation

The PDS, which was created by Charles A. Powell (1969a, b), is so called because it incorporates the type of dilemma characteristic of PD: upon the initiation of a PDS operation, the actors in an initially two-nation system are faced with a choice between (a) inaction, (b) arming against each other (as might be dictated by *classical rationality*), or (c) trading with each other (as might be dictated by *collective rationality*). In relation to the arming and trading options, actors must decide on one or the other. They cannot arm against and trade with each other at the same time. Hence, players may frequently be confronted with conflicts of mixed motives: to trust the members of another group and trade with them or to distrust them and arm against them. The reasoning of members of Group A, therefore, may be analogous to that of Prisoner A: they are better off arming, no matter what the others do, because (a) if they do not arm and the others do, they stand to suffer a loss (e.g. make themselves vulnerable to conventional or nuclear blackmail) or (b) if they do arm and the others do not, they will gain and the others will lose.

Once again, both parties may reason the same way, each ending up in this case not only with the opportunity costs associated with forfeited trading opportunities, but also with confirmation of their suspicions that the others were "out to get them," which may facilitate a conflict spiral, further opportunity costs, and eventual war. If they trusted each other, on the other hand, they would end up with the material benefits of increased trade.

As the PDS operation continues, it develops into a "multination" situation in which each group can attempt to resolve this either-or problem by singling out one other group against which it will arm and then trading with all other groups. In contrast to the noncooperative or cooperative versions of the two-group PDS, therefore, the multigroup PDS tends to encompass elements of both renditions of PD, usually with noncooperative elements contained within a cooperative framework.

Even here, however, there will always be some temptation for actors to defect from trade agreements. Assuming the dominance within the actors of zero-sum rationality – which is one of the tenets of realism (see Morgenthau, 1973, Chapter 1) – there will always be some chance that positive-sum, *benign* outcomes will be replaced by zero-sum, *conflict* outcomes. Once this has occurred, the loser in each case may feel highly motivated to reciprocate in kind, either alone or in counter-alliance with other groups. This would tend to encourage, as in the two-nation system, the locking-in of the relationship to a conflict spiral – very much like the runaway arms race of Lewis Richardson's (1939, 1960a) unstable-equilibrium model – in which the actors generate successive negative-sum, *malign* outcomes.[19]

PDS Model and Script

Before we justify our selection of the *Prisoners' Dilemma Simulation*, in lieu of other operations listed in Table 3.1, it would be helpful if we first discussed the nature of the PDS "world" and its development.

According to the *Basic Simulation Manual* (Appendix A.1), the PDS world at "time zero" consists of two nation-groups, each comprising decision-makers and "validators," credited with a basic gross national product (GNP) of $500 billion, and unarmed. Although GNP is comprised of "gross national consumption product" (GNCP) and "gross national armaments product" (GNAP), the initially unarmed status of the two groups means that the basic GNP of $500 billion is credited to each group only in terms of its GNCP account. Activation of the GNAP category, therefore, is a function of actor choice.

The payoff which accrues to each nation-group at the end of a decision period is a function of a programmed growth rate of $20 billion (GNCP), plus – if both groups traded – the "gross national trade product" (GNTP) for that period, which is also $20 billion. Hence, if both groups traded during the very first decision period, each would begin the second period with $540 billion in GNP *qua* GNCP ($500b + $20b [GNCP] + $20b [GNTP]). On the other hand, if one group armed for $50 billion and the other traded, the arming group would begin the second decision period with $470 billion in GNCP and $50 billion in GNAP ($500b + $20b [GNCP] − $50b [GNAP]), while the trading group would begin with $520 billion in GNCP ($500b + $20b [GNCP]). And if both groups armed for $50 billion, each would begin the second period with $470 billion in GNCP and $50 billion in GNAP. As already indicated, the groups cannot simultaneously trade with and arm against each other: they must select one or the other option and indicate their decision on a *Decision Form* (Appendix A.2).

The successful implementation of decisions to trade or to arm (or even to "do nothing") during the early stages of a PDS operation is contingent completely on the level of validator satisfaction. This is obtained for each group at the end of each decision period by calculating, in accordance with Part 7.A of the *Basic Simulation Manual*, the mean validator response to the third item of the *Validator Form – Part B* (Appendix A.12(a)). For instance, if validator satisfaction is registered at the 4.2 level, the decisions taken by the group's decision-makers will be implemented without qualification. A reading of 1.3, on the other hand, specifies an orderly transference of power (see Part 7.B of the *Manual*); i.e. the "ruling clique" will be replaced by an equal number of persons drawn from the ranks of the validators (and selected by the validators themselves). The ousted decision-makers will, in turn, assume the status of validators.

The decision-makers of either group can declare war at any time by completing and submitting a *War Form* (Appendix A.3). In such cases, the target group can respond in either of two ways: (a) it can surrender immediately or (b) it can elect to defend itself, in which case it must submit a counter declaration of war. Determinations of winner and loser in any given war are made on the basis of which side has a 10 percent GNAP advantage. If neither side has such a GNAP advantage, the conflict will be stalemated and each group will lose 25 percent of its GNCP and GNAP. On the other hand, if one group does possess such a lead, it will be proclaimed the victor and to it will accrue all but $50 billion of the defeated group's GNCP. The losing side will also forfeit all of its GNAP, which will be written off as "destroyed capability."

Simulation Manual Addendum No. One (Appendix A.4) increases the scope of behavior by specifying conditions under which coups and revolutions can occur. It also specifies the conditions under which new nation-groups can be formed. Effectively, this addendum is the basis for a "multination" system.

According to *Simulation Manual Addendum No. Two* (Appendix A.5), whenever a group is classified as underdeveloped, it must select one of three programs to structure and pace its rate of economic growth or recovery. *Addendum No. Two* also provides information on alliance formation, the development of international organizations, and disarmament schedules.

Once the evolution of the multigroup system has exhausted the supply of human validators, all groups operate in terms of programmed validation. *Simulation Manual Addendum No. Three* (Appendix A.6) specifies that the ratio of each group's GNAP to its total GNP (i.e. GNCP + GNAP) determines its validation level for any given decision period. However, once a certain validation level has been registered, the feedback consequences associated with it are not automatically implemented. There is only about one chance in six that the feedback consequences will actually take effect. For example, if a group's decision to arm at a certain level produces a GNAP/GNP ratio of 510:850, the group's programmed validation routine will record a level-four validation which portends the group's forfeiture of 75 percent of its GNAP and 50 percent of its GNCP. Whether or not these forfeitures are actually implemented depends on the outcome of a toss-of-the dice procedure, e.g. which slip of paper is drawn from a pile of six, five of which have "no" marked on them, and one of which is marked "yes." If "yes" is drawn, then the forfeitures are implemented. Appendix A.6 also provides information on GNAP redeployment and interbloc wars.

Simulation Manual Addendum No. Four (Appendix A.7) provides a niche for a universal actor by establishing an international bargaining room. Although apparently nonpolitical in nature – given its express purpose to provide an appropriate ambience within which international trade can be conducted – the international bargaining room nevertheless constitutes a forum for intergroup dialogue in general and conflict prevention and resolution in particular. Consistent and accurate communication between delegates and their respective groups becomes essential at this point because of the increased risk of trading with and arming against the same group at the same time (including trading with a group against which one's group had armed during previous decision periods). If this were to occur, the erring group's decisions with respect to all other groups at that point would be nullified. It would also lose the GNAP it had accumulated if it traded with another against which it had been previously armed.

Whereas Appendix A.1 specifies a relatively simple arming schedule, *Simulation Manual Addendum No. Five* (Appendix A.8) adds to the progressive complexity of the decision-making environment by specifying an arming schedule which is related directly to GNP levels. For instance, if a group is in possession of a GNP of $1305 billion and its decision-makers decide to arm for the first time, they cannot arm in excess of $420 billion. And if they decide to arm a second time while their total GNP is still under $1400 billion, they cannot convert more than $280 billion of their GNCP into GNAP. And if they wish to continue arming, they cannot arm in excess of $140 billion during each of the remaining periods that their total GNP is under $1400 billion. Attempts to arm in excess of the prescribed levels would result in nullification of the group's decisions. In addition, the programmed validation routines and corresponding potential outcomes of *Addendum No. Three* (Appendix A.6) would still apply.

Simulation Manual Addendum No. Six (Appendix A.9) provides each group with the opportunity to "go nuclear." In this regard, decision-makers can, with 100 percent certainty, initiate a nuclear armaments program only if they have already invested $100 billion of their GNAP in research and development. This investment is not itself converted into nuclear GNAP. Nor is a group's conventional GNAP. However, once a group has made this investment, all of its subsequent defense expenditures can be in terms of nuclear weapons. The status of "effective nuclear power" – i.e. a group which is able to launch nuclear attacks – is achieved only when a group has acquired at least $200 billion in nuclear weapons.

In a war between a group with only conventional arms and a group with at least $100 (but less than $200) billion in nuclear GNAP, there is no winner and loser but, instead, two losers, i.e. both groups forfeit their respective arsenals. On the other hand, in a war between an effective nuclear power and a group with only conventional arms, the former, because of its distinct GNAP superiority, would be proclaimed the victor and enjoy some of the spoils of victory. Victory in this case, however, is not as absolute as it is for conventional war because, although the defeated group forfeits all of its GNAP and all but $50 billion of its GNCP, only 50 percent of its forfeited GNCP accrues to the victor. The rest is just written off as destroyed capability. And in a war between effective nuclear powers, the group or bloc with a 50 percent (no longer 10 percent) advantage over its adversary will win, in which case it will also acquire only 50 percent of the loser's GNCP (minus $50 billion which the loser retains). In the event of a stalemate, each group will forfeit 50 percent of its GNCP and GNAP.

The final attempt to add to the complexity of the decision-makers' environment in PDS is represented by *Simulation Manual Addendum No. Seven* (Appendix A.10), which provides actors with the option of "transnational" integration (as well as subsequent disintegration).[20]

Throughout a PDS operation, communication is virtually unlimited. Decision-makers in each group can communicate among themselves, and with their validators, as well as with their counterparts in other groups, via face-to-face exchange, written message, and, when facilities permit, telephone. Moreover, when the proceedings of the international bargaining room are televised, the delegates can use the TV medium to signal to their respective groups. The validators, on the other hand, are somewhat constrained in this regard: they are permitted to communicate among themselves and with their decision-makers, but not with their counterparts or the decision-makers in other groups.

Operating the PDS

Prior to the first decision period of a PDS operation, the actors are administered a questionnaire (Appendix B) to determine, among other things, which of them are high in "need for achievement" and "need for power."[21] Those who are so identified are assigned to the role of decision-makers for the two incipient groups, usually labelled *Ergo* and *Sumo*. This practice reflects the assumptions and empirical findings of some scholars that decision-makers tend to be high in one or both of these motives (see Powell, 1969b, p. 321; Raser, 1966; Browning, 1968a, b; Winter, 1976). The remaining actors are assigned as validators to the two groups.

The actors assigned to decision-making and validation roles receive no role specification other than the titles *Decision-maker* and *Validator*. In this way, the development of authority structures within each of, as well as between, the two components of a group is left entirely to the actors themselves. This, coupled with the selective juxtapositioning of motivationally different decision-makers and validators, is designed to stimulate *intra*nation interaction and conflict and, consequently, the development of a multigroup system.[22]

From the outset of a PDS operation, each decision-making and each validation component is usually located in a separate room. Whenever available, a telephone and a closed-circuit television receiver are located in each room. One or two laboratory staff (i.e. *Administrators*) are assigned to each component in order to: (a) explicate the contents of the *Basic Simulation Manual* and subsequent addenda, when necessary; (b) administer *Forms A* (Appendices A.11(a)–(b)) after each decision has been submitted to the *Computer*; (c) administer *Forms B* (Appendices A.12(a)–(b)) after the actors have been informed, by either courier or televised newscast, of the outcomes of all decisions; (d) act as couriers and deliver messages to other groups or escort actors (usually decision-makers) to other groups, to conferences, or to the international bargaining room; and (e) make observations, usually on special forms (Appendix A.13), of intra- or intercomponent processes. They are not, as indicated in Appendix A.1, to participate in these processes as decision-makers or validators themselves.[23]

Other laboratory staff are assigned to the *Computer* (i.e. to compute the programmed feedback and "vital statistics" of each group), to operate a switchboard (when a telephone system is available), to deliver televised reports (when television services are available), to deliver messages, and to act as the *Administrators* for the delegates to the international bargaining room (which is usually located in, or adjacent to, a television studio when such services are available).

When the PDS is operated over relatively long periods, e.g. for up to fifteen weeks with one two-hour session per week, the *Basic Simulation Manual* is administered to the actors approximately one week before the operation begins. This is followed by the administration of the first addendum, usually during the first week, and by the administration of the remaining addenda on a successive weekly basis, so that, for instance, by the sixth week the actors have received the sixth addendum.

The Selected PDS Operations

Each of the five PDS operations included in this study (PDS 1, 2, 3, 4 and 5) was conducted once each week for two hours during a thirteen- to fifteen-week period as a laboratory supplement to undergraduate courses in American foreign policy and in international politics at Temple University, Philadelphia, from spring 1966 until spring 1968. The actors in these operations, therefore, were the students enrolled in these classes. They were neither paid cash for their participation nor graded for their performance. They were, however, graded for their written analyses of each weekly run of the PDS (a grade which did figure into the calculation of their final grade for the course which encompassed the PDS).[24]

Powell and his coworkers operated PDS 1–3.[25] I was an actor in PDS 1 and an *Administrator* in PDS 2 and 3. PDS 4 and 5 were operated by me together with my coworkers.

Why the PDS?

The PDS falls into the *symbiotic format* or gaming-simulation category of Table 3.1. I selected it for the present study in order to avail myself of, and to build upon, the raw database developed by PDS designer Powell. Even if the PDS had not already been used to generate a database, it still had advantages – for me, at least – over *formal-format* and *casual-format* operations, as well as over the most widely used symbiotic-format operation in international relations, the *Inter-Nation Simulation* (INS).

The PDS was preferred to *formal-format* operations simply because it involved "real people" as actors. Given the objectives of this study, plus the state of corresponding theory and the nature of formal-format operations, a simulation involving real human components was decided on in order to avoid "premature closure" – imposing rigid parameters on an empirically weak theoretical base (see Kaplan, 1964, pp. 278–80) – as well as to generate information about those areas where the corresponding theory was in fact deficient.

The PDS was preferred to *casual-format* operations, which also employ humans as actors, because: first, the imposition of specific personalities (e.g. Kaiser Wilhelm) on the actors, which is common practice in these operations, could have contaminated the effects of the actors' own personalities on their behavior; and, second, the use of human control teams (in lieu of human or programmed validators), which is also common practice, meant that agents of the experimenters would have been involved in such operations as players. While the implications of the latter are difficult to assess, it seems that the actors in casual-format operations would have to constantly consider the possible reactions of "Control" as well as of other actors to each decision they contemplate taking. This constant juggling of exogenous (real-world) and endogenous (game-world) considerations could serve as a constant reminder that the actors are "only playing a game" and, perhaps, prevent them from getting wrapped up in the "reality" of their intergroup system.[26]

Within the *symbiotic-format* category itself, the PDS was preferred to the most prominent member of that category, the INS, for three reasons. First, although the INS does not involve actors playing specific persons, it does involve them playing specific roles (*Central Decision-maker*, *Aspiring Decision-maker*, *External Decision-maker*), which can also influence the impact of actor-personalities on decision-making behavior, although probably not to the same extent as would the imposition of specific personalities. This is not to suggest that a study of the effects of certain role-types on behavior within simulated or real-world settings would not be a proper research undertaking, that role variables do not affect behavior, or that the PDS is wholly role-free. But, given my intention to investigate, among other things, the relationships between certain personality variables and conflict, the PDS seemed more relevant in this regard than did the INS (or any other operation).

A second reason why the PDS was preferred to the INS is because the latter appears to contain a systematic bias based upon realist assumptions, i.e. the INS seems to directly encourage arming as an instrument of survival and the development of tight bipolar structures as a consequence of the need to maximize security. According to Powell (1969b, pp. 314–15):

> the basic rationality assumption for the INS and most micro-macro or market-type simulations is that the players maximize some basic value in their allocation decisions. In the INS the "market" is the total amount of force capability in the international system. Now, one quick way for the "market" to punish a non-competitive player or group is through an attack on them, particularly if the unit is at a decisive disadvantage. But in addition to this, there is the force ratio, or index of "relative security," which has a strong effect upon [programmed] validator satisfaction, and thus upon the probability of office-retention. Unless no "market" exists (general disarmament), the decision-maker is forced by the model to maximize security by an appropriate transformation of basic capability to force capability. Moreover, security can be even more easily maximized through alliance formation, since bloc force capability is aggregated. (Of course, war is the simplest way to achieve monopoly.) This routine is explicitly designed, as Chadwick admits, "to represent a relatively tight bipolar system" (1967, p. 189). This is the problem with the INS, basically. Its "free" activity must operate within a pretty tightly defined "market" structure and with a basic competitive rationality. This is the mid-1950s "realist" position, and these are the basic facts of international life that the INS is supposed to teach its participants.
>
> ... *if life is really that way, it is unnecessary to have the model force the player to adopt this sort of rationality*. (Emphasis added)

The PDS, in contrast, has been designed by Powell to avoid this problem. Indeed, it may even be argued that the PDS is structurally biased toward cooperative rationality, in that it directly encourages trading rather than arming. (Although some players have argued that when the PDS has been operated over a long period of time, it tends to encourage arming as a counter-measure to "creeping boredom." This may say more about some of the players, however, than about the PDS "forcing" them to behave in a certain way.)

The final reason why the PDS was preferred to the INS concerns our earlier comment that the INS and at least two of its derivatives (the IPS and SIPER) are among the few gaming-simulations in the field of international relations whose outputs have been submitted to validity checks. Specifically regarding the INS, Harold Guetzkow (1966, 1968b; Guetzkow and Valadez, 1981b) has completed a comprehensive assessment of INS findings and has found that, in general, they compare rather favorably with findings from corresponding, mostly real-world, studies. On the one hand, one could argue that the widespread use of INS and the relative success of Guetzkow's findings (which we will discuss further in Chapter 4) should have motivated me to prefer the INS to the PDS, in order to build upon a validated database. On the other hand, however, I would argue that, if part of one's overall research objective is to explore whether small-group systems *in general*, rather than any one particular operation, are capable of replicating (and therefore, revealing) real-world processes, then one should employ operations in addition to the INS and submit their outputs to validity checks as well. If validity assessments of these were to prove as successful as those for the INS, then a stronger case could be made for the value of simulation in general as a source of insight into real-world processes.

Some Possible Concerns

The validation issue relates to two questions one might have about the use of simulation in this study, the most obvious of which is that the PDS operations used to generate our data were run from 1966 to 1968, at a time when the U.S.A. was prosecuting its controversial war in Vietnam, the subject of many campus and other protest demonstrations. One might well assume that those particular runs were affected by the nature of the times in a way different from, say, runs of 1986 to 1988. The second, less obvious, question is raised by the view that simulation is no longer the "done thing" in international relations. *Simulation and Gaming* editor David Crookall (1997) captures this sense in his overview of the differential use of simulation in various fields during the past thirty years:

> The use of simulation/gaming in business education and training is perhaps the most consistent and best documented area in which simulation/gaming is used. In the early years (1960s and 1970s), international relations and politics figured prominently in simulation/gaming. This was followed by a surge of interest in the social sciences (1970s and 1980s). Other areas of considerable development in the last decade that come to mind include policy issues, environmental problems, language learning, human resources, and cross-cultural communication. However, the area of business education and training has probably overtaken all other areas (put together?) in the application of simulation/gaming. This

is probably true for the amount of use and is certainly the case in regard to research conducted into its use.

Simply put, the two questions are: (a) do the "age" of, and *Zeitgeist* surrounding, the PDS data invalidate them from informing our quest to develop theory of complex conflict processes; and (b) do data generated by a technique no longer widely used in international relations, except by a few "diehards," have anything to say about violent conflict and war? A tempting response is to argue that the "unfashionable" is not necessarily invalid, and the "old" may not necessarily be outdated. In any case, these two questions make it all the more imperative to subject the PDS data to comprehensive real-world and other lab/sim validation assessments, which we have done and report on in Chapter 5.

Conclusion

In this chapter, we have discussed experimentation and simulation in general, the *Prisoners' Dilemma Simulation* in particular, and why the PDS was selected for use in this study. In the next two chapters, we move further into the operational setting by presenting and discussing the multilevel, multivariate conflict models developed from data generated by the PDS, and by considering to what extent the findings correspond to those from other, mostly real-world, studies.

Notes

1. In general, debates on the "scientific" status of a field center on whether the behaviors of the relevant subject matter have been conceptualized as being determined by *causal laws*; moreover, on whether members of the field have discovered (or "invented") some of those laws, which indicates the extent to which the subject matter is accessible to the manipulation and control associated with controlled experimentation.

   For some, causal laws may underlie social phenomena but complexity renders the detection of these laws especially problematic. For instance: (a) too many variables may characterize social phenomena; (b) even if a researcher knows which of these variables are the important ones, it may be difficult, if not impossible, to measure them precisely; (c) even if the researcher can measure some of them, precisely or otherwise, his or her measurements may reflect not only the nature of the thing being measured, but also its "reaction" to the process of observation/measurement; (d) the measured factors may make sense only within the particular cultural-temporal context within which the measurements have been made; and (e) even if a scientist gets this far without much error contaminating his or her study, the findings will always be colored by his or her values – the social scientist cannot be value-free (see Nagel, 1961, Chapters 13–15; Popper, 1961, 1972a, Chapter 16; Kaplan, 1964; Rudner, 1966; Ryan, 1970).

   For others, the search for causal laws is a misconceived goal, representing a misconception of the nature of social phenomena, and the search for such via scientific method is a misconceived means, representing a misconception of the methodology of social science. This view, argued eloquently by Peter Winch (1958), has been reinforced by *postmodernists* who, according to Pauline Marie Rosenau (1992, pp. 8–9), "rearrange the whole social science enterprise. . . . They offer indeterminacy rather than determinism, diversity rather than unity, difference rather than synthesis, complexity rather than simplification. They look to the unique rather than to the general, to intertextual relations rather than causality, and to the unrepeatable rather than the re-occurring, the habitual, or the routine. Within a post-modern perspective social science becomes a more subjective and humble enterprise as truth gives way to tentativeness. Confidence in emotion replaces efforts at impartial observation. Relativism is preferred to objectivity, fragmentation to totalization. Attempts to apply the model of natural science inquiry in the social sciences are rejected because post-modernists consider such methods to be part of the larger techno-scientific corrupting cultural imperative, originating in the West but spreading out to encompass the planet (Lyotard 1984)."

2. Statistical transformation involves changing the values of variables so that the resulting distributions of values fulfill certain criteria. For instance, by *standardizing* the values on the selected variables, we would have, in each case, a distribution of values which is characterized by a *mean* of zero and a *standard deviation* of one. The purpose of transformation is usually to make the values of variables relevant to subsequent analysis. Standardized values, for instance, can be used in *multiple regression analysis* (which has been performed in this study; see Chapter 4) in order to compute *beta weights* (*standardized regression coefficients*), which can then be used as a basis for rank-ordering independent variables in terms of the relative degrees of variation they explain in the behavior of given dependent variables. On transformation in this sense, see Gurr (1972, pp. 116–17, 154–5).
3. A partial correlation coefficient is "a measure of the *amount of variation explained* by one independent variable after the others have explained all they could" (Blalock, 1960, p. 345).
4. For these and other views on measurement and statistical analyses in the field of international relations, see the articles in Knorr and Rosenau (1969).
5. On field studies, see Katz (1953). James Patrick's (1973) participant observation of an urban gang in Glasgow, Scotland, is an example of the use of field studies in conflict situations.
6. On verbal experiments, see Kaplan (1964, pp. 163–4), and Selltiz *et al.* (1976, Chapters 9 and 10 and Appendices A and B). Although, as a point of departure, I have used Nagel's (1961) model of controlled empirical inquiry, which locates survey questionnaires and interviews (verbal experiments) under controlled investigations (pp. 457–9), I nevertheless find Kaplan's (1964, p. 163) argument that they are "experiments" compelling: "Merely providing a stimulus that would otherwise not be acting, or not acting then and there, is also a type of manipulation of the observational materials. Thus, questionnaires, tests, and interviews . . . must all be regarded as experiments, and even as manipulative ones." See Alcock (1972, Chapters 7 and 8) for examples of the use of verbal experiments in conflict studies (i.e. surveys of attitudes toward war and peace held by members of various populations).
7. On field experiments, see French (1953). Perhaps the classic use of this technique in conflict studies is the work of Muzafer and Carolyn W. Sherif (1953).
8. On laboratory experiments, see Festinger (1953). Examples of the employment of this approach in the study of conflict can be found in Rapoport and Chammah (1965).
9. "Internal validity" is the extent to which a causal relationship between independent and dependent variables has been established, in contrast to "external validity," which is the extent to which the findings are generalizable from one level to another (see Frankfort-Nachmias and Nachmias, 1996, pp. 105–15).
10. "[It] *is* a sound observation that no generalizations concerning social phenomena based exclusively on laboratory experiments can be safely assumed without further inquiry to hold in natural social environments" (Nagel, 1961, p. 456). Nevertheless, the need for external validation may also apply to field experiments, where researchers may want to

generalize from one level to another within the overall "natural social environment," e.g. from findings on conflict and cooperation in a boys' camp to relations between states.

11. On content analysis, see Holsti (1969), and on structured observation, Heyns and Zander (1953) and Miller (1970, pp. 200–30). Structured observation is similar to content analysis in that it involves observation of a subject matter in terms of explicit categories (*coding*) and, within categories, determination of degrees of attribute possession (*scaling*).
12. On simulation in general in the social sciences, see Guetzkow (1962), Coplin (1968), Raser (1969), Duke (1974), Greenblatt and Duke (1975), and Crookall and Saunders (1989). For descriptive summaries of nearly 2000 simulation operations, see Gibbs (1974, Chapter 5). On simulation in the study of international conflict processes, see Guetzkow *et al.* (1963), Rapoport (1964, Chapter 13), Guetzkow (1968a, 1976), Smoker (1970, 1976), Bremer (1977, 1987a), Guetzkow and Valadez (1981a) and Karl Deutsch (1987a, b).
13. Alternatively, one can imagine a situation where a theory exists, is empirically valid, and is technically adequate for translation into model-input, but where the model-output is not empirically valid.
14. Most of the specific simulations listed in Table 3.1 have been subjected to various kinds and degrees of *input* assessment. The INS – perhaps the most widely used simulation of international processes – and at least two of its derivatives, the IPS and SIPER, have also been subjected to *output* assessment (see Smoker, 1970; Guetzkow and Valadez, 1981b). Evaluations ("verisimilitude assessments") have also been conducted of GLOBUS (see Bremer, 1987b).
15. See Guetzkow (1968a, pp. 9–10) for a brief discussion and justification of the use of simulation in "theoretically destitute" fields such as political science and international relations.
16. Game theory is a branch of *decision theory*. It provides no information about what people actually do in certain situations and therefore, is not a *descriptive (empirical) theory*. It is primarily a *prescriptive (normative) theory*, a theory of rational decision-making, dealing with what people should do in certain (conflict) situations. It can be – and has been – viewed as a theory, or the science, of rational conflict. There are, however, conflict situations in which current game theory *qua* normative theory does not apply and is actually rather dangerous for the parties involved in such situations. To say that game theory is normative, therefore, is to be only partially accurate: game theory *qua* normative theory applies only to a certain class of games.

    Attempting to provide a definition which applies to game theory in terms of all of its dimensions, Rapoport (1965, p. 196) has suggested that game theory is "essentially a structural theory. It uncovers the logical structure of a great variety of conflict situations and describes this structure in mathematical terms. Sometimes the logical structure of a conflict situation admits rational decisions; sometimes it does not." (Also see Luce and Raiffa, 1957; Rapoport, 1960, Chapters VI–XIV; 1964, Chapters 1–8; Schelling, 1967; Shubik, 1967. For the classic treatise on game theory, see von Neumann and Morgenstern, 1944.)
17. A representation of a game in terms of a rectangular array or matrix of the totality of strategies and corresponding outcomes available to players is the *normal form* of the game (see Rapoport and Chammah, 1965, p. 20). The first number in each quadrant of the matrix represents the value of the payoff which accrues to Prisoner A (the (horizontal) row-chooser) if the decisions taken by both players reflect that particular quadrant. The second number in each quadrant represents the value of the payoff which accrues to Prisoner B (the (vertical) column-chooser) under the same conditions.
18. On this theme, Rapoport (1974, p. 234) writes: "The purpose of formulating [a] conflict as a game is not that of resolving the conflict by 'solving the game.' It is that of

displaying the structure of the conflict and thereby exposing features of it that may be concealed by rhetoric. In particular, appreciation of the peculiar structure of some of the so-called *mixed-motive* conflicts represented by nonzero-sum games may change the conflicting parties' perception of their situation" (emphasis added).

19. On *benign*, *conflict*, and *malign* outcomes, see Boulding (1965).
20. In contrast to Addenda 1–6, which were employed in each of the five operations (PDS 1–5) whose data have been used in this study, *Simulation Manual Addendum No. Seven* was used only once, in PDS 5, as part of the PhD-related research of a simulation coworker and colleague, Jerwyn L. Schatz. Also, in contrast to Addenda 1–6, which were designed by Powell, Addendum 7 was designed by Schatz. The title of Schatz's project was, "Problems of Coalition Maintenance at the International Level: A Study Utilizing Simulation and Real-World Data."
21. See items 102, 103, 108, and 111 of Appendix B. Powell had selected these items, presumably on intuitive grounds, as rough indicators of "need for achievement" and "need for power." When I began to operate the PDS, I continued this practice in order to maintain, as much as possible, consistency of starting conditions.
22. Lincoln Bloomfield has noted in his work with the PME (or PE) that a "balanced distribution of attitudes [within groups] had the effect of stimulating discussion and encouraging consideration of sharply different alternatives" (Bloomfield and Gearin, 1971, p. 19).
23. It is often difficult for *Administrators* to avoid assuming the role of participant, not just because of their physical proximity to – and the contagion generated by – the actors over time, but also because they are active in the operation of the model. For instance, when an *Administrator* runs through a maze of corridors to get a decision form to the *Computer* before a particular decision period terminates, it may be a moot point whether she or he is an "actor" or an "observer" with respect to *her* or *his* group. These caveats notwithstanding, *Administrators* tend not to participate as decision-makers or validators. Nevertheless, the implications here for third party conflict resolution practitioners are clear: it is difficult, if not impossible, to remain "neutral" in the conflicts in which one intervenes (see Cobb and Rifkin, 1991).
24. In these reports, the actors attempted to discern similarities/dissimilarities between their *in vitro* settings and the real world, and to describe, analyze, and explain simulation developments and events in terms of the concepts they were being exposed to in their courses. In this way, the actors were encouraged to develop analytical skills as well as to provide a rich source of actor-perceptions of simulation worlds.
25. Powell's classification scheme for these PDS operations is somewhat different from mine, i.e. his Temple II–IV were reclassified as PDS 1–3. I did not include Temple I (as well as other PDS operations which Powell conducted earlier at the University of Oregon) because my access to the output of these operations was not as complete as it was for Temple II–IV.
26. According to Bloomfield and Gearin (1971), however, getting "wrapped up" in the casual-format PME (or PE), especially in the case of real-life professionals (i.e. senior officials from the foreign policy/defense communities), does not seem to have been a problem: "[PE's] most unequivocal value lay in its effect on the individual participant. Evidence accumulated that a well-designed and executed PE could have a substantial impact on a professionally trained person in loosening up some of his policy assumptions by virtue of forcing him to realistically 'live' with an artificial situation not of his own choosing" (p. 7). "The most highly valued quality of the PE is that professional players act essentially as they act in real life" (p. 30).

4 Modelling Violent Conflict and War[1]

Introduction

This chapter deals with the conflict models developed from data generated by five PDS operations (PDS 1–5). Observations were made on the selected independent and dependent variables within each of the five PDS operations on the basis of the operational definitions spelled out in Appendix C. Sources of observations were, in large part, players' responses to the PDS questionnaire (Appendix B), their actions as expressed on decision and war forms (Appendices A.2 and A.3), their written analyses, and observational forms completed by *Administrators* (Appendix A.13).

For each of the five runs, *time-series* observations were made on the same actors in terms of the same variables over successive weekly runs (for up to fifteen weeks). Observations on twelve of the 23 independent variables (DI, RES, RED, MD, %MD, BEL, %BEL, ALL, ATT, %ATT, VICT, and SAC) were lagged with respect to observations on the dependent variables.[2] Since observations were made on all actors for each run, analyses of the relationships between the independent and dependent variables reflect a combination of *cross-sectional* as well as *longitudinal* (time-series) data.

Bivariate Analysis

Data analysis initially involved the computation of *product-moment correlation coefficients* – bivariate measures of strength of relationship (on a 0 to ±1.0 scale) – for nonlinear as well as linear values of the variables. *Logarithmic transformations* were performed on the values of each variable to test for nonlinearity.[3]

There were 138 relationships between the 23 independent and six dependent variables (23 × 6 = 138). Each relationship was measured twice in order to explore for nonlinearity, and each was measured in six different settings (i.e. PDS 1, 2, 3, 4, and 5, plus PDS 1–5 combined); hence, a minimum of 1656 product–moment coefficients was computed (138 × 2 = 276 × 6 = 1656).

The "best" bivariate correlation coefficients – i.e. in each case the higher of the two (linear and nonlinear) coefficients – were then compared with the findings from other studies to determine what Charles Hermann (1967, pp. 223–4) calls *hypothesis validity*: the extent to which the PDS findings were compatible with the findings generated by corresponding (mostly real-world) studies.

Validation of Bivariate PDS Findings

As mentioned in Chapter 3, the outputs of most simulations have not been subjected to validity checks. Guetzkow and Valadez (1981b, p. 326) characterize the situation as follows:

> To date, emphasis among simulation builders has been more upon the venture of model construction, with the scholar working as an artist, rather than upon involvement in checking correspondences between the simulations and their respective reference systems, as is incumbent upon the scholar who works as a social scientist or policy-influencer.

One of the few individuals to conduct comprehensive validation assessments of simulation has been Harold Guetzkow (1966, 1968b; Guetzkow and Valadez, 1981b). He compared the outputs generated by his own *Inter-Nation Simulation* (INS), and two of its derivatives, the *International Processes Simulation* (IPS) and *Simulated International ProcessER* (SIPER), with the findings produced by other, mostly real-world studies. In the concluding section of his original validation assessment, Guetzkow (1966, p. 44) commented that:

> Perhaps the most serious limitation in the assessments of correspondences between simulations and "realities" in international relations in this essay is found in its almost total – albeit reluctant – reliance upon Inter-Nation Simulations. It is to be regretted that those developing political-military exercises and all-computer simulations have not produced more assessments of the validity of their contributions so that the homomorphic relations could be checked out for more than the INS simulations.

By 1981, Guetzkow and Valadez (1981b, p. 258) reported:

> Inasmuch as but one work (Bonham, 1967) on the validation of either the RAND/MIT political exercises or TEMPER has been recorded thus far, the studies to be surveyed in this chapter center largely on the Inter-Nation Simulation (INS) and its variations: the International Processes Simulation (IPS) and the Simulated International ProcessER (SIPER).

According to the literature cited here, therefore, the INS is virtually the only gaming-simulation in international relations whose results have been subjected to validation assessments. Again, this was one of the reasons why I preferred the PDS to the INS: to explore the extent to which another gaming-simulation of international relations was capable of capturing real-world systems. Hence the need to validate the PDS, initially at the bivariate level.

There were 122 comparisons made between the PDS findings and the results of corresponding real-world and other laboratory/simulation studies. Of the corresponding studies, 60 (50 percent) were about foreign conflict in general and not about specific dimensions of foreign conflict comparable to MD, BEL,

%BEL, ALL, or ATT. Hence, to render the PDS findings comparable to these studies, a relationship for each of the 23 independent variables and foreign conflict *in general* was inferred from the PDS findings. One consequence of this was that quite a few of the specific categories of PDS findings were not assessed.

Nonassessed findings included those on five (22 percent) of the independent variables (POLC, PERC, SSEC, %MD, and %ATT), whose relationships with conflict did not figure in the evaluation because corresponding relationships were not found in the studies consulted. Of the remaining eighteen independent variables that were included in the assessment, three (ACH, RES, and RED) were reflective of more validation "misses" than "hits."[4] Hence, fifteen of the eighteen included independent variables (83 percent) survived the validation assessment.

Of the 122 comparisons, there was agreement between the PDS and real-world and other lab/sim findings, in terms of *direction of relationship* (+ or −), in 92 (75 percent) of the cases. Given that 28 of the 92 "hits" involved precise correlation coefficients (in contrast to summarized findings associated with the remaining "hits," which revealed only the direction of relationship), it was possible, in these cases, to determine the *strength of relationship* as well: the extent to which the magnitudes of the corresponding PDS and reference coefficients were similar. In each of 24 of the 28 cases (86 percent), at least one of the PDS coefficients was found to be within 0.10 of at least one of the corresponding reference coefficients.

Also concerning comparative magnitudes, 3.2 percent of the coefficients for PDS 1, 2, 3, 4, and 5 and 1.45 percent of the coefficients for PDS 1–5 combined were greater than 0.50. Although these percentages are somewhat higher than John Vasquez's (1976, p. 194) finding that 0.7 percent of the selected coefficients for international conflict were greater than 0.50 (see Chapter 1), the implication here is that, whether in the real world or in the PDS, few variables seem to qualify for *primacy*; or as Bremer (1995b, p. 271) puts it, "war . . . arises out of the *concatenation* of *many weak forces* rather than the operation of one or even a few strong forces" (emphasis added).

Accordingly, the bivariate PDS findings came through the assessment rather well: for the 78 percent (18/23) of the independent variables included, there were many PDS and corresponding findings from real-world and lab/sim studies which shared the same direction of relationship (75 percent) and, in those cases where precise correlational comparisons were possible, the same or similar strength of relationship (86 percent) as well.

This degree of "fit" between the PDS and corresponding real-world and lab/sim studies is particularly striking, especially if we take into account the differences between them in terms of (a) scale, (b) measurement of variables, and (c) treatment of time. Also striking are the similarities between Guetzkow's INS and the PDS validation studies, even though both sets of assessments made use of different real-world and lab/sim and other field reference materials. For instance, in his original assessment study, Guetzkow (1966, p. 42) reported that approximately three-fourths of his comparisons were made with findings from real-world studies. By 1981, this proportion increased to slightly higher than four-fifths, or 81 percent (see Guetzkow and Valadez, 1981b, Tables 8.3, 8.5, and 8.11 on pp. 273–4, 285–6, and 302–3, respectively). These figures compare favorably with the PDS, where between three-fourths and four-fifths (95/122 = 78 percent) of the comparisons also involved real-world reference materials.

Guetzkow pointed out in his original assessment (1966, p. 42) that there was "greater congruence among the materials assembled in assessing the validation related to 'DECISION-MAKERS AND THEIR NATIONS' than among entries concerned with 'RELATIONS AMONG NATIONS'." Although, by 1981, the distance between the two categories had narrowed (76 and 75 percent, respectively), it still held (Guetzkow and Valadez, 1981b). In the PDS study, the proportion of validated findings on decision-makers (88 percent) is also greater than the proportion of validated societal findings (65 percent).

More importantly, in terms of direction of relationship, the proportion of validated INS findings in Guetzkow's original assessment was 82 percent (Guetzkow, 1966, p. 41tb). By 1981, this fell slightly to 75 percent (Guetzkow and Valadez, 1981b). These figures, especially the more recent ones, are remarkably similar to the proportion of validated PDS findings: 75 percent.

Accordingly, not only does the PDS seem to be capable of replicating (and therefore revealing) real-world processes, but given the similarity between the PDS and INS validation assessments, *small-group systems in general may be so capable*. Hence, a reasonable hypothesis is that simulations comprised of "real" human beings (particularly, the PDS and INS) may be more than merely heuristic devices for generating insights into complex (multilevel, multi-dimensional) conflict processes. One test of this proposition would be to use PDS findings to develop models of such conflict processes and then to subject those models to a *multivariate* validation assessment. The remainder of this chapter deals with the development of such models, while Chapter 5 deals with their assessment.

Multivariate Analysis

One is led from bivariate to multivariate analysis not just because one assumes that behavior is the result of many factors at many levels, but also because an apparent relationship between two variables may be *spurious*, i.e. it may be weaker than what has been indicated by the bivariate coefficient, or even nonexistent, because the independent and dependent variables may themselves have been "caused" or otherwise influenced by a third or more variables which have not been brought explicitly into the relational system.[5]

There is also the opposite problem, where a relationship between an independent variable and a dependent variable will not register unless other variables are brought into the relational system, i.e. the value of a bivariate coefficient may indicate that the corresponding relationship between two variables is low or nonexistent, whereas if other variables were brought into the relational system, the resulting coefficient might indicate that the relationship was rather strong. As Ezekiel and Fox (1959, p. 195) point out:

> Investigators sometimes think they are doing "research" when they study the relation of a given variable . . . to a number of other factors, discard all those factors that show no correlation with [the dependent variable], and select for further study by multiple correlation the factors that show the highest simple correlation with [the dependent variable]. [Such a] procedure may result in discarding factors which would show a truly important relation to [the dependent variable] after the effect of other associated factors had been allowed for.

This problem, plus spuriousness, can be dealt with to some extent through the use of multivariate techniques such as *partial correlation* and *standardized regression*, both of which involve the computation of the value of a relationship between an independent variable and a dependent variable, while taking into account the effect on the dependent variable of other independent variables.[6]

Partial correlation coefficients and standardized regression coefficients ("beta weights") also provide a researcher with a basis for *ranking* independent variables, i.e. determining, for a given dependent variable, which, among a number of independent variables, appears to be the primary source of influence on the dependent variable, followed by the second most important source, etc. However, despite the fact that both types of coefficients can generate rankings:

> As a general rule, we might rather dogmatically assert that whenever one's attention is to be focused on the nature of *causal laws*, he [or she] will be on safer grounds comparing the behavior of *regression coefficients* rather than *correlation coefficients*. (Blalock, 1961, p. 87; emphasis added)[7]

Accordingly, although both types of coefficients will be presented for purposes of comparison, beta weights will constitute the main basis for rank-ordering the independent variables in each of the PDS conflict models presented below.

That six of the independent variables in our analysis are time-lagged versions of the dependent variables suggests the possibility of models comprising variables which at one point in time are treated as dependent variables, but which at an earlier or later point in time are treated as independent variables. This introduces the possibility of *reciprocal causation*, where, in our case, dependent variables may be influenced by each other *qua* independent variables *over time*.[8]

Reciprocal (two-way) causation, especially when it occurs more or less *instantaneously*, implies *nonrecursive models*, which can be developed through *two-* or *three-stage least squares regression*. Alternatively, one can use *ordinary least squares* (OLS) to develop *recursive* models, "in which we [normally] rule out two-way causation" (Blalock, 1961, p. 54). A contradiction? Apparently not, as "Recursive systems can actually be used to handle instances in which we imagine causation to be reciprocal, provided we are in a position to '*lag*' some of the variables" (*ibid.*, p. 55; emphasis added), as has been done in this study:

> By treating the same variables at different time periods as though they were distinct, the problem can be handled in terms of recursive equations. Thus certain variables at $t - 1$ may be taken as . . . independent, while

these same variables at time *t* may be considered to be causally dependent on some of the other variables. (*Ibid.*, p. 56)

Because we fulfilled this lag criterion, we were able to use OLS to estimate the values of coefficients in relational systems involving the possibility of reciprocal causation.[9] Consequently, we were able to avoid the *identification problem* associated with nonrecursive models: estimating unique values for coefficients on relationships in which observations on possibly reciprocally causal variables have been made at the *same point in time*.[10]

A particular version of OLS, *stepwise regression*, was used to develop the models of complex conflict processes that appear below. Stepwise regression selects variables which account for less and less of the variation in the behavior of the dependent variable until some cutoff point is reached.[11] A model so developed, therefore, is comprised of one variable that explains the greatest proportion of the variation in the behavior of the dependent variable and – if the cutoff point has not yet been reached – another variable which, taking into account the proportion of variation explained by the first independent variable, accounts for the second highest proportion of variation, etc.[12]

Prior to the regression analysis for this study, the values on all the variables were *standardized*, so that the subsequent regression coefficients, the "beta weights," would facilitate the ranking of the explanatory variables on the basis of their relative potencies.[13]

PDS 1–5 Combined

Initially, conflict models were developed for each of the dependent variables for PDS 1–5 combined, rather than on each of the five data-sets taken separately, to explore whether or not there were patterns common to all five PDS operations. The expectation was that, if "laws of conflict behavior" were operative in the PDS, these would – and should – be evident in the models for PDS 1–5 combined, which appear in Table 4.1.[14]

So, how does Waltz fare for PDS 1–5 combined? In terms of the beta weights (as well as partial *r*s), the trans-societal level (SEC) is dominant for two of the models (DI and MD), one of which (MD) is supportive of Waltz's hypothesis that the international level is more potent as a source of influence on international conflict than are either the societal or individual levels. The second and third levels of primacy for the MD model comprise factors operative at the decision-making level (PERC, TO).

The models for Bellicosity (BEL), Alliances (ALL), and Aggressive Attacks (ATT) suggest an alternative hypothesis: *self-stimulation/self-perpetuation* of violent conflict and war. For each of these models, the major source of influence on the dependent variable is the variable itself, as expressed (lagged) at earlier points in time. The second and third levels of primacy are comprised of other societal factors (VICT, BEL), the trans-societal factors (SEC, SAC), and, lastly, a decision-making factor (TO).

A model for Change in Bellicosity (%BEL) was "deductively" developed, using the same three independent variables that were "inductively" selected for

Table 4.1 Models for PDS 1–5 ($N = 342$)

DI =	+0.16ACH +	0.10RED +	0.17MD −	0.31SEC	($R^2 = 0.19$)
	(+0.18)	(+0.11)	(+0.18)	(−0.32)	(partial *r*)
	(−)	(+n.1.)	(−n.1.)	(−n.1.)	(pred. rel.)
MD =	+0.16PERC −	0.12TO −	0.37SEC		($R^2 = 0.12$)
	(+0.16)	(−0.12)	(−0.34)		(partial *r*)
	(+)	(+)	(+n.1.)		(pred. rel.)
BEL =	+0.49BEL −	0.21VICT +	0.15SAC		($R^2 = 0.27$)
	(+0.49)	(−0.16)	(+0.11)		(partial *r*)
	(+)	(+)	(+)		(pred. rel.)
ALL =	+0.10POLC −	0.16PERC −	0.11TO +	0.37ALL	
	(+0.12)	(−0.19)	(−0.14)	(+0.43)	(partial *r*)
	(+)	(+)	(+)	(+)	(pred. rel.)
	−0.10%ATT +	0.21VICT +	0.33SEC		($R^2 = 0.47$)
	(−0.13)	(+0.27)	(+0.36)		(partial *r*)
	(+)	(+)	(+n.1.)		(pred. rel.)
ATT =	+0.11TO +	0.12BEL +	0.50ATT		($R^2 = 0.29$)
	(+0.13)	(+0.13)	(+0.50)		(partial *r*)
	(+)	(+n.1.)	(+)		(pred. rel.)

Note: See Table 4.2 for a glossary of labels of variables included in the models for PDS 1–5.

BEL by the stepwise procedure.[15] Reading the two patterns together in Table 4.2, increases in (lagged) BEL and decreases in VICT are associated with *increases* in BEL at *decreasing* rates, while increases in SAC are associated with *increases* in BEL at *increasing* rates. The comparative rankings, coupled with the clear dominance of BEL, suggest that, for PDS 1–5, arming dynamics were characterized more by increases in BEL at *decreasing* rates associated with increases in (lagged) BEL and decreases in VICT than by increases in BEL at *increasing* rates associated with increases in SAC.

Returning to Table 4.1, an evolving "culture of aggression" (increases in lagged ATT), coupled with increases in arming (lagged BEL) and increases in time pressures (TO) – when decision-makers "would not have time to think" – appears to have made war (ATT) and, indeed, *positive feedback*-driven conflict spirals, more likely. Viewing ATT in conjunction with the BEL and %BEL models in Table 4.2, therefore, warfare for PDS 1–5 appears to have been more of a *self-* than an *other-* or *mutually stimulating* phenomenon: driven more by previous warfare than by arms race dynamics.[16]

Table 4.2 Bellicosity and change in bellicosity for PDS 1–5

BEL =	+0.49BEL	− 0.21VICT	+ 0.15SAC	(R^2 = 0.27)
	(+0.49)	(−0.16)	(+0.11)	(partial *r*)
	(+)	(+)	(+)	(pred. rel.)
%BEL =	−0.29BEL	+ 0.10VICT	+ 0.13SAC	(R^2 = 0.14)
	(−0.30)	(+0.07)	(+0.09)	(partial *r*)
	(+)	(+)	(n.1.)	(pred. rel.)

Decision-making level: ACH, Need for Achievement; POLC, Political Cynicism; PERC, Personal Cynicism; TO, Temporal Overload.

Societal level: DI, Domestic Instability; BEL, Bellicosity; ALL, Alliances; ATT, Aggressive Attacks; MD, Manifest Distrust; VICT, Attack Victim; %ATT, Change in Aggressive Attacks.

Trans-societal level: SEC, Systemic Environmental Complexity; SAC, Systemic Attack Contagion.

Disaggregation: Successive Stages of Systems Development

As mentioned above, if "laws of conflict behavior" were operative in the PDS, they would (and should) have been observable in the models for PDS 1–5 combined. The relatively low R^2s for these models, however, suggest that: (a) the relevant variables were not included in the analysis; (b) if they were, they were not adequately measured; (c) time may have been treated inappropriately; (d) the independent variables may have *multiplicative* rather than *additive*, nonlinear rather than linear, relationships with the dependent variables; (e) the relatively impressive results of the PDS *bivariate* validation assessment notwithstanding, multiple regression-generated *multivariate* models may not be getting at real conflict behavior; and/or (f) the *level of aggregation* inherent in PDS 1–5 combined may simply be too high, rendering as "invisible" otherwise important relationships.

We will take up the aggregation issue now, followed by the PDS models perhaps not getting at real behavior in Chapter 5, and by other possible sources of low R^2s in Chapter 8.

PDS 1–5 represents the combination of five separate PDS operations, each with different groups and persons, and each of which was run over a different four-month period, with a "beginning," an "end," and something in between. It is quite conceivable that by aggregating the five operations, we have inadvertently concealed the operation of processes which were peculiar to certain operations or to certain phases in the development of systems, thereby producing models of relatively low coefficients of multiple determination (R^2s). Rather than looking for "laws" at the aggregate level of PDS 1–5 combined, perhaps we should have been looking for them at successive levels of PDS "world" development.

In Chapter 1, our discussion indicated that many studies of war have produced contradictory findings. In Chapter 2, we suggested that some of these apparently contradictory relationships may be due to nonlinearity: to *complex* relationships that are characterized by different directions of relationship at different points in time. For example, in the Correlates-of-War (COW) project, J. David Singer and his associates found conflicting relationships for certain variables when they compared the international system of the nineteenth century with that of the twentieth: relationships which were concealed when coefficients were computed for the nineteenth and twentieth centuries combined. For instance, they tended to find positive relationships between alliances and war for the two centuries combined, but when they disaggregated their data, they found negative relationships for the nineteenth century and positive relationships for the twentieth century (see Singer and Small, 1968).

Perhaps one of the most interesting examples of aggregated findings concealing conflicting relationships on the same variables is found in the results of Jonathan Wilkenfeld's (1973) investigation of the relationships between domestic and foreign conflict, in which he used data originally collected and analyzed by Rudolph Rummel (1963, 1964) and Raymond Tanter (1966). In contrast to Rummel, who found little evidence of a relationship between domestic and foreign conflict for 1955–57, which Tanter basically replicated for 1958–60, Wilkenfeld found some significant relationships for 1955–60.

Although Wilkenfeld used Rummel's and Tanter's data, his research design was different in some important respects from theirs. For instance, in addition to combining the two data-sets and using one-year temporal units of analysis, he introduced one- and two-year time lags and investigated the relationships between domestic and foreign conflict for different types of nations: *polyarchic*, over half of which were economically developed Western nations; *centrist*, which were dictatorial and highly centralized; and *personalist*, most of which were Latin American dictatorships.

Wilkenfeld found not only some significant relationships between domestic and foreign conflict, but also different relationships for the different types of nations. For example, whereas the polyarchic nations had positive relationships between turmoil and foreign conflict, the centrist nations had some positive and some negative, and the personalist group tended to have near-zero relationships.

A significant implication of these studies is that if we confine our investigations to monolithic aggregates, such as PDS 1–5 combined, we risk not only concealing conflicting relationships on the same variables at different levels or different points in time, but committing what W. S. Robinson (1950) called the *ecological fallacy*: making inferences about units at disaggregated levels on the basis of observations on units at aggregate levels.

Given that conflicting relationships on the same variables might be indicated for disaggregated levels not only by relatively low coefficients of determination, but also by nonlinear coefficients at aggregated levels, the case for disaggregating PDS 1–5 was strengthened by the observation that 51 (37 percent) of the 138 bivariate coefficients for PDS 1–5 contained some degree of nonlinearity.

Accordingly, the disaggregation of PDS 1–5 seemed justified, but there was one major problem: in terms of what criteria – what levels or points in time – should PDS 1–5 be subdivided? Nazli Choucri and Robert North (1975, p. 171) helped to provide a solution with their discussion of *breakpoints*, or:

> discrete points at which transformations can be identified. [These] may be viewed in either of two ways: as changes in trend-lines due to nonlinear relationships, or, more commonly, as evidence of change in the system. Such breaks represent changes in the relationships among the variables, which can be either the result of unique events or the cumulative effect of minor changes.

Finding such points in PDS 1–5, revealing *three* successive stages of development, was facilitated by the evolutionary nature of PDS. As indicated in Chapter 3, during the first three weeks of each operation, the typical PDS "world" consisted basically of two groups, each relatively underdeveloped and comprising decision-maker and validator components. *Simulation Manual Addendum Number One* (Appendix A.4), which was administered during this period, specified conditions under which coups and revolutions among the validators could occur. It also specified conditions under which new nations could be formed. Runs 1–3, therefore, were characterized primarily by the transition from a two- to a multigroup system, an interval which has been designated in this study as the *early* stage of development.

During runs 4–7 of each operation, the PDS world was a multigroup system, with each group tending to consist of players in only one role: decision-maker. "Live" domestic conflict during this interval (as well as during runs 8–11), therefore, tended to occur only among the decision-makers in each group. Moreover, an addendum administered during this interval allowed the groups to become "nuclear powers" (Appendix A.9). Runs 4–7, therefore, were characterized primarily by nuclear technology availability in a multigroup system. This interval was designated as the *intermediate* stage of development.

During runs 8–11,[17] the flow of addenda to the players ceased, and some of them, apparently with a need for environmental stimulation – which had been encouraged and satisfied previously to some extent by the progressive complexity introduced by the addenda – appear to have attempted to fill this "stimulation-gap" by creating their own environmental complexity: by devising and implementing "New World Orders." One player in a later PDS operation, for example, commented during the debriefing session that he continued his efforts to formulate and disseminate proposals for avoiding war among the "nations" in the system because: "We were initially given our own system – a tabula rasa – in effect, a rare opportunity for building our own world, and I'd be damned if I would let a war occur or upset our plans."[18] Runs 8–11, therefore, appear to have been characterized primarily by an increase in the scope of attempts by actors to intervene into, and to control, their systemic environment. This interval was designated as the *late* phase of development.

Accordingly, PDS 1–5 combined was disaggregated into three successive blocks: *early*, *intermediate*, and *late* stages of societal and system development. The stepwise procedure was then used to develop models for each of the dependent variables for each of the three developmental stages: models which might differ from the above general models not only in terms of values of coefficients and direction of relationships, but also in terms of content.

In addition to exploring possible differences between the aggregated and disaggregated models, one objective here was to test Waltz at different levels of development: when systems were relatively youthful, when they were into their "middle years," and when they were mature, experientially as well as chronologically.

Table 4.3 contains the conflict models for the early stage.[19] For each of these, the apparent primary variable is not only at the trans-societal level but is the same in each case: Systemic Environmental Complexity (SEC), the number of other actors in the external environment. The MD, BEL, ALL, and ATT models for the early period, therefore, are consistent with Waltz's hypothesis that the international system is dominant in the genesis of international conflict and war.

The societal level appears to dominate secondary rankings at the early stage: Relative Economic Deprivation (RED) for Domestic Instability (DI); Relative Economic Status (RES) for Manifest Distrust (MD); (lagged) Aggressive Attacks (ATT) for Bellicosity (BEL); Change in (lagged) Aggressive Attacks (%ATT) for Alliances (ALL); and (lagged) Bellicosity (BEL) for Aggressive Attacks (ATT). There is only one case at the early stage where there is a tertiary explanatory variable: Attack Victim (VICT) in the ALL model, which is also at the societal level.

Table 4.3 Early stage models (N = 50)

DI =	+0.32RED	− 0.38SEC		(R^2 = 0.22)
	(+0.34)	(−0.39)		(partial r)
	(+n.l.)	(−n.l.)		(pred. rel.)
MD =	−0.27RES	− 0.48SEC		(R^2 = 0.29)
	(−0.30)	(−0.49)		(partial r)
	(+)	(+n.l.)		(pred. rel.)
BEL =	−0.28ATT	+ 0.52SEC		(R^2 = 0.26)
	(−0.30)	(+0.49)		(partial r)
	(+)	(+n.l.)		(pred. rel.)
ALL =	+0.22%ATT	+ 0.18VICT	+ 0.63SEC	(R^2 = 0.64)
	(+0.34)	(+0.28)	(+0.69)	(partial r)
	(+)	(+)	(+n.l.)	(pred. rel.)
ATT =	+0.32BEL	+ 0.39SEC		(R^2 = 0.31)
	(+0.35)	(+0.41)		(partial r)
	(+n.l.)	(+n.l.)		(pred. rel.)

Decision-making level: none.

Societal level: DI, Domestic Instability; MD, Manifest Distrust; BEL, Bellicosity; ALL, Alliances; ATT, Aggressive Attacks; RED, Relative Economic Deprivation; RES, Relative Economic Status; %ATT, Change in Aggressive Attacks; VICT, Attack Victim.

Trans-societal level: SEC, Systemic Environmental Complexity.

Moving on to the models for the intermediate stage in Table 4.4, there is somewhat of a mix with regard to primary rankings, although with a societal edge. For the Domestic Instability (DI) model, Need for Achievement (ACH), a decision-making variable, is dominant; for Manifest Distrust (MD), Relative Economic Status (RES), a societal variable, is dominant; for Bellicosity (BEL), Relative Economic Status (RES), a societal variable, is again dominant; for Alliances (ALL), Systemic Attack Contagion (SAC), a trans-societal variable, is dominant; and for Aggressive Attacks (ATT), (lagged) Aggressive Attacks (ATT), a societal variable, is dominant.

Primary rankings at the intermediate stage, therefore, comprise one instance of decision-making, three instances of societal, and one instance of trans-societal dominance – with only the ALL model compatible with Waltz for this period.

For three of the models at the intermediate stage, the decision-making level seems to dominate second place. For Domestic Instability (DI), the appropriate variable is Sub-Systemic Environmental Complexity (SSEC); for Bellicosity (BEL), it is Political Cynicism (POLC); and for Alliances (ALL), it is Temporal

Table 4.4 Intermediate stage models (N = 130)

DI =	+0.21ACH	+ 0.19SSEC	− 0.17SEC			(R^2 = 0.11)
	(+0.22)	(+0.20)	(−0.18)			(partial r)
	(−)	(+n.l.)	(−n.l.)			(pred. rel.)
MD =	+0.22RES					(R^2 = 0.05)
	(+)					(pred. rel.)
BEL =	−0.21DOG	− 0.27POLC	− 0.23TO	+ 0.37RES		(R^2 = 0.27)
	(−0.22)	(−0.28)	(−0.26)	(+0.39)		(partial r)
	(+)	(+)	(+)	(+)		(pred. rel.)
ALL =	−0.33TO	− 0.13BEL	+ 0.21ALL	− 0.23ATT	+ 0.48SAC	(R^2 = 0.63)
	(−0.42)	(−0.19)	(+0.31)	(−0.31)	(+0.56)	(partial r)
	(+)	(+)	(+)	(+)	(+n.l.)	(pred. rel.)
ATT =	−0.16DOG	− 0.17POLC	+ 0.26TO	+ 0.22BEL		
	(−0.18)	(−0.19)	(+0.29)	(+0.25)		(partial r)
	(+)	(+)	(+)	(+n.l.)		(pred. rel.)
	+0.38ATT	+ 0.30SEC				(R^2 = 0.41)
	(+0.39)	(+0.31)				(partial r)
	(+)	(+n.l.)				

Decision-making level: ACH, Need for Achievement; SSEC, Sub-systemic Environmental Complexity; DOG, Dogmatism; POLC, Political Cynicism; TO, Temporal Overload.

Societal level: DI, Domestic Instability; MD, Manifest Distrust; BEL, Bellicosity; ALL, Alliances; ATT, Aggressive Attacks; RES, Relative Economic Status.

Trans-societal level: SEC, Systemic Environmental Complexity; SAC, Systemic Attack Contagion.

Overload (TO). For Aggressive Attacks (ATT), Systemic Environmental Complexity (SEC), a trans-societal variable, appears to be the second most influential variable. Hence, for the intermediate stage, secondary rankings comprise three instances of decision-making and one instance of trans-societal dominance.

For third-place rankings at the intermediate stage, there are two instances of the decision-making level (TO in both BEL and ATT), one instance of the societal level (lagged ATT in ALL), and one instance of the trans-societal level (SEC in DI).

Looking at the models for the late stage in Table 4.5, we can see that societal variables appear to be primary in four of the five cases (lagged MD in DI and MD, lagged BEL in BEL, and lagged ATT in ATT). In the remaining model, that for ALL, Systemic Environmental Complexity (SEC), a trans-societal variable, is primary.

In the three models with more than one explanatory variable there is, with regard to secondary rankings, one instance of societal dominance (lagged ALL in ALL), and two instances of decision-making dominance (SSEC in BEL and POLE in ATT).

Table 4.5 Late stage models (N = 147)

DI =	+0.26MD				(R^2 = 0.07)
	(−n.l.)				(pred. rel.)
MD =	+0.32MD				(R^2 = 0.10)
	(+)				(pred. rel.)
BEL =	−0.20SSEC	+ 0.12TO	− 0.12RED	+ 0.65BEL	(R^2 = 0.53)
	(−0.28)	(+0.17)	(−0.16)	(+0.68)	(partial *r*)
	(+)	(+)	(+)	(+)	(pred. rel.)
ALL =	+0.18POLC	− 0.38PERC	+ 0.15DI	+ 0.41ALL	
	(+0.24)	(−0.41)	(+0.22)	(+0.49)	(partial *r*)
	(+)	(+)	(n.l.)	(+)	(pred rel.)
	−0.17VICT	+ 0.49sec			(R^2 = 0.58)
	(−0.24)	(+0.51)			(partial *r*)
	(+)	(+n.l.)			(pred. rel.)
ATT =	+0.18AUTH	+ 0.19POLC	+ 0.21POLE	+ 0.24ATT	(R^2 = 0.14)
	(+0.18)	(+0.19)	(+0.20)	(+0.24)	(partial *r*)
	(+)	(+)	(−)	(+)	(pred. rel.)

Decision-making level: SSEC, Sub-systemic Environmental Complexity; TO, Temporal Overload; POLC, Political Cynicism; PERC, Personal Cynicism; AUTH, Authoritarianism; POLE, Political Efficacy.

Societal level: DI, Domestic Instability; MD, Manifest Distrust; BEL, Bellicosity; ALL, Alliances; ATT, Aggressive Attacks; RED, Relative Economic Deprivation; VICT, Attack Victim.

Trans-societal level: SEC, Systemic Environmental Complexity.

Finally, with regard to tertiary rankings at the late stage, the decision-making level seems to dominate: TO in BEL (whose beta-weight coefficient is tied with that for societal-level RED), PERC in ALL, and POLC in ATT.

What Does It All Mean – If Anything?

Examining the summary of the above findings in Table 4.6, we can see clearly that, at the early stage, the trans-societal level dominates the primary rankings for the five PDS conflict models; followed by the societal level, which just as clearly dominates the secondary rankings; and again by the societal level, which barely registers, and occupies third place almost by default.

Across the early, intermediate and late stages, there is an increasing trend toward societal-level primacy, followed by various degrees of decision-making dominance in second and third place. The trans-societal level is primary across the three stages for only one of the four foreign conflict models: Alliances (ALL). Accordingly, Waltz's hypothesis has been explicitly supported in only some cases: for the four foreign conflict models at the early stage and for the ALL models across the three stages, as well as for the MD model for PDS 1–5 combined.

Table 4.6 Distribution of best-predicting variables in the PDS conflict models by rank and level

Stage		Ranking		
		Primary	Secondary	Tertiary
Early	DM	0	0	0
	Soc	0	5	1
	T-S	5	0	0
Intermediate	DM	1	3	2
	Soc	3	0	1
	T-S	1	1	1
Late	DM	0	2	2.5
	Soc	4	1	0.5
	T-S	1	0	0
PDS 1–5	DM	0	1	3
	Soc	3	3	1
	T-S	2	1	1

DM, decision-making level; Soc, societal level; T-S, trans-societal level. Numbers indicate the number of variables classified under each ranking for each level.

Nevertheless, the overall PDS patterns are interesting. Under the primary rankings, for instance, there was apparently movement from trans-societal dominance at the early stage to societal dominance by the late stage. Under the secondary rankings, there was movement from societal influence at the early stage to increasing and then decreasing decision-making influence by the late stage. And under the tertiary rankings, there was movement from bare societal influence at the early stage to increasing decision-making influence by the late stage.

A developmental interpretation could be put on these patterns. That is, in the very beginning of each of the PDS worlds, the actors may have fumbled around, trying to make sense of, in William James's phrase, the "bloomin' buzzin' confusion" (cited in Kuhn, 1970, p. 113) inherent in their new identities, roles, relationships, and environments. All that any particular person may have known was that he or she belonged to a certain group comprised of, and shared with, other persons ("us"), while other persons belonged, initially, to one other group and, subsequently, to other groups ("them").

This sense of group identity may have proven to be a relatively powerful source of influence on behavior, but not as powerful initially as the trans-societal (trans-group) level, which, unlike the group, lacked form and "knowability." As such, the larger environment would not have been conducive to fulfilling needs for *predictability*, *regularity*, and *stability* (see Sandole, 1984, p. 46). This was, in a sense, the "last frontier" or "state of nature" where actors could either tread carefully or play out their never adequately defined "human nature" in relatively unrestrained fashion.

Over time, as the decision-makers in each group got to know more about their counterparts in other groups, their environment may have become more familiar and predictable. As this development proceeded, the trans-societal environment, while still important, may have started to lose its potency as an influence on behavior. The society (group), which emerged as the highest and final level of effective political organization, would have gradually moved in to assume this role.

If we return to Tables 4.3–4.5, we can see that not only did the societal replace the trans-societal level, but it was particular variables at the societal level that replaced variables (primarily SEC) at the trans-societal level. The first hint of this trend appears in the Aggressive Attacks (ATT) model for the intermediate stage, where the primary source of influence on ATT appears to have been lagged ATT. By the late stage, the trend appears to have been in full swing: the primary (and only) source of influence on Manifest Distrust (MD) appears to have been lagged MD; the primary source of influence on Bellicosity (BEL) appears to have been lagged BEL; the secondary source of influence on Alliances (ALL) appears to have been lagged ALL; and the primary source of influence on Aggressive Attacks appears again to have been lagged ATT, although at a lower level of magnitude than for the intermediate stage. Hence, it was not only the societal level but apparent *self-stimulating/self-perpetuating conflict processes* which developed into a dominant trend across the three stages and which also dominate the BEL, ALL, and ATT models for PDS 1–5 combined.

The phenomenon of self-stimulating/self-perpetuating conflict processes at the societal level suggests that there may be dynamics inherent at that and other levels which, over time, can become more and more independent of conscious or "rational" intentionality. This can be problematic because, as Anatol Rapoport (1974, p. 133) suggests:

> Problems arise when organized aggregates appear to acquire goals and purposes of "their own," independent of those of the individuals comprising them. Problems arise also when the behavior of large systems seems to be determined by *quasi-mechanical* interactions that do not reflect any goals or purposes, not even of the systems. (Emphasis added)

The fact that behavioral systems can operate independently of human design does not, however, mean that they are not nevertheless supported and sustained by human agents. Such support is suggested by Table 4.6, where, as the societal level moves into first place, the decision-making level follows right behind, moving from a position of no influence to a strong second and moderate third place for the intermediate stage, and then to a moderate second and slightly stronger third place position for the late stage.

Hence, returning to our developmental scenario, perhaps as decision-makers in the PDS got to know more and more about their counterparts in other groups and about their environment in general, and felt more secure in their roles and relationships, they themselves may have become more powerful as influences on their own behavior. Again, this influence appears to have come in second and third behind the primary phenomenon of self-stimulating/self-perpetuating conflict processes. The question arises, therefore: how might the decision-making level, the "human dimension," play a role in facilitating apparently self-stimulating, or quasi-mechanical, conflict systems?

The Realist Paradigm Revisited

Rapoport (1974, pp. 7, 134) tells us that "what men think or say about human conflict has a great bearing on the nature of human conflict and its consequences." What do men (perhaps more so than women) think about conflict, particularly international conflict?

Given the dominance of realism in the study and practice of international relations (see Chapter 1), we can assume that "men," male decision-makers, think of conflict in *Realpolitik* terms. I have argued elsewhere (Sandole, 1980a, 1984, 1986, 1987, 1990, 1993a) that realist belief-value systems play a major role, via the insidious dynamic of the *negative self-fulfilling prophecy*, in sustaining the very conflict systems which are the concern and subject matter of realists and others – consequences which may be counterproductive and independent of the conscious intentions of the actors concerned.

If it is the case that realism fuels the engine of self-stimulating conflict processes, then we would expect to find some evidence of this in the PDS conflict models, assuming, of course, that aspects of realist belief-value systems have been incorporated into our study. We can argue, without making too much of a leap of imagination, that Dogmatism (DOG), Authoritarianism (AUTH), Political Cynicism (POLC), Personal Cynicism (PERC), and Need for Power (POW) relate to realism in some way. None of these – indeed, no decision-making variables at all – appear in the conflict models for the early stage, where the trans-societal level is primary. As the trans-societal level begins to lose its primacy, two of these, DOG and POLC, appear in the Bellicosity (BEL) and Aggressive Attacks (ATT) models for the intermediate stage, but in terms of *negative* relationships. By the late stage, when self-stimulating/self-perpetuating conflict processes appear to be a clear trend, PERC appears in the Alliances (ALL) model, but also in terms of a negative relationship. However, POLC is also in the ALL model, and in the ATT model as well – in terms of *positive* relationships.

AUTH is also in the ATT model for the late stage, and in terms of a positive relationship. The same is true for Political Efficacy (POLE). Although not necessarily a realist variable, POLE could, in combination with other variables, make for either a passive or an active form of realism. In this case, the presence of AUTH and POLC along with POLE and lagged ATT – all with positive relations with ATT – suggests an active form of realism (see Sandole, 1980a).

Conclusion

In this chapter, we have discussed additional elements of research design, the results of validation assessments of bivariate PDS findings, and other reasons for moving from bivariate to multivariate analysis. We have also presented and discussed multivariate models of complex conflict processes comprising data generated by the PDS for PDS 1–5 combined and for the early, intermediate, and late stages of societal and system development.

Disaggregating PDS 1–5 into three successive stages of development did not result in the discovery of any "laws" of violent conflict and war. Nevertheless, the findings on the four foreign conflict models for the early stage and for the Alliances (ALL) models across all three stages, as well as for the Manifest Distrust (MD) model for PDS 1–5 combined, *are* compatible with Waltz's hypothesis that the international system is primary in the genesis of international conflict and war.[20]

The findings have also revealed a trend across the three stages of self-stimulating/self-perpetuating conflict processes. There is some evidence that this trend may have been accompanied (and facilitated) by the growing presence of elements of realist belief-value systems which, by the late stage, were appropriately linked with some conflict variables.

Quasi-mechanical conflict processes, whether of the *self-stimulating* (Lambelet and Luterbacher, 1978) or *mutually stimulating* kind (Richardson, 1939, 1960a), also occur in the real world. Similarly, the association between realist belief-value systems and the use of coercion also seems to hold in the real world (Leng, 1982, 1983, 1986; Vasquez, 1993). But we are getting ahead of ourselves: to what extent *do* the multivariate findings presented in this chapter hold up in other (mostly real-world) settings? We turn to this question in Chapter 5.

Notes

1. Chapters 4 and 5 are "somewhat technical," yet because they deal with the PDS findings and the extent to which they are compatible with other studies, and influence the remaining – admittedly more "reader-friendly" – chapters of the volume, readers are encouraged to stay the course and to go through them.
2. DI, Domestic Instability; RES, Relative Economic Status; RED, Relative Economic Deprivation; MD, Manifest Distrust; %MD, Change in Manifest Distrust; BEL, Bellicosity; %BEL, Change in Bellicosity; ALL, Alliances; ATT, Aggressive Attacks; %ATT, Change in Aggressive Attacks; VICT, Attack Victim; and SAC, Systemic Attack Contagion. It was felt that some passage of time was necessary for these independent variables to affect the behavior of the dependent variables: a question about which most social science theory is deficient. As the unit of time in the PDS was the two-hour simulation run, in most cases, the conflict or dependent variables were measured at "present time" (t), while the lagged explanatory or independent variables were measured for the previous week's run, at t - 1, or for two runs prior to "present time," at t - 2.
3. On logarithmic and other transformations, see Draper and Smith (1966, pp. 128–34).
4. A "hit" was recorded if a finding from a real-world or laboratory/simulation study reflected the same *direction of relationship* (+ or −) as a comparable PDS finding. Only one "hit" per PDS bivariate relationship was recorded for each real-world or lab/sim study. Hence, if one study reported 40 product–moment correlation coefficients in support of a PDS relationship between BEL and ATT, it was counted as one "hit" for that PDS relationship. The same criterion applied to "misses." Further, if a finding from a real-world or lab/sim study was reported, or otherwise appeared, to be nonlinear, but without any direction of relationship specified, or with a 50–50 distribution between positive and negative relationships, it was recorded as 1/2 in the "hit" category and 1/2 in the "miss" category.
5. On spuriousness and other problems associated with the interpretation of "simple" bivariate relationships, see Blalock (1961, Chapter 3).
6. "The *partial correlation* is a measure of the *amount of variation* explained by one independent variable after the others have explained all they could. The *beta weights* [i.e. *standardized regression coefficients*], on the other hand, indicate how much change in the dependent variable is produced by a *standardized change* in one of the independent variables *when the others are controlled*" (Blalock, 1960, p. 345; emphasis added).
7. Although partial correlation coefficients and standardized regression coefficients will usually "rank variables in the same order of importance," this is not always the case because of "the mathematical differences in the meaning of the two sets" (Blalock, 1960, p. 345; Ezekiel and Fox, 1959, p. 197).
8. Each dependent variable may also be reflective of *self-causation*: its behavior at one point in time may be influenced by its behavior at an earlier point in time.
9. On various forms of regression, see Ezekiel and Fox (1959) and Draper and Smith (1966).
10. On the "identification problem" and its avoidance, see Blalock (1969, Chapters 4 and 5).
11. The minimum condition that an independent variable had to fulfill in order to be included in a model generated by the stepwise procedure was that its relationship with the dependent variable was *due to chance* in one out of 20 cases (1/20 = 0.05), i.e. the probability that its relationship with the dependent variable was due to chance was 5 percent.
12. On stepwise regression as well as other "specific statistical procedures for selecting variables in regression," see Draper and Smith (1966, Chapter 6).

13. Standardization involves subtracting from each value on a variable the mean value for that variable, and then dividing the result by the *standard deviation*. According to Blalock (1960, pp. 344–5), "If the partial b's [*unstandardized regression coefficients*] are to be used to compare various independent variables as to their relative abilities to produce changes in the dependent variable, we must correct for the fact that there will undoubtedly be differences in scale involved. One variable may be measured in terms of dollars, another in terms of years. It would therefore be meaningless to compare a unit change in one variable with a unit change in another. If each variable is *standardized* [on the other hand] we can obtain adjusted slopes which are comparable from one variable to the next. We thus measure changes in the dependent variable in terms of standard deviation units for each of the [independent] variables, a fact which assures us of the *same variability* in each of these variables" (emphasis added).
14. Each of these (and the models in Tables 4.2–4.5) is comprised of standardized regression coefficients (beta weights), corresponding partial correlation coefficients, predicted relationships (from Chapter 2) and *coefficients of multiple determination* (R^2). Coefficients of multiple determination – in each case, formed by squaring the *multiple correlation coefficient* (R) – indicate the proportion of variation in the behavior of the dependent variable explained by all the independent variables *combined* in any given multivariate relational system. Hence, the closer that R^2 is to 100 percent (a rare event in the social sciences), the more likely it is that the relational system includes most of the major explanatory variables for that particular dependent variable. Similarly, squaring each partial correlation coefficient (located in parentheses under each beta-weight coefficient in Tables 4.1–4.5) produces the *coefficient of partial determination* (partial r^2), which indicates the proportion of variation in the behavior of the dependent variable that has been accounted for by each independent variable, once the other independent variables in the relational system have explained all they could.
15. This was done because the stepwise procedure selected a different model for %BEL:

    $$\%BEL = +0.10RES + 0.14RED - 0.29BEL - 0.10\%ATT + 0.18SAC \ (R^2 = 0.16)$$

    Although inclusive of two of the variables that were selected by the procedure for the BEL model (BEL and SAC), the original %BEL model did not share *all* variables with the BEL model, thereby precluding a meaningful discussion of BEL and %BEL together.
16. Apropos a "culture of aggression" leading to war in the real world, Bremer's (1980) "analysis suggests that the most powerful states in the system are caught in a *culture of war* and that the more powerful they are, the more they are unable to avoid war" (Vasquez, 1993, p. 162; emphasis added). And, in general, "War and the steps and practices that lead to it must be seen as part of a *culture of violence* that has given birth to these practices" (*ibid.*, p. 197; emphasis added).
17. Runs 12 and beyond for the five PDS operations were not included in the analysis because most of these had been subjected to experimental interventions and manipulation by students employing various research designs.
18. The PDS operation in which this student participated took place over a period of ten weeks in conjunction with the course "International Bargaining Processes," which I taught for the University of Southern California, School of International Relations, United Kingdom Graduate Programme, at the Royal Institute of International Affairs, London, England, during fall semester 1978.
19. %BEL models are not presented for the early, intermediate, and late stages because the %BEL models generated "inductively" by the stepwise procedure were different from the corresponding BEL models. Again, this was why we developed, "deductively," a model for %BEL for PDS 1–5, which included the same variables as those selected "inductively" for BEL. It was decided not to create "deductive" %BEL models for the three successive stages because the problem of noncomparable variables for BEL and

%BEL was even more extreme for the disaggregated cases than it was for PDS 1–5 combined. Nevertheless, as a point of departure for future research, the fact that the correlates of rates of change in arming (%BEL) were different from the correlates of arming (BEL) suggests that the causes of accelerating and decelerating arms increases may be very complex, with different sets of factors operating on each of the two dimensions involved (BEL and %BEL).

20. The primacy of the international level in the genesis of war has also been a major hypothesis in the COW project. Although COW principal investigators Singer and Small have worked under the assumption that any theory of war will be *multilevel*, they have nevertheless "urge[d] that considerable exploration of *systemic* properties be given high priority" (1968, p. 286; emphasis added). Singer has also mentioned his "strong suspicion that variables of a systemic and dyadic sort will turn out to be more powerful than those at the national and the decision-making levels" (1981, p. 7). Recently, however, as noted in Chapter 1, Singer has acknowledged that the decision-making level may play a more important role: "I strongly suspect that our most powerful explanations for war – and most other eventualities in world politics – will rest on assumptions about the decision process" (1995, p. 229).

5 Validated Research Design: Relationship of PDS Findings to Other Studies

Introduction

In this chapter, we will discuss additional problems that may have influenced the multivariate findings presented in Chapter 4, followed by a discussion of *multivariate validation*: the extent to which the relationships in the multivariate models correspond to findings in real-world and other studies. The validation discussion sets the stage for the final section of the chapter, which is concerned with offering some answers to the question: "What variables are worth looking at with respect to violent conflict and war?"

Methodological Problems in the Model-building Process

In Chapter 4, we discussed high levels of aggregation as one possible reason for models accounting for low levels of variation (i.e. less than 50 percent) in the behavior of dependent variables and, in general, for relationships falling short of being law-like regularities. We decided, therefore, to disaggregate PDS 1–5 and develop models for the *early*, *intermediate*, and *late* stages.

Although disaggregation of PDS 1–5 led to partial confirmation of Waltz's hypothesis and to the serendipitous discovery of *self-stimulating/self-perpetuating conflict processes*, the resulting R^2s indicate that it, too, did not result in the discovery of "laws" of violent conflict and war. Accordingly, methodological problems in addition to aggregation (e.g. the failure to include (other) relevant variables in the analysis) may have beset the analysis. As mentioned in Chapter 4, these will be addressed in the concluding chapter, with one exception: the possibility that multiple regression-generated PDS models might not be getting at "real" conflict behavior. This issue, which will be covered in this chapter, concerns assumptions underlying the use of *ordinary least squares regression*. The extent to which such assumptions are/are not adhered to could affect the composition of multivariate models and the values of their R^2s, as well as the outcomes of corresponding multivariate validation assessments.

One of these assumptions is that the data to which ordinary least squares procedures are applied have been measured at the *interval* level: scales of measurement characterized by *equal intervals* between the units of measurement. Variables measured in terms of interval scales permit researchers to determine by *how much* more or less one actor relative to another possesses a particular attribute (e.g. population or land size) or behaves in a certain way (e.g. GNP per capita).

Examining, in Appendix C, the operational definitions of the first eight independent variables – the *decision-making* (psychological) variables – we can observe that these have been measured *not* at the interval but at the *ordinal* level. One possible consequence of having applied an interval-level technique – ordinary least squares regression – to these data is that various degrees of error may have crept in, thereby influencing the values of the resulting coefficients. The degree to which such error has been introduced depends, in part, upon the distance between these measurements and "interval-ness."

Although it would be meaningless to say that one group in the PDS was *more dogmatic* than another group, say, by "20 units of Dogmatism," the particular manner in which DOG and the other psychological variables have been measured suggests that the amount of error which may have been introduced is minimal. The psychological variables for each group were measured not in terms of one-digit ordinal rankings ("most" dogmatic, second most dogmatic, etc.), but in terms of three-digit averages for all members of a group (e.g. 3.20, 3.75). Given that variables whose operational definitions did involve interval-level measurements (e.g. RES) were also measured in terms of three-digit averages – so that a group could be characterized by an RES of $320 billion as well as by a DOG of 3.20 – the measurements of the psychological variables could be viewed as *interval-like* and, therefore, as appropriate for treatment by interval-level techniques of analysis without significant error creeping into the analysis.

There is some justification for such "mixed methodological marriages" between data measured at one level and techniques of analysis suitable primarily for data measured at another level. Hubert Blalock, who at one point appeared to be against such unions (1960, pp. 16–20), seemed, at another point, to accept them (1961, p. 94):

> for exploratory purposes it may not be entirely unwise to make use of the rationale developed in connection with higher levels of measurement, even where actual measurement cannot be nearly so precise. Such methods [e.g. ordinary least squares] might best be used in a highly exploratory manner, with the recognition that the required assumptions are being only very imperfectly met.

Similarly, John Tukey has argued that, by using relatively powerful techniques of analysis on data which are not interval in a strict sense, the results of our analysis may not be too precise, but we may nevertheless increase our knowledge:

> we must recognize that many crucial variables in social and political analysis can be measured at present only with ordinal, usually judgmental scales. If we therefore restrict ourselves to low-level analysis of important

variables, reserving powerful techniques for precisely measured variables, the price is mathematically self-righteous ignorance. (Cited in Gurr, 1972, p. 63)

Another assumption underlying the use of ordinary least squares regression is that of *homoscedasticity* or equal population variances: a condition where the standard deviations of the values on the dependent variable for each value of a given independent variable are the same regardless of the value of the independent variable (see Blalock, 1960, p. 279). Given that the PDS 1–5 data-set represents a combination of *longitudinal* and *cross-sectional* data – and that there are sizeable differences in the variances of measures when they are taken over time or in cross-sections (see Midlarsky, 1975, p. 135) – there would seem to be some degree of *heteroscedasticity* or unequal variance in PDS 1–5, which, in turn, could have biased the values of the coefficients in the general models. Since, however, as indicated in Chapter 4, the data on all variables were *standardized* prior to the regression-based development of the PDS models, this potential problem would seem to have been nipped in the bud: Standardization enables us to "measure changes in the dependent variable in terms of standard deviation units for each of the [independent] variables, a fact which assures us of the *same variability* in each of these variables" (Blalock, 1960, pp. 344–5; emphasis added).

Ordinary least squares regression also involves the assumption that the cases included in a data-set are independent of each other: that the choice of each case had no bearing on the choice of any other case included in the set (see *ibid.*, p. 109). *Time-series analysis*, in which observations are made on the same actors in terms of the same variables at different points in time, as in the PDS study, could be a violation of this assumption. The potential violation here concerns the *autocorrelation of error terms*: the intercorrelation of unmeasured influences on a given dependent variable at different points in time (see Miller, 1971, pp. 290–3).

There are a number of ways to control for autocorrelation of error terms, one of which is discussed by Blalock (1969, pp. 84, 98):

> In general, autocorrelations are apt to be most serious for short intervals because of the fact that the error terms are more likely to be dominated by disturbances that act continuously throughout a brief interval. As the time between observations is increased, errors are more likely to behave randomly unless there are a few major disturbances of prolonged duration. . . . [Hence, the] longer the interval between the first and second observations the more reasonable it would be to assume no autocorrelation.

The selection of the two-hour weekly PDS run as our temporal unit of analysis reflects this particular approach to dealing with the problem of autocorrelation: one week of "real time" separated each operation of the PDS and, consequently, each set of observations on the selected variables within the PDS. It is difficult to imagine, therefore, a set of unmeasured factors, which influenced a given variable during one two-hour run, carrying over across successive, "discontinuous" weekly intervals to influence that same variable during subsequent runs; in contrast to situations where the basic temporal units were adjacent to each other in a continuous temporal process.

There is another problem, one not necessarily associated with an assumption underlying the use of least squares regression, but which can nevertheless create havoc if a researcher wishes to rank, in terms of relative degrees of potency, independent variables comprising regression-generated models. *Multicollinearity*, or the problem of intercorrelations between independent variables in a given model, becomes significant when correlations between independent variables are in excess of 0.85, although "lesser degrees of multicollinearity can [also] pose problems for the substantive interpretation of regression coefficients" (Althauser, 1971, p. 453).

Using Althauser's qualified definition of significant multicollinearity as a basic criterion, any intercorrelation of independent variables beyond 0.50 could cause difficulties in interpretation. Only one pair of independent variables in this study had the problem to that extent, their intercorrelation reaching + 0.76, nearly as high as Althauser's initial 0.85 criterion: Attack Victim (VICT) and Systemic Attack Contagion (SAC) in the BEL model for PDS 1–5. Such a level of multicollinearity could have distorted the values of the VICT–BEL and SAC–BEL coefficients, thereby making it difficult to determine accurately the relative influences of each variable on BEL.

One way to manage multicollinearity is to exclude one of the multicollinear variables from the model. But on the basis of what criteria? Also, according to Choucri and North (1975, pp. 310–11):

> we cannot rule out the use of a particular variable or the estimation of a particular equation simply because of multicollinearity. Other problems might arise. High intercorrelations result in the loss of precision, but the exclusion of a theoretically relevant variable on these grounds might exacerbate serial correlation in the disturbances.

Another approach to the management of multicollinearity is to combine longitudinal with cross-sectional data (see Johnston, 1963, pp. 201–7). However, given that the models presented in Chapter 4 already represent that kind of combination, the VICT–SAC intercorrelation of + 0.76 suggests that this approach, with respect to the BEL model for PDS 1–5, may have failed. In any case, combining longitudinal with cross-sectional data can lead, as already noted, to the problem of heteroscedasticity.

Accordingly, various methodological problems, notwithstanding our attempts to deal with them or to otherwise "explain them away," may have influenced the values of the coefficients in the general (aggregate) and developmental (disaggregated) models, as well as the rankings of the independent variables in each case. This seems to be particularly true for the general model for BEL, where the VICT–SAC relationship scores high on multicollinearity. It is interesting to note that VICT and SAC do not appear in any of the three developmental models for BEL. Disaggregation, therefore, may have reduced the significance of multicollinearity in the PDS. In any case – and this is the point of this somewhat "technical" discussion – even the remotest possibility that some of these problems may have influenced the multivariate PDS findings was another reason to subject them to a comprehensive validation assessment.

Our discussion of the multivariate validation assessment of the PDS conflict models proceeds as follows:

1. Examining the adequacy of the reference materials: the extent to which the selected comparison studies mirror the universe of real-world and other laboratory/simulation studies corresponding to the PDS study.
2. Comparing the relationships in the PDS models with corresponding relationships found in real-world and other simulation/laboratory studies, in terms of both *direction* and *strength* of relationship.
3. Comparing *best-predicted* dependent variables in the PDS with best-predicted dependent variables in real-world and other studies.
4. Comparing *best-predicting* independent variables in the PDS with best-predicting independent variables in real-world and other studies.

Multivariate Validation of the PDS Conflict Models

Adequacy of the Reference Materials

Comparisons between the relationships in the PDS models and corresponding relationships found in other studies are indicated in Appendix D.[1] Table 5.1 summarizes the information presented in Appendix D. One striking aspect of Table 5.1 is the differences between the five sets of models in terms of number of relationships tested (column 2) as a proportion of number of distinct relationships (column 1) in each model: 60 percent of the relationships in the DI models; 50 percent of the relationships in the MD models; 42 percent of the relationships in the BEL models; 15 percent of the relationships in the ALL models and 78 percent of the relationships in the ATT models have been tested. Clearly, the ATT models are the most tested and the ALL models the least tested in this study, with the DI, MD, and BEL models in between.

These differences are indicative of the preferences of researchers whose works were consulted. Hence, according to our reference materials, interstate warfare has clearly been researched more often than alliances. Although it cannot be claimed, as indicated in note 1, that the selection of real-world and other studies outlined in Appendix D constitutes a *representative sample* of the universe of studies corresponding to PDS findings, the ranking implicit in the ATT/ALL pattern in Table 5.1 does approximate findings in John Vasquez's (1976) comprehensive assessment of statistics-based research in international relations. Ranking his dependent variables on the basis of the frequency of their inclusion in the hypotheses in his sample, Vasquez found that his internation negative interactions (our MD) had been researched more often than internation alliances (ALL), with internation violence (ATT), internal stress within nations (DI) and national military power (BEL) in between (Vasquez, 1976, p. 192, fn. 27).

Accordingly, Vasquez's data-set as well as the PDS reference materials indicate that research on interstate war exceeds that on alliances, with research on domestic instability and military expenditures in between. The implication,

Table 5.1 Summary of findings on agreement/disagreement between relationships in PDS models and corresponding relationships in other studies

Models	(1) No. distinct relationships	(2) Number tested	(3)[a,b] No. rel'ships supported	(4) (3) as a % of (2)	(5) (3) as a % of (1)	(6)[c] Number of comparisons	(7)[a] Supportive comparisons	(8) (7) as a % of (6)
DI	5	3 (60%)	2	67	40	6	5	83
MD	6	3 (50%)	3	100	50	5	5	100
BEL	12	5 (42%)	4	80	33	6	5	83
ALL	13	2 (15%)	1	50	8	2	1	50
ATT	9	7 (78%)	4.5	64	50	19	13.5	71
Totals	45	20	14.5	72.5	32	38	29.5	77.6

Notes: [a] If a finding from a reference study appeared to be nonlinear, but without direction of relationship specified, or consisted of a 50–50 distribution between positive and negative relationships, it was coded as: supported = 0.5; not supported = 0.5.

[b] When a number of studies was involved in the assessment of a particular PDS relationship (e.g. BEL–ATT, where eight studies were involved), the number of confirmations as a proportion of the total number of studies involved was recorded (e.g. for BEL–ATT, 5/8 or 0.625) and added to the remaining indicators of support to arrive at a total confirmation index for the dependent variable concerned (e.g. for ATT, 4.5 relationships were supported).

[c] The difference between (2) and (6) is that the former refers to the number of distinct relationships that were tested, while the latter refers to the number of studies used to test the PDS relationships. Since more than one study was sometimes used to assess a given PDS relationship, the number of comparisons tends to exceed the corresponding number of relationships tested.

therefore, is that the reference materials used in the PDS multivariate validation assessment constitute an acceptable *convenience sample*, at least with regard to the universe of corresponding studies published during the 1960s and 1970s.

Direction and Strength of Relationships

The figures in column (4) of Table 5.1 – number of relationships supported as a percentage of number of relationships tested – suggest that the PDS relationships have fared rather well. Although these figures are a more accurate reading of the validity of the PDS models than are the figures in column (8) – supportive comparisons as a percentage of number of comparisons[2] – the aggregate figure for column (4), 72.5 percent, is fairly close to that for column (8), 77.6 percent. And both are roughly the same distance from, and nearly identical to, the figure recorded in Chapter 4 for the percentage of comparisons supportive of the bivariate PDS relationships in terms of direction of relationship: 75 percent.

Also, as can be seen in the final column of Table 5.2, the percentages of relationships in the PDS 1–5 general (aggregate) and combined developmental (disaggregated) models which are in agreement with corresponding relationships *hypothesized* in Chapter 2 are 60 percent in each case. Specifically, the early stage, where Waltz's hypothesis was confirmed for all four foreign conflict models, is characterized by the highest agreement score between our pretheory-derived predicted relationships and the corresponding PDS findings: 73 percent, which is nearly identical to the 75 percent norm.[3]

Before we get too carried away with our discovery of a "75 percent norm," which, thus far, applies to the PDS findings only in terms of sign or *direction* of relationship, we should also discuss the validity of the multivariate findings in terms of *strength* of relationship. John Vasquez's comprehensive assessment provides us with some assistance in this regard as well. At the end of his study, Vasquez (1976, pp. 199–207) lists three categories of findings that are indicative of the level of knowledge in international relations: (a) *null* findings, or hypotheses that have been tested using *N*s of 20 cases in which less than 2.3

Table 5.2 Compatibility of PDS findings with predicted relationships

	"Hits"	"Misses"	Hits as % of pred. rel.	
PDS 1–5	12	8	12/20	(60%)
Early	8	3	8/11	(73%)
Intermediate	10	9	10/19	(53%)
Late	9.5	6.5	9.5/16	(59%)
Three stages combined	27.5	18.5	27.5/46	(60%)

Note: See predicted and actual PDS relationships in Tables 4.1 and 4.3–4.5 of Chapter 4.

percent of the results were coefficients of 0.72 and above; (b) *possible* findings, or hypotheses that have been tested using *N*s of fewer than 20 cases in which at least 2.3 percent of the results were coefficients of 0.72 and above; and (c) *promising* findings, or hypotheses that have been tested using *N*s of at least 20 cases in which 2.3 percent of the results were coefficients of 0.72 and above.

We collapsed Vasquez's possible and promising categories into one category, subsumed the hypotheses in his sample under the null and possible–promising categories, as appropriate, and matched his variables with corresponding PDS variables. The relevant Vasquez–PDS comparisons appear in Table 5.3, which allowed us to explore to what extent, if any, the values of the partial *r*s for the PDS relationships in the possible–promising category exceeded the values of the partial *r*s for the PDS relationships in the null category.

An examination of the coefficients in Table 5.3 indicates that nine out of twelve PDS relationships in the possible–promising category are higher in magnitude than the highest magnitude recorded for a PDS coefficient in the null category (0.30). For *75 percent* of the relationships in the possible–promising category, therefore, the hypothesis that the magnitudes of PDS relationships in the possible–promising category are higher than the magnitudes of relationships in the null category has not been disconfirmed.[4] Accordingly, the *75 percent norm* applies to the multivariate findings in terms of strength as well as direction of relationship.

Best-predicted Dependent Variables

The R^2s for the conflict models enabled us to rank the PDS dependent variables in terms of proportion of variation explained. We were able to rank corresponding variables from Vasquez's study on the basis of his *Predictive Power Index* (Vasquez, 1976, pp. 176–9); specifically, the proportion of findings on each of his dependent variables in which a coefficient of determination of at least 0.52 (0.72 x 0.72 = 0.52) was produced (*ibid.*, pp. 192–8). Table 5.4 provides comparisons of the rankings of both sets of dependent variables and, therefore, a basis for determining whether, and to what extent, there was agreement in this regard.

The rankings of Vasquez's dependent variables for the general and intermediate PDS models in Table 5.4 are exactly the same. Moreover, with the sole exception that BEL occupies third place in the PDS rankings, while its counterpart, Military Power, occupies first place in Vasquez's rankings, Vasquez's dependent variables are ranked in the same general order of importance as are the PDS dependent variables for the general and intermediate models. Also, the BEL exception virtually disappears, as the proportion of variation explained in BEL increases from the early to the late stages. Indeed, across the three developmental stages, the location of BEL in the PDS rankings gets progressively closer to the location of Military Power in the ranking of Vasquez's variables.

The ranks of some of the PDS dependent variables are identical to the ranks of their counterparts in Vasquez's study. In the general and intermediate models, DI and Internal Stress occupy fourth place and MD and Internation Negative Interactions occupy fifth place in their respective rankings. For the late models, ATT and Internation Violence occupy third place in their respective rankings.

There are some near-identities as well, i.e. comparisons in which the rank of

Table 5.3 Comparisons of PDS relationships with Vasquez's null and possible–promising hypotheses[a]

Vasquez's hypotheses with matched PDS variables	Magnitudes of corresponding PDS relationships
Null findings	
1. There appears to be no strong relationship between negative interactions between nations (MD) and internal stress within nations (DI)	MD–DI = + 0.18, + 0.26
2. There appears to be no strong relationship between violence among nations (VICT, SAC, ATT) and the military power of nations (BEL)	VICT–BEL = − 0.16[b] SAC–BEL = + 0.11[b] ATT–BEL = − 0.30[b]
3. There appears to be no strong relationship between military power of nations (BEL) and internation alliances (ALL)	BEL–ALL = − 0.19
Possible–promising findings	
4. There could be a strong relationship between internation alignment (ALL) and internation alignment (ALL)	ALL–ALL = + 0.43, + 0.31, + 0.49[b]
5. There may be a strong relationship between military power (BEL) and military power (BEL)	BEL–BEL = + 0.49, + 0.68
6. There may be a strong relationship between negative interactions (MD) and negative interactions (MD)	MD–MD = + 0.32[b]
7. There may be a strong relationship between military power (BEL) and violence (ATT)	BEL–ATT = + 0.13, + 0.35, + 0.25
8. There may be a strong relationship between violence (ATT) and violence (ATT)	ATT–ATT = + 0.50, + 0.39, + 0.24

Notes: [a] Partial *r*s were used as indicators of strength of relationship, except where a model contained only one independent variable, in which case the product–moment *r* was used.

[b] These relationships are not included among the assessments in Appendix D (in terms of direction of relationship) because, at the time that those assessments were conducted, corresponding studies could not be located. They are included here (in terms of strength of relationship) because of the opportunity provided by Vasquez (1976).

Table 5.4 Comparisons of rankings of best-predicted dependent variables in the PDS models with rankings of corresponding variables in Vasquez's study

	PDS			Vasquez		
Model	Dependent variable	R^2	Rank	Dependent variable	% of total findings with min. coeff. of det. of 0.52	Rank
General	Alliances (ALL)	0.47	1	Internation Alliances	2.16	2
	Aggressive Attacks (ATT)	0.29	2	Internation Violence	1.41	3
	Bellicosity (BEL)	0.27	3	Military Power	21.90	1
	Domestic Instability (DI)	0.19	4	Internal Stress	0.72	4
	Manifest Distrust (MD)	0.12	5	Internation Neg. Intractns	0.32	5
Early	ALL	0.64	1	Internation Alliances	2.16	2
	ATT	0.31	2	Internation Violence	1.41	3
	MD	0.29	3	Internation Neg. Intractns	0.32	5
	BEL	0.26	4	Military Power	21.90	1
	DI	0.22	5	Internal Stress	0.72	4
Intermediate	ALL	0.63	1	Internation Alliances	2.16	2
	ATT	0.41	2	Internation Violence	1.41	3
	BEL	0.27	3	Military Power	21.90	1
	DI	0.11	4	Internal Stress	0.72	4
	MD	0.05[a]	5	Internation Neg. Intractns	0.32	5
Late	ALL	0.58	1	Internation Alliances	2.16	2
	BEL	0.53	2	Military Power	21.90	1
	ATT	0.14	3	Internation Violence	1.41	3
	MD	0.10[a]	4	Internation Neg. Intractns	0.32	5
	DI	0.07[a]	5	Internal Stress	0.72	4

Note: Because these models consisted of only one independent variable, r^2 was used to determine the location of the dependent variable in the ranking.

a PDS variable is one rank removed from that of its counterpart in Vasquez's study. For the general, early, and intermediate models, ALL occupies first place while Internation Alliances occupies second place, and ATT occupies second place while Internation Violence occupies third place in their respective rankings. For the late models, ALL again occupies first place while Internation Alliances occupies second place, and BEL occupies second place while Military Power occupies first place; MD occupies fourth place while Internation Negative Interactions occupies fifth place; and DI occupies fifth place while Internal Stress occupies fourth place in their respective rankings.

There are similar ranks between PDS and Vasquez for "best-predicted" and "less well predicted" dependent variables. For the general, early, and intermediate models, ALL (Internation Alliances) and ATT (Internation Violence) are among the best-predicted dependent variables and, for the general, intermediate, and late models, DI (Internal Stress) and MD (Internation Negative Interactions) are among the less well predicted dependent variables.

While Table 5.4 deals with comparisons between ranks on individual variables, Table 5.5 deals with comparisons between *clusters* of rankings. For example, 10 comparisons could be, and were, made for the general models in Table 5.4, of which eight yielded parallel orderings.[5] Following this procedure for the whole of Table 5.4, we have the observations recorded in Table 5.5, where it can be seen that the PDS dependent variables in general improve across the early and late stages with regard to the fit between their ranks and those of their counterparts in Vasquez's study.[6] Moreover, the extent of agreement, on average, between the PDS dependent variables and their counterparts in Vasquez's study, in terms of clusters of ranks based on variation explained, is *75 percent*.

Accordingly, the *75 percent norm* continues to hold, for best-predicted dependent variables as well as for direction and strength of relationship. We now move on to consider the fourth and final phase of our comprehensive validation assessment of the multivariate PDS findings: a comparison between the PDS independent variables and those of corresponding real-world studies in terms of rankings based on predictive potencies.

Table 5.5 Comparisons between clusters of rankings of PDS dependent variables and clusters of rankings of corresponding dependent variables in Vasquez's study

Model	(1) Number of comparisons	(2) Number of parallel orderings	(3) (2) as % of (1)
General	10	8	80
Early	10	6	60
Intermediate	10	8	80
Late	10	8	80
Totals	40	30	75

Best-predicting Independent Variables

Vasquez's comprehensive study provides us with yet another barometer of validation assessment; in this case, one that facilitates comparisons between the predictive potencies of PDS independent variables and those of comparable real-world studies. Just as Vasquez listed his dependent variables in terms of percentage of total findings which accounted for at least 52 percent of the behavior of each dependent variable, so he listed his independent variables in terms of percentage of total findings which accounted for at least 52 percent of the behavior of a number of dependent variables (Vasquez, 1976, pp. 181–9).

By grouping together all PDS independent variables which corresponded to Vasquez's independent variables, and ranking his in terms of the 0.52 criterion and ours on the basis of mean beta weights, we were able to determine whether, and to what extent, there was agreement in this regard between the PDS and the real world, again as sampled by Vasquez. Rankings for both sets of independent variables are provided in Table 5.6.

We can note, first of all, that there are some identities between the two sets of rankings in Table 5.6. For the general models, ATT/%ATT/VICT/SAC and Internation Violence occupy third place, and RED/TO and Internal Stress occupy sixth place in their respective rankings. For the early models, RES and Economic Attributes occupy third place in their respective rankings. For the intermediate models, ALL and Internation Alliances occupy fourth place in their respective rankings. And for the late models, BEL and Military Power occupy first place, POLC/PERC/AUTH/POLE and Characteristics of National Leaders occupy fourth place, and RED/DI/TO/SSEC and Internal Stress occupy sixth place in their respective rankings.

There are some near-identities here as well. For the general models, BEL occupies second place while Military Power occupies first place, and ACH/POLC/PERC occupies fifth place while Characteristics of National Leaders occupies fourth place in the respective rankings. For the early models, BEL shares first-place ranking with RED while Military Power alone occupies first place in the respective rankings. For the intermediate models, ATT/SAC occupies first place while Internation Violence occupies second place in the respective rankings. And for the late models, MD occupies third place while Internation Negative Interactions occupies second place in the respective rankings.

Extending our comparisons to clusters of rankings, as we did for the dependent variables, we have the data recorded in Table 5.7, where the extent of agreement, on average, between the independent variables in the PDS and their counterparts in Vasquez's study, in terms of predictive potency, is 57 percent: not quite in the vicinity of our 75 percent norm.[7] On the other hand, the findings for the general and, especially, the late models *are* in the vicinity of 75 percent, thereby suggesting that the real world, as sampled by Vasquez, may, in terms of independent as well as dependent variables, reflect a "late" developmental period (see note 6).

Given that multicollinearity may have had more of an effect on the general (aggregate) models than on the developmental (disaggregated) models, it is also

Table 5.6 Comparisons of rankings of best-predicting independent variables in the PDS models with rankings of corresponding variables in Vasquez's study

Model	PDS			Vasquez		
	Independent variable	Mean beta weight[a]	Rank	Independent variable	% of total findings with min. coeff. det. of 0.52	Rank
General	ALL = 0.37	0.37	1	Internation alliances	1.78	5
	BEL = 0.49, 0.12 ATT = 0.50, VICT = 0.21, 0.21	0.30	2	Military power	7.51	1
	%ATT = 0.10, SAC = 0.15	0.23	3	Internation violence	3.96	3
	MD = 0.17	0.17	4	Internation negative interactions	4.16	2
	ACH = 0.16, POLC = 0.10, PERC = 0.16, 0.16	0.14	5	Characteristics of national leaders	2.97	4
	RED = 0.10, TO = 0.11, 0.11, 0.12	0.11	6	Internal stress	0.20	6
	SEC = 0.31, 0.33, 0.37	0.34[b]	–	–	–	–
Early	BEL = 0.32	0.32	1.5	Military power	7.51	1
	RED = 0.32	0.32	1.5	Internal stress	0.20	4
	RES = 0.27	0.27	3	Economic attributes	1.71	3
	ATT = 0.28, VICT = 0.18, %ATT = 0.22	0.23	4	Internation violence	3.96	2
	SEC = 0.38, 0.63, 0.39, 0.52, 0.48	0.48[b]	–	–	–	–

Table 5.6 *(continued)*

Intermediate	ATT = 0.23, 0.38, SAC = 0.48	0.36	1	Internation violence	3.96	2
	RES = 0.37, 0.22	0.29	2	Economic attributes	1.71	5
	TO = 0.23, 0.33, 0.26, SSEC = 0.19	0.25	3	Internal stress	0.20	6
	ALL = 0.21	0.21	4	Internation alliances	1.78	4
	ACH = 0.21, DOG = 0.16, 0.21, POLC = 0.27, 0.17	0.20	5	Characteristics of national leaders	2.97	3
	BEL = 0.13, 0.22	0.17	6	Military power	7.51	1
	SEC = 0.17, 0.30	0.23[b]	–	–	–	–
Late	BEL = 0.65	0.65	1	Military power	7.51	1
	ALL = 0.41	0.41	2	Internation alliances	1.78	5
	MD = 0.26, 0.32	0.29	3	Internation negative interactions	4.16	2
	POLC = 0.18, 0.19, PERC = 0.38, AUTH = 0.18, POLE = 0.21	0.23	4	Characteristics of national leaders	2.97	4
	ATT = 0.24, VICT = 0.17	0.20	5	Internation violence	3.96	3
	RED = 0.12, DI = 0.15, TO = 0.12, SSEC = 0.20	0.15	6	Internal stress	0.20	6
	SEC = 0.49	0.49[b]	–	–	–	–

Notes: [a] Beta weights were used instead of partial *r* because they are additive, while partial *r* is not. Beta weights, therefore, lent themselves to computation of means, which provided a basis for ranking the PDS independent variables. [b] Although SEC does not figure in the rankings, because there was nothing in Vasquez's (1976) study that seemed to correspond to it, it appears as the last item for each set of models to indicate its potency relative to other independent variables. Had it been included in the rankings, it would have ranked second in the general models, first in the early models, fourth in the intermediate models and second in the late models.

Table 5.7 Comparisons between clusters of rankings of PDS independent variables and clusters of rankings of corresponding independent variables in Vasquez's study

Model	(1) Number of comparisons	(2) Number of parallel orderings	(3) (2) as % of (1)
General	15	10	67
Early	6	3	50
Intermediate	15	5	33
Late	15	11	73
Totals	51	29	57

interesting that the second highest agreement-score between the PDS independent variables and those drawn from Vasquez's study has occurred for the general models. In any case, whatever agreement has obtained for any of the models between the PDS independent variables and those from Vasquez's study is relevant to the next section of this chapter, which is concerned with exploring answers to the question: "What variables are worth looking at with respect to violent conflict and war?"

Ingredients of Complex Conflict Processes

Just as Table 5.4 revealed similarities between PDS and Vasquez with regard to best- and less well *predicted* dependent variables, so Table 5.6 reveals similarities between PDS and Vasquez with regard to best- and less well *predicting* independent variables. For the general models, for example, BEL (Military Power) and ATT/%ATT/VICT/SAC (Internation Violence) are among the highest ranked, while ACH/POLC/PERC (Characteristics of National Leaders) and RED/TO (Internal Stress) are among the lowest ranked predictors of conflict in general.

For the early models, BEL (Military Power) is among the most potent predictors, while RES (Economic Attributes) is among the least potent predictors. For the intermediate models, ATT/SAC (Internation Violence) are among the most potent predictors, while ALL (Internation Alliances) is among the least potent predictors. And for the late models, BEL (Military Power) is the most potent predictor, MD (Internation Negative Interactions) is among the most potent predictors, POLC/PERC/AUTH/POLE (Characteristics of National Leaders) are among the least potent predictors and RED/DI/TO/SSEC (Internal Stress) are the least potent predictors of conflict in general.

In terms of the PDS–Vasquez nexus, therefore, the most important sources of conflict in general in the PDS were four societal variables (BEL(3), ATT(2), VICT(1), and MD(1)) and one trans-societal variable (SAC(2)).[8] The least important sources were five psychological variables (POLC(2), PERC(2), AUTH(1), ACH(1), and POLE(1)); the two spatial-temporal variables (TO(2) and SSEC(1)); and five societal variables (RED(2), DI(1), RES(1), and ALL(1)).[9] In effect, the trans-societal level was one of the most dominant, albeit infrequent, general predictors; the societal level was both one of the most dominant and one of the least dominant general predictors; and the decision-making level (both the psychological and spatial-temporal dimensions) was one of the least dominant predictors of conflict in this study.

Even when we include relationships on variables which did not figure in the validation assessment, we get much the same line-up of levels in terms of general predictive potencies. It is clear from Table 5.8 that one trans-societal variable, SEC, was the dominant source of influence on all conflict variables during the early stage. During the intermediate stage, a mixture of levels prevailed: the trans-societal level was dominant for one of the conflict variables (SAC–ALL); the societal was dominant for another three (RES–MD, RES–BEL, and ATT–ATT); and the decision-making level (psychological) was dominant for one (ACH–DI). And during the late stage, for all conflict variables but one (where the trans-societal level prevailed (SEC-ALL)), the societal level was dominant (MD–DI, MD–MD, BEL–BEL, and ATT–ATT).

Discussing each of the levels in detail, we can see that the trans-societal level has often been a primary (or nearly primary) source of influence in this study: for all of the conflict variables during the early stage (SEC–DI, SEC–MD, SEC–BEL, SEC–ALL, SEC–ATT); for one during the intermediate stage (SAC–ALL) and another where the trans-societal level occupied second place (SEC–ATT); for one during the late stage (SEC–ALL); and for two in the general models (SEC–DI, SEC–MD) and one other where the trans-societal occupied second place (SEC–ALL). To this we can add that, had SEC been included in the PDS–Vasquez comparisons, it would have ranked second in the general models, first in the early models, fourth in the intermediate models, and second in the late models (see note b of Table 5.6).

The PDS findings on the role of the trans-societal level are supported by corresponding real-world studies. In addition to those included in our original validation assessment – by Michael Haas (1970) and Manus Midlarsky (1975) (see Appendix D, Table D.5) – recent studies reported by Vasquez (1993, p. 143) are even more supportive. Maoz (1989, p. 202), for example, has found an impressive positive relationship between the number of states in the system (SEC) and the number of disputes in the system. Also, Small and Singer (1982, pp. 130, 141) have found that as the number of states in the system (SEC) increases, so does the number of wars.[10]

These findings, together with the positive relationships between SEC and BEL, and SEC and ATT for the early stage, and between SEC and ALL for the early and late stages, are clearly supportive of the Rosecrance (1966) thesis that increases in the number of independent actors in the system make for increases in complexity, incalculability, uncertainty and, therefore, for increases in the number of international conflicts.

There is, nevertheless, some support for the Deutsch–Singer (1964) thesis as well: the negative relationships between SEC and MD for the early stage and for PDS 1–5 are compatible with the proposition that increases in the number of actors make for increased stability in the system. In general, however, in terms

Table 5.8 Ranked levels and primary variables in the PDS conflict models

Model		Rankings of levels[a]				No. indep. vars. in model	Primary[b] variable	Partial r^2 of primary variable	R^2 of model
		1st	2nd	3rd	4th				
DI:	Early	t-s	soc	–	–	2	- 0.38SEC	0.15	0.22
	Inter.	d-m (p)	d-m (st)	t-s	–	3	+ 0.21ACH	0.05	0.11
	Late	soc	–	–	–	1	+ 0.26MD	–	0.07
	General	t-s	soc	d-m (p)	soc	4	- 0.31SEC	0.10	0.19
MD:	Early	t-s	soc	–	–	2	- 0.48SEC	0.24	0.29
	Inter.	soc	–	–	–	1	+ 0.22RES	–	0.05
	Late	soc	–	–	–	1	+ 0.32MD	–	0.10
	General	t-s	d-m (p)	d-m (st)	–	3	- 0.37SEC	0.12	0.12
BEL:	Early	t-s	soc	–	–	2	+ 0.52SEC	0.24	0.26
	Inter.	soc	d-m (p)	d-m (st)	d-m (p)	4	+ 0.37RES	0.15	0.27
	Late	soc	d-m (st)	d-m (st)	soc	4	+ 0.65BEL	0.46	0.53
	General	soc	soc	t-s	–	3	+ 0.49BEL	0.24	0.27

Table 5.8 *(continued)*

Model		Rankings of levels[a]				No. indep. vars. in model	Primary[b] variable	Partial r^2 of primary variable	R^2 of model
		1st	2nd	3rd	4th				
ALL:	Early	t-s	soc	soc	–	3	+ 0.63SEC	0.48	0.64
	Inter.	t-s	d-m (st)	soc	soc	5	+ 0.48SAC	0.31	0.63
	Late	t-s	soc	d-m (p)	d-m (p)	6	+ 0.49SEC	0.26	0.58
	General	soc	t-s	soc	d-m (p)	7	+ 0.37ALL	0.18	0.47
ATT:	Early	t-s	soc	–	–	2	+ 0.39SEC	0.17	0.31
	Inter.	soc	t-s	d-m (st)	soc	6	+ 0.38ATT	0.15	0.41
	Late	soc	d-m (p)	d-m (p)	d-m (p)	4	+ 0.24ATT	0.06	0.14
	General	soc	soc	d-m (st)	–	3	+ 0.50ATT	0.25	0.29

Notes: [a]The bases of the rankings were the mean beta weights of the independent variables operative at each level. The coding employed was: t-s, trans-societal level; soc, societal level; d-m (st), decision-making (spatial-temporal) level; and d-m (p), decision-making (psychological) level.

[b] Each primary independent variable is accompanied by the beta weight on its relationship with the conflict variable.

of both the PDS and corresponding real-world findings (including those of Singer himself: Small and Singer, 1982), the Rosecrance view has fared better than that of Deutsch and Singer.[11]

The societal level has also achieved primacy or near-primacy in this study and, arguably, more so than the trans-societal level. For three of the models during the intermediate stage, for four during the late stage, and for three of the general models, variables at this level appear to have dominated the behavior of their respective dependent variables. In addition, the societal level has ranked second in the five models for the early stage, one model for the late stage, and three models for PDS 1–5. These overall findings could be taken as justification for researchers who have tended to focus their attention on independent variables operative only at the societal level,[12] especially since the findings emerged from a study in which the societal was one of a number of levels, any one of which (e.g. the trans-societal) could have emerged as dominant.

In addition to perpetuating the reign of single-level studies, however, enthusiasm for concentrating only on independent variables at the societal level might be premature, given Vasquez's (1976, p. 190) observation that such variables in his survey had the poorest predictive potency: of the 7347 independent variables operative at this level, 92.7 percent produced findings which were statistically insignificant and/or had measures of association less than 0.501. Only 2.2 percent involved stronger associations. Our finding here, therefore, certainly justifies looking for independent variables at the societal level, but, as in the case of the trans-societal, not at that level alone.[13]

Whereas the trans-societal and societal levels have each been primary in a number of cases, the decision-making level has achieved primacy in only one case: the DI model for the intermediate stage, where the psychological dimension was operative. The psychological dimension also came in second for one intermediate, one late, and one general model, as did the spatial-temporal dimensions for two models at the intermediate stage and for one model at the late stage.

In a far-ranging survey and assessment of the impact of personality factors on cooperative and conflictful behavior, Kenneth Terhune (1970, pp. 217–18) posed the question:

> Given the demonstrated effects of personality variables, are the *magnitudes* of those effects really very significant in comparison to the effects of situational variations? . . . Too few studies have varied both personality and situational parameters to arrive at a definitive answer to the question.

In the PDS study, we have varied both personality and situational factors and, clearly, the magnitudes of the effects of personality variables have not been very significant. But there may be more to this story than meets the eye.

We have generated, via the stepwise procedure, 20 models: four for each of the five conflict variables. In twelve of these models (see Tables 4.1 and 4.3–4.5), psychological variables are *not* included. This tends to confirm Terhune's (1970, pp. 204–6) own experience that the effect of personality factors on behavior is relatively difficult to detect in complex situations such as simulations with multiple decision periods, in contrast to one-trial and multitrial two-person laboratory games. In the eight remaining models, however, personality factors are included: in one model, as already indicated, the personality dimension is dominant; in three models (including one general model), it is the second most dominant; in three other models, it is the third most potent; and in four models, it is the fourth most potent dimension.

Even allowing for this apparently not negligible presence of psychological factors in some of the models, their average predictive potency is low. This may be due to the way in which the psychological variables were operationally defined, which involved computing average scores on the variables for the individuals in each group. The scores were not weighted by dominant personalities, as Fred Greenstein (1969, p. 137) has suggested they might have been. In effect, we computed averages for a relatively full range of personalities, rather than focusing, to any extent, on dominant or extreme personality types. And as Terhune (1970, p. 219) has indicated, "In studies where a fuller range of personalities was used, . . . correlation coefficients between personality variables and behavioral indices are often low."

Sidney Verba (1961, p. 97) posed a question some time ago, similar to Terhune's, in which he considered the benefits of incorporating "nonlogical" (i.e. psychological) factors into models of international relations: "Does the increase in explanatory power that would accompany the introduction of such variables into a model of the international system justify the increased complexity of the model?" Considering the low predictive potency of the psychological variables in this study, especially the observation in Table 5.8 that, for the general MD model, the psychological dimension, which was the second most dominant, apparently accounted for a minute proportion of variance,[14] one might be tempted to respond with a "no!" On the other hand, there are some considerations which might prompt us to respond with a "yes!"

We cannot, for instance, dismiss as negligible the fact that psychological factors appear in 40 percent of the models: in one case as the most potent dimension and in three other cases as the second most potent dimension. Nor can we lose sight of the possibility, implicit in the quote from Ezekiel and Fox (1959, p. 195) in Chapter 4, that certain high-potency independent variables may enter a model only because other variables, like the psychological ones, have been brought into the relational system. In other words, in a given model, low-potency relationships between some independent variables and the dependent variable may be a prerequisite for high-potency relationships occurring between other independent variables and the dependent variable.

Further, assuming that relationships between certain variables might be revealed only during certain time periods (see Burrowes and Spector, 1973, p. 317), the observation that three of the models containing psychological variables were for the intermediate stage and another two were for the late stage, while three were general models, suggests that "Further inquiry in this area will require that these and other conditions be identified and built into our theoretical frameworks and research designs" (*ibid.*).[15] Among those "other conditions" might be the suggestion from Chapter 4 that the increasing trend across the three stages of *self-stimulating/self-perpetuating conflict processes* may have been accompanied (and facilitated) by the growing presence of elements of realist belief-value systems (which, by the late stage, were appropriately linked with some of the conflict variables).

In general, then, although the psychological variables proved to be of relatively low predictive potency, it seems that they should continue to be incorporated into our research designs, but only as part of multilevel strategies. As Terhune (1970, p. 219) puts it, "more complex situations necessitate the *inclusion* of more factors, but do not justify the *exclusion* of personality factors, in order to understand behavior."

Accordingly, whether we look at the predictive potencies of all the independent variables in the PDS study or only at the independent variables whose potencies have been supported by Vasquez's study, we find that, with respect to violent conflict and war, variables operative at the trans-societal and societal levels were the most dominant, while variables operative at the decision-making level (spatial-temporal as well as psychological) were the least potent.

The PDS and the "Steps to War"

In his comprehensive assessment of empirical studies of war, John Vasquez (1993, p. 155; 1987, p. 117) has delineated "the typical path by which relatively equal states have become embroiled in wars with one another in the modern global system." His "steps to war" comprise variables corresponding to those of the PDS. For instance, decision-makers can respond to crises by increasing "their military power through alliances [ALL] and/or military buildup [BEL] (Wallace, 1972; Most and Siverson, 1987)." In such tense situations, increases in BEL can lead to arms races (BEL/%BEL) and increases in ALL can lead to polarization, "both of which may increase insecurity." Under such conditions, actors may employ *Realpolitik* tactics in "militarized disputes between equals" (Leng, 1983). Eventually in such a tense environment, a dispute may arise that escalates to war:

> Disputes or crises are most likely to escalate if there is an ongoing arms race [BEL/%BEL] (Wallace, 1979), and if (1) they are triggered by physical threats to vital issues (Gochman and Leng, 1983); (2) they are the second or third crisis with the same rival (with realpolitik tactics becoming more coercive and hostile in each succeeding crisis) (Leng, 1983); (3) a hostile interaction spiral emerges during the crisis (Holsti, North, and Brody, 1968); and (4) hard-liners dominate the leadership of at least one side.

To what extent are the PDS findings compatible with Vasquez's "steps to war"? First of all, Alliances (ALL) do not appear in any of the PDS models for Aggressive Attacks (ATT). This is compatible with Vasquez's (1993, p. 159, 168) observation that, although alliances are often "followed by war, [they] are probably not a direct cause of war. . . . Instead [they are probably] a step toward war that aggravates an already tense relationship."

Bellicosity (BEL) is the second dominant variable in the ATT model for PDS 1–5 combined, the second dominant variable in the ATT model for the early stage and the fourth dominant variable in the ATT model for the intermediate stage. As indicated in Table D.5 (see Appendix D), the BEL–ATT relationship has been fairly well supported by corresponding real-world studies. It has also been supported by more recent studies: for instance, Bremer's (1980) study, which "suggests that the most powerful states . . . are caught in a *culture of war* and that the more powerful they are, the more they are unable to avoid war" (Vasquez, 1993, p. 162; emphasis added). Bremer's study has been extended by Eberwein (1982) and Gochman and Maoz (1984, pp. 606–9), who "have found that the more powerful states are, the more involved they become in militarized disputes" (Vasquez, 1993, p. 162).

There do not appear to have been any significant arms race processes (BEL/%BEL) in the PDS, although the "culture of war" does seem to have been a feature across developmental stages as well as for PDS 1–5 combined. One aspect of this *Realpolitik* culture, in addition to the growing presence of elements of realist belief-value systems, is the SAC–foreign conflict connection. SAC is in the BEL model for PDS 1–5 combined as the least dominant variable, as well as in the ALL model for the intermediate stage as the dominant variable: the "presence of a series of disputes that might escalate to war may encourage others to arm [SAC–BEL] [and/or conceivably to enter into alliances (SAC–ALL)] because of the threatening environment" (Vasquez, 1993, p. 182).

By far, the most salient indicator of the war culture in the PDS was the phenomenon of self-stimulating/self-perpetuating violent conflict.[16] As indicated in Table D.3 (Appendix D), Lambelet and Luterbacher (1978) provide empirical support for BEL–BEL. Choucri and North (1975) do as well (cited in Vasquez, 1993, p. 172). And as indicated in Table D.5, Moyal (1949), Tanter (1966), and Singer *et al.* (1972) provide empirical support for ATT–ATT. More recent support has come from Thompson's (1989) argument that the violence in Northern Ireland has been self-perpetuating.

Overall, then, there appears to be quite a good fit between the PDS results and Vasquez's "steps to war."

Conclusion

We began this chapter by discussing some methodological problems which may have influenced the multivariate findings in Chapter 4. Partially because of those potential problems, we subjected the findings to a comprehensive validation assessment, comparing PDS findings to findings from real-world and other studies in terms of direction and strength of relationship, rankings of best-predicted dependent variables, and rankings of best-predicting independent variables.

Despite vast differences between the PDS findings and those of other studies, including the fact that the PDS findings are multivariate (beta weights and partial *r*s), whereas those of other studies tended to be bivariate (e.g. product–moment correlations), the agreement-scores between the PDS and other (mostly real-world) findings tended to fall within the range of the *75 percent norm*.

The validation of the PDS findings in terms of rankings of best-predicting independent variables led to the discussion of what variables seemed to be worth looking at with regard to violent conflict and war. This revealed the relatively high potency of variables operative at the trans-societal and societal levels and the relatively low potency of variables operative at the decision-making level.

The final section of the chapter dealt with the correspondence between the PDS findings and Vasquez's "steps to war."

Perhaps the most significant consequence of the multivariate validation assessment of PDS findings has been the observation that it is not only the *static* identification of what variables might be worth looking at – *conflict-as-startup conditions* (see Sandole, 1993a, p. 21) – but also the identification of *dynamic* processes that might overtake these static startup conditions: *conflict-as-process* (*ibid.*). This distinction plays a major role in the theory articulated in Chapter 6.

Notes

1. The PDS findings were assessed primarily through comparisons with findings generated by other studies published during the 1960s and 1970s, in part to maintain "temporal proximity" with Guetzkow's INS assessments. Hence, the validation assessment of the PDS reported here is partial and, by implication, incomplete. Nevertheless, the assessment is fairly comprehensive, demonstrating a methodology for validating gaming-simulations in general as well as some impressive results for the PDS in particular. And in any case, some updating of the basic assessment is done toward the end of the chapter.
2. See note c for Table 5.1.
3. Hence, perhaps our pretheory reflects an "early" developmental period (see note 6).
4. Even if we were to withdraw hypothesis no. 4 and the ALL–ALL findings from the analysis, because ALL is not quite the same thing as Vasquez's internation alignment, we would find that six out of nine relationships (67 percent) in the possible–promising category are of higher magnitudes than 0.30.
5. On the basis of the PDS rankings for the general models: (a) Vasquez's Internation Alliances, Internation Violence, Military Power, and Internal Stress should be, and are, ranked higher than Internation Negative Interactions (four comparisons and four "hits"); (b) Internation Alliances, Internation Violence, and Military Power should be, and are, ranked higher than Internal Stress (three comparisons and three "hits"); (c) Internation Alliances and Internation Violence should be, but are not, ranked higher than Military Power (two comparisons and two "misses"); and (d) Internation Alliances should be, and is, ranked higher than Internation Violence (one comparison and one "hit"). Hence, for the general models, there are eight parallel rankings (or "hits") out of ten comparisons, producing an agreement score of 80 percent.
6. Hence, in contrast to the hypotheses derived from the pretheory in Chapter 2, which, given the level of their agreement with PDS findings, may reflect an "early" developmental period (see note 3), Vasquez's comprehensive assessment of quantitative international relations studies, given the level of their agreement with PDS findings, may, with regard to dependent variables, reflect "intermediate" and "late" developmental periods. What this suggests is a possible lack of fit between theory and research in international relations.

7. On the basis of the PDS rankings in Table 5.6 for the general models, for example: (a) Vasquez's Internation Alliances, Military Power, Internation Violence, Internation Negative Interactions, and Characteristics of National Leaders should be, and are, ranked higher than Internal Stress (five comparisons and five parallel rankings, or "hits"); (b) Internation Alliances, Military Power, Internation Violence, and Internation Negative Interactions should be, and with one exception (Internation Alliances) are, ranked higher than Characteristics of National Leaders (four comparisons and three "hits"); (c) Internation Alliances, Military Power, and Internation Violence should be, but with one exception (Military Power) are not, ranked higher than Internation Negative interactions (three comparisons and one "hit"); (d) Internation Alliances and Military Power should be, and in one case (Military Power) are, ranked higher than Internation Violence (two comparisons and one "hit"); and (e) Internation Alliances should be, but is not, ranked higher than Military Power (one comparison and one "miss"). Hence, for the general models, there are ten parallel rankings or "hits" out of fifteen comparisons, producing an agreement score of 67 percent.
8. It is important to keep in mind that SAC appears here because of its association with ATT and VICT, and *not* because something like it appeared in Vasquez's data-set.
9. The number in parentheses after each variable indicates how often the variable (matched with Vasquez) appeared in the PDS models as a best- or less well predicting independent variable.
10. Vasquez (1993, p. 143) uses the "territoriality axiom" to explain the "well-established association between system size [SEC] and conflict": "If it is the case that territoriality makes states prone to use violence to establish their boundaries, then as the number of states in the system [SEC] increase, the number of militarized disputes should also increase, since the establishment of new borders will entail more disputes."
11. For a fuller account of the "size/stability controversy" (which includes others besides Deutsch/Singer and Waltz/Rosecrance) and empirical tests of the corresponding hypotheses, see Ostrom and Aldrich (1978).
12. Vasquez (1976, p. 190) reports that 96 percent (7347) of the independent variables in his sample are located at the national (societal) level, "which clearly reflects an overwhelming consensus among quantitative scholars on the importance of this [level]."
13. In any case, as Jack Levy (1996, p. 18) maintains, we should look for societal-level variables of certain kinds: "In terms of levels of analysis, far more attention needs to be directed to societal-level variables [e.g. ethnonational and other identity-based conflicts; economic variables; resource scarcities exacerbated by environmental degradation and resulting population migrations; democratization processes]. These have been important but neglected in the past, and in all probability they will become increasingly important in the future in shaping the preferences of state leaders and the constraints on their actions."
14. The rounded-off value of the partial r^2 for the dominant variable (0.12) is the same as that of the R^2 for all variables in the model (0.12).
15. Although Burrowes and Spector (1973, p. 317) were addressing specifically "relationships ... between the domestic and external politics of nations," which they believe exist "probably . . . only for certain types of nations, at certain times, and under certain circumstances," their recommendation for further research in this regard would also seem to apply to research on the relationship between psychological factors and conflict.
16. That self-stimulating/self-perpetuating violent conflict processes, and not "other-stimulated conflict" (i.e. action–reaction) processes, were the dominant process theme in the PDS is suggested by the observation that Attack Victim (VICT) is not included in any of the models for ATT. It appears only in the general and early models for ALL in a positive relational sense (as the third dominant variable in each case), and in the late model for ALL and the general model for BEL in a negative relational sense.

6 Implications for Theory: A Generic Theory of Violent Conflict and War

Introduction

Thus far in this study, we have: (a) identified violent conflict and war as problems (still!) in need of solution; (b) developed a multilevel framework and pretheory for analyzing and explaining violent conflict and war; (c) discussed simulation in general and the Prisoners' Dilemma Simulation (PDS) in particular as a method for generating data on variables drawn from the pretheory; (d) presented and discussed models of complex conflict processes generated by stepwise regression from the PDS data; and (e) subjected the models to a comprehensive validation assessment, enabling us to respond more fully to the question "what variables are worth looking at?" as possible causes and conditions of violent conflict and war.

Whether we looked at the predictive potencies of all the independent variables in the general (aggregate) and developmental (disaggregated) models or only at the independent variables whose relative potencies were supported by Vasquez's (1976) study, we found that variables operative at the trans-societal and societal levels were dominant, while variables operative at the decision-making level (spatial–temporal as well as psychological) were the least potent sources of influence on the conflict variables.

One trans-societal variable, SEC, was the dominant source of influence on all conflict variables during the early stage. During the intermediate stage, a mixture of levels prevailed, with the trans-societal achieving dominance in one case (SAC–ALL); the societal in three (RES–MD, RES–BEL, ATT–ATT); and the decision-making level (psychological) in one (ACH–DI). During the late stage, the societal level was dominant for all conflict variables (MD–DI, MD–MD, BEL–BEL, ATT–ATT) except one (ALL), where the trans-societal level (SEC) prevailed.

The "Waltzean Hypothesis" of international system dominance in the genesis of war was compatible with the MD model for PDS 1–5, all foreign conflict models for the early stage, and the ALL models across all three developmental stages.

A finding which emerged serendipitously from the study – making compelling the distinction between *conflict-as-startup conditions* and *conflict-as-process* – was the observed trend across the three stages of apparently *self-stimulating/self-perpetuating conflict processes* (MD–MD, BEL–BEL, ATT–ATT), perhaps facilitated in part by *Realpolitik* perspectives, perceptions, and behaviors.

With these findings, we are at a point where we can return to the realm of theory – the current conflict/conflict resolution literature as well as the pretheory of Chapter 2 – to explore to what extent the ingredients of a *generic theory of violent conflict and war* exist among these various elements. The premise here is that a "generic theory" will be useful, not just for explaining, but for responding to, violent conflict and war at all levels, including the violent ethnic conflict and warfare of the post-Cold War era.

Generic theory in conflict and conflict resolution has been a contentious issue (e.g. see Burton and Sandole, 1986; Avruch and Black, 1987), with no clear resolution in sight. On the one hand, Kenneth Boulding (1962) thought such a theory possible, differences between levels notwithstanding, and went some way toward developing one. On the other hand, Anatol Rapoport (1974, pp. 7–10) – despite (or precisely because of) his own efforts in this regard – had his doubts about a general theory of war as well as a general theory of conflict. Somewhere in between is John Vasquez (1993, p. 306), who, while he believes that a "unified theory of conflict and violence" is possible, does not feel the same about a generic theory of war (*ibid.*, p. 49):

> [Given] the assumption of multicausality, or equifinality, ... trying to delineate the causes of war by only studying wars in the hopes of finding a common pattern will not be successful. ... In terms of policy relevance, this means that even if some causal sequences of war are identified and eliminated, war may still be caused by other factors. This makes the task of bringing about permanent peace arduous and complicated.

Our study reflects Boulding's (1962, pp. viii, 1–2) view that:

> It seems reasonable to suppose that conflict [of which war is a special case] does exhibit many general patterns, that the patterns of conflict in industrial relations, international relations, interpersonal relations and even animal life are not wholly different from one another, and that it is, therefore, worth looking for the common element.

Accordingly, what do the current literature and the study reported here have to say about that "common element" – what Christopher Mitchell (1981, pp. 4, 314) calls the "unity of the [*multidisciplinary, multilevel*] subject matter" – particularly with regard to violent conflict and war?

Beyond "Pretheory" (I): Paradigms of Conflict and Conflict Resolution[1]

In his significant assault on the 300-year reign of the Cartesian dogma of "immaculate perception," Thomas Kuhn (1970) argued that the realities perceived by the "high priests of truth" – scientists – are a function of their collective, internalized "maps" (or *paradigms*). Different paradigms, different mappings of the "same thing," mean different realities, whether for members of different communities at one point in time or for members of the same community over time.

Clearly, whatever applies to scientists must apply to the rest of us as well, since, as Sir Karl Popper (1959, p. 22) put it, scientific knowledge is "common-sense knowledge writ large." That there may be multiple, and indeed, competing conceptions/reconstructions of reality, even (but clearly not only) for scientists, makes the concept of paradigms particularly relevant to conflict and conflict resolution where parties are quite prepared to die and to kill to defend their competing worldviews.

There are at least four paradigms relevant to conflict and conflict resolution at all levels: (a) political realism (*Realpolitik*), (b) political idealism (*Idealpolitik*), (c) Marxism, and (d) "non-Marxist radical thought" (NMRT).

The first two, the subject of "The Great Debates" recounted by Carr (1939), are polar opposites; indeed, each can be viewed as a reaction to the other. Political realism (*Realpolitik*), as discussed in Chapter 1, tends to be the dominant system (also see Sandole, 1984). Its view of the world is clearly a bleak one, encouraging the use of what Morton Deutsch (1973) calls the *competitive* processes: power-based, adversarial, confrontational, zero-sum, "win–lose" approaches to dealing with conflict. As Vasquez (1993) argues in his "steps to war," *Realpolitik* and the corresponding competitive processes tend to be associated with destructive outcomes.

Proponents of political idealism (*Idealpolitik*), on the other hand, may be in agreement with realists about the alarming frequency and intensity of violent conflict and war ("descriptive realism") and about the absence of appropriate mechanisms for dealing with such ("explanatory realism (b)"), but disagree that a fixed "evil" human nature is part of the explanation ("explanatory realism (a)") and disagree with *Realpolitik* responses to the problem ("prescriptive realism"). For idealists, violent conflict and war can be the result of many contributory factors, including learned responses to frustrated goal-seeking behavior. The range of responses to violence is fairly broad, including "counter-violence" (in self-defense), but also nonviolent means for bringing about change in political, social, economic, and other systems to eliminate causes and conditions of violent conflict and war.

Idealpolitik encourages the use of Deutsch's *cooperative* processes: non-adversarial, nonconfrontational, nonzero-sum (positive-sum), "win–win" approaches to dealing with conflict. *Idealpolitik* and the corresponding cooperative processes tend to be associated with constructive outcomes.

The basic difference between *Realpolitik* and *Idealpolitik* is, quite simply, "nature versus nurture": while one stresses containing, deterring, and making the best of a basically negative, biologically driven situation, the other emphasizes the changeability of environment and, therefore, of behavior. As Waltz (1959) indicates, one orientation is clearly pessimistic in outlook, while the other is optimistic.

The two remaining paradigms represent various combinations of political realism and idealism. Like realism, Marxism stresses the inevitability of conflict (but for different reasons and between socioeconomic classes). Marxism is also like idealism, however, in its emphasis on structural change (in the system of ownership of the means of production) as the way to bring about behavioral change. Correspondingly, Marxism, like idealism, has a variable conception of human nature which is dependent on environment, in contrast to realism's fixed conception of human nature (irrespective of environment).

Non-Marxist radical thought (NMRT) is like realism in that it recognizes the potency of our biological nature (e.g. the "power of human needs in world society": see Coate and Rosati, 1988), but like idealism in that it puts emphasis on structural change (to bring social, political, economic, and other institutions more in line with *basic human needs*). NMRT is also very much like Marxism in its recognition that the changes necessary to (re)align institutions with needs – environment with "human nature" – are often radical and, therefore, attempts to effect such change, coupled with the *role-defense* response to such by supporters of a threatened status quo (see Burton, 1979), are likely to generate and sustain violent conflict cycles.

Both Marxism and NMRT are like realism in that they see competitive processes of conflict resolution (and often destructive outcomes) characterizing the efforts of disenfranchised, disempowered, needs-violated persons and minority outgroups generally, attempting to redefine their relationships with resistant supporters of a status quo which has tended to benefit only the ingroup. NMRT also shares with idealism, however, a sense of the validity, power, and rationality of cooperative processes (and constructive outcomes) as the only way to achieve fair, long-lasting, durable solutions to problems underlying manifest conflict. The paradox (for Marxist as well as NMRT theorists and practitioners) is that the use of competitive processes, intentionally or ostensibly to clear the way for structural change and cooperative processes, may generate *self-stimulating/self-perpetuating* violent conflict processes which reinforce the realist definition of things (a fate which could also befall idealists who become involved in "wars to end war").

Accordingly, there are at least four orientations to conflict and conflict resolution (realism (*Realpolitik*), idealism (*Idealpolitik*), Marxism, and NMRT), suggestive of two different approaches to dealing with conflict (competitive and cooperative). Although analytically distinct as static points of departure, there is sufficient overlap among the four orientations to blur their fine points of distinction once static conditions are overwhelmed by dynamic conflict processes over time. What is important to realize here is that, although parties to conflict may wind up killing each other, they may have come to that point from different "startup conditions" (*equifinality*). What is also important is that conflict analysts, conflict resolution theorists and practitioners, peace researchers, and others can embody or otherwise use any or some combination of the conflict and conflict resolution perspectives in order to make sense of, and to deal with, conflict.

The preference in this study is to combine the (4 + 2) perspectives into an overall basis for looking at a wide range of causes and conditions of conflict, plus strategies for dealing with them.[2] In what follows, therefore, we attempt such a "multi-paradigm" based integration of the current literature, the pretheory of Chapter 2, the PDS findings of Chapter 4 and the validation results of Chapter 5, primarily with regard to conflict causes and conditions, but with implications for conflict resolution as well.

Beyond Pretheory (II): Toward a Generic Theory of Violent Conflict and War

Waltz's (1959) framework, as modified by Robert North (1990) and Nazli Choucri (Choucri and North, 1990),[3] remains a useful device for shaping this integration and organizing our search for a generic theory of violent conflict and war: for answers to the question, what do theory and research, including the research reported in this volume, tell us about the transition from MCPs to AMCPs?

The Individual Level[4]

Many theorists and researchers have worked at this level, producing such variety that we have subdivided it into four subcategories: *biological*, *physiological*, *learning*, and *dissonance*.

Biological

Both the biological and the physiological subcategories are concerned with "human nature," the biological tending to reflect the work of philosophers, theologians, and others who discuss the "nature of the Beast" conceptually, without necessarily attempting or being able to measure or otherwise systematically observe aspects of that nature.[5] The physiological, on the other hand, reflects the work of physiologists, psychologists, and others who have attempted empirically to measure or otherwise systematically observe (as well as intervene into) aspects of human nature.

Among the biological theorists and researchers are the classic realist thinkers. For Hans Morgenthau (1973), probably the dominant realist thinker during the Cold War period, power politics (*Machtpolitik*) – the defense, increase, or demonstration of power, in pursuit of "interest defined as power" (i.e. survival) – "is governed by objective laws that have their roots in human nature" (p. 4). Morgenthau's fellow realist, the Protestant theologian Reinhold Niebuhr (1940, 1953), conceived of humans as corrupted by original sin and, therefore, capable of evil behavior, especially given their "will-to-live"/"will-to-power," which encourages them to seek security and to reduce failure-generated *anxiety* by enhancing their power, usually at the expense of others.

Earlier thinkers, such as St Augustine (1948), also argued that negative human behavior was a function of original sin. Spinoza (1951), on the other hand, argued that violence was the result of passion overwhelming reason.

Following the end of World War I, Sigmund Freud (1922, 1959, 1961) viewed human destructiveness as the result of a dialectical struggle between two opposing forces, one associated with life (*Eros*) and the other with death (*Thanatos*). When *Eros* dominates, aggression tends to be directed outward (to "explode"), whereas when *Thanatos* is in the ascendancy, aggression tends to be directed inward (to "implode"). This energy is always present and always seeking release, if not externally, then internally. Hence, "the recurrence of war and conflict becomes a necessary periodic release by which groups preserve themselves through diverting their self-destructive tendencies to outsiders" (Dougherty and Pfaltzgraff, 1990, p. 277).

The biological subcategory also includes ethologists: for example, Konrad Lorenz (1967). Although Lorenz believed that aggression was innate to humans as well as to other forms of life, he also believed that, *within* species, aggression tended not to be lethal, but to have survival value (e.g. to prevent bunching-up of a species within its habitat). Among humans, however, this characteristic has broken down. Because our rate of technological/cultural evolution has surpassed our rate of phylogenetic evolution, especially in the "natural" development of mechanisms of ritualized aggression and inhibitions to lethal aggression found in other species, human aggression has tended not to have survival value, but instead to be clearly lethal and dysfunctional.

Given that political realists are included in the biological subcategory, and that the remaining thinkers there tend to share the assumption that violent human behavior is a function of a biologically determined human nature, the biological subcategory lends itself easily to a *Realpolitik* interpretation of conflict and corresponding approach to conflict resolution.

Physiological

This subcategory applies to theorists and researchers who deal with efforts to measure or otherwise systematically observe "symptoms" of human nature; specifically, those who actually intervene into parts of the organism to explore the effects of certain interventions. John Paul Scott (1958), for example, has argued that humans have "an internal physiological mechanism which has only to be stimulated to produce fighting" (pp. 62–3). The mechanism, therefore, is not spontaneous. Also, the form of its expression is dependent on *learning*: "we find that motivation for fighting is strongly increased by success, and that the longer success continues, the stronger the motivation becomes" (*ibid.*, p. 126). Scott's theory locates the physiological sources of aggressive behavior within a multifactor framework which allows for the *interaction* between the organism ("nature") and its environment ("nurture") – "we must not forget that in any real situation behavior will be the result of factors from all levels" (*ibid.*, p. 2).

Paul MacLean (1975, 1978) has argued that humans have a *triune brain*, composed of *reptilian*, *limbic*, and *neocortical (cerebral cortex)* subsystems, which correspond to progressive levels of phylogenetic evolution (with the "reptilian" subcomponent being the most primitive part). In animals other than humans, stimulation of either of two parts of the brain "concerned primarily with self- and species-preservation" (Restak, 1979, p. 41) – the *hypothalamus* in the reptilian section or the *amygdala* in the limbic section – produces physiological reactions associated with "preparation for attack" (e.g. hissing, pupil dilation, arching of the back, salivation) (see Hilgard *et al.*, 1979, p. 321; Restak, 1979, p. 46).

By observing reptilian- and limbic-dominant behaviors in other animals, MacLean believes that we can have a glimpse of *paleopsychic* processes: ancient forms of behavior that we have inherited from our reptilian and mammalian antecedents (Restak, 1979, p. 36). But humans are also characterized by the cerebral cortex, which "is more highly developed in human beings than in any other organism" (Hilgard *et al.*, 1979, p. 42); hence, we might expect human behavior to be governed more by the cerebral cortex than by the reptilian and limbic brains.

MacLean tells us that in any particular social situation, "all three brains [reptilian, limbic, and neocortical] would be experiencing the same thing [but, as in the case of competing paradigms] each in a different way" (Restak, 1979, p. 51); and that the experiences mediated by one or two of these brains might be in conflict with those mediated by the remaining brain(s). MacLean has developed the concept of *schizophysiology* to refer to the conflict between *feelings* (the limbic brain) and *thinking* (the neocortical brain). If the limbic brain gains the ascendancy in such ("interbrain") conflicts, and starts to control and dictate behavior, then actors may "feel" strongly about something but be completely in error. Such powerful feelings "may be the basis for some forms of paranoid psychosis: a schizophysiology where believing is seeing rather than seeing is believing" (*ibid.*, p. 52). Wittingly or otherwise, MacLean provides a physiological basis for Spinoza's argument that violence can result when passion overwhelms reason.

The argument that, under stress, *reptilian/limbic rationality* might not be under the control of what "common sense" might dictate, *neocortical rationality*, is compatible with Arthur Koestler's (1978) argument "that there is a flaw, some potentially fatal engineering error built into ... the circuits of our nervous system." What drives all this for Koestler, "The Ghost in the Machine," is MacLean's schizophysiology between the limbic and neocortical brains (Koestler, 1967, pp. 281–2).

Implicit in Koestler's argument are *basic needs*, e.g. the need for belongingness: the "excessive capacity and urge" among humans "to become identified with a tribe, nation, church, or cause" (Koestler, 1978). He identifies these integrative, *self-transcending* tendencies, rather than the *self-assertive* ones, as major factors contributing to violence throughout human history (Koestler, 1967, p. 234): "the crimes of violence committed for selfish, personal motives are historically insignificant compared to those committed ... out of a self-sacrificing devotion to a flag, a leader, a religious faith or a political conviction."

In Koestler's scheme, "war is a ritual, a deadly ritual, not the result of aggressive self-assertion, but of self-transcending identification" (p. 253), where, in the process of transcending the Self, one identifies with a tribe, church, flag, or ideal and then one may experience "vicarious ... violent emotions on behalf of the entity" (pp. 244, 245); where one also surrenders responsibility for one's behavior to the entity, thereby encouraging acting "with ruthless cruelty towards the enemy or victim of the [entity]" (pp. 248, 251). Personal hating is not part of this process: "The individual victim ... is punished not as an individual, but as a symbolic representation of [the 'enemy']" (pp. 252, 253). This is all evidence of "The Ghost," the "fatal flaw," the schizophysiology between the limbic and neocortical brains: a physiological argument in support of the doctrine of original sin.

Koestler's general pessimism, plus his particular reconstruction of MacLean's work, not only renders that work as compatible with *Realpolitik*, but further encourages its use by realists as evidence that their assumption of a violence-prone, flawed human nature is valid.

Learning

Albert Bandura (1973), like John Paul Scott, sees aggression as a function of the interaction between a physiological mechanism, stimulation of that mechanism, and *learning*. Whereas Scott "roots the aggressive impulse in physiological processes, but demands a stimulus from the environment" (Dougherty and Pfaltzgraff, 1990, p. 278), Bandura bases his theory "not on inner impulses or drives, but on social learning, social contexts and roles, response feedback influences, modeling and reinforcement, and the learned ability to assess the rewarding and punishing consequences of any given action" (*ibid.*, p. 288).

Given MacLean's observation that the limbic system dominates the cerebral cortex in stressful situations, if a "schizophysiology" produces a violent response to a stressful stimulus – perhaps a response "modeled" on the behavior of someone else or others in a similar situation – and should that violent response succeed in containing, destroying, or otherwise eliminating the stimulus as a threat, then the organism may "learn" a particular relationship between a certain stimulus (x) and response (y). This is *discriminant learning*. Once the connection has been made and begins to serve as a norm for the individual, to be used in similar situations, and further successes are experienced, then the successive experiences of positive reinforcement of the x–y connection may have the effect of virtually "wiring" the connection into his or her nervous system. As this *response generalization* occurs over time, it will become progressively more difficult to undermine that internalized x–y connection, even in cases where it no longer applies.

This may explain why, in cases of perceived threats to security, learned (internalized) *Realpolitik* theory is so compelling a normative guide to action: why it (perhaps as a limbic-dominated framework) tends to dominate behavior in international (and other) conflict situations where "wars [seem to] occur because there is nothing to prevent them."

Accordingly, *learning* can play a powerful role in conflict, especially in the escalation and perpetuation of violent conflict processes. According to Vasquez (1993, pp. 195–6):

> From its *lessons of history*, realism has given rise to a set of power politics practices and recommendations which ... against equals ... do not produce peace and security, as realists maintain, but increased insecurity,

> coercion, and entanglement in a process and series of steps that may lead to war. (Emphasis added)

However, on the assumption that even "wired" *Realpolitik* behavior can be unlearned, learning theorists in conflict and conflict resolution tend to be optimistic and, therefore, identified with *Idealpolitik*.

Dissonance

This subcategory concerns violence as a reaction to felt discrepancies between *preferred* and *actual* states of affairs. It has been derived from Leon Festinger's (1962) concept of *cognitive dissonance*, which concerns discordant relationships between beliefs and values, behavior, and/or environment as they actually are and as we think or prefer them to be. "Dissonance," which is experienced as *anxiety* (which plays a role in Niebuhr's realism), can be managed, if not reduced and eliminated, by avoiding further dissonance-provoking situations, and/or by making appropriate changes in our beliefs and values, behavior, and/or environment, to reach new equilibria between the preferred and actual. As the connections noted in Chapter 2 between anxiety and a number of variables imply, dissonance management/reduction behavior can exacerbate existing, or generate new, tensions, which can be expressed violently, either internally or externally (especially if the limbic dominates the neocortical brain).

A number of theorists and researchers belong here, starting with Johan Galtung, whose *structural violence* (1969) still ranks as one of the most provocative contributions to understanding and dealing with violent conflict and war. Defined as a structurally based discrepancy between actual and potential states of somatic and mental well-being, it need not be perceived by its "victims" or involve physical violence. What it does constitute, however, is a system of differential, unequal access to the means for closing the gap between the actual and the potential, where those at "the bottom" of some hierarchically structured relational system cannot – by reason of *involuntary membership* in certain ethnic, class, religious, gender and/or other groups – obtain fair access to the social, economic, political, educational, legal, and/or other systems and corresponding resources typically enjoyed, and presided over, by the mainstream. Structural violence is what exists in situations of institutionalized racism within, and imperialism across, societies: "Above all the power to decide over the distribution of resources is unevenly distributed" (*ibid.*, p. 171).

When structural violence makes the transition from the objective to the subjective realms – when it gets to be perceived by those who have been suffering, or are about to suffer, from it – the limbic system may, indeed, become exercised, predisposing affected actors toward violent reactions against those (or surrogates of those) perceived to have been oppressing them, or as about to attempt to oppress them.

Ted Robert Gurr (1970) has conceptualized one variation on the perceived structural violence theme, *relative deprivation* (RD), as a perceived discrepancy between "value expectations" (VE) (resources to which one feels entitled) and "value capabilities" (VC) (resources which one feels capable of acquiring and keeping). The greater the average degree of perceived discrepancy between VE and VC, the greater the RD; the greater the intensity and scope of RD among members of some collectivity, the greater the potential for collective violence, including political violence (*ibid.*, Chapters 2, 3, 6, 8; and pp. 360–7).

Galtung's *rank disequilibrium* (1964) refers to discordant locations of actors along various indicators of socio-economic (and other) measurement. One may, for example, be high on some indicators (e.g. education), but low on others (employment, income, housing). In Galtung's scheme, it is not the actor who is low across all indicators, but the one who is *mixed* between "topdog" and "underdog" statuses, who is most likely to respond violently to the perceived source of the imbalance (Galtung, 1964; in Smith, 1971, p. 275):

> Aggression is most likely to arise in social positions in rank-disequilibrium. In a system of individuals it may take the form of crime, in a system of groups the form of revolutions, and in a system of nations the form of war. But these extreme forms of aggression are unlikely to occur unless (1) other means of equilibration towards a complete topdog configuration have been tried, and (2) the culture has some practice in violent aggression.

When *perceived* structural violence – e.g. relative deprivation or rank disequilibrium – leads to the contemplation or manifestation of violence as a means for changing one's situation, then *frustration–aggression* may be involved. According to John Dollard and his colleagues, whose *Frustration and Aggression* (1939) "has stimulated more empirical research than any other theory of aggression" (Megargee and Hokanson, 1970, p. 22), frustration is the "interference with the occurrence of an instigated goal-response at its proper time in the behavior sequence" (Dollard *et al.*, 1939, p. 7). Frustration was, in the original formulation, both a necessary and a sufficient condition of aggression (*ibid.*, p. 1):

> This study takes as its point of departure the assumption that *aggression is always a consequence of frustration.* More specifically the proposition is that the occurrence of aggressive behavior always presupposes the existence of frustration and contrariwise, that the existence of frustration always leads to some form of aggression.

This fairly tight causal connection between frustration and aggression may be less ambitious than it might otherwise appear, if seen against the background of the comprehensive, multidimensional view of aggression put forward by Dollard and his colleagues: aggression could be overt or nonovert, direct or indirect (and if indirect, involving *object-* and/or *response-displacement*), physical or ideational, conscious or unconscious, external or internal. Also, whatever forms of aggression occur (if any) are a function of a complex interplay between the strength of instigation to aggression and the inhibition of acts of aggression:

> The strength of instigation to aggression varies directly with the amount of frustration. Variation in the amount of frustration is a function of three factors: (1) strength of instigation to the frustrated response; (2) degree of interference with the frustrated response; and (3) the number of response sequences frustrated. (Dollard *et al.*, 1939/1970, p. 29)

If, however, through prior *learning*, the frustrated individual associates punishment with certain acts committed against certain actors or things, then, depending upon whether the weight comes down more on one side than the other in the instigation-to-aggression/anticipation-of-punishment relationship, he or she may be inhibited, deterred from behaving in certain ways toward certain objects.

This "interference" with an instigation to aggression sets up further frustrations (in addition to the original frustration), which can fuel a *frustration–aggression–interference with aggression–more frustration cycle*, manageable to some extent through object- and/or response-displacement: the frustrated individual can substitute targets and/or means in his or her attempts to reduce the instigation to aggression, and to experience "catharsis."

Depending upon circumstances, object displacement may include self-punishment: "the tendency to self-aggression is stronger both when the individual believes himself, rather than an external agent, to be responsible for the original frustration and when direct aggression is restrained by the self rather than by an external agent" (*ibid.*, p. 32).

Over the years, in part because of reformulations by the Dollard group itself and critiques by others (e.g. Bandura and Walters, 1963), frustration has, for many, taken on the status of a *contributory condition* of aggression. In any case, whatever the causal status of frustration, what is it that is being frustrated that can cause conflict to be expressed violently?

James Chowning Davies (1962, 1973, 1986) makes an explicit theoretical connection between the Dollard group's formulation of frustration–aggression and his (Davies's) modification of the *hierarchy of needs* developed by Abraham Maslow (1987). For Davies, it is the frustration of *substantive needs* (physical, social-affectional (AFF), self-esteem, and self-actualization (ACH)) or *implemental needs* (security, knowledge, and power (POW)) that can facilitate the transition from MCPs to AMCPs: "Violence ... is produced when certain innate needs or demands are deeply frustrated" (Davies, 1973, p. 251).

John Burton (1979, 1990a, b) has hypothesized a link between frustration and basic needs for identity, security, recognition, autonomy, dignity, and bonding:

> Human needs theory argues ... that there are certain ontological and genetic needs that will be pursued, and that socialization processes, if not compatible with such human needs, far from socializing, will lead to frustrations, and to disturbed and anti-social personal and group behaviors. Individuals cannot be socialized into behaviors that destroy their identity and other need goals and, therefore, must react against environments that do this. ... Behaviors that are a response to frustration of such human needs will often seem aggressive and counterproductive, but they are understandable in this context. (Burton, 1990a, pp. 33–4)

All four of the conflict paradigms are reflected in the dissonance subcategory: structural violence (including relative deprivation and rank disequilibrium), especially when manifested as institutionalized racism or imperialism, can easily find a niche within political idealism, Marxism, or NMRT; however, it can also find a home under political realism (e.g. in a hegemonic balance-of-power system). Frustration–aggression can clearly be subsumed under all four. And while basic needs are explicitly linked to NMRT, they are certainly implied in the other three orientations as well, e.g. a need for security, especially a frustrated one, will always make sense to realists.

Whether one's focus is violent conflict at the interpersonal, intergroup, interorganizational, international, or other levels, the actors in each case, at each level, are likely to be impacted by factors from other levels. This is part of the value of the Waltz/North four-level framework: it forces us to consider John Paul Scott's (1958, p. 2) proposition, "that in any real situation behavior will be the result of factors from all levels." We continue our cross-level journey, therefore, keeping in mind Jack Levy's (1996, p. 17) caution that:

> although the levels-of-analysis framework serves as a useful organizing framework, we must not apply it so rigidly that it distracts attention from the important task of understanding how variables at different levels of analysis *interact* in the processes contributing to international [and other] conflict. (Emphasis added)

The Societal Level

Much of what applies to the individual level has been or can be applied to the societal level and beyond. While there are clear differences of scale and appearance between, say, a divorcing couple and an international war, individuals are still involved across the spectrum of different levels of analysis, as *decision-makers*; by implication, so are individual-level causes and conditions. This is why, for John Burton (1990a, p. 135), "the individual is the unit of explanation of social and political development": a generic, cross-level variable which constitutes "the basis of an explanation of social change and of the consequences of resistance to social change" (Burton, 1984, p. 19). This is not, however, an argument in favor of reductionism (in this regard, see Kelman, 1965, pp. 5–6): the causes and conditions of marital strife may not necessarily be the same as those for war (although there may be similarities, e.g. in processes of escalation).

One particular societal (intersocietal) application of individual (interpersonal) processes can be found in the studies conducted by Robert North and his colleagues of the crisis which escalated into World War I. Using content analysis to transform qualitative information into quantitative data, the researchers explored relationships between perceptions and actions, and uncovered evidence to support the following propositions:

- if perceptions of anxiety, fear, threat, or injury are great enough, even the perception of one's own inferior capability will fail to deter a nation from going to war (Zinnes *et al.*, 1961);
- in situations of high involvement, actors will tend to *overperceive* the level of violence in the actions of their adversary, and to *overreact* to the actions of the adversary (Holsti *et al.*, 1968).

Intense involvement and overperception of, and overreaction to threatened or actual attacks, are consistent with

1. Spinoza's argument that violence is the result of reason being overwhelmed by the passions.
2. MacLean's schizophysiology – that under the stress of threatened or actual attacks, the limbic brain will come to dominate the neocortical brain, thereby increasing the probability of an emotional (violent) reaction to the threatened or actual frustration of basic needs for security, identity, and the like.
3. Leng's (1983) observation that, even in cases of reduced "capability from one crisis to the next ... the weaker state moves to more coercive bargaining" (Vasquez, 1993, p. 186).

Clearly, in crises and other aspects of the realist "steps to war" (Vasquez, 1993, Chapter 5; 1987, p. 117), actors behave in ways which increase the probability of war. This was also the case in the PDS where, in Chapter 4, the ATT–ATT relationship for PDS 1–5 was observed to be suggestive of an "evolving culture of aggression." In Chapter 5, we observed, across the three developmental stages, further evidence of such *self-stimulating/self-perpetuating conflict processes*, not just for ATT, but for MD and BEL, and nearly ALL as well. We also observed examples of contagion-stimulated conflict, i.e. the SAC–BEL relationship for PDS 1–5 and the SAC–ALL relationship for the intermediate stage. A number of real-world studies were observed to be supportive of these PDS findings.

Whenever a "culture of war" (Bremer, 1980) or "culture of violence" (Vasquez, 1993, pp. 162, 197) prevails, highly involved actors might, indeed, tend to overperceive, and to overreact to threatening situations. Under the circumstances, it would not be surprising that, "in the long run there is a positive association between the possession of military capability [BEL] and its ultimate use [ATT]" (Bremer, 1980, p. 79; cited in Vasquez, 1993, p. 162), a well-supported finding which occurs for the ATT models for PDS 1–5 and the early and intermediate stages, and which, apropos our search here for *generic theory*, may have validity at other levels as well (e.g. see Berkowitz and LePage, 1967).[6]

When two or more actors continue to arm against each other, especially as part of the "steps to war," their conflict relationship may become transformed into an apparently deterministic, escalatory spiral, beyond their ability to halt or reverse. Lewis Richardson (1939, 1960a) has attempted, with his action–reaction models, to capture mathematically the dynamics of such processes, which he believed occur when people do not stop to think. The view held in this study is that people, especially men, *do* "stop to think" during periods of conflict escalation, but within the context of the (limbic-dominated) *Realpolitik* framework.[7]

Although neither "arms races" (BEL/%BEL–BEL/%BEL) nor other forms of action–reaction processes (VICT–ATT) were observed in the PDS, they have been observed in various real-world settings. On arms races, the empirical record supports "the conclusion that military buildups that occur within a rivalry, where the states are contiguous, are an important step toward war" (Vasquez, 1993, pp. 183–4). On action–reaction in general, there "is considerable evidence in international relations that behavior, particularly conflict behavior, follows an action–reaction model" (*ibid.*, p. 187).

If such dynamics are occurring *within* a society, between the defenders and attackers of the political status quo, the defenders may elect to enjoy the assumed benefits of the *functions-of-conflict thesis*, and operationalize the "oldest hypothesis in politics": "when the natives are restless, find an enemy!" As mentioned in Chapter 2, Georg Simmel (1955, p. 98) has even prescribed that elites in "certain groups . . . see to it that there be some enemies in order for the unity of the members to remain effective and for the group to remain conscious of this unity as its vital interest."

That one should feel compelled to invent enemies in order to protect and preserve one's Self, role, and "identity group" is reminiscent of Freud's theory: to avoid a *Thanatos*-driven "implosion," actors may have to engineer an *Eros*-dominant "explosion" and externalize their hostilities onto others. This is also compatible with Vamik Volkan's (1985, 1988) thesis that there is a "need for enemies" as well as allies, fulfillment of which is essential to the development of one's identity.

The idea (and perhaps drive) to externalize aggression, at all levels, in order to maintain one's Self and/or ingroup, may be an expression of *ethnocentrism*, which William Graham Sumner (1906) thought was a universal human trait: where "each group nourishes its own pride and vanity, boasts itself superior, exalts its own divinities, and looks with contempt on outsiders" (*ibid.*, pp. 12–13; cited in LeVine and Campbell, 1972, p. 8).

The tendency to bifurcate people into "them" and "us" and to reserve most of our wrath for "them" may, according to John Pfeiffer (1984, p. 92), "have been inherited from times past and wired in from birth." Edward Wilson (1979, pp. 122–3) tells us that "Our brains do appear to be programmed to the following extent: we are inclined to partition other people into friends and aliens, . . . [and] we tend to fear deeply the actions of strangers and to solve conflict by aggression." The "problem is that our built-in universe was formed largely in prehistoric . . . times [when] the sight of a stranger . . . meant real trouble – and triggered swift, generally violent action" (Pfeiffer, 1984, p. 92). Nowadays, "large-scale violence may be a throwback," something that made sense in earlier times, but not now.

Although domestic conflict did not appear to stimulate foreign conflict in the PDS, which is consistent with Rummel's (1968, p. 208) finding that "domestic instability has little relation to a nation's foreign conflict behavior," we will, for reasons mentioned in Chapter 5, continue to assume the possibility of a connection between domestic and foreign conflict.

The assumption that conflict *within* can spill over *without*, "for certain types of nations, at certain times, and under certain circumstances" (Burrowes and Spector, 1973, p. 317), is compatible with Burton's (1984, pp. 3, 6–7) thesis "that the major sources of potential conflict [between capitalism and socialism] are the shortcomings *within* each system that render each insecure, even without any external threat" (emphasis added), e.g. ethnic conflicts, race riots, high levels of street violence, high levels of unemployment and growing inequalities of income and opportunity. The Serbian–Croatian–Muslim wars in former Yugoslavia, Armenian–Azerbaijani hostilities in and over Nagorno-Karabakh, and Russian–Chechen war are just three examples of "system failures and inadequacies" in the post-Cold War era, capable of spilling over and drawing in other actors (see Sandole, 1991).

As Burton indicates, the "shortcomings" within social systems can include economic inequalities. John Hobson (1965) has argued in this regard that imperialism was the result of maladjustments in capitalism: (a) overproduction on the part of a wealthy elite and (b) underconsumption on the part of an impoverished majority – "objective" symptoms of structural violence *within* a society.

Borrowing from Hobson and others, Lenin (1939) argued that imperialism was the inevitable consequence of "the highest stage of capitalism," in which the world's more powerful capitalist states, requiring ever more resources to sustain further economic growth, would compete for cheap sources of raw materials and labor, and guaranteed markets. In a world of shrinking colonial opportunities, relationships between the competing capitalist states would resemble a perpetual state of potential (and often, actual) war (see "Descriptive Realism"), while relationships between the "exploiting" and the "exploited" would constitute objective conditions of structural violence *between* societies. For Lenin, therefore, an international system dominated basically by capitalist states would be rife with international conflict.

Similarly, Nazli Choucri and Robert North (1975) have argued that increases in population and advances in technology, plus corresponding increases in demands for resources, can lead to *lateral pressures* for societies to move beyond their borders to get what they want. A good deal of conflict potential inheres in lateral pressures, especially if, as in the picture of imperialism drawn by Hobson and Lenin, potential sources of the desired resources are less and less available. This means that, more and more, states might attempt to get what they want by force. Choucri and North did, in fact, find that "domestic growth . . . is a strong determinant of national expansion, and that these are linked to military expenditures, alliances, and international violence" (Dougherty and Pfaltzgraff, 1990, p. 346).

PDS findings relevant to imperialism and lateral pressures, and corresponding real-world studies, include the following:

1. The positive relationship between RES and MD for the intermediate period is generally supported by East and Hermann's (1974) finding of a positive relationship between economic development and percentage of foreign conflict events, and by Moore's (1974) finding of a positive relationship between economic development and foreign conflict, which was stronger for undeveloped than for developed nations (see Appendix D, Table D.2).
2. The positive relationship between RES and BEL for the intermediate period is generally supported by Moore's (1974) finding of a positive relationship between economic development and defense expenditures as a

percentage of GNP, which was also stronger for undeveloped than for developed nations (see Appendix D, Table D.3).

3. The negative relationship between RES and MD for the early period is specifically supported by the Feierabends' (1969) finding of a negative relationship between economic development and foreign conflict for mid-modern nations, while the aforementioned positive relationship between RES and MD for the intermediate period is specifically supported by the Feierabends' (1969) finding of a positive relationship between economic development and foreign conflict for high-modern nations (see Appendix D, Table D.2).

These PDS and corresponding real-world findings suggest, therefore, a *non-linear* positive relationship between economic development (RES) and foreign conflict (MD and BEL): positive during undeveloped periods, negative during mid-modern (early) periods and again positive during high-modern (intermediate) periods.

When we factor in the positive relationships between RED and DI for PDS 1–5 and the early stage, generally supported by Gurr's (1968) finding of a positive relationship between economic deprivation and total strife, and the Feierabends' (1966) finding of a positive relationship between systemic frustration and political instability (see Appendix D, Table D.1), the following scenario may be plausible:

> Economic development for undeveloped nations in a global environment of diminishing resources could lead to more aggressive international behavior on their part in order to compete effectively with the more developed nations. Once development reaches a certain (e.g. mid-modern) stage, nations may cut back on their foreign adventurism to consolidate gains at home. As they start to fall behind in the international competition, however, experiencing reductions in relative economic status, increasing deprivation (unfulfilled rising expectations), and a rise in domestic conflict, they may increase their foreign conflict behavior to activate the "functions-of-conflict thesis" and attempt to nip domestic conflict in the bud. With further economic development and increases in economic status (to, e.g. the high-modern stage), they may, along with other nations, increase their foreign conflict behavior in order to hold on to, and to increase, their share of a cake of diminishing size, plus to further dampen the causes and conditions of domestic conflict.

A reworking of the imperialist and lateral pressures theories into an integrated theory, therefore, could include a nonlinear positive relationship between economic development and foreign conflict, and a positive relationship between economic deprivation and domestic conflict.

The International Level

The more the international environment reflects the *Hobbesian black hole of international anarchy*, the more it is what Rapoport (1974, p. 175) refers to as an *exogenous* (in contrast to *endogenous*) conflict environment: "*Endogenous* conflicts are . . . those wherein the conflicting systems are parts of a larger system that has its own mechanisms for . . . controlling or resolving conflict," versus *exogenous* conflicts, where there are no such mechanisms. The more exogenous the conflict environment, therefore, the more that "wars [will] occur because there is nothing to prevent them" (Waltz, 1959, p. 232).

The war-facilitating nature of the international system can vary, depending on the extent to which its various international political systems are, among other things, bipolar or multipolar. As we noted in Chapter 2, Karl Deutsch and J. David Singer (1964) have equated multipolarity in the international system with increased "interaction opportunities," pluralistic possibilities for cross-cutting loyalties, stability, and therefore, less war (in terms of frequency and intensity). Kenneth Waltz (1964), on the other hand, has argued that bipolarity means simplicity, predictability, manageability, stability, and therefore less war.

Attempts to resolve the system polarity-stability debate in other than a theoretical way have led to empirical inconclusiveness, matching the state of affairs in theory. One of the participants in the theoretical debate, J. David Singer, and one of his main coworkers in the Correlates-of-War project, Melvin Small (Singer and Small, 1968), found that bipolarity (as well as alliance aggregation) correlated negatively with war in the nineteenth century, but positively with war in the twentieth century, whether war was measured "by number of wars, the nation-months involved, or battle deaths incurred" (*ibid.*, p. 283). In terms of Singer's own COW results, therefore, his and Deutsch's theoretical multipolarity-stability argument is valid only for the twentieth century (up to 1945), whereas the Waltz (1964) bipolarity-stability and Rosecrance (1966) multipolarity-instability arguments hold for the nineteenth century.

Since the ending of the Cold War, the replacement of the East–West bipolar relationship by "creeping" multipolarity has been accompanied by a resurrection of ethnic conflict and nationalist sentiments in Eastern Europe and the former Soviet Union. These developments caused concern for some even prior to the implosion of former Yugoslavia, including Lawrence Eagleburger (see Tarnoff, 1989), John Mearsheimer (1990a, b) and Robert Hunter (1989), who, as mentioned in Chapter 1, commented prophetically that "we have more chance of a [European] war now than we had during the last thirty years."

As indicated in Chapter 5, the PDS and corresponding real-world findings are more supportive of Waltz/Rosecrance than of Deutsch/Singer. The relationship between the number of actors in the system (SEC) and war (ATT), therefore, would appear to be a predominantly positive one: as the former increases, so does the latter (and vice versa). This may be explained, to some extent, by Vasquez's (1993) *territoriality* thesis:

> of all the possible issues that could end in war, issues involving territorial

> contiguity are indeed the most war prone (p. 125). ... The logic of this analysis implies that states with more borders should experience more wars (p. 142). ... [Hence,] the more states in the system [SEC], the more wars [ATT] that can be expected (p. 145).

What makes the territoriality issue provocative is that, for Vasquez (*ibid.*, pp. 139–40), "This tendency is deeply ingrained and is part of humanity's collective genetic inheritance," not in a "hard-wired," but a "soft-wired" sense. Hence, the SEC–ATT relationship, like the tendency to bifurcate people into "them" and "us," appears to be grounded in "human nature."

The more actors in the system (SEC) and the more war (ATT), the more "contagion": the more likely that the "steps to war" and the use of violence in any part of the system will be replicated ("imitated") by others, e.g. the SAC–BEL and SAC–ALL relationships in the PDS.[8]

Further suggestions that the "new multipolarity" might be a harbinger of more intense as well as more frequent warfare can be found in the evidence documenting the proliferation of nuclear as well as chemical, biological and even conventional weapons of mass destruction, plus missile technology. For example,

> [U.S.] Secretary of State Madeleine K. Albright [has] urged the NATO alliance to recognize the spread of nuclear, biological and chemical weapons in the Middle East and Persian Gulf region as its most pressing strategic priority in the post-Cold War era.
>
> Citing the proliferation danger as "the most overriding security interest of our time," Albright told NATO foreign ministers at their annual meeting that the spread of weapons of mass destruction should be the new *"unifying threat"* that binds the [U.S.A.] and Europe. (Drozdiak, 1997b, p. A1; emphasis added)

Just looking at trends in nuclear proliferation (see Spector, 1987; *Economist*, 1992; Budiansky, 1992; Robbins, 1992), and threats to use nuclear weapons – e.g. by China against the United States (see Clark, 1996; O'Neill, 1996), and by India and Pakistan against each other (see Haass and Rose, 1997; Hoagland, 1997) – plus the ongoing, Iraq-inspired biological threat (see Chevrier, 1997), the international system seems to be moving in the direction of Morton Kaplan's (1957) *unit veto state*, where many, most, or all states will have the capacity to destroy everyone else.

One reason for proliferation is that it may enable the developing world (the South) to compensate partially (in a military sense) for the massive economic disparity it suffers from in its relationship with the North. According to the first Brandt Commission Report (1980), one-fourth of the world's population (the North) has four-fifths of the world's income, while three-fourths of the world's population (the South) has one-fifth of the world's income. Also:

> In the North, the average person can expect to live for more than seventy years; he or she will rarely be hungry, and will be educated at least up to secondary level. In the countries of the South the great majority of people have a life expectancy of closer to fifty years; in the poorest countries one

> out of every four children dies before the age of five; one-fifth or more of all the people in the South suffer from hunger and malnutrition; fifty per cent have no chance to become literate. (*Ibid.*, p. 32)

Arguably, these data fit neatly into a Marxist (but also an idealist, NMRT, or realist) framework and constitute objective conditions of Galtung's structural violence on a grand scale and, according to Willy Brandt (1980, p. 7), the "great social challenge of our time. [Hence,] the two decades ahead of us may be fateful for mankind."

The Global (Ecological) Level

The "fourth, or global image," as Robert North (1990, p. 25) defines it, "distinguishes between natural and social environments and allows for the systematic investigation of the ways they interact on land, in the sea, and in space and for the outcomes." North is particularly concerned about the outcomes of the first three images on the global level:

> the planet and the delicate balances of its natural features. Even relatively minor alterations in natural environment ... could make our survival difficult, if not impossible. Meanwhile, our expanding activities and interests exert increasingly threatening pressures on both social and natural environments.

In a very important sense, the fourth, or global, level is under assault by lateral pressures that "are directly traceable to the growth of human populations, the advancement of their technologies (including organizations), and their search for resources" (North, 1990, p. 188). In the context of the "Malthusian nightmare" that is likely to result, violent conflict is a distinct possibility:

> Poverty and environmental decline are tightly linked. Neither is conducive to stable democracy. Where the land's capacity to produce is ebbing under the pressure of rapidly growing numbers of people who have no alternative means of survival, the result is economic stagnation or decline. This in turn can lead to frustration, resentment, political turmoil and violence. (Mathews, 1992)

Although this "new" level of analysis is less "invisible" now than it was, say, twenty years ago, it still does not command the attention of the political and industrial elites, or of the numbers of people in general which the problems it addresses would seem to demand, partly for emotional-ideological and partly for cognitive-conceptual reasons (see Sandole, 1987). As North (1990, p. 24) puts it, "the fourth image, or global system, has not been extensively developed or widely accepted as an analytical concept, even though there seems to be an increasing need for it."

A small group of researchers has been responding to this problem in the "Project on Environmental Change and Acute Conflict":

> evidence that they [have] gathered points to a disturbing conclusion:

> scarcities of renewable resources are already contributing to violent conflicts in many parts of the developing world. These conflicts may foreshadow a surge of similar violence in coming decades, particularly in poor countries where shortages of water, forests and, especially, fertile land, coupled with rapidly expanding populations, already cause great hardship. (Homer-Dixon *et al.*, 1993, p. 38; also see Homer-Dixon, 1991)

In this setting, global interests *are* national interests, a prescriptive imperative that is slowly developing into a descriptive reality. North's book, Mary Clark's "search for new modes of thinking" (1989), and the efforts of Homer-Dixon and others are facilitating this "paradigm shift."

Conceptual Integration or Confusion: Generic Theory or Disparate "Islands of Theory"?

We have attempted, in the above discussion, to weave into an integrative tapestry aspects of theory, the PDS findings and validation results: to develop from these inputs a generic theory of violent conflict and war that might be useful for the parties to protracted, violent conflict situations, those trying to help them, and, in general, those trying to understand such conflicts. To what extent, if any, have we succeeded?

The discussion thus far suggests that we have broken some significant ground. Beginning with the prescriptions of both John Paul Scott and Kenneth Waltz to employ a framework that recognizes and allows for the potential contribution of factors from all levels to the development of conflict, the following, distilled from the above, would seem to cohere into the basis of a generic theory on the initiation and escalation of violent conflict, with implications for conflict resolution:

1. There does appear to be a physiological mechanism (inclusive of, for example, the hypothalamus and amygdala) that requires some kind of stimulation to be activated to produce violent reactions, which can nevertheless be influenced by learning (Scott, Bandura).
2. During periods of threatened or actual violations of an actor's basic needs for security, identity, and the like, which may reflect territoriality (Vasquez), elements of this physiological mechanism (specifically, the limbic system) may come to dominate the actor's "neocortical rationality" (MacLean's schizophysiology), increasing the probability of a violent response to the perceived source (or a surrogate of the source) of the frustrated needs (Davies, Burton, Dollard *et al.*).
3. Frustration can be fed by perceived structural violence (Galtung) at various levels of the actor's external environment, e.g. rank disequilibrium (Galtung) or relative deprivation (Gurr).
4. The frustration-of-needs/aggression nexus is both stimulated by, and in turn stimulates, ethnocentrism (Sumner) and *Realpolitik*.
5. When two or more actors so characterized are parties to a conflict, then

frustration-of-needs/aggression can generate a quasi-deterministic spiral, reflective of Richardson's action–reaction processes (where, again, "men" in particular do "stop to think," but in terms of *Realpolitik*), with reciprocal, "imitated" increases in the capability to wage war, and in other "steps to war" (Vasquez). The more involved in this process the actors become, the more they will tend to overperceive and overreact to threatened and actual assaults to needs (North *et al.*), even in cases where their capabilities have been reduced (Leng). This will fuel further the spiral (and MacLean's schizophysiology/Koestler's "Ghost in the Machine"), and increase the probability of generating "negative self-fulfilling prophecies" (NSFPs) (Sandole, 1984, 1986, 1987).

6. These NSFPs may be reflective of self-stimulating/self-perpetuating conflict processes as well as of action–reaction processes, or a combination of both. Action–reaction processes can operate independently of self-stimulating/self-perpetuating conflict processes (*Eigendynamik*), but over time, in protracted conflict situations, will probably give rise to the latter (a "culture of violence"). These can then either operate independently of action–reaction processes or encourage their development, such that action–reaction processes can be viewed as a special case of self-stimulating/self-perpetuating conflict processes. In either case, regardless of which is "chicken" and which is "egg," each of the two variants of NSFPs would seem to be able to give rise to, and interact with, the other.
7. NSFPs, or "conflicts-as-process" (as well as "conflicts-as-startup conditions", e.g. relative deprivation), can be further exacerbated by environmental "shocks" and uncertainties associated with developments at the international and global level: among others, proliferation of weapons of mass destruction (Kaplan); the "Malthusian nightmare revisited" (Choucri and North, Clark, Mathews, Homer-Dixon); the collapse of previously existing political and other systems, and corresponding increases in the number of political units and in territorial contiguity; and increases in the amount of violence and war worldwide.
8. "Conflict-as-process" is where third parties enter the scene, and their "trick" is to create the "magic" by which *Realpolitik*-driven competitive processes can be replaced (or supplemented) by *Idealpolitik*-based cooperative processes of conflict resolution.

Conflict-as-startup Conditions and Conflict-as-process: A "Two-culture Problem"

"Conflict-as-startup conditions" generates "conflict-as-process," and once process comes to characterize conflict, it does not matter how (or when) the conflict started. As indicated earlier, *equifinality* is the operative concept here: different startup conditions can lead to the same process (initiation, escalation, controlled maintenance, etc.).[9]

Beyond some critical point in escalation or controlled maintenance, conflict-as-process can take on a life of its own, in which case it itself becomes a source of the continuation and further development of conflict.[10] As Lund (1996, pp. 133–4) puts it:

> The existing theoretical literature does not seem to suggest that parties have an ineluctable desire or tendency when a dispute arises to prosecute it to the bitter end through armed force. This literature suggests instead that, *once some level of significant violence has begun* [emphasis in the original], it is prone to escalate because an interactive process of attack and retaliation leads to a *self-perpetuating cycle* [emphasis added].[11]

Hence, over time, conflict-as-process may be more important than conflict-as-startup conditions. But while process may "drive" the conflict (like Richardson's (1939, 1960a) *defense coefficients*), if the conflict is undergirded by long-term startup conditions (e.g. the *grievances* in Richardson's model), even if conflict-as-process were to cease (e.g. in Cyprus), it might be resurrected unless the corresponding conflict-as-startup conditions were dealt with meaningfully for all concerned.[12]

Conflict-as-startup conditions can remain in the long-term memories and folklore of the actors concerned, surfacing from time to time through the various modes of cultural expression (e.g. songs and stories): "buttons" to be pushed in the event that certain conditions are present (e.g. unemployment, minority groups as candidates for scapegoat status, collapse of political and other systems).

Northern Ireland and former Yugoslavia, among others, come to mind here. Apropos the former, Richard Rose (1971, pp. 354–5) has observed that:

> Londonderry on August 12, 1969, aptly illustrates how time past and time present can fuse together in an explosive way. Protestants there that day were commemorating the 280th anniversary of the liberation of the besieged Protestant bastion within the old walled city from Catholic hordes surrounding it. As they looked over Derry's walls, the marchers could see that Catholics, as in Jacobite times, were present in great numbers in the Bogside just below their fortifications. Catholics did not have to turn their minds further back than the previous twelve months to anticipate what might happen next. In that period, the Royal Ulster Constabulary several times entered the Bogside in large numbers, assaulting Catholics on the streets and in their homes in ways that official enquiries could later amnesty but not excuse. The Catholics began to build barricades to prevent a recurrence of this. This recalled Protestants from ancient history to the present. The barricades were interpreted as the beginning of yet another Catholic insurrection. The approach of the police to the barricades was seen by the Catholics behind the lines as yet another instance in which Protestants sought, in the words of an eighteenth-century Irish song, to make "Croppies lie down." In such circumstances, *it hardly matters whether an individual interpreted events in seventeenth, eighteenth or twentieth-century terms.* In Northern Ireland, the conclusions

> drawn – for or against the regime – are much the same in one century as in the next. (Emphasis added)

Under such circumstances, when previous process interacts with, blends into, and strengthens conflict-as-startup conditions, conflict-as-process is never far from the surface: a latent fire always ready to be rekindled. Hence, Thompson's (1989, p. 691) observation "that Northern Irish society generates cycles of violence that escalate rapidly. The escalation is independent of socioeconomic changes and is strongly *self-perpetuating*" (emphasis added).

Muzafer Sherif's (1967, p. 29) discussion of the "heavy hand of the past" is relevant here: "each child in time acquires from his cultural heritage a past in human relationships that becomes his own, in the sense that he experiences its facets as his personal tastes, preferences, likes and dislikes." Hence, " 'myths, traditions, and symbols of national pride handed down from one generation to another' are among the factors conducive to 'modern wars between nations and groups of nations' " (Cantril, 1950, p. 18; cited in Sherif, 1967, p. 26). They help to keep conflicts-as-process in an ongoing or resurrectable state.

As in the treatment of phobias and anxiety/panic attacks, each of which, like our conflicts-as-process, can take "on a life of its own" (Mathias, 1994), there is a version of the "two-culture problem" operative here. There are those in the field (e.g. conflict analysts, peace researchers) who concentrate on conflicts-as-startup conditions, as psychoanalysts do in the treatment of phobias, while there are others (e.g. conflict resolution theorists/researchers, facilitators, conciliators, mediators) who concentrate on conflicts-as-process, as cognitive behavior therapists do in the treatment of phobias.

This division of labor is fine as far as it goes; however, there is little, if any, constructive connection between those who concentrate on conflict-as-startup conditions and those who deal with conflict-as-process. There are also few who deal with both.[13] Accordingly, more should be done about process – in theory as well as in practice – but in a way which connects it to startup conditions. Conflict resolution *theory* should take into account conflict-as-process as well as conflict-as-startup conditions, with the recognition that, over time in the development of any particular conflict system, the emphasis may shift from startup to process as the dominant driving force. And although *practice* must concentrate initially on process, subsequently it should deal with the startup conditions as well (e.g. "victimhood": see Montville, 1993), lest process be resurrected and return to haunt us all (e.g. the brutal ethnic warfare and genocide in former Yugoslavia).

Conclusion

In this chapter, we have attempted to sketch out the outlines of a *generic theory of violent conflict and war*, using as input the PDS findings of Chapter 4 and the results of the validation assessment of Chapter 5, against the background of current theory and the pretheory of Chapter 2.

Toward the end of the proposed generic theory, we revisited a distinction made in Chapter 5 between "conflict-as-startup condition" and "conflict-as-process," noting the operation of a "two-culture problem" in which startup conditions and process are not well integrated, either in theory or in practice. Until they are, efforts to intervene in protracted, violent conflict may – good intentions to the contrary – backfire, actually making matters worse.

Accordingly, dealing effectively with the "two-culture" problem is requisite to dealing effectively with violent conflict and war. In Chapter 7, we keep this in mind as we attempt to apply some of the theory developed here, not only to *understanding*, but also to *dealing with*, the resurrected violent ethnic conflict of the post-Cold War era.

Notes

1. Much of the discussion in this chapter is a revised version of Sandole (1993a).
2. This is compatible with Linda Brady's (1997, pp. 10–11) assessment of the broad field of security studies, where, given the "Turbulence in both the international environment and in the intellectual milieu within which scholars operate ... the security studies community should avoid prematurely reaching closure on the application of the appropriate paradigm, theory, or framework. Acknowledgement of the value of diverse perspectives, including realism, neo-realism, neo-institutionalism, and post-modernism, will expand the horizons of the field in needed ways."
3. Choucri and North have added the "global [ecological] level" to Waltz's framework, to capture those events, processes, and systems (natural and social) that are truly "global," either as effects of the first three images and/or as sources of influence on them, e.g. destruction of the world's rain forests, depletion of the ozone layer, the greenhouse effect, the AIDS pandemic, and other global problems in need of solution.
4. Although this level achieved primacy in the PDS on only one occasion (in the intermediate model for DI), and in any case had low predictive potencies – which is compatible with the corresponding empirical literature (e.g. Vasquez, 1976; Druckman, 1993) – for reasons discussed in Chapter 5 (e.g. Terhune, 1970), it remains a part of our efforts to develop a generic theory of violent conflict and war.
5. The selection of most of those who appear in the biological subcategory has been influenced by Waltz's (1959, Chapter 2) discussion of "first-image pessimists."
6. Berkowitz and LePage's (1967) experimental research implies such a relationship at the interpersonal level, especially in the presence of anger, which is strengthened by observations in the United States suggesting a positive relationship between handgun availability and the incidence of homicide and suicide (see Harwood, 1997; Havemann, 1997; Suro, 1997; Vobejda, 1997).
7. The role of gender in the etiology of violent conflict will be addressed in Chapter 8.
8. We address this phenomenon in Chapter 7 as a form of "spillover": *multiplier-effect systemic contagion.*
9. This recognition suggests, among other things, the possibility of reconciling, at least "in theory," apparently competing startup conditions.
10. In his "analysis of protracted intergroup conflicts ... rooted in the denial of basic human needs," Ronald Fisher (1993, p. 248) tells us that: "such conflicts are highly resistant to de-escalation, in part because of a host of social-psychological processes, including cognitive rigidities and distortions, self-fulfilling prophecies, and irrational commitment mechanisms. It is also due to the complexities of such conflicts, that is, to a set of interlocking ethnic, political, and economic factors in which no one issue can be

resolved by itself. *In such a situation, the conflict is not an event, but a process in which the process itself becomes a major source of continuing conflict*" (emphasis added).

11. That such processes are a *generic, cross-level* phenomenon is suggested by the study of delinquency conducted by Thornberry *et al.* (1991): "Because of its reciprocal relationships with . . . bonding variables, delinquent behavior contributes, in a very real sense, to its *own* causation. . . . After some initial impetus is provided, the reciprocal nature of the causal system tends to be *self-perpetuating*, and delinquency becomes more and more likely" (pp. 31, 33; emphasis added).
12. "Meaningful" here means, for example, the satisfaction of the parties' *procedural, substantive*, and *psychological* interests (see Moore, 1986, pp. 35–9).
13. For a variety of responses to this condition, see the readings in Sandole and van der Merwe (1993).

7 Implications for Practice: Dealing with Ethnic Conflict in Post-Cold War Europe[1]

Introduction

The ending of the Cold War has become associated not with the advent of a new era – a collaborative "New World Order" – but with the outbreak of violent conflict in various parts of Eastern Europe, the former Soviet Union, and elsewhere. It has been almost as if a certain "conflict equilibrium" must be maintained worldwide: when conflict at one level subsides, it picks up elsewhere.[2]

Many of these conflicts existed before as well as during the Cold War but, in the latter case, were latent and prevented from being expressed by the suppressive power of the state. Many of these conflicts were, and still are, of an *ethnic* nature, where members of various linguistic, religious, and/or racial groups have attempted to prevail against, and at the expense of, each other, e.g. in former Yugoslavia, where some of the most virulent of these conflicts have occurred.

Although these conflicts include other dimensions in addition to the ethnic one – e.g. political, economic, environmental – they are referred to here as ethnic conflicts because members of certain groups are being assaulted, killed or otherwise "removed" from certain areas and symbols of their cultural identity destroyed by members of other groups in large part because of their involuntary membership in those groups: they are killed, and their villages and cities are leveled, not because of what they have done, but because of who they are. "Ethnic cleansing" is, among other things, a sign that genocide, while not on the scale of the Nazi Holocaust, has nevertheless returned to Europe: an epiphenomenon of the ending of the Cold War, the collapse of Communist regimes in Eastern Europe and the collapse of the Soviet Union itself; in effect, the collapse of systems which had previously kept violent ethnic conflict in check.[3]

The CSCE as Background to Yugoslavia

During March 24 to July 8, 1992, the fourth review meeting of the principal regional security actor linking the (by then, former) Cold War adversaries, the *Conference on Security and Cooperation in Europe* (CSCE) – later renamed the *Organization for Security and Cooperation in Europe* (OSCE) – took place in Helsinki, followed by a summit meeting during July 9–10. The objectives of Helsinki '92 were to build further upon previous CSCE efforts to "institutionalize" the CSCE and contribute to post-Cold War developments in the three traditional areas of the CSCE process – (a) security, (b) economics and environmental, and (c) humanitarian – including new mechanisms for early warning, conflict prevention, crisis management, peacekeeping, and the peaceful settlement of disputes. Helsinki '92 was to go beyond the confidence- and security-building activities with which the CSCE had been associated since its advent in the early 1970s, by laying further groundwork for the development of a collaborative peace and security system for post-Cold War Europe.[4]

Also during March to July 1992, the Yugoslavian war, which had been raging between Serbia and Croatia since the summer of 1991, resulting in some 10,000 deaths, spilled over from Croatia into Bosnia-Hercegovina. By mid-1994, the Yugoslavian wars had resulted in, according to some estimates, more than 200,000 fatalities, mostly Slavic Muslims, plus in excess of two million refugees: a refugee problem unlike anything seen in Europe since World War II (Battiata, 1992a; CSCE Helsinki '92, 1992, p. 12; Maass, 1992; Nullis, 1994; Post *et al.*, 1995, p. 38).

Clearly, despite the hopes of some (e.g. Lewis, 1991), the new and evolving CSCE institutions for dealing with conflict in post-Cold War Europe did not prevent the outbreak of ethnic warfare in former Yugoslavia. (Nor did any other international organization for that matter.) Much the same could be said for other violent ethnic conflicts which have re-emerged in the wake of, or are otherwise associated with, the ending of the Cold War (e.g. the Armenian–Azerbaijani war over Nagorno-Karabakh and the Russian–Chechen war).

This chapter sets out to explore to what extent (if any) the generic theory presented in Chapter 6 accounts for the re-emergence of the ethnic violence and warfare in post-Cold War Europe, particularly the wars in former Yugoslavia, and whether it says anything about how to deal with such conflicts, including "future Yugoslavias." Specifically, the chapter explores answers to five questions:

1. What are some of the likely causes and conditions of violent expressions of ethnic conflict in Europe, especially the wars in former Yugoslavia?
2. What are some of the likely consequences of the continuation of these violent ethnic conflicts?
3. Why have existing institutions and processes, especially those associated with the principal regional security actor, the CSCE/OSCE, proven to be ineffective in either preventing or otherwise dealing with the violent manifestations of these conflicts?

4. How can these institutions and processes be made more effective in dealing with these conflicts?
5. What else can, or should, be done to deal with these manifestations of the "New World Disorder" in Europe?

Wars and Rumors of War Revisited

The resurrection of violent ethnic conflict in post-Cold War Europe reflects a global trend already under way during the Cold War: the progressive increase in *domestic* major armed conflicts as a proportion of total (domestic and foreign) major armed conflicts worldwide.[5] According to figures reported by Peter Wallensteen and others (see Table 7.1), not only was the number of domestic much larger than the number of foreign major armed conflicts between 1986 (one year following Mikhail Gorbachev's assumption of power in the former Soviet Union) and 1991 (the year in which the wars in former Yugoslavia began), but the number of domestic as a proportion of total (domestic and foreign) major armed conflicts increased during that period.

Wallensteen's figures are compatible with conclusions reached by Ted Robert Gurr (1993) in his study of 233 minority groups at risk of oppression in 93 countries. For example:

1. "Since the end of the Cold War, conflicts between communal groups and states have come to be recognized as the major challenge to domestic and international security in most parts of the world" (p. 314).
2. "Every form of ethnopolitical conflict has increased sharply since the 1950s" (p. 316).
3. "Ethnonationalist civil wars are the most protracted deadly conflicts of the late twentieth century" (p. 319).

Clearly, ethnic-based violent conflict *within* states seems to be one discernible wave of the post-Cold War future – among the "low intensity conflicts" that, for Martin van Creveld (1991), are replacing conventional interstate war (also see Holsti, 1996). Former UN Secretary General Boutros Boutros-Ghali, reflecting the first of the above conclusions cited from Gurr's (1993) study, warned that "ethnic conflict poses as great a danger to common world security as did the Cold War" (cited in Preston, 1993).

Table 7.1 Domestic as a proportion of total major armed conflicts worldwide, 1986–1991

	1986	1987	1988	1989	1990	1991
Domestic conflict	32	32	33	33	36	33
Foreign conflict	5	7	6	3	2	2
Domestic/total conflict (%)	86.5	82.0	84.6	91.7	94.7	94.3

Source: From *State of World Conflict Report 1991–1992*, pp. 16–18.

Ethnic Conflict in Eastern Europe and the Former Soviet Union

The revolutionary changes that have taken place in Eastern Europe and the former Soviet Union, and in East–West relations generally, have led to the thawing of long-suppressed ethnic conflicts and nationalist sentiments frozen in place by nearly fifty years of Cold War. Although the most violent example in Eastern Europe thus far has been the ethnic warfare in former Yugoslavia, potential or actual ethnic "fault-lines" exist elsewhere (e.g. in Romania, which contains a sizable Hungarian minority).[6]

In the former Soviet Union, violent conflicts have occurred between, among others: (a) Abkhazians and Georgians in Georgia; (b) Armenians and Azerbaijanis in Azerbaijan; (c) Ossetians and Georgians in Georgia; (d) ethnic Romanians and ethnic Russians in Moldova; and (e) Chechens and Russians in the Russian Federation. In each case, the conflict has threatened to facilitate the kind of state disintegration that occurred earlier in the former Soviet Union.[7] The implications for European peace and security, particularly of the conflicts in the Russian Federation, are ominous. But before we deal with these, let us explore the causes and conditions of such conflicts.

Ethnic Conflict: Causes and Conditions

Ethnic conflict occurs between representatives of groups, each of whose members shares significant aspects of history, tradition, language, worldview, perhaps race and religion, and an ingroup identity which includes "the other" (outgroup) as "out to get them."[8]

There is nothing inherently wrong with conflict itself. At certain levels, conflict can be an "early warning" that something has gone wrong in an otherwise important relationship and that the time has come for the parties to take appropriate action. We are concerned, therefore, with whether parties elect to deal with conflict by *competitive* or *cooperative* means (Deutsch, 1973). And if competitive, we are concerned with the escalation of manifest conflict processes (MCPs) into aggressive manifest conflict processes (AMCPs) (e.g. the ethnic warfare in former Yugoslavia). To what extent does the theory presented in Chapter 6 provide any insights into the development of violent ethnic conflict and warfare in post-Cold War Europe?

Basic Human Needs, Frustration and Ethnic Conflict

Our definition of MCP (see Chapter 2) includes, in addition to *disagreement*, parties' attempts to *undermine* each other, to "win," or at least not to "lose." This means that each must do something about, or to, the other to prevent it from winning. As suggested by Rapoport (1960), this undermining can be achieved by one or some combination of three modes: "Fights, Games, [or] Debates." *Debates* involve attempts to *convert* the opponent or some important third party; *games* involve attempts to *outwit* the opponent; and *fights* (AMCPs) involve attempts to *destroy* the "enemy."

It does not matter how the parties attempt to undermine one another because fights, games, and debates all involve various degrees of *frustration*: "To undermine one's opponent is to prevent him/her/them from achieving their objective. And the closer the process of undermining is to a fight, the more intense should be the frustration" (Sandole, 1986, pp. 119–20). Contrariwise: "the more intense the frustration, the more likely it is that some kind of experience or expression of aggression will occur – whether internal or external, physical or verbal, direct or indirect" (*ibid.*, pp. 120–1).

Basic human needs are what appear to be frustrated, causing conflict to be expressed violently – MCPs to be transformed into AMCPs. John Burton's (1979, 1990a, b) emphasis on the need for *identity* (and his use of the concept *identity group*) renders his framework particularly relevant to "conflicts in multi-ethnic societies [which] account for most of the protracted violent conflicts in the world society" (1990a, p. 137). Hence, according to Don Podestra's (1987) analysis of ethnic and religious conflict in 25 countries during 1987, "These simmering conflicts [are] rooted in the most basic forms of human *identity*," reflecting "the need to assert group *identity*" (emphasis added), and originating in one particular emotion: *a fear of group extinction*.

"The fear of [group] extinction" (see Horowitz, 1985, pp. 175–81) has a basis in reality: in addition to the millions of Armenians, Jews, Native Americans, and others subjected to genocidal policies before 1945, Harff and Gurr (1988) have determined that there have been 44 instances of genocide and politicide in all world regions since 1945, with estimated casualties ranging between 7 and 16 million people. Rummel (1987, p. 28) has calculated that "the worldwide risk of being killed by one's own government because of one's race, ethnic group, politics, etc., is more than three times greater than the risk of war." And, as already indicated, Gurr (1993) has estimated that there are presently at least 233 minority groups at risk of oppression in 93 countries.

Clearly, "Genocides and politicides are brutal efforts to maintain the security of one's 'identity group' at the total expense of other groups" (Sandole, 1990, p. 63). Perhaps because of this connection between ethnic conflict and *group extinction*, Burton (1990a, p. 138) has commented that:

> So far there has been no solution to any major multi-cultural or multi-ethnic conflict. Ethnic and cultural conflicts persist and either become an on-going part of a social-political system, or erupt, leading to violence and the destruction of the system.[9]

Conflict Resolution and "Pr*o*vention"

The basic human needs involved in violent ethnic conflict are ontological imperatives that transcend culture, personality, time, and situation. Everyone (including other forms of life) has needs in some sense: they are requisite to survival, of self, identity group, and species. Hence, there is an important – and, we hasten to add, *nondeterministic* – biological element here (see Burton and Sandole, 1986; Sandole, 1990). What *are* influenced by culture, personality, time, and situation are the ways in which people experience, define, express and attempt to fulfill their needs (see Avruch and Black, 1987, 1993; Burton and Sandole, 1987; Avruch *et al.*, 1991).

No matter what barriers they may encounter, people will aspire to meet their needs, one way or another, even to the point of being defined – and reacted to – by others as deviant, criminal or *terrorist*. In this regard, Jenonne Walker (1993b, pp. 104, 113) tells us that, for many, "a conflicting sense of *identity* is irreconcilable . . . It is far harder to compromise conflicting senses of *identity*" (emphasis added). This may explain, to some extent, those Bosnian and Croatian Serbs who feel that their needs for identity *and* security cannot be met in any political arrangement in which they are, or could be, a minority.

Minority groups are, with respect to majority groups, often in a state of *structural violence* (Galtung, 1969): situations of disadvantaged access to the political, legal, educational, economic, and other resources typically enjoyed by the mainstream. Structural violence is not always perceived by minorities, in which case "false consciousness" or the "happy slave" phenomenon may be operative. However, if or when it ceases to be a *latent conflict* – a conflict which should exist but does not (Deutsch, 1973, p. 14) – and finds its way into minority consciousness, *rank disequilibrium* (Galtung, 1964) and/or *relative deprivation* (Gurr, 1970), or some other experience of "felt dissonance," may result. In the event, minorities may attempt, within the mainstream, to fulfill their needs for security as well as identity, recognition, and others, but without success. Subsequently, via frustration–aggression-based escalation, they may "explode" their way into mainstream consciousness.

When violence does occur, there may be a *Realpolitik*, "law-and-order" response in the short run: state or even international authorities may feel that they must respond forcefully to prevent loss of life, destruction to property, and the like. This may lead (perhaps, only temporarily) to *negative peace*: the absence of hostilities (Galtung, 1969). This is not, however, conflict *resolution*: a collaborative problem-solving process leading to a durable agreement that deals, to the satisfaction of all concerned, with the issues that lead to the violence.

For practical, and not "only" ethical, reasons, therefore, parties to conflicts should move toward *positive peace*: the absence of structural violence, and pursuit of *social justice* for all concerned.[10] This means facilitating the access of minorities into the mainstream from which they were previously systematically excluded, or preventing the collapse of a group's status into that of a minority threatened with such exclusion; alternatively, creating new systems in which all can satisfy their respective needs for security, identity, and the like: this is the challenge that has yet to be met in former Yugoslavia, Azerbaijan, the Russian Federation, and elsewhere in Eastern Europe and the former Soviet Union.

Incorporating minorities into the mainstream may initially involve bringing people "to the table" to enter into a dialogue, e.g. to negotiate a ceasefire or otherwise agree to stop the killing (negative peace), in order to check the insidious dynamic of the *negative self-fulfilling prophecy* (NSFP) implicit in *other-stimulating* (action–reaction) or *self-stimulating* conflict spirals. The parties can then begin to collaboratively pursue social justice (positive peace), which, in the long run, will require significant changes in the political, legal, educational, economic, and/or other structures and processes that would otherwise continue to reflect and maintain actual or potential structural violence. This is the meaning of Burton's conflict *provention*: "prevention of an undesired event by removing its causes, and by creating conditions in which it cannot occur" (1990a, p. 233); in effect, promoting "conditions that create cooperative relationships" (*ibid.* p. 3).

A fundamental problem, however, is that political elites, in pursuit of their own needs for identity, security, and the like, tend toward maintenance of the status quo and of their hegemonic power position within it – what Burton (1979, p. 73 and Chapter 7) calls *role defense* – resisting efforts to empower actual or potential minorities, usually because they (and not surprisingly, the minorities as well) see the world through *Realpolitik*, confrontational, zero-sum (win-lose) lenses:

> In practice the most violent role defense situations are where there are no acknowledged processes for change: [in such cases] a power confrontation seems inevitable. While demands are made for change on those occupying authoritative roles, they are not accompanied by any recognition of the legitimate human needs of those to be displaced. (*Ibid.*, p. 144)

In such cases, therefore, there is a need for new mechanisms (conflict *resolution*) as well as new systems (conflict *provention/transformation*) – imperatives which apply clearly to former Yugoslavia and elsewhere in Eastern Europe and the former Soviet Union.

The Internal–External Conflict Nexus

The *functions-of-conflict thesis* associated with, among others, Bodin (1955), Simmel (1955), and Coser (1956) – that conflict with the outside can have internal value, preventing or nipping in the bud internal disarray and disintegration, thereby defending and preserving roles – seems to be generic, applying to all systems levels, including the *intrapsychic*. Vamik Volkan's (1985, 1988) argument in this regard, that there is a *need for enemies* as well as allies, fulfillment of which is requisite to the development of one's sense of *identity*, may be more compelling when we recall that a "hostile other" seems to be a major component of the identities of those involved in ethnic conflict: "people actually use and "need" enemies as *external stabilizers* of their sense of *identity* and *inner control*. [Hence, they] sometimes have a psychological investment in the continuation of a given conflict" (Montville, 1988, p. ix; emphasis added).[11]

As the democratization of Eastern Europe and the former Soviet Union continues, the needs for identity, recognition, autonomy, dignity, and security of those pursuing change are likely to intensify, exacerbating ongoing, or creating new, conflicts with others who, given their own role defense, will want to maintain the current, or re-establish an earlier, status quo (e.g. the stated desire of the Communist Party of the Russian Federation to reconstitute the Soviet Union: see Erlanger, 1996).

In view of the hypothesized and potentially real connection between internal and external conflict (and not only in repressive systems), there are disturbing implications for European security of increases in ethnic and other conflicts in Eastern Europe and the former Soviet Union: unless conflicts *within* ethnically divided societies are dealt with meaningfully for all concerned, they could, via *spillover*, exacerbate ongoing, or lead to new, conflicts *between* the affected states and some of their neighbors, as well as exacerbate or lead to similar conflicts elsewhere.

The Post-Cold War *Zeitgeist* According to Fukuyama *et al.*

Significant though the aforementioned trends in conflict and their implications may be, there are those who argue that there really is not much cause for alarm because, for a variety of reasons, the long-term future looks brighter and more promising. Francis Fukuyama (1989), for example, provoked intense debate by pronouncing that, with the ending of the Cold War, liberal democracy had triumphed over Communism and, in effect, "History" had come to an end (*ibid.*, p. 4):

> What we may be missing is not just the end of the Cold War, or the passing of a particular period of postwar history, but the end of history as such . . . the end point of mankind's ideological evolution and the universalization of Western liberal democracy as the final form of human government.

The "end of history" for Fukuyama also meant "the growing 'Common Marketization' of international relations, and the diminution of the likelihood of large-scale conflict between states" (*ibid.*, p. 18):

> This does not by any means imply the end of international conflict *per se*. For the world at that point would be divided between a part that was *historical* and a part that was *post-historical*. Conflict between states *still in history*, and between those states and those *at the end of history*, would still be possible. There would still be a high and perhaps rising level of ethnic and nationalist violence, since those are impulses incompletely played out, even in parts of the post-historical world. Palestinians and Kurds, Sikhs and Tamils, Irish Catholics and Walloons, Armenians and Azeris, will continue to have their unresolved grievances. This implies that terrorism and wars of national liberation will continue to be an important item on the international agenda. *But large-scale conflict must involve large states still caught in the grip of history, and they are what appear to be passing from the scene*. (Emphasis added)

Hence, history may be "dead" or dying for East–West *inter*state relations, but, as already indicated, is very much alive at the *intra*state level. Overlapping with, but going beyond, the data presented in Table 7.1, Wallensteen and Axell (1993, pp. 332–3) report that, for the period 1989–92,

> a total of 82 armed conflicts were recorded . . . 35 [of which] were . . . wars, resulting in at least 1000 battle-related deaths in a single year. . . . *very few of the armed conflicts were "classic" inter-state conflicts.* Only [four conflicts] pitted two internationally and mutually recognized states against each other. (Emphasis added)

Fukuyama's argument is a complex one, as he also maintains (1989, p. 18) that "The end of history will be a very sad time" and that "Such nostalgia . . . will continue to fuel competition and conflict even in the post-historical world for some time to come." In effect, the constellation of factors making for a reduction of large-scale, ideologically based conflict between large states will clash with, and perhaps be overwhelmed by, a longing for such conflicts (a theme to which we will return in Chapter 8). What this means, quite simply, is that history may not end.

But history may not "end" for another reason as well: although ideological tensions between East and West have clearly diminished, Fukuyama seems to have overlooked the *spillover potential* of the ethnic and other conflicts that he admits will continue to occur. This also seems to be a problem with Max Singer and Aaron Wildavsky (1993):

> In the post-Cold War world, there is no longer a single decisive threat. But there is a new framework to world politics: Its essential feature is that the world is divided between *zones of turmoil and development* and *zones of peace and democracy*. (Singer, 1993; emphasis added)

Zones of peace and democracy (Fukuyama's *post-historical* world) include Western Europe, North America, Japan, and Australia/New Zealand. The rest of the world comprises zones of turmoil and development (Fukuyama's *historical* world). But, by the year 2100, "the zones of war and turmoil are likely to be much smaller than they are today. . . . In the long run . . . these zones of turmoil will be dominated by the spread of wealth, democracy, and peace" (*ibid.*). Singer and Wildavsky's argument is similar to John Mueller's (1989), that major war – war between developed countries – is becoming obsolete, in part because of the spread worldwide of economic prosperity:

> The prospects look rather good for the foreseeable future not only because war has lost its evident appeal but also because substantial agreement has arisen around the twin propositions that prosperity and economic growth should be central national goals and that war is a particularly counter-productive device for achieving these goals. Associated with this are changes in perspectives about how a country achieves status and "power" in the modern world. Increasingly, economic strength is being used as the central measure, replacing military prowess and success in war. (p. 219)

These are "rational" arguments, that, yes, there will continue to be "a great deal of war and tragedy" (Singer, 1993) in the "zones of turmoil," the historical world, but, as liberal democracy and free-market prosperity continue to spread worldwide, *ecological imperatives permitting*, the incidence of major war between major powers will diminish. There is some validity to these arguments as well, as indicated by the "intellectual growth industry" of research on the effects worldwide of the spread of democracy (see Kegley and Hermann, 1995, pp. 5–6). For example, research on the relationship between democracy and war suggests (without a clear explanation) "that democracies' refusal to resolve their conflicts among themselves by the use of force is 'as close as anything we have to an empirical law in international relations' (Levy, 1989[a]: 270)" (Kegley and Hermann, 1995, p. 8).

Accordingly, Fukuyama, Singer and Wildavsky, and Mueller may be right in the *long run* (again, ecological imperatives permitting). But what about the wars taking place in the "zones of turmoil" in the short to middle run? Michael Mandelbaum might argue that these will not threaten the "vital interests" of those living in the "zones of peace" – that "even though there may be more crises rooted in ethnic conflicts than we've seen in years, in most cases it won't matter to us that much" (cited in Goshko, 1991).

Richard Ullman (1991, pp. 144–5), in apparent agreement with Mandelbaum, Fukuyama, and others, has commented: "Violent conflicts will certainly occur. . . . [but] they will be sufficiently confined so that they will be very unlikely to escalate across the threshold of war among the major European powers." But, given the "spillover potential" inherent in the ethnic and other *intra*national conflicts occurring in Eastern Europe and the former Soviet Union, they *could* escalate and, in the process, undermine further democratization and reform in those areas, ultimately sabotaging the development of a post-Cold War *peace and security commons*.

Spillover: An Expanded View and Typology

Spillover can mean conflict spreading within a given area, between it and contiguous areas, or simply elsewhere, suggesting various kinds of conflict escalation or expansion of conflict-as-process, e.g. *functional spillover*, *external intervention*, and *multiplier-effect systemic contagion*.

Functional Spillover

Functional spillover is associated with scapegoating (conscious or unconscious) and role defense. Its objective is to find or otherwise "invent" enemies in order to reintegrate or reunify a group which is, or is likely to come, under internal stress, so that otherwise threatened elites can remain in power. This is the functions-of-conflict thesis of Bodin (1955), Simmel (1955), and Coser (1956), or *conflict-cohesion hypothesis*, which "has been so widely accepted among social scientists . . . that Dahrendorf (1964, p. 58) suggests that . . . 'It appears to be a general law' " (Levy, 1989b, p. 261; emphasis added). It is, perhaps, the oldest hypothesis (and principle) in the study (and practice) of politics: "when the natives are restless, find an enemy and go to war!"

A case in point: former President Slobodan Milosevic of Serbia manipulated for many Serbs the meaning of Kosovo in order to remain in power. Kosovo is the "Jerusalem" of the Serbian people, their "holy ground . . . where [their] most historic and religious monuments are located" (Dragnich and Todorovich, 1984, p. 1). Kosovo is the Serbs' medieval kingdom, the "cradle of their nationhood, when they were virtually its sole occupants . . . the center of [their] empire of the middle ages, at one time the strongest empire in the Balkans" (*ibid.*; also see Dragnich, 1992, Chapter 9).

On June 28, 1987, Milosevic made a speech in "a field in Kosovo called Kosovo Polje, the Field of Black Birds, on the anniversary of the defeat there of a Serbian commander" (Rosenberg, 1993, p. 1):

> "They'll never do this to you again," he pledged to the crowd. "Never again will anyone defeat you." . . . The defeat on that field took place in 1389.
>
> A year later, the coffin of the defeated Serb commander began a year-long pilgrimage through every village in Serbia, followed by multitudes of sobbing mourners dressed in black in every town. For many in Serbia, the year 1989 marked not the fall of communism, but the 600th anniversary of the defeat of Knez Lazar at Kosovo Polje.

The Serbs did not regain Kosovo until some five centuries later, during the Balkan Wars of 1912–13. Nevertheless, 74 years later, in 1987, some 90 percent of Kosovo's population was comprised of the "Ottoman legacy": nearly two million ethnic Albanians who are predominately *Muslim*. For many Serbs, therefore, nothing had changed in Kosovo in 600 years: the Muslims – and therefore the "Turks" – were still there; and more to the point, as the dominant group!

In Chapter 6, we quoted Richard Rose (1971, pp. 354–5) on Northern Ireland, where "time past and time present can fuse together in an explosive way . . . [where] the conclusions drawn . . . are much the same in one century as in the next." The same clearly applies to the Balkans, where,

> for most Serbs, the war in Bosnia is simply one more battle in a long struggle that began six centuries ago in a battle on the field of Kosovo in southern Serbia. They are driven by a conviction that the war is just and that it will not end until all Serbs are safely united in one state and the territory of Kosovo is permanently under Serbian control. . . . this war is no different from their struggle against the Turks over the centuries. (Emmert, 1993, p. C1)

Apparently, for many Serbs, once the Kosovo "button" was pushed, the resurrected conflict-as-process would not cease until a major conflict-as-startup condition was dealt with – the return of Kosovo to permanent Serbian rule:

> Over the centuries, the cult of Kosovo evolved to celebrate martyrdom on the one hand but also to demand of all generations of Serbs that they avenge the loss of Kosovo and liberate all Serbs from oppression. During Ottoman rule . . . the Serbs believed that God would protect His people and return them one day from captivity. They also came to believe that there can be no free state without a struggle. Their epic poetry idealized those who sacrifice themselves in order to strike a blow against the oppressor. In the words of the epic: "Whoever is a Serb and of Serbian

> blood and comes not to fight at Kosovo ... Let nothing grow from his hand ... until his name is extinguished forever." (*ibid.*, p. C4)

For Serbs worldwide, therefore, Kosovo has the status of what Vamik Volkan (1991, 1992) calls a *chosen trauma*:

> an event that causes a large group of people (i.e. an ethnic group) to feel helpless and victimized by another group and to share a humiliating narcissistic injury. A group does not really elect the loss of shared self-esteem, but it does "choose," consciously as well as unconsciously, to psychologize and mythologize what has occurred. The group draws into its *identity* the mental representation of the "chosen trauma" and passes it along to the next generation along with related feelings of hurt and shame and associated defenses. Each successive generation gets a modified account of the event, but its place in the overall psychology of the group changes very little, and it continues to influence attitudes toward any other group directly or indirectly associated with those responsible for this historic offense. Once a shared trauma is "chosen," its historical truth is no longer important; what matters is its place in the *identity* formation of the victims and their establishment of mental representations of victimizers. (Volkan and Itzkowitz, 1993, p. 129; emphasis added)

In other words, the wars in former Yugoslavia may spread full-circle back to Kosovo, where, in many ways, the current round began, to "ethnically cleanse" it of "The Turk":

> It is this spirit that makes the world nervous about Serbia's intentions in Kosovo today. For the time being, the Albanian population there has not mounted an armed resistance to martial law. If they were to do so or if the government in Belgrade were to encourage the ethnic cleansing of the province, there is little doubt that the war in the Balkans would spread beyond the borders of the former Yugoslavia. The ... leadership in Albania (and President Clinton for that matter) has made it clear that it will not stand idly by if Albania's co-nationals in Kosovo become the next victims. (Emmert, 1993, p. C4)[12]

But this takes us into the second category of spillover.

External Intervention

As a form or source of spillover, external intervention can occur on behalf of ethnic (or racial or religious) kin or on humanitarian grounds.

Intervention on Behalf of Ethnic Kin

Approximately one year before Slovenia and Croatia declared their independence from the Yugoslav federation on June 25, 1991, the U.S. Institute of Peace (USIP, 1990, p. 26) reported:

> Although problems in Romania, Bulgaria, and even ... Albania would

> probably prevent Yugoslavia's neighbors from taking immediate advantage of its slide toward dissolution, it is not impossible that the Balkans will revert to the confusion of the late nineteenth and early twentieth centuries over the next three to five years. Should foreign adventurism become useful to neighboring governments and should the Yugoslavs lose the ability to police [their] borders, a struggle could ensue among Serbs, Albanians, Bulgarians and even Greeks over the Southern regions of the Yugoslav state. While the Serbs are focused on problems there, the Romanians could make further trouble by stirring up their brothers in Banat, and the Hungarians could do the same in Voivodina in the North.

In other words, should Milosevic or others decide to "ethnically cleanse" Kosovo of its roughly two million ethnic Albanians, with the latter fleeing into neighboring Albania and Macedonia (where relations have been tense between Slavic Macedonians and an ethnic Albanian minority), Albania could get involved, intervening on behalf of its "ethnic kin" in Kosovo and Macedonia.[13] More importantly, however, Greece, which earlier had imposed economic blockades on Macedonia,[14] might decide, perhaps together with its "religious kin," the Serbs, to exploit the situation, which could bring in Bulgaria and even Turkey. With two NATO "allies" involved, but on opposite sides, it would be difficult to imagine how Russia could avoid intervening more actively on behalf of its fellow Cyrillic Slavs and Orthodox Christians, the Serbs.

This admittedly worst-case scenario – which, since Greece and Turkey "went to the brink of war" in January 1996 (Lippman, 1996; IHT, 1996), is not all that far-fetched[15] – could mean another Balkan, if not general European, war before the century (and millennium!) comes to an end.[16]

Although the wars in former Yugoslavia have posed the most immediate spillover threat for Europe in the post-Cold War period, they are not the only threat to peace and security in the region. In addition to other *intra*national (ethnic) conflicts in Eastern Europe, which reflect the "spillover factor" (e.g. tensions between Slovaks and ethnic Hungarians in the Slovak Republic affecting relations between the Slovak Republic and Hungary), there are conflicts in the former Soviet Union which dwarf these and even the wars in former Yugoslavia. For example, prior to a ceasefire that has more or less held since May 1994, the war between ethnic Armenians and Azeris in Nagorno-Karabakh (in Azerbaijan) had escalated to war between Armenia and Azerbaijan, affecting relations between Turkey and Russia to such an extent that some Russians threatened that Turkish intervention on behalf of the Turkic Azeris could bring about *World War III* (Shapiro, 1992).

Further, tensions between ethnic Russians and Ukrainians in Ukraine have exacerbated, and have been exacerbated by, the conflict between Russia and Ukraine over how to divide up the military assets left over by the collapse of the former Soviet Union (e.g. the Black Sea Fleet): "Beside a war between [these] two great eastern Slav nations, the conflict in Yugoslavia would pale into insignificance" (Bromke, 1993, p. 37).[17]

Whether in former Yugoslavia, the former Soviet Union or anywhere else in the post-Cold War world, spillover as intervention on behalf of ethnic kin plays a major role in Samuel Huntington's "Clash of Civilizations" through what he (borrowing from H. D. S. Greenway) calls the *kin-country syndrome*, or "civilizational rallying" (1993, pp. 35–9; 1996, pp. 272–91):

> In the post-Cold War world, multiple communal conflicts have superseded the single superpower conflict. When these communal conflicts involve groups from different civilizations, they tend to expand and to escalate. As the conflict becomes more intense, each side attempts to rally support from countries and groups belonging to its civilization. Support in one form or another, official or unofficial, overt or covert, material, human, diplomatic, financial, symbolic, or military, is always forthcoming from one or more kin countries or groups. The longer a fault line conflict continues the more kin countries are likely to become involved in supporting, constraining, and mediating roles. As a result of this "kin-country syndrome," fault line conflicts have a much higher potential for escalation than do intracivilizational conflicts and usually require intercivilizational cooperation to contain and end them. In contrast to the Cold War, conflict does not flow down from above, it bubbles up from below. (Huntington, 1996, p. 272)

Humanitarian Intervention

By November 30, 1994, there were 38,130 troops, 727 police, and 680 observers participating in the UNPROFOR (United Nations Protection Force) missions in former Yugoslavia – "the largest peace-keeping operation in the history of the United Nations" – with military and civilian personnel provided by 37 UN member states (UN, 1995, p. 108).[18] Although this was not "peace-keeping" in the traditional sense – as there was no *negative peace* to keep – it certainly constituted further internationalization of the wars in former Yugoslavia, with implications for spillover: there were then forces on the ground whose governments had been historically linked with, as well as supportive of, different combatants, thereby creating a possibility for "taking sides" and, in the extreme, even for confrontations between some of the "peace-keepers" themselves.[19]

A never-ending problem for third parties is that, even though they may not actually take sides, they might still be *perceived* by some of the conflicting parties as if they were, "in fact," biased toward one side or the other. UNPROFOR as a whole encountered this problem: it was criticized by some (including the Bosnian Muslims) for facilitating "ethnic cleansing" operations conducted by the Bosnian Serbs (e.g. by assisting fleeing refugees to evacuate besieged areas); for assisting the Bosnian Serbs in the realization of their military objectives (e.g. by taking up positions which Bosnian Serbs had seized and from which they had withdrawn, thereby (inadvertently?) allowing them to redeploy elsewhere); and for keeping otherwise doomed residents of besieged villages and cities alive through food and medical aid, only for them to be killed or otherwise "ethnically cleansed" later on (Anderson and Binstein, 1994; Chalmers, 1993, p. 437; Posen, 1993, pp. 33–4; Rieff, 1994).

Clearly, what may have begun as a noble humanitarian mission may have ended up contributing to a worsening of the situation, as happened in Somalia, which – prior to the fall of Srebrenica in Bosnia, in July 1995 – had been defined as "the costliest, bloodiest and so far most futile UN exercise in global peacekeeping" (Richburg, 1994, p. A1).[20]

Multiplier-effect Systemic Contagion

Multiplier-effect systemic contagion concerns a less direct form of spillover reminiscent of Systemic Attack Contagion (SAC) and the spread of violent conflict through *demonstration-* and *bandwagon-effects* (see Chapter 2), whereby ethnic and other conflicts in some parts of the world exacerbate or stimulate the development of similar conflicts elsewhere. In this regard, David Gompert (1994, p. 42), a former U.S. National Security Council (NSC) official, has warned that "the crisis, in Bosnia especially, [has set] the worst possible *precedents* for the [post-Cold War] era" (emphasis added). Indeed, the wars in former Yugoslavia may be a wave of the future: a *model* for ethnic and other wars *in* – and through functional and/or "ethnic kin" spillover, *between* – Russia and other republics of the former Soviet Union.

A link between ethnic conflicts in former Yugoslavia and in the former Soviet Union has been noticed for some time. In March 1988, for instance, some three years prior to the collapse of former Yugoslavia, Diehl (1988, p. A29), reported:

> Soviet leader Mikhail Gorbachev . . . is due to spend four days traveling through Yugoslavia next week, . . . As he flies from Moscow to Belgrade . . . [he] will leave behind bitter ethnic conflicts in Soviet Central Asia and rising nationalism in the western Baltic republics. In Yugoslavia, meanwhile, he will encounter nationalist problems that are *remarkably similar* in their dynamics and origin. (Emphasis added)

In October 1991, some four months after the Yugoslavian wars began, during the siege of the Croatian city of Vukovar, Dobbs (1991c, p. A19) observed:

> A recent confidential memorandum prepared by the KGB security police and leaked to the Soviet press warned that ethnic clashes and extensive internal migration could lead to the establishment of "national regimes of a populist, semi-fascist type." It added that the *Soviet Union is going down "the same path as Yugoslavia, repeating almost step by step events that happened there a year to 18 months ago."* (Emphasis added)

A major reason for these developments in the former Soviet Union is not only the large number of different nations and ethnic groups, but also their distribution throughout the country. According to a 1989 census, there are

> 102 separate nations and ethnic groups. More than 65 million [former] Soviet citizens – out of a total population of 287 million – live *outside* their titular republics. Of the 23 inter-republic borders in the former Soviet

> Union ... only three are not contested. *Similar disputes are at the heart of Yugoslavia's civil war.* (Dobbs, 1991a, p. A32; emphasis added)

Hence, Gurr's (1993, p. 322) proposition that "The immediate potential for escalating ethnopolitical conflict is greatest in the Soviet successor states." This applies especially to Russia, with its sixteen autonomous republics:

> When former Soviet prime minister Nikolai Ryzkhov paid a visit to the Croatian city of Vukovar [the "Hiroshima of Yugoslavia": a city totally leveled during a three-month siege in 1991] he was startled by the physical devastation and ethnic hatred left behind by the war. *But what disturbed him most were the parallels between Yugoslavia's descent into violence and the political crisis in Russia.*
>
> "If Russian leaders are unable to find a solution to our political and economic problems [e.g. concerning Chechnya], the result could be something 100 times worse than what has happened in Yugoslavia. *I do not exclude the possibility of Vukovar happening many times over in Russia.*" (Dobbs, 1993; emphasis added)

Paralleling the disintegration of the former Soviet Union, therefore, has been the threatened disintegration of the Russian Federation itself, facilitated, in part, by one particular "Vukovar": the war between Moscow and Chechnya, the "self-proclaimed [Muslim] republic ... landlocked in the Caucasus Mountains," which declared its "independence" in November 1991 (Hockstader, 1994):

> Chechenia [Chechnya] is a headache for Russian President Boris Yeltsin that will not go away. Attempting to keep it inside the Russian Federation promises nothing but trouble. *But letting it go altogether could encourage dozens of other regions populated by restive nationalities to follow suit by breaking with Moscow.* And Yeltsin has made it clear he will not tolerate Russia's unraveling. (Emphasis added; also see Dobbs, 1991c; LeVine, 1994; WP, 1994)

In an apparent effort to save the Federation (and his presidency!), President Yeltsin launched a military assault on Chechnya on December 11, 1994, which has been disastrously counterproductive: by July 30, 1995, when "the two sides signed an agreement aimed at ending the killing" (which subsequently collapsed), some 30,000 people had been killed, "most of them civilians, Chechen and Russian alike" (Zucchino, 1995, p. A1). The war continued until August 31, 1996 – "with estimates of the number of dead [then] ranging from 30,000 to 80,000" – when General Alexander Lebed, "acting in his brief incarnation as ... Yeltsin's security chief and special peace envoy to Chechnya," brokered a peace agreement, which deferred until 2001 the question "about whether Chechnya is legally still part of Russia" (Hockstader, 1997a; also see Hoffman, 1996).

As the Russian–Chechen and similar conflicts continue to threaten to pull the Russian Federation apart,[21] it is likely that existing tendencies toward role defense and the playing out of the functions-of-conflict thesis will be reinforced as guides to action, spurring further calls for a "reconstitution of the former

Soviet Union," including by other than "voluntary" means. One ostensible (if not, in some cases, "real") reason offered would be the 27 million or so Russians living in other former Soviet republics as *minorities* – a situation already exploited by ultranationalist Vladimir Zhirinovsky, who has promised "to create a unitary Russian state from the Baltic Sea to the Bering Strait" (Dobbs, 1991c, p. A19).[22]

Complementing the problem of Russians as minorities in the "near-abroad" and providing even more arguments for Russian ultranationalists, is that the same situation exists *within* the Russian Federation itself: for example, before the Russian–Chechen war, some 150,000 ethnic Russians lived within Chechnya (whose total population was 1.2 million people) (Hockstader, 1994).

No matter where the "Yugoslav model" is operative or otherwise applicable – *within* Russia or other republics or, through spillover, *between* Russia and other republics or, as seems likely, at all levels within the former Soviet Union – we can appreciate, with Griffiths (1993, p. 124),

> [the] fear, which seems well-founded, that a combination of economic, nationalist, ethnic and other social factors might produce some kind of *post-cold war "domino-effect" of conflict and societal collapse from region to region and level to level.* This scenario is most credible in terms of processes in the former Soviet Union. (Emphasis added)

A "domino effect" of instability and an increased threat of war in post-Cold War Europe, facilitated by "Yugoslav contagion," is clearly what Egon Bahr, foreign policy analyst for Germany's Social Democratic Party (SPD), had in mind when he warned:

> *What happened in Yugoslavia is a foretaste of what can happen and is already happening elsewhere. ... Europe will see many Yugoslavias*, with huge numbers of refugees that could throw even countries that are stable today into disorder. Europe simply cannot wait for Eastern Europe to become as stable economically and politically as Western Europe is now. Organizing security in the classic sense must be started immediately. (NYT, 1993; emphasis added)

Just how has security been organized in Europe, in the "classic" or any other sense, in response to these and other post-Cold War developments?

The New Europe: Toward a Post-Cold War Peace and Security System

Part and parcel of the dramatic changes that have been taking place in Europe are developments which constitute explicit attempts to guarantee the ending of the Cold War and to plug the "Hobbesian black hole of international anarchy." These developments include the Paris Summit of the Conference on Security and Cooperation in Europe (CSCE), which met on November 19–21, 1990, and the products of that summit and subsequent developments.

The Paris CSCE Summit

One of the products of the Paris CSCE summit was the (U.S.) criterion-event for holding the summit, the *Treaty on Conventional Armed Forces in Europe* (CFE), which limited each of the former Cold War blocs (NATO and the former Warsaw Treaty Organization, or WTO) to equal numbers of tanks (20,000), armored combat vehicles (30,000), artillery (20,000), combat aircraft (6800), and attack helicopters (2000) (see ACDA, 1990). Ambassador Jonathan Dean, former chief U.S. negotiator at the Mutual and Balanced Force Reduction (MBFR) talks which preceded CFE, defined the CFE Treaty as "the definitive end of the surprise attack option" (cited in Leopold, 1990).

Another product of the Paris summit was the *Joint Declaration*, in which the sixteen members of NATO and six members of the WTO solemnly pledged that they were "no longer adversaries" but, instead, determined to "build new partnerships and extend to each other the hand of friendship." They agreed further to recognize that "the security of each of their countries is inextricably linked to the security of all the States participating in the [CSCE]" (*ibid.*). In effect, they were attempting to neutralize the *prisoners'* and *security dilemmas* (Rapoport, 1960; Herz, 1959), whereby states in the *Realpolitik* frame tend to counterproductively pursue their own security interests at the expense of others.

The *Document of the Vienna Negotiations on Confidence- and Security-building Measures* (CSBMs) (CSBMs Vienna Document, 1990), issued right before the Paris summit, contributed further to the confidence-building process begun during the initial meetings of the CSCE in 1973–5, and improved upon during the Stockholm Conference on CSBMs and Disarmament in Europe (Stockholm Document, 1986). By enhancing *transparency* within the CSCE concerning otherwise potentially suspicious military activities, these new CSBMs built upon a "conflict-resolution-friendly" tradition that had developed over the years within the CSCE, by providing the former Cold War adversaries with further "*opportunities to falsify their worst-case assumptions* about each other" (Sandole, 1991, p. 10).

The remaining, and in some ways most important, development associated with the Paris CSCE summit was the *Charter of Paris for a New Europe*, which, on behalf of all (then 34) CSCE participating states, formally brought the Cold War to an end: "The era of confrontation and division of Europe has ended. We declare that henceforth our relations will be founded on respect and co-operation" (*Charter of Paris*, 1990, p. 13).

The Charter also took initial steps to "institutionalize" the CSCE, which, until the Paris summit, had been a "process" with no fixed address, secretariat, or regularly scheduled meetings. Hence, the Charter called for regular meetings of CSCE heads of state or government during CSCE follow-up meetings (approximately once every two years); and for meetings of CSCE foreign ministers, in the form of the newly created Council of Ministers for Foreign Affairs, to take place at least once each year. To prepare the meetings of the Council (including reviewing current issues and making recommendations), the Charter created a Committee of Senior Officials (CSO), which would also implement the Council's decisions.

In addition, the Charter created: (a) a CSCE Secretariat in Prague (which was subsequently relocated to Vienna, but with an office remaining in Prague); (b) an Office for Free Elections in Warsaw (subsequently renamed the Office for Democratic Institutions and Human Rights, or ODIHR); and (c) a Conflict Prevention Centre (CPC) in Vienna.[23]

The CPC was tasked initially to provide support for the implementation of a number of the newly created CSBMs: (a) annual exchange of military information; (b) consultation and cooperation regarding unusual military activities; (c) communications network; (d) cooperation regarding hazardous incidents of a military nature; and (e) the annual implementation assessment meetings. Left open was the possibility that the CPC might constitute a forum for dispute settlement. The Charter affirmed the commitment of the participating states, not only to prevent conflicts, but to define and seek "appropriate mechanisms for the resolution of any disputes which may arise" (*Charter of Paris*, 1990, p. 18). It mentioned the opportunity provided by the CSCE experts meeting scheduled to meet in Valletta, Malta, from January 15 to February 8, 1991, whose objective was to create a mechanism for the peaceful settlement of disputes.

The Valletta meeting took place and established the "CSCE Procedure for Peaceful Settlement of Disputes" (Valletta Report, 1991). It did not, however, assign the Procedure to the CPC. That task was left to the first meeting of the Council of Ministers for Foreign Affairs, which took place in Berlin on June 19–20, 1991. Among other things (accepting Albania into the CSCE and adopting a mechanism for consultation and cooperation regarding emergency situations: the *Berlin Mechanism*), it designated the CPC as the "nominating institution" for the CSCE Procedure (the *Valletta Mechanism*), i.e. for any given dispute, the CPC director could preside over the creation, but not the functioning, of a "CSCE Dispute Settlement Mechanism." Hence, the Berlin meeting of the Council provided the CPC with a conflict-resolution supplement to its original crisis-prevention/management function.

The Charter also affirmed "that the ethnic, cultural, linguistic and religious *identity* of national minorities will be protected and that persons belonging to national minorities have the right freely to express, preserve and develop that *identity* without any discrimination and in full equality before the law" (*Charter of Paris*, 1990, p. 14; emphasis added). The signatories also expressed their "determination to combat all forms of racial and ethnic hatred, anti-semitism, xenophobia and discrimination against anyone as well as persecution on religious and ideological grounds" (*ibid.*, p. 17), a concern which – especially in view of certain right-extremist developments in Austria, France, Germany, and elsewhere (see Kitschelt, 1995; Merkl and Weinberg, 1997) – led to the CSCE Experts Meeting on National Minorities in Geneva on July 1–19, 1991, "to hold a thorough discussion on the issue of national minorities and of the rights of persons belonging to them" (*Charter of Paris*, Supplementary Document, 1990, p. 21; Geneva Report, 1991).

Post-Paris CSCE Developments: Helsinki and Beyond!

Shortly after the abortive coup attempt against Gorbachev during August 19–21, 1991, the Moscow Meeting of the Conference on the Human Dimension of the CSCE took place from September 10 to October 4, 1991, contributing further to the development of the evolving human dimension mechanism (the *Moscow Mechanism*), including conditions under which "A state may ... be forced to receive a rapporteur mission ... for fact-finding" (CSCE Commission, 1992, p. 27).

Also, during January 30–31, 1992, the CSCE Council of Foreign Ministers met in Prague. One of the decisions it took was to establish the possibility of *consensus-minus-one* decision-making in cases of egregious violations of CSCE principles and commitments (*ibid.*, p. 22). Specifically, in cases of "clear, gross and uncorrected violations" of CSCE commitments, the CSCE Council of Foreign Ministers or CSO could take "appropriate action," even, if necessary, "in the absence of the consent of the State concerned." But this particular encroachment on national sovereignty went only so far: "Such actions would consist of political declarations or other political steps to apply *outside* the territory of the State concerned" (Prague CSCE ("Prague Document"), 1992, p. 4; emphasis added).[24]

By the time the fourth CSCE review conference convened in Helsinki, a package of additional CSBMs had been produced, adopted by consensus on March 4, 1992, inclusive of new provisions on, among others, information exchange, notification, constraints on the size of military exercises, and inspections (see CSBMs Vienna Document, 1992). Also, an *Open Skies Treaty* had been concluded on March 21, 1992, permitting overflights of the territories of the 24 signatory states (covering the area from Vancouver to Vladivostock), thereby providing additional (and "equal") opportunities for "falsifying worst-case assumptions." The stage was set for more to come.

The Helsinki CSCE review conference met from March 24 to July 8, 1992, concluding with a two-day summit during July 9–10 and a declaration which reflected the call of the 1991 NATO Rome summit to improve CSCE conflict prevention and crisis management mechanisms (NATO Rome Summit, 1991). In this regard, the Helsinki CSCE created a High Commissioner on National Minorities (HCNM), which, using the resources of the Warsaw-based ODIHR, would have two functions – (a) *early warning* and (b) *early action* – to be performed

> at the earliest possible stage in regard to tensions involving national minority issues which have not yet developed beyond an early warning stage, but, in the judgement of the Commissioner, have the potential to develop [*spill over*] into a conflict within the CSCE area, affecting peace, stability or relations between participating States. (*CSCE Helsinki Document 1992*, Ch. 2, p. 7)

At the "early warning" level, the HCNM would collect and assess information concerning minority issues, "from any source, including the media and nongovernmental organizations" (*ibid.*, p. 11), which could include data such as those generated by Gurr's (1993) "Minorities at Risk" project. Also at this stage, the HCNM could visit any CSCE state and "communicate in person . . . with parties directly concerned to obtain first-hand information about the situation," e.g. the "role of the parties directly concerned, the nature of the tensions and recent developments . . . and . . . the potential consequences for peace and stability within the CSCE area" (*CSCE Helsinki Document 1992*, Ch. 2, pp. 8–9). If the HCNM were to determine "that there [was] a *prima facie* risk of potential conflict . . . he/she [could then] issue an early warning, which [would] be communicated promptly . . . to the CSO" (*ibid.*, p. 9).

Part of the HCNM's "early action" function might be "to enter into further contact and closer consultation with the parties concerned with a view to possible solutions, according to a mandate to be decided by the CSO" (*ibid.*). Suggestive of opportunities for nongovernmental conflict resolution specialists to work collaboratively with the CSCE, the HCNM can consult up to three experts "with relevant expertise in specific matters" (*ibid.*, p. 13). Such persons would "be selected by the [HCNM] with the assistance of the ODIHR from the resource list" maintained by the ODIHR for the Human Dimension Mechanism (the Moscow Mechanism) (*ibid.*).

Once it receives an early warning from the HCNM or any other prescribed source (e.g. other CSCE offices, or a state directly involved in a dispute), the CSO may also "seek independent advice and counsel from relevant experts [as well as from] institutions, and international organizations" (*ibid.*, Ch. 3, p. 16). Thereafter, the CSO, acting on behalf of the Council of Foreign Ministers, would have "overall CSCE responsibility for managing [any] crisis with a view to its resolution":

> It may, *inter alia*, decide to set up a framework for a negotiated settlement, or to dispatch a rapporteur or fact-finding mission. The CSO may also initiate or promote the exercise of good offices, mediation or conciliation. (*ibid.*, pp. 16–17)

The Helsinki review conference also provided for the possibility of CSCE peace-keeping operations: a development prompted by the escalation of violent ethnic conflict in former Yugoslavia and the former Soviet Union.[25] Taken together with the new and enhanced conflict prevention and crisis management mechanisms, plus references in the concluding document to *social justice, basic human needs*, and – reflecting John Burton's (1990a) *provention* – to "the CSCE [as] crucial to our efforts to forestall aggression and violence by addressing the *root causes* of problems" (*CSCE Helsinki Document 1992* ("Helsinki Summit Declaration"), pp. 2, 5, 6; (emphasis added), CSCE negotiators appear to have concluded at Helsinki that a post-Cold War peace and security system in Europe would require elements of both *negative* and *positive peace*: the former to stop or prevent the killing and the latter to deal with the often deep-rooted problems underlying violent expressions of conflict.

By the end of Helsinki, on July 10, 1992, problems with the CFE Treaty resulting from the breakup of the Soviet Union into the three Baltic states and twelve other successor states had been resolved, with the relevant states (Armenia, Azerbaijan, Belarus, Georgia, Kazakhstan, Moldova, Russia, and

Ukraine) accepting a redistribution of the obligations incurred by the former USSR. By that time, although Armenia, Belarus, Kazakhstan, and Russia had yet to ratify the CFE,[26] "all states parties signed the Provisional Application of the CFE Treaty, which brought the Treaty provisionally into force" (Sharp, 1993, p. 598).[27] The followup to the CFE negotiations, the CFE-1A Talks, dealing with personnel limitations, produced an agreement that was signed in Helsinki on July 10, 1992 as well.[28]

Also at Helsinki, the CSCE participating states decided to continue the momentum generated, in part, by the CSBMs and CFE negotiations, by combining them into one set of negotiations: the CSCE *Forum for Security Cooperation* (FSC), which began in Vienna on September 22, 1992 (see *CSCE Helsinki Document 1992*, Chapter V). The FSC is

> less concerned with negotiating force reductions than with establishing a *continuing dialogue* on security perceptions and policies, not least the military's role in a democracy. High on the agenda [was] the negotiation of [the] code of conduct ... prescrib[ing] limits on a government's use of force on its own territory [which was later agreed upon as part of the Budapest CSCE 1994 decisions; see below]. (Walker, 1993b, p. 110; emphasis added)

Attempting to further develop CSCE capabilities for the peaceful settlement of disputes, the participating states also decided at Helsinki to convene a meeting at Geneva, from October 12 to 23, 1992, to work toward the creation of a CSCE *Conciliation and Arbitration Court*, enhancing the Valletta Mechanism and establishing "a CSCE procedure for conciliation, including directed conciliation" (*CSCE Helsinki Document 1992*, Ch. 3, p. 24). By the time the fifth CSCE review conference and accompanying CSCE summit concluded in Budapest, in December 1994, the *Convention on Conciliation and Arbitration* had come into force.[29]

Decisions taken at the Budapest CSCE summit on December 5–6, 1994 included, among others: (a) the CSCE becoming the body of *first resort* for dealing with conflicts, "a primary instrument for early warning, conflict prevention and crisis management in the region"; (b) agreement on a *Code of Conduct on Politico-Military Aspects of Security*, setting forth guidelines for the "role of armed forces in democratic societies"; (c) agreement on the "political will to provide, with an appropriate resolution from the [UN] Security Council, a multinational peacekeeping force [for Nagorno-Karabakh] following agreement among the parties for cessation of the armed conflict"; and (d) as of January 1, 1995, "the CSCE [being] known as the Organization for Security and Cooperation in Europe (OSCE)" (*CSCE Budapest Document 1994*, "Budapest Summit Declaration" and "Budapest Decisions," Chapters I, II, IV).[30] An agreement on confidence- and security-building measures (CSBMs Vienna Document, 1994) was adopted at Budapest as well: "Together with many additions and improvements, completely new texts [were] added, for instance the annual exchange of information on defence planning, to be given not later than two months after the adoption of the defence budget" (*CSCE '94*, no. 4, p. 10).

This is rather impressive, especially the "historical first" for the CSCE: agreeing in principle to provide a peace-keeping force to help maintain the negative peace, in effect since May 12, 1994, between the Armenian and Azerbaijani parties to the Nagorno-Karabakh war. However, at least two developments dampen the enthusiasm one might otherwise experience upon reviewing the results of CSCE Budapest: (a) the CSCE representatives could not agree on either a common position or common policy on the war in Bosnia-Hercegovina; and (b) slightly less than a week after the conclusion of the Budapest CSCE summit, on December 11, 1994, Russia initiated its disastrous war against Chechnya.

Taken together with (then) CSCE Secretary General Wilhelm Höynck's (1994a, p. 5) observation that "to date none of the CSCE's procedures for the peaceful settlement of disputes [including the Valletta Mechanism] has been used by the participating States," the CSCE's overall efforts to plug the "Hobbesian black hole of international anarchy" may reflect more illusion than reality. Their potential has not been fully realized because of, among other reasons: (a) the lack of "political will" to make difficult decisions, e.g. regarding the wars in former Yugoslavia; (b) the existence of competitive (*interblocking* instead of *interlocking*) relations between the CSCE and other international organizations, e.g. the UN (see Sandole, 1994a, 1995a); and (c) the resolution-inhibiting aspects of the conflicts themselves, e.g. the *interaction-effects* of "history" and recent brutalities on parties' willingness to continue fighting to "settle" the conflict on the battlefield.

In addition, the "temporal immaturity" and jurisdiction of the new CSCE institutions and processes have rendered them relatively impotent in either preventing or otherwise dealing with violent ethnic conflicts in post-Cold War Europe. At the time of the Geneva meeting on national minorities in July 1991, for instance, the first round of the Yugoslavian wars had begun. The new CSCE institutions and processes were either nonexistent (e.g. the HCNM) or not sufficiently developed (e.g. the CPC, ODIHR) to be of any use: they were, and in some cases still are, "too" new.

Except for those few cases where the new mechanisms deal specifically with relations *within* CSCE participating states (e.g. the Moscow Mechanism and the HCNM), the CSCE – now the OSCE – deals with relations *between* member states. This is a major example of Muzafer Sherif's (1967) "heavy hand of the past," in this case the sovereignty-protecting tradition of international law. Although there have been some attempts at "paradigm-shifting" on this issue,[31] the CSCE/OSCE and other international governmental organizations (IGOs) have been, and in some significant ways remain, *irrelevant* to what has been occurring in Bosnia-Hercegovina, Chechnya, and elsewhere in Eastern Europe and the former Soviet Union. This potentially fatal flaw has been a major challenge facing the architects of peace and security in post-Cold War Europe.

The situation has not improved dramatically with the "reinvention" of the CSCE as the OSCE. The results of the OSCE summit at Lisbon during December 1996, for example, were basically uninspiring, in part because of a lack of consensus on how to frame efforts to deal with the Nagorno-Karabakh conflict. One possible exception to an otherwise lackluster final document was the *Lisbon Declaration on a Common and Comprehensive Security Model for Europe for the Twenty-first Century*, comprising, among other things, a *Platform for Cooperative Security* which would define "modalities for cooperation between the OSCE and other security organizations," and a *Charter on European Security* (see *OSCE Lisbon Document 1996*; CSCE Commission, 1997b).

Enhancing Conflict Resolution: A "Track-2" Complement to "Track-1"

As part of its good offices, the CSO could have drawn – and since Budapest 1994, its successor, the Senior Council, could still draw – upon national and international *nongovernmental* (i.e. *track-2*) conflict resolution resources to assist in dealing with the violent ethnic conflicts taking place in post-Cold War Europe. Track-2 attempts to get a constructive dialogue going between conflicting parties, often in situations where *track-1 governmental* processes have failed to do so (see Davidson and Montville, 1981/2; Montville, 1990a; Volkan *et al.*, 1991a, b; McDonald and Bendahmane, 1987; Diamond and McDonald, 1996). A major objective of such dialogues is to substitute *problem-solving* conflict resolution for confrontation, cooperative for competitive processes (see Burton, 1969, 1979, 1990a; Burton and Dukes, 1990; Deutsch, 1973; Fisher and Keashly, 1991; Kelman, 1986, 1991; Mitchell and Banks, 1996).

Track-2 processes could be used in the short term to help avert or reduce and terminate hostilities (negative peace), and in the middle to long term to facilitate the collaborative solving of problems underlying violent conflict situations and reconciliation among the parties (positive peace). In either case, parties to conflicts would have to invite second-track practitioners to enter their "space" as third parties (e.g. facilitators) to assist them in establishing and maintaining collaborative processes, complementing and/or linking up with corresponding track-1 processes (of, for example, the UN, OSCE, EU, and NATO) whenever appropriate and possible.

The number of possible practitioners of problem-solving conflict resolution is growing.[32] Their names could be included in the registers of qualified candidates maintained by the CPC for the Valletta Mechanism and by the ODIHR for the Moscow Mechanism and the HCNM. Through the good offices of the OSCE, EU, UN, or others, these practitioners could be made available to conflicting parties considering use of any of the various OSCE mechanisms for conflict prevention or peaceful settlement of disputes.[33]

The promise (and corresponding hypothesis) of the second-track option is that effective collaboration between the OSCE (and other IGOs) and nongovernmental conflict resolution resources could enhance the prospects for originally "local" conflicts to be dealt with to the satisfaction of all concerned, thereby preventing them from spilling over to neighboring and other areas within and outside the OSCE.

The New European Peace and Security System

Given the theory articulated in Chapter 6 and the utility of track-2 mechanisms argued here, one approach to such collaboration – for dealing effectively with ethnic conflict in former Yugoslavia and preventing "future Yugoslavias" elsewhere – can be found in the *new European peace and security system* (NEPSS) (see Sandole, 1993d, 1995b, 1998). NEPSS is a model for a post-Cold War peace and security system in Europe that calls for making use of, and integrating, existing institutions and mechanisms within the overall context of the OSCE.[34] OSCE plays a pivotal role in NEPSS because, in addition to its (now) 55 participating states, representing all of the former Cold War adversaries and the neutral and nonaligned (NNA), its traditional three "basket" structure provides a basis for integrating existing European and trans-Atlantic institutions and processes into interdependent components of a post-Cold War peace and security system:

Basket 1 (security in general; political/ military dimension in particular)	NATO/NACC [EAPC]/ Partnership for Peace, WEU, CIS
Basket 2 (economic dimension)	EU/EFTA
Basket 3 (human dimension)	Council of Europe

Western organizations corresponding to each of these three "baskets" have, in recent years, been reaching out to former adversaries in the East, if not to explicitly encourage their membership, then certainly to otherwise liaise and collaborate with them in heretofore unprecedented ways, which augurs well for their membership later on. Under Basket 1, for instance, the North Atlantic Treaty Organization (NATO) has been collaborating with its former adversaries, first in the form of the North Atlantic Cooperation Council (NACC), then the Partnership for Peace (PfP), and, more recently, the Euro-Atlantic Partnership Council (EAPC), which has replaced the NACC.

The NACC was created at the NATO Rome summit of November 7–8, 1991, to facilitate consultations and cooperation in security matters among the former Cold War adversaries (see NATO Rome Summit, 1991). It represented a concretization of sentiments expressed in the *Joint Declaration* of the Paris CSCE summit, furthering the paradigm shift from competitive (*national* security) to cooperative (*common* security) processes.[35]

The PfP, created at the NATO Brussels summit of January 10–11, 1994, is open to all members of the OSCE, and not just, as in the case of NACC, to the former Cold War adversaries. The PfP builds upon NACC (and the paradigm shift) by inviting the neutral and nonaligned (NNA) to join with NATO and the former WTO countries in developing a common security system through bilateral arrangements between NATO and each partner country for, among others, joint planning, training and exercises to facilitate PfP participation in peace-keeping, search and rescue, humanitarian, and other operations.[36] PfP also encourages the expectation that membership will ultimately lead to entry into an expanding and, undoubtedly, "reinvented" NATO (see NATO Brussels Summit, 1994): a source of concern to Russians who feel that, notwithstanding their membership in the partnership, eventual NATO membership does not apply to them, and who, in any case, still define NATO in Cold War terms.

At its July 8–9, 1997 summit in Madrid, NATO invited three former WTO members – the Czech Republic, Hungary, and Poland – to negotiate entry into NATO. Given Russian sensitivities to NATO "enlargement" (*expansion*),[37] the Madrid invitation was preceded by the *Founding Act on Mutual Relations, Cooperation and Security between [NATO] and the Russian Federation*, signed in Paris on May 27, 1997, which effectively allows a Russian voice, but not a veto, in NATO deliberations. Madrid was also preceded by a meeting on May 29 of NATO foreign ministers in Sintra, Portugal, establishing the Euro-Atlantic Partnership Council (EAPC), which succeeded and went beyond the NACC, and enhances the PfP, by promising to "bring NATO and its Partners even closer together with more intensive military exercises, planning, consultations and other activities" (White, 1997, p. 13). Together with the NATO–Ukraine Charter, also agreed to at Sintra and signed at Madrid, these developments have furthered the "paradigm shift" from national to common security (see AP, 1997; *OSCE Newsletter*, 1997; *OSCE Review*, 1997).[38]

The *European Union* (EU) is the premier organization for facilitating realization of the goals implicit in the OSCE's Basket 2 emphasis on promoting "economic and social progress and the improvement of the conditions of life" (CSCE Helsinki Final Act, 1975, p. 89). Despite crises over the Maastricht Treaty on European Union (e.g. see Levinson *et al.*, 1992), the EU has been pursuing the further development of a "common economic space", e.g. negotiations between the (then) European Community (EC) and the *European Free Trade Association* (EFTA) during 1989–92, to create a *European Economic Area* (EEA), "which was to come into force on 1 January 1993 and include 19 countries" (*Europe in Figures*, 1995, p. 24), representing "the world's biggest and wealthiest single market [380 million population]" (Drozdiak, 1991):[39]

> [This] agreement breaking down the barriers between the remaining economic blocs in Western Europe also is expected to accelerate the process of eventually incorporating the impoverished new democracies in the eastern part of the continent. . . .
>
> Jacques Delors, the [former] president of the [then] EC's executive commission, [has] said . . . that the Community may include as many as 30 member states in the future.

The EU, therefore, is very likely to take in additional members,[40] including states which were formerly adversaries, e.g. those involved in the *Pact on Stability in Europe*: Bulgaria, the Czech Republic, Estonia, Hungary, Latvia, Lithuania, Poland, Romania and Slovakia (see Helenius, 1995). Indeed, at its summit meeting in Luxembourg in December 1997, the EU invited the three candidates for NATO membership – the Czech Republic, Hungary, and Poland – one other Pact country, Estonia, plus Slovenia and Cyprus, to begin to negotiate entry into the EU. In addition:

> the EU will . . . be working closely with another five states that have expressed an interest in joining the union: Bulgaria, Latvia, Lithuania, Romania and Slovakia [the remaining Pact countries]. These states will be

offered expanded political and economic assistance from the EU with an eye toward eventual membership (*The Week in Germany*, 1997, p. 1).[41]

Reflecting, in part, the assumption that increases in living standards in these and other areas will undermine some of the factors that encourage the violent expression of ethnic and other conflicts, Walker (1993a, p. 50) suggests that "As the [EU] gradually encompasses many of Europe's new democracies at least in closer association arrangements, and some of them as full members, it could become the most important European organization for mitigating ethnic tensions."[42]

The humanitarian objectives associated with Basket 3 are to further:

> the spiritual enrichment of the human personality without distinction as to race, sex, language or religion, [through] increased cultural and educational exchanges, broader dissemination of information, contacts between people, and the solution of humanitarian problems. (CSCE Helsinki Final Act, 1975, p. 113)

The realization of these goals is meant to occur "in full respect for the principles guiding relations among participating states," listed as part of Basket 1, where Principle VII deals with "Respect for human rights and fundamental freedoms, including the freedom of thought, conscience, religion or belief"; and Principle VIII, "Equal rights and self-determination of peoples" (*ibid.*, pp. 80–1).[43]

The *Council of Europe* (COE), which "makes being a functioning democracy a condition of membership" (Walker, 1993a, pp. 47–8), has been instrumental in achieving these goals:

> In considering applications for membership the Council conducts detailed examinations of national and local government laws, regulations and behavior to ensure conformity not only with electoral, police, judicial and civil service practices of member states, but also with the European Convention on Human Rights. The Council also offers extensive information, training programmes and practical help to enable aspiring members to meet its standards, as well as to understand the practical problems of enforcing the European Convention on Human Rights [through the European Court of Human Rights which renders binding judgements on members' compliance with the Convention].[44]

The actual or potential expansion of, among others, NATO, the EU, and the Council of Europe within the framework of the OSCE is compatible with a major feature of NEPSS: *no one* – ethnic and other groups within states as well as states themselves (*including* the Russian Federation) – should be left out in terms of systems designed to enhance the political/military, economic/environmental, and humanitarian/human rights dimensions of overall security. For post-Cold War Europe to "work," therefore, it must reflect, *for all concerned*, "peace, security *and* justice" (CSCE Helsinki Final Act, 1975, p. 77 and passim; emphasis added): to leave any party outside the "European house" would be to ensure that they have no stake in preserving it; worse, to encourage them to try to burn it down!

So far, so good, but as articulated thus far, NEPSS is basically a model for an *inter*state peace and security system: the existing institutions and processes it would integrate in terms of OSCE's three "baskets" are basically interstate international governmental organizations. As such, it would merely perpetuate international "business as usual." Hence, NEPSS also needs something that deals with the *intra*state level, e.g. issues involving minority relations with dominant ingroups *within* states. This is where *integrated systems of conflict resolution networks*, encompassing track-2 as well as track-1 mechanisms and processes, enter the picture.

"Integrated systems of conflict resolution networks" comprise vertical as well as horizontal dimensions (see Sandole, 1993c, 1995b, 1998; Lund, 1996, Chapters 4 and 5). *Vertical integration* involves systems of conflict prevention, management, settlement, resolution, and provention/transformation operating, for instance, at levels somewhat similar to those in our multilevel framework and theory – local, societal, subregional, regional (EU/WEU, COE, NATO/EAPC/PfP, CIS, OSCE), and global (UN) – with track-2 (nongovernmental) mechanisms complementing track-1 (governmental) processes whenever possible. The premise here is, just as the causes and conditions of a violent conflict can be found at different levels, so an effective response to such a conflict would have to take into account factors at those levels as well.

Hence, following early warning of a developing conflict within the OSCE area that could spread to other levels, appropriate track-1 and track-2 conflict resolution resources could be brought together – perhaps by the HCNM assisted by a track-2 NGO (e.g. the *Foundation on Inter-Ethnic Relations*: see Zaagman and Thorburn, 1997) – to deal with the conflict at its initial ("local") level of incidence/observation, but including communication and collaboration with, and resources from, other levels as well, such that the conflict does not spill over to any of them. As Michael Lund (1996), anticipating the OSCE's "Platform for Cooperative Security" (*OSCE Lisbon Document 1996*), puts it:

> the international community needs to think in terms of appropriate *divisions of labor* and *complementarities* (p. 144). . . . The *vertical division of labor* . . . would be achieved by pushing explicit direct responsibility and accountability downward . . . to the parties to the conflicts themselves and to subregional and regional actors. At the same time, extralocal and extraregional states and the [UN] would provide appropriate facilitative, technical, political, and (if necessary) military support. (p. 183; emphasis added)

That both track 1 (e.g. military support) and track 2 may be necessary for dealing with protracted ethnic conflicts applies as well to the second component of integrated systems of conflict resolution networks: *horizontal integration*. For NEPSS to succeed, it should also include an "embedded" *Realpolitik* option for use as part of a larger whole consisting primarily of *Idealpolitik* measures and processes, to move to, but then beyond, negative, and toward positive peace. For instance, track-1 peace-keeping forces, representing the UN, the OSCE, or at least something approaching a "representative sample" of the EAPC/PfP, might, under very clear conditions, enter a war zone to effect and/or enforce a negative peace, as a necessary (but clearly not sufficient) condition for moving toward positive peace. Such clear conditions should include the attempted imposition by one party of a genocidal "final solution" on another. In the event, the objectives of the peace-keeping operation would not include a "Balkan Storm," the bombing of civilian centers, and the killing of tens of thousands in order to "win," or to "impose solutions," or – what is, in any case, impossible – to "solve" (through *military* means) the conflict, but (a) to prevent genocide, (b) to permit international relief operations to get through to threatened populations, and (c) to separate the warring factions in order to afford them a "cooling-off" opportunity, as a necessary (but again, not sufficient) condition of collaborative resolution of the conflict they have been expressing through violent means.

What might the horizontal dimension of integrated systems look like, especially in comparison with the way force has traditionally been used by the international community? Sir Brian Urquhart (1991b) provides some insight in this regard:

> At the moment, the U.N. has basically two military options. The first is *traditional peacekeeping* – that is, forces that can only be deployed after a cease-fire is in place, that are accepted by the parties to the conflict and that may only use force in self-defense. The second option is a *large-scale collective enforcement action* like that in Korea in 1950 or, under Chapter VII of the Charter, in Kuwait in 1991 – both under the leadership of the United States.
>
> *A third category of international military operation is needed*, somewhere between peacekeeping [Chapter VI] and large-scale enforcement [Chapter VII]. It would be intended to put an end to random violence and to *provide a reasonable degree of peace and order so that humanitarian relief work could go forward and a conciliation process could commence.* The forces involved would be relatively small, *representatively international* and would not have military objectives as such. *But, unlike [traditional] peacekeeping forces, such troops would be required to take, initially at least, certain combat risks in bringing the violence under control.* They would essentially be armed police actions. (Emphasis added)

"The aim [of the third option]," Urquhart continues, "would be to enable the Security Council [under Article 43 of the Charter] to deploy an international force quickly in a situation where the *cycle of violence could not be broken except by firm intervention.* Such a situation [has existed] in Somalia and . . . in Yugoslavia" (*ibid.*; emphasis added). But the need transcends these two cases:

> The unraveling of national sovereignty seems to be a feature of the post-cold war period. In more and more situations, *only firm and even-handed intervention from the outside is likely to put an end to self-perpetuating bloodshed* and the progressive ruin of once peaceful societies.
>
> Can the United Nations do something to meet this challenge? Or must the world continue to stand by and watch the carnage on television? (*ibid.*, emphasis added)

In terms of the language employed in this study, Urquhart's message is clear:

mechanisms or procedures *other* than (or at least in addition to) currently existing ones are required for situations where *conflicts-as-startup conditions* have been overtaken by escalating *conflicts-as-process*, with quasi-deterministic lives of their own; where the combatants, in negatively self-fulfilling fashion, endeavor to impose violent, often "final" solutions on one another.[45]

But there is a potential "fatal flaw" here: unless Urquhart's option for negative peace, or any other embodiment of the horizontal dimension, establishes the conditions for positive peace, leading to resolution of the conflicts which have been violently pursued, a peace-keeping operation (traditionally or otherwise defined) might constitute merely a holding operation that could collapse "back into history" at any time: violence, no matter how justifiable on humanitarian and other grounds, may serve merely to stimulate further violence. For these and other reasons, many in the conflict resolution community, who are, in any case, committed to nonviolent alternatives to the traditional means associated with *Realpolitik*, would have difficulties with Urquhart's proposition in particular and the horizontal dimension in general.

Reprehensible though even a "writ small" rendering of *Realpolitik* may be, however, it is, at least for me, *less* reprehensible than watching various degrees of genocide being played out or otherwise reported on television without doing anything to stop the slaughter. Less viscerally, as part of a larger, *Idealpolitik*-oriented package, a "judicious" amount of *Realpolitik* is compatible with current thinking among other track-1 and track-2 researchers and/or practitioners than Urquhart. In Fisher and Keashly's (1991, p. 36) *contingency model of third party intervention*, for example:

> the overall strategy ... is to intervene with the appropriate third party method at the appropriate time in order to de-escalate the conflict. ... This is potentially accomplished by initially *matching a particular intervention to a specific stage* and then by combining further interventions, if necessary, in appropriate sequences, to further de-escalate the conflict. (Emphasis added)

At the fourth and final stage of conflict escalation in Fisher and Keashly's model, *destruction*, the corresponding appropriate intervention is *peace-keeping*. At this stage,

> the conflict has escalated to [a "fight":] the point where the parties attempt to destroy each other. ... The third party strategy of choice at this point is that of peace-keeping, a power intervention designed to assist in the separation of the parties and the control of the violence. ... When the interaction between the parties can be stabilized and some initial commitment to joint effort can be obtained, the path is cleared for other third party interventions. (*Ibid.*, p. 39)

John Vasquez (1993, p. 289) has thought along similar lines: "A successful peace system will have several accepted channels for resolving issues and rules that tell actors *which channel to use at what stage of contention*" (emphasis added). Also, according to former OSCE Secretary General Wilhelm Höynck (1994a, p. 4):

> the response to emerging conflict must be gradual. *The action taken should at every stage be commensurate with the magnitude of the problem and adequate to the nature of the risks.* Low-key, advisory and fully co-operative instruments should in general precede more intensive political pressure. Discreet diplomacy or public condemnation, delicate persuasion or clear-cut ultimate, co-operation or confrontation can present very delicate choices when it comes to finding the *right means for preventing existing disputes from escalating into conflicts and for containing conflicts before they spread.* (Emphasis added)

Jennone Walker, former Special Assistant to President Clinton and Senior Director for Europe on the National Security Staff, put it this way (1993b, pp. 105, 115):

> perhaps [the] most important guideline is that neither hard nor soft mediation is likely to be successful if it only consists of diplomats proposing solutions and urging reasoned compromise. *Mediation efforts must be supported by a combination of political, economic and military muscle* that promises (or threatens) an effective mix of pain and gain. . . . [But it] cannot be emphasized too strongly that the *credible threat of economic or military action should be an aid to mediation, not an alternative to it.* (Emphasis added)

Michael Lund (1996, p. 154) summarizes this overlap in track-1/track-2, researcher/practitioner thinking as follows:

> Preventive diplomacy thus . . . needs to be modulated, not only from place to place but also as a single conflict situation evolves. The sequence over time in which *coercive* and/or *conciliatory* or positive inducements are used is therefore important. *Elements of both may need to be present at every stage of a conflict* but their relative proportions within a particular "preventive package" may well have to be graduated as a dispute intensifies. (Emphasis added)[46]

As this volume approached completion, the wars in former Yugoslavia stopped, with overall grim statistics including "300,000 people . . . killed and countless more 'ethnically cleansed' from land and homes they had lived in for generations" (Elliott, 1998). Following debacles such as the fall of the UN "safe areas" of Srebrenica and Zepa in July 1995, negative peace has been achieved, at least temporarily, precisely because of mediation efforts (the U.S.-led Holbrooke mission) supported by "military muscle" (the NATO bombing of Bosnian Serb positions), culminating in the Dayton (and related) agreements of November–December 1995 (see Holbrooke, 1998).

In addition to the "Erdut Agreement" – the *Basic Agreement on Eastern Slavonia, Baranja and Western Sirmium* (1995) – whereby Serbia agreed "to the peaceful restoration of Croatian sovereignty in Eastern Slavonia over a two year period" (Gutman, 1995, p. 6),[47] the "Dayton Peace Accords" – the *General Framework Agreement for Peace in Bosnia and Herzegovina* (1995) – called for, among other things, the replacement of UNPROFOR by a U.S.-led NATO

"Implementation Force" (IFOR) – subsequently succeeded by a "Stabilization Force" (SFOR) – to police the separation of the parties while the political and economic reconstruction of Bosnia-Hercegovina got underway.

While we should not be too quick to be critical of a process that has halted a deplorable genocidal war, at least for the two and one-half years of IFOR's and SFOR's combined tenure in Bosnia-Hercegovina,[48] there is at least one problem with Dayton in addition to the clearly unrealistic time lines: although the horizontal, *Realpolitik* dimension – the NATO-maintained negative peace – has been proceeding fairly well, it has not been matched by equal success along the *Idealpolitik* front, which would include the vertical dimension to optimize prospects for achieving positive peace.

Important elements relevant to positive peace have, however, been incorporated into Dayton: (a) a High Representative responsible for the civilian-led reconstruction of Bosnia-Hercegovina and (b) the OSCE Mission to Bosnia-Hercegovina, responsible for the preparation, conduct, and monitoring of elections, monitoring of compliance with human rights provisions, and the facilitation of negotiations dealing with confidence- and security-building measures (CSBMs) and arms control (see *OSCE Review*, 1995c). But former High Representative (and earlier Swedish prime minister) Carl Bildt lamented the international community's lack of enthusiasm to provide the vast resources his office required to do its job (Whitney, 1996):

> "The popular perception is that after the elections, we go home because it's all over," Mr. Bildt said. But on the civilian side, work has barely begun on the hardest tasks – organizing elections, rebuilding shattered homes, roads and power lines, and organizing the return of 2.2 million refugees. And unless there are signs of success soon, all the billions of dollars that went into the NATO achievement could be money down the drain.
>
> "We need money," he said. "We don't have the money. The election is not funded. Refugee returns are not funded. There are an estimated 3 million uncleared mines scattered all across the country. More than 60 percent of all housing units are damaged, and 18 percent are destroyed. All of these problems will take many years and a lot of money to solve, and I don't see where it's coming from."

Some improvement in the funding of the reconstruction of Bosnia occurred at a "high-level conference of donors [meeting] in Brussels on April 12 and 13 [1996]" (*ibid.*), where

> Representatives of 50 countries [attending the] two-day conference, at which the World Bank and European Union played host, pledged $1.23 billion, while vowing to accelerate the flow of aid in coming months so that the Bosnian people will be able to reap tangible peace dividends by the time elections are held in early September. (Drozdiak, 1996)

But financing is only part, albeit a significant part, of the overall reconstruction of Bosnia. All the money necessary to fulfill the tasks outlined by Carl Bildt, plus the creation of jobs for the "250,000 soldiers being demobilized in ...

Bosnia-Herzegovina," as urged at the donors' conference by World Bank president James Wolfensohn (Friedman, 1996), might count for little if meaningful *reconciliation* does not take place among the warring parties.[49] As Bildt (1996) has said, "Bosnia is one of the most bitterly divided societies there has ever been, and its task in achieving reconciliation will be immense."

Elaborating on this point in a way reminiscent of Richard Rose's (1971) account of the fusion of past and present in Northern Ireland, and the role of this dynamic in the "legacy of Kosovo," John Pomfret (1995, p. A34) tells us:

> One of the most striking things about the Balkans today is the *power of the past in everyday life*. Most conversations begin with a history lesson. This is because, psychologically, Yugoslavia, like much of the region, was locked in a deep freeze during 45 years of Communist rule – questions about ethnic rivalries were suppressed by Tito to keep the country together. As a result, they remained unresolved and the *mentality of Balkan warriors in 1995 is little different than it was in 1945*. . . .
>
> The last four years, however, have added another legacy of violence . . . that one war crimes investigator described as "possessing an almost intimate brutality." So just as the unresolved legacy of World War II helped fuel the post-Communist outbreak of war, this new toll of violence and suffering has created bitterness that could be used to fire future battles. (Emphasis added)[50]

The intensity of these aggravated grievances (conflict-as-startup conditions) is unlikely to abate after only two-to-three years of enforced negative peace (suppressed conflict-as-process), especially given Carl Bildt's fears "that governments attending the donors' conference might not come up with the remaining $1.2 billion of the $1.8 billion that is needed this year" (Friedman, 1996). Hence, prior to the termination of IFOR in December 1996,

> The Pentagon . . . offered its grimmest assessment to date of the prospects for peace in Bosnia, warning that without an enormous international aid program to rebuild its economy and political institutions the country will probably fragment after the withdrawal of NATO peacekeeping troops late this year. . . . the civilian reconstruction effort there is barely under way [and the] economy and physical infrastructure [are] still in ruins. . . . [Also,] the strategic goals of the warring factions [have] not fundamentally changed since the days of the civil war and . . . tensions among them [will] probably grow in the months leading up to the NATO pullout. (Shenon, 1996)

Despite – or, perhaps, because of – national and local elections and other developments, the situation in Bosnia remains much the same as of this writing, prior to the termination of SFOR in June 1998 (see Drozdiak, 1997a; Hockstader, 1997b; Ryan, 1997).

Accordingly, in terms of Boutros-Ghali's (1992) categories of intervention, Dayton represents for Bosnia-Hercegovina fairly successful *peace-making* (both military (the NATO bombing) and political (Holbrooke's mission)) and *peace-keeping* (NATO's IFOR and SFOR), with, as of this writing, *peace-building* lagging far behind. *Operationally* speaking, therefore, Dayton is a track-1/*Realpolitik*-only agreement in search of a track-2/*Idealpolitik* component. And that is part of the challenge for the international community: to design such a component, initially within the context of existing arrangements such as the OSCE Mission's Coordinating Group and the High Representative's Joint Civilian Commission (see *OSCE Newsletter*, 1996, p. 8).

The other part of the challenge is to persuade the Americans, Europeans, and others to keep a credible, effective peace-keeping force in Bosnia beyond any politically motivated, unrealistically short time lines – long enough to ensure that negative peace holds.[51] Bosnia is a clear case of where negative peace is a necessary (but not sufficient) condition of positive peace. The reconstruction of Bosnia – in emotional/reconciliative as well as physical/economic terms – will take years, and an appropriate peace-keeping force should stay long enough to ensure that the job gets done.

Conclusion

This chapter set out to explore answers to five questions, the first of which was: given the theory presented in Chapter 6, what are some of the likely causes and conditions of violent ethnic conflict in Europe, especially the brutal wars in former Yugoslavia? We have mentioned some possible examples of conflict-as-startup conditions, e.g. frustrated basic needs for, among others, identity, esteem, and security, often experienced as victimhood and fear of group extinction, one response to which is role defense-based aggression. We have also mentioned conflict-as-process, which, via the negative rendition of the self-fulfilling prophecy (NSFP), tends toward self-stimulating/self-perpetuating conflict spirals. Once a manifest conflict process (MCP) has escalated, via competitive means, to a violent conflict-as-process – an AMCP or a "fight" – it no longer matters what the startup conditions were because then the conflict is kept alive by its own dynamics (*Eigendynamik*).

The second question was: what are some of the likely consequences of the continuation of these violent ethnic conflicts? In a word, "spillover": to other parts within the original conflict-affected areas; to neighboring countries; and to other areas worldwide. The asymmetrical relationship between the outcomes of *Realpolitik* and *Idealpolitik* measures and the unrealistic deadlines associated with the implementation of the Dayton Peace Accords suggest that the wars in Bosnia-Hercegovina could start up again and spill over to other areas within former Yugoslavia (Kosovo,[52] Macedonia) and neighboring countries (Albania, Hungary, Romania, Bulgaria, Greece, Turkey), and, in general, contaminate other levels of the human decision-making environment, especially in the former Soviet Union, making violent means for dealing with conflict – "lethal conflict management" – more rather than less likely.

The third question was: why have existing institutions and processes, especially those associated with the principal regional security actor, the CSCE/OSCE, proven to be ineffective in either preventing or otherwise dealing with these violent conflicts? The Conflict Prevention Centre, the

Procedure for the Peaceful Settlement of Disputes (the Valletta Mechanism), the Human Dimension Mechanism (the Moscow Mechanism), and the High Commissioner on National Minorities are, along with the OSCE peace-keeping provision, all on the right track. However, the potential of these mechanisms has not been fully realized, in part because of: (a) the absence of political will on the part of the international community to deal comprehensively and effectively with the wars in former Yugoslavia; (b) the absence of effective collaboration between the OSCE and other international governmental organizations (e.g. the UN); and (c) the absence of track-1/track-2 collaboration and new approaches to peace-keeping (Urquhart's "third option") to deal specifically with the resolution-inhibiting aspects of the conflicts themselves. In addition, the mechanisms themselves are "too new" and "respectful of state sovereignty," rendering them impotent in the face of, and basically irrelevant to, the core conflicts in former Yugoslavia and elsewhere.[53]

The fourth question was: how can these institutions and processes be made more effective in dealing with these conflicts? And the fifth was: what else can, or should, be done to deal with these manifestations of the "New World Disorder" in Europe? Given the (threatened or actual) violent ethnic conflicts in Europe and elsewhere, it is clear that state governments and international governmental organizations *alone* are ill-equipped to deal with them. Within the context of the new European peace and security system (NEPSS), however, especially the vertical dimension of integrated systems of conflict resolution networks, track-2 mechanisms and processes can complement and link up with track-1 to enhance the probability of dealing effectively with developing conflicts (preventive diplomacy), preventing spillover (*Idealpolitik* peace-making, peace-keeping) and achieving positive peace (peace-building). If the effective use of track-2 is held hostage by hostilities, the threat of genocide, or other humanitarian imperatives, then the horizontal dimension of integrated systems can become operational to forcibly separate the parties (*Realpolitik* peace-making, peace-keeping) in order to facilitate achieving negative peace as a necessary (but again, not sufficient) condition of positive peace.

But, recalling Rapoport's (1974, p. 133) comment that problems arise "when the behavior of large systems seems to be determined by *quasi-mechanical* interactions that do not reflect any goals or purposes, not even of the systems" (emphasis added), how can *Realpolitik* be used to deal with self-stimulating/self-perpetuating conflict processes without making matters worse? Although Brian Urquhart (1991b) was probably correct in his assessment that former Yugoslavia was a "situation where the cycle of violence [could not] be broken except by firm intervention," how can *Realpolitik* continue to be applied there in the absence of resources to support an overall *Idealpolitik* strategy, without conducing to a new round of war?

Also, even if negative peace can be maintained, other interventions designed to improve the relationship in order to move toward positive peace may not be possible, at least not in the foreseeable future. Early in the Bosnian war, combat veteran David Hackworth (1992) observed that, "viewed from almost any angle, [it] makes no sense at all. ... This is indiscriminate violence and mindless slaughter. ... After fighting like this, the only thing sure to survive is hatred."

Malcolm Chalmers (1993, p. 432) agrees: " 'ethnic cleansing' by Croatian and Serbian forces in Bosnia will produce a legacy of bitterness and continued conflict far into the future." Mostar, in many ways a microcosm of the rest of Bosnia-Hercegovina, is a case in point: former enemies and current federation "allies," the Bosnian Croats and Bosnian Muslims, have not been able to put their recent past behind them, despite a fairly significant amount of European Union investment in administering and resurrecting the divided city (see Fitchett, 1996): their "mutual bitterness is as great as that with the Serbs" (Ryan, 1997, p. C2). The brutality of the Russian–Chechen war has created the same problem for the future of Russian and Chechen relations.

Clearly, with Chechnya, the threat of future Yugoslavias has already been realized in the Russian Federation, as anticipated by former Soviet prime minister Nikolai Ryzkhov. In general, although recent research by Peter Wallensteen and his colleagues (see Sollenberg, 1996) and by Ted Robert Gurr (forthcoming) suggests a less bleak future than their studies cited earlier might otherwise indicate,[54] so-called "low intensity conflicts" nevertheless appear to be a trend which is likely to carry us into the twenty-first century. However, rather than replace Clausewitzean interstate wars, as Martin van Creveld (1991) has argued, they may, via spillover, constitute one important factor in their etiology.

The wars in former Yugoslavia and the former Soviet Union have occurred, in large part, because "there [was and] is nothing to prevent them." We have argued in this chapter, however, that this condition need not remain in place indefinitely. The prevention of future Yugoslavias will be dependent on the existence of appropriate mindsets and mechanisms, other supportive environments, and the political will to use the mechanisms. Despite some significant problems, the new European peace and security system (NEPSS) outlined here, with its integrated systems of conflict resolution networks, deserves serious consideration by track-1 and track-2 architects of peace and security in post-Cold War Europe.

Notes

1. As my most recent effort to respond to a "moving target" – peace and security developments in post-Cold War Europe – Chapter 7 represents to varying degrees mergers, revisions, expansions and updating of Sandole (1991, 1992a, b, 1993c, d, 1995b, 1998).
2. This idea clearly inheres in one of the most controversial propositions of the post-Cold War era: Samuel Huntington's (1993, 1996) "Clash of Civilizations" (see CFR, 1993; Barber, 1997/8, for some sense of the debate around this issue).
3. As part of his advocacy of a bipolar (versus a multipolar) international system, Waltz (1979, pp. 208–9) argued, during the Cold War, that "Although we would prefer that East Europeans freely choose their governors, we may nevertheless understand that the Soviet Union's managing a traditionally volatile part of the world has its good points."
4. See Maresca (1985) for an insider's account of the development of the CSCE within the context of the Cold War; Bloed (1993) for an "extensive analysis of the origin,

development and basic features of the Helsinki Process," from 1972 until 1993, with accompanying official documents; and Rotfeld (1997) for an analysis and accompanying documents of the CSCE/OSCE from 1973 to 1996. For discussions of the role of the CSCE/OSCE in the post-Cold War world, see, among others, Lucas (1990, 1993) and Kemp (1996).

5. A "major armed conflict," according to Peter Wallensteen, is "a prolonged combat between the military forces of two or more governments or of one government and organized armed opposition forces, involving the use of manufactured weapons and incurring battle-related deaths of at least 1,000 persons [during the course of the conflict]" (cited in *State of World Conflict Report 1991–1992*, p. 11; also see Wallensteen and Axell, 1993).
6. For background to the Yugoslavian and other conflicts in Eastern Europe see, among others, Borden *et al.* (1992), Bradley (1997), Bromke (1993, pp. 34–6), Csepell (1996), Danforth (1997), Deak (1990), Denitch (1994), Dobbs (1991a), Dragnich and Todorovich (1984), Dragnich (1992, 1996), Elsie (1997), Fine and Donia (1995), Gallagher (1995), Glenny (1993), Griffiths (1993, Chapters 1–3), Gurr (1993, Chapter 7), Gutman (1993), Job (1992), Judah (1997), Kaplan (1993), Kuzmanic and Truger (1992), Lampe (1996), Lukic and Lynch (1996), Magas (1993), Rieff (1995), Ronen (1997), Silber and Little (1997), Stein (1997), Tanner (1997), USIP (1990, 1992a, b), and Woodward (1995).
7. For background to the ethnic conflicts in the former Soviet Union see, among others, Bromke (1993, pp. 36–8), Cox (1991), Dillon (1990), Dobbs (1991a, c), FT (1993), Glynn (1989), Goldman (1990), Griffiths (1993, Chapter 4), Karklins (1986), Lukic and Lynch (1996), Motyl (1995a, b), Nahaylo and Swoboda (1990), Starovoitova (1997), Suny (1996), Tishkov (1997), Tutuncu (1998), Walker (1991), and Wright *et al.* (1996).
8. The literature dealing with ethnic conflict and conflict resolution includes, among others, Bächler (1997), Berberoglu (1995), Boucher, *et al.* (1987), Brown (1993), Brown *et al.* (1997), Carment and James (1997), Coakley (1993), Conner (1994), Enloe (1973), Forbes (1997), Groom (1986), Gurr (1993, forthcoming), Gurr and Harff (1994), Heraclides (1989, 1991), Horowitz (1985), Lapidoth (1997), Montville (1990a), Sisk (1996), and Stavanhagen (1996).
9. Burton clearly captures here the gist of the "cultures of violence" associated with the ethnic conflict in former Yugoslavia, the former Soviet Union and elsewhere in the post-Cold War world.
10. For a survey and critique of Johan Galtung's work, which is associated with these and other concepts, see Peter Lawler (1995).
11. Samuel Huntington's (1993, 1996) work on the "Clash of Civilizations," with its clear ingroup/outgroup distinctions between "us" and "them" – between Western and non-Western (e.g. Confucian and Islamic) civilizations – implies this need: "We know who we are only when we know who we are not and often only when we know whom we are against" (Huntington, 1996, p. 21).
12. In mid-February 1998, as writing of this volume was coming to an end, Morton Abramowitz (1998) warned that: "Every year for the past eight years, articles have been written that Kosovo is about to explode – that mass violence and the expulsion of vast numbers of Albanians are approaching – and that the West has to do something. So far Kosovo has been the dog that has not barked, despite the execrable situation that exists between the province's 1.8 million Albanians and the Belgrade regime. Nevertheless, Kosovo steadily deteriorates. Serb repression increases, and violence in the province is rising. . . . Nobody knows when Kosovo will 'erupt.' But it is clear that one day that will happen, and that day is drawing closer." Some three weeks later, there were ominous signs that the "Kosovo Prophecy" was unfolding, including a brutal Serbian campaign "to stamp out an armed independence movement" (Nordland and Watson, 1998), resulting in "the worst bloodletting in Kosovo this decade" (Spolar, 1998c): "In this

place, the latest Balkan war – and perhaps the most dangerous one – is gathering day by day" (Hockstader, 1998, p. A1). By January 1999, nearly one year later, "Some 2000 Kosovars [had] been killed. Hundreds of thousands ... burned and bombed out of their homes. So many villages have been destroyed that, even under ideal circumstances, it would take years for Kosovo to recover from Mr. Milosevic's depredations" (WP, 1999).

13. By mid-March 1998, following the then recent Serbian "military campaign against ethnic Albanian rebels, ... using helicopter gunships, armored vehicles and heavy artillery to demolish villages and hunt down pro-independence leaders" (Soloway and Stephen, 1998, p. A1), "nerves rather than sabers appear[ed] to be rattling in Albania. No refugees [were] pouring into the country [one of the poorest in Europe] or into neighboring Macedonia, which has a sizable Albanian population" (Spolar, 1998c). Although "Western diplomats fear the ethnic violence [in Kosovo] is spinning out of control and [still] risks destabilizing Albania as well as neighboring Macedonia" (Dinmore, 1998), by January 1999 this had not occurred. Of the up to 300,000 Albanians displaced as refugees by the end of October 1998 (see Loeb, 1998), "Some moved to the Yugoslav republic of Montenegro; others crossed the border into Albania or Macedonia, but most stayed in Kosovo" (WP, 1998d).
14. The Greek blockades of Macedonia occurred during August to December 1992 and February 1994 to September 1995 (Macedonian Embassy, 1996).
15. Two years later, as this volume was nearing completion, Greek–Turkish tensions were again high: "Recently Greece and Turkey have engaged in provocative military maneuvers [in which] both parties violated a six-month-old moratorium on military overflights of Cyprus. More threateningly, Turkish military planes more than once buzzed the C-130 aircraft carrying the Greek defense minister. ... As recently as yesterday [1 January 1998], Greek warships reportedly challenged two Turkish cargo vessels in international waters in the Aegean Sea" (Klarevas, 1998).
16. Misha Glenny (1995, p. 106) disagrees with the proposition that Kosovo would play a pivotal role in such a regional conflict expansion scenario, arguing: "during the Bush administration and the first half of President Clinton's term ... U.S. policymakers appeared to believe that the spark that could light a wider Balkan war was not Macedonia but Kosovo. This was due in part to the misperception that irrational blood lust rather than calculated territorial expansion was the cause of the Balkan conflict. ... Milosevic had no intention of opening up a southern front of military conflict on territory that the Serbs already controlled."
17. By late May 1997, however, "After years of frustrating diplomacy, Russia and Ukraine ... ended their tug-of-war over the Black Sea Fleet" (Gordon, 1997). Nevertheless, at least from the point of view of Ukrainians, Russian–Ukrainian relations continue to reflect, in the words of James Mace, a "gaping, unhealed wound," the result of "Stalin's forced collectivization in the early 1930s in which millions of Ukrainians died. The metaphor of a gaping, unhealed wound could not be more apt for understanding the depth of pain, fear, and hatred a history of unatoned violence creates in a *victimized* people" (Montville, 1993, pp. 112–13). Against the background of this particular *genotypic* "conflict-as-startup condition," therefore, other *phenotypic* issues could threaten to stimulate the development of a "conflict-as-process" between the Russian Federation and Ukraine.
18. The 28 contributors of the 38,130 troops participating in UNPROFOR's missions in Bosnia-Hercegovina, Croatia, and Macedonia as of November 30, 1994, were (in descending order): (1) France, 4493; (2) Britain, 3405; (3) Jordan, 3367; (4) Pakistan, 3017; (5) Canada, 2091; (6) Netherlands, 1803; (7) Malaysia, 1550; (8.5) Russian Federation, 1464; (8.5) Turkey, 1464; (10) Spain, 1267; (11) Bangladesh, 1235; (12) Denmark, 1230; (13) Sweden, 1212; (14) Ukraine, 1147; (15) Poland, 1109; (16) Belgium, 1038; (17) Czech Republic, 971; (18) Kenya, 967; (19) Nepal, 899; (20) Argentina, 854; (21) Norway, 826; (22) U.S.A., 748; (23) Slovak Republic, 582;

(24) Finland, 463; (25) Egypt, 427; (26) New Zealand, 249; (27) Indonesia, 220; and (28) Lithuania, 32. The arrival of the Turkish contingent in 1994 was not without controversy, in part because, "At the peak of the Ottoman Empire, Turkish soldiers occupied parts of the Balkans for more than five centuries" (Pomfret, 1994a). This may be why the Turkish contingent was numerically matched and perhaps "neutralized" by the contingent of one of Turkey's traditional enemies, the pro-Serbian Russians.

19. Russia, as already indicated, tended to speak on behalf of Serbia and the Bosnian Serbs, while Turkey spoke for the Bosnian Muslims as well as Kosovar/Macedonian Albanians.
20. "The fall of Srebrenica," according to Daniel Williams (1996), "was one of the lowest points in the history of international pledges to protect civilians during the 3 and 1/2 year Bosnian war . . . The town was among six designated UN 'safe areas' for refugees; if the Serbs attacked, NATO planes were supposed to bomb. But as the Serbs shelled the town, NATO held back. Srebrenica and nearby Zepa both fell. Women and children were trucked out. Men, however, were left in the hands of the Serbs. . . . About 7,000 men . . . are missing, and most are presumed dead" (also see Honig and Both, 1996).
21. General Lebed (1996) has warned that the "chances are rather high that the [Russian–Chechen] war may resume with fresh force and on an even larger scale." However, on May 12, 1997, Mr Yeltsin and his Chechen counterpart, Aslan Maskhadov, signed a peace treaty formalizing the ceasefire reached some eight months earlier, one objective being "to present a united front against rejectionists who have staged a series of bombing attacks and kidnappings." Yeltsin pledged that both parties would "reject forever the use of force or threat of force" (Hoffman, 1997).
22. According to some estimates, the proportion of Russians in the Russian Federation is 82.6%; Kazakhstan, 38%; Kyrgyzstan, 21.5%; Ukraine, 20.3%; Belarus, 13.2%; Moldova, 12.8%; Turkmenistan, 12.6%; Uzbekistan, 10.8%; Tajikistan, 10.4%; Azerbaijan, 7.9%; Georgia, 7.4%; Armenia, 1.5%; and, in the three Baltic states, Lithuania, 8.6%, Estonia, 30.3%, and Latvia, 33% (CT, 1991; Bromke, 1993, pp. 36–8; Russian Embassy, 1995).
23. A CSCE Parliamentary Assembly was established later, in April 1991 (see *CSCE Digest*, 1991), with a secretariat in Copenhagen.
24. The "consensus-minus-one" procedure was used by the CSO at the end of the Fourth CSCE review conference in Helsinki, on July 8, 1992, to "suspend the presence" of Yugoslavia (then comprising only Serbia and Montenegro) at the CSCE Summit, held on July 9–10, "and [at] all CSCE meetings." As of this writing, the suspension still holds.
25. Two of the conditions necessary for CSCE peace-keeping (which could include the "resources and possible experience and expertise of . . . the [EU], NATO and the WEU, . . . [and] the peacekeeping mechanism of the Commonwealth of Independent States") are that "the parties directly concerned" must consent to a peace-keeping operation, and "an effective and durable cease-fire" must first be in place (*CSCE Helsinki Document 1992*, Ch. 3, pp. 19–20, 23).
26. Russia ratified the CFE Treaty on September 3, 1992; Armenia on October 12; Belarus on October 30; and Kazakhstan also on October 30 (Sharp, 1993, p. 592).
27. The CFE "entered into force *de jure* on 9 Nov. 1992, when all [29] signatory states had deposited their instruments of ratification" (Walker, 1994, p. 29, fn. 20). Some three years later, however, problems with CFE implementation persisted: "The November 16 [1995] deadline for full implementation of the [CFE Treaty] passed amid continuing concern over non-compliance, particularly over Russia's failure to reduce its military border strength to levels, or so-called 'flank limitations,' called for under the accord. . . . the issue has taken on increased significance and sensitivity since Russia launched a large-scale military campaign against separatist elements in Chechnya last December, swelling its force levels in its southern flank and contributing to its

violation. . . . The impasse has been further complicated by attempts by several high-ranking Russian military officials and others to link CFE and planned NATO expansion, threatening abrogation or replacement of the treaty" (McNamara, 1995). Implementation problems have also been noted for Ukraine and Belarus. For a review and update of the CFE, see CSCE Commission (1997a).

28. According to this agreement, the U.S.A. would be allowed to station 250,000 troops in Europe; Russia 1,450,000, Ukraine 450,000, Germany 345,000, France 325,000, Britain 260,000, Poland 234,000, Hungary 100,000, and Czechoslovakia 140,000 (*CSCE Helsinki '92*, 1992, p. 6; for a more comprehensive listing, see Walker, 1994, p. 157).

29. Some five months later, on 29 May 1995, the Court on Conciliation and Arbitration was established in Geneva, to settle disputes submitted to it by the (then fifteen) states which had ratified the Convention (*OSCE Newsletter*, May 1995, p. 7).

30. Other name-changes included (a) the CSCE Council of Ministers becoming the Ministerial Council, the CSCE's "central decision-making and governing body [to] meet, as a rule, towards the end of every [one-year] term of chairmanship at the level of Foreign Ministers"; (b) the CSO becoming the Senior Council, to "meet in Prague twice a year, at the minimum [to] discuss and set forth policy and broad budgetary guidelines"; and (c) the Permanent Committee becoming the Permanent Council, "the regular body for political consultation and decision-making [which meets weekly and] can also be convened for emergency purposes." The PC comprises the permanent representatives of the participating States and hence, meets in Vienna (*CSCE Budapest Document 1994*, "Budapest Decisions").

31. Former UN Under Secretary General for Special Political Affairs, Sir Brian Urquhart (1991a), for example, has argued that "National sovereignty is almost everywhere in retreat [and should] become a thing of the past."

32. Nongovernmental conflict resolution resources include the Berghof Research Center for Constructive Conflict Management in Berlin (see Ropers, 1995); the Conflict Management Group (CMG) in Cambridge, Massachusetts (which has worked with the OSCE, especially the High Commissioner on National Minorities [HCNM]. See Chigas, 1994a, b; Chigas *et al.*, 1996; CMG, 1993, 1994); the Helsinki Citizens' Assembly in Prague (see HCA, 1990, 1992); the Institute for Multi-Track Diplomacy (IMTD) in Washington, DC (see Diamond and McDonald, 1996); International Alert in London (see IA, 1996; for an evaluation of IA's activities, see Sørbø *et al.*, 1997); the International Negotiation Network (INN) of the Carter Center at Emory University in Atlanta (see *State of World Conflict Report 1991–1992, 1995–1996*); the National Peace Foundation in Washington, DC (see NPF, 1997); Partners for Democratic Change in San Francisco, with centers in Bulgaria, the Czech Republic, Hungary, Lithuania, Poland, the Russian Federation, and the Slovak Republic (see PDC, 1992; Shonholtz and Shapiro, 1997); and Search for Common Ground in Washington, DC and Brussels (see SFCG, 1997). For further information about nongovernmental conflict resolution resources and their activities, see the articles in Shonholtz and Linzer (1997).

33. One source of potentially relevant practitioners is *Who's Who in Europe, in Peacemaking and Conflict Resolution*, prepared by Mehmet Gürkaynak (1993) for the European Conference on Peacemaking and Conflict Resolution (ECPCR). Also see the U.S. Institute of Peace's *Guide to Specialists '97–98* (USIP, 1997–8).

34. "Within the overall context of" means within the *framework* of, but *not* subsumed (in a hierarchical relationship) to, the OSCE.

35. By January 1, 1993, NACC comprised 38 members: (a) the sixteen members of NATO (Belgium, Canada, Denmark, France, Germany, Greece, Iceland, Italy, Luxembourg, Netherlands, Norway, Portugal, Spain, Turkey, the United States, and the United Kingdom); (b) the six Eastern European former members of the Warsaw Treaty Organization (Bulgaria, the Czech Republic, Hungary, Poland, Romania, and Slovakia); (c) Albania; (d) the three Baltic states (Estonia, Latvia, and Lithuania); (e) Russia

and the eleven remaining former Soviet republics (Armenia, Azerbaijan, Belarus, Georgia, Kazakhstan, Kyrgyzstan, Moldova, Tajikistan, Turkmenistan, Ukraine, and Uzbekistan); plus (f) one observer, Finland (see Rotfeld, 1993, p. 177).

By 1997, NACC membership climbed to 40 with the addition of Slovenia and the former Yugoslav Republic of Macedonia, plus four observers, with Austria, Sweden, and Switzerland joining Finland in that role (see *NATO Basic Fact Sheet No. 2*, 1997).

The Western European Union (WEU) – possibly the "European pillar" of an expanding NATO as well as the likely security arm of the EU – created a similar organization in 1992, the WEU Consultative Forum, with Central and Southeast European states. In addition to the ten WEU members (Belgium, France, Germany, Greece, Italy, Luxembourg, the Netherlands, Portugal, Spain, and the United Kingdom) and three associate members (Iceland, Norway, and Turkey), the Consultative Forum includes ten associate partners (Bulgaria, the Czech Republic, Estonia, Hungary, Latvia, Lithuania, Poland, Romania, Slovakia, and Slovenia) and five observers (Austria, Denmark, Finland, Ireland, and Sweden) (see Walker, 1993a, pp. 50–1; Walker, 1994, pp. 48, 54; YIO, 1997/8, pp. 1656–7).

36. By summer 1996, the Partnership for Peace (PfP) included the NATO 16 and 27 others, including (after months of tense delays) Russia, for a total of 43 members (see Williams, 1994; *CSCE Digest*, 1996). Among the 27 non-NATO members were the six Eastern European members of the former WTO (Bulgaria, the Czech Republic, Hungary, Poland, Romania, and Slovakia); fourteen former Soviet successor states (i.e. all with the exception of Tajikistan); two former Yugoslav republics (Macedonia and Slovenia); Albania; and four neutral and nonaligned (Austria, Finland, Malta, and Sweden). Malta has since withdrawn, while another member of the neutral and nonaligned, Switzerland, has joined.

By 1998, Tajikistan was a member as well, for a total of 44 PfP members: the same as the 40 members of the (now defunct) NACC and its four observers or, currently, the 44 members of the Euro-Atlantic Partnership Council (EAPC) which has replaced the NACC (see *NATO Fact Sheet No. 9*, 1997; PfP, 1998).

37. On September 8, 1995, Russian President Boris Yeltsin, perhaps in part to defuse criticism of his policies by ultranationalists and others, condemned, in the wake of the fall of Srebrenica, NATO's bombing of Bosnian Serb positions, even hinting that in addition to humanitarian aid for Serbian refugees from Croatia, "Russia might consider also sending military aid if the NATO attacks continue." He also made a connection between NATO's bombing and its planned expansion up to Russia's borders, arguing that the latter "will mean a conflagration of war throughout all Europe" (see Hoffman, 1995). Further: "In Moscow, . . . antagonism towards NATO's expansion is growing. Polish and Hungarian accession to NATO would be unwelcome but tolerated; the Baltics would be a different matter. Leading Russian military strategists have warned that Moscow could respond by repositioning tactical short-range nuclear missiles on its western borders. Viktor Mikhailov, Russia's atomic energy minister, has even suggested bombing Czech bases if the republic becomes part of NATO's military infrastructure" (Hearst, 1996).

38. The first meeting of the Euro-Atlantic Partnership Council (EAPC) took place at the Madrid NATO summit on July 9, 1997 (the same day that the NATO–Ukraine Charter was signed) with the 44 member nations discussing the role of the EAPC in conflict resolution and crisis management, and its relationships with the UN, OSCE, and NATO (see Marshall, 1997). As already indicated, the 44 EAPC members are the same as the 40 members and four observers of the former NACC and the same as the 44 members of the PfP. In other words, "All members of PfP are also members of the [post-NACC] EAPC," the overarching framework within which PfP activities occur (see Balanzino, 1997; *NATO Fact Sheet No. 9*, 1997; PfP, 1998).

39. By January 1, 1995, the EEA had eighteen members – the fifteen EU members, plus

Iceland, Norway, and Liechtenstein – but not Switzerland, which had rejected membership through a referendum (see *Europe in Figures*, 1995, p. 24).

40. By January 1, 1995, EU membership climbed to fifteen with the addition of Austria, Finland, and Sweden to Belgium, Denmark, France, Germany, Greece, Ireland, Italy, Luxembourg, Netherlands, Portugal, Spain, and the United Kingdom (*Europe in Figures*, 1995, p. 24).
41. As a reflection of, among other things, the "Clash of Civilizations" *within* NATO: "the EU leaders decided in Luxembourg against including [Turkey] in the expansion process. . . . Turkey, an associate member of the EU and its predecessors since 1964, has been seeking to join the EU for the past ten years" (*The Week in Germany*, 1997, pp. 1, 2; also see Hockstader, 1997c; Hockstader and Couturier, 1997; IHT, 1997).
42. Walker (1993a, p. 50) adds: "This will be true as much because of the 'socializing' effect of constant contact and cooperation among interior, justice, social affairs or other ministries, as well as those responsible for economic and foreign policy, as because of specific agreements."
43. Strictly speaking, therefore, the Human Dimension combines the humanitarian concerns of Basket 3 and the human rights concerns of Basket 1.
44. By 1989–90, as the Cold War was coming to an end, the COE consisted of 23 members: Austria, Belgium, Cyprus, Denmark, Finland, France, Germany, Greece, Iceland, Ireland, Italy, Liechtenstein, Luxembourg, Malta, Netherlands, Norway, Portugal, San Marino, Spain, Sweden, Switzerland, Turkey, and the United Kingdom (see COE, 1998). By the end of 1993, Bulgaria, the Czech Republic, Estonia, Hungary, Lithuania, Poland, Romania, Slovakia, and Slovenia – former adversaries of the West – had become members as well, bringing COE membership up to 32 (*ibid.*). Many others had also applied, "including Russia and other member states of the Commonwealth of Independent States (CIS)" (Walker, 1993a, p. 47). By the end of 1995, the Council's membership stood at 38 countries, including Albania, Andorra, Latvia, Macedonia, Moldova, and Ukraine (see COE, 1998). Russia was admitted in 1996, despite its continuing brutal campaign in Chechyna, because "there was also broad consensus within the council that denying Russia membership would be a blow to the country's advocates of democracy" (*The Week in Germany*, 1996). Croatia was also admitted in 1996, bringing total COE membership up to 40 countries, which has remained constant up to the present time (see COE, 1998).
45. Others have put forward similar arguments, creating, in the process, a "Great Debate" about the role of peace-keeping (broadly or narrowly defined) in the post-Cold War era. See, for example, former UN Secretary General Boutros Boutros-Ghali's effort in *An Agenda for Peace* (1992) to make the UN more relevant to post-Cold War realities, featuring four major categories of intervention: *preventive diplomacy*, *peace-making* (including a discussion of armed deployments like those advocated by Urquhart), *peace-keeping*, and *post-conflict peace-building* (which has a clear positive peace connotation). Also see Akashi (1995/6), Bertram (1995/6), Chalmers (1993), Gardner (1992), Hoffmann (1995/6), Lorenz (1992), Rikhye (1992), Roberts (1995/6), Ropers and Schlotter (1993, Chapter 4), and Tharoor (1995/6).
46. In his *Preventing Violent Conflicts: A Strategy for Preventive Diplomacy* (1996), Lund distinguishes between "vertical" and "horizontal" components of preventive diplomacy systems, as I have done here with regard to NEPSS's integrated systems of conflict resolution networks. However, although my "vertical dimension" is similar to his "vertical division of labor," the comparability between my "horizontal dimension" and his "horizontal division of labor" is not nearly so neat: "The division of labor necessary to institute a multilateral system of conflict prevention must operate through a *horizontal* division of tasks, as well as *vertically*. This means that at *each of the vertical levels* – local, regional, and global – third parties involved must engage in greater *lateral cooperation*, coordinating their actions, pooling their resources, and assigning responsibilities as required by the circumstances of a given conflict. Thus a number of actors

[*including NGOs*] would be working at *each* level to keep the dispute within the bounds of that level" (Lund, 1996, p. 189; emphasis added).

Accordingly, as the stage upon which "lateral cooperation" is played out, Lund's horizontal division can be viewed as a special case of both his vertical division and my vertical dimension. In some cases, my horizontal dimension could be viewed as a special case of Lund's horizontal division, in that, at *particular levels* and intensities of conflict, track-1 military action might have to be undertaken to effect negative peace as a necessary (but not sufficient) condition of track-2 efforts to achieve positive peace. In other cases, however, track-1 military action may be applied "vertically," as in the case of external intervention in Bosnia. In both scenarios, the use of a "judicious" amount of *Realpolitik* is "horizontal" because, along the path to positive peace, military action (track-1) may have to be undertaken prior to the use of other means (track-2) to facilitate reaching the desired end-state (which seems to have more of a "lateral" than a "hierarchical" quality to it).

In any case, in both Lund's and my schema, the vertical division of labor/dimension *is* the overarching framework: lateral actions of any kind along Lund's horizontal axis and, within NEPSS, military actions designed to achieve negative peace as a necessary (but not sufficient) condition of positive peace are *tactical* means for achieving larger *strategic* objectives. The "complex" relationship between the *Realpolitik*-based horizontal dimension and *Idealpolitik*-based vertical dimension in NEPSS will be discussed further in Chapter 8.

47. Although "key details of [this] agreement were worked out in face-to-face negotiations between Serbian President Slobodan Milosevic and Croatian President Franjo Tudjman in the Balkans peace talks near Dayton, Ohio [the] agreement itself . . . was concluded between local negotiators in the Croatian town of Erdut" (Dobbs, 1995, p. A1). This component of the Balkans peace process came to an end on January 15, 1998, when the UN terminated its two-year peace mission in Croatia, "returning to Croatia control of the last piece of land [there] seized by minority Serbs" (Spolar, 1998b). This area (Eastern Slavonia) includes "Vukovar, a city of Serbs, Croats, Hungarians and other nationalities [which] was nearly flattened in a siege [during] autumn [1991] by the Yugoslav military" (Spolar, 1998a).

48. Shortly after the U.S. presidential elections in November 1996, President Clinton announced that the U.S.A. would be participating in a NATO-led follow-on force to IFOR (due to end the following month): SFOR would be roughly half the size of IFOR and remain in Bosnia at least until June 1998 (see Dobbs, 1996b; Dobbs and Baker, 1996; Baker and Graham, 1996).

49. Note, for example, the less-than-positive results of the European Union's efforts to reunify the Croatian and Muslim sectors of Mostar: "Aid pumped into Mostar – an estimated $50 million – has succeeded in restoring water supplies, electricity and other infrastructure, and the sum is far higher spending per person than other Bosnian localities can expect. [But] Economic treatment has proved . . . ineffective in producing political changes" (Fitchett, 1996).

50. As mentioned in Chapter 6, "when previous process interacts with, blends into, and strengthens conflict-as-startup conditions, conflict-as-process is never far from the surface: a latent fire always ready to be rekindled."

51. On December 18, 1997, President Clinton decided to extend the U.S. presence in Bosnia beyond the June 1998 deadline for SFOR: "With a blunt admission that he misjudged how long it would take to build *lasting peace* in Bosnia, President Clinton . . . announced that he has decided in principle to keep U.S. military forces there past a June 1998 deadline and *into the indefinite future*. . . . [He] said pulling out the U.S. force now would invite a return to . . . ethnic violence" (Harris, 1997, p. A1; emphasis added). Two months later, on February 18, 1998, "NATO decided . . . to extend its military mission in Bosnia beyond June at roughly the current strength of 34,000 troops, although it may be reduced significantly after national elections there this fall"

(WP, 1998a). Two days later, the "20 non-NATO countries that participate in the operation [also] approved extending the force's mandate beyond its June expiration date" (WP, 1998b). Among these, Partnership for Peace members include Albania, Austria, Bulgaria, the Czech Republic, Estonia, Finland, Hungary, Latvia, Lithuania, Poland, Romania, Russia, Slovenia, Sweden, and Ukraine. Non-PfP participants are Egypt, Ireland, Jordan, Malaysia, and Morocco (see Balanzino, 1997, p. 11).

52. Alternatively, reversing the causal sequence, "a major change in Kosovo – large-scale violence, a massive outflow of Albanians, a change in borders – could wreck Dayton by its impact on Serbia's leadership, on the Bosnian Serbs and on the region in general. The international management of such a disaster would be enormously difficult and costly" (Abramowitz, 1998).
53. Although we have focused in this chapter on the CSCE/OSCE as the principal regional security actor linking the former Cold War adversaries and neutral and nonaligned, its failures to deal effectively with the wars in former Yugoslavia and elsewhere are also the failures of the international community in general, including the UN, which has the authority to mandate peace enforcement missions, and NATO, which has the means to implement them.
54. Paralleling Sollenberg's (1996) conclusion, based upon a longitudinal analysis of armed conflict between 1989 and 1995, that "the turbulent initial phase of the post-Cold War period now seems to have come to an end" (cited by Darby, 1998), is Gurr's finding, reported in an update to his 1993 *Minorities at Risk*, that, from 1990 to 1995, there was a decline worldwide in economic, political, and cultural discrimination against national, ethnocultural, and religious minorities; in short, an improvement in the observance of human rights (Gurr, forthcoming, Chapter 5).

8 Violent Conflict and War: Further Implications for Theory, Research, and Practice

Introduction

At the end of the twentieth century – of the millennium – the *global problematique* appears to comprise a growing list of seemingly intractable problems. In addition to AIDS, population growth, hunger, deforestation, ozone layer depletion, and global warming, among others, migratory pressures, refugee movements, nuclear theft, and land mine proliferation – with approximately three million in Bosnia-Hercegovina alone – have come to characterize the post-Cold War world, possibly with complex, mutually exacerbating interactions between them. One set of those problems has been addressed to some extent in this study: violent conflict and war, at *all* levels (war "writ large"), but particularly between and within states (war "writ small").

In his classic study of war ("writ small"), Quincy Wright (1964, pp. 331–2) issued the following challenge:

> Is it possible to develop an analysis more adequate than those of the past for dealing with war in our time? Such an analysis should, in a *single formula*, relate the factors emphasized in each of the points of view about war. Each point of view with respect to war, to some extent, falsifies reality. [Hence,] efforts to predict or to control war must estimate the *relative weight* to be given to each point of view and to numerous causal factors. (Emphasis added)

This study is a response to Wright's challenge, consisting of a number of steps taken to develop such an analysis.

First, in response to the fragmented, bivariate nature of quantitative studies of war (Chapter 1), we developed a multilevel map and pretheory of variables operative at the trans-societal, societal, and decision-making levels that may be relevant to the initiation and escalation of violent conflict and war (Chapter 2).

Second, we developed from the pretheory hypotheses on the relationships between 23 potential independent variables and five dependent (conflict) variables (Chapter 2).

Third, we tested the hypotheses derived from the pretheory by measuring the selected variables over time in terms of data generated by the *Prisoners' Dilemma Simulation* (PDS) (Chapter 3), and then computed product–moment correlation coefficients to determine, for each hypothesis, the strength and direction of relationship between the variables (Chapter 4).

Fourth, we subjected the bivariate PDS findings to validation assessment by comparing them with findings produced by corresponding (mostly real-world) studies, resulting in an agreement score of 75 percent for direction of relationship and 86 percent for strength of relationship, which compared favorably with Harold Guetzkow's (1966, 1968b; Guetzkow and Valadez, 1981b) validation assessment of the INS (Chapter 4).

Fifth, given the results of the bivariate validation assessment, we conducted a multivariate analysis to explore the validity of the hypothesized multiplicity of factors involved in the "genesis of war," in which it would be possible to rank the explanatory variables (and their corresponding levels) in terms of relative potency.

This involved combining the data on five separate PDS operations into one data-set, subsequently dividing that into three successive periods – early, intermediate, and late stages of development – and then using standardized regression analysis, which facilitates the ranking of explanatory variables, to develop models for each of the five dependent variables for the combined data-set as well as for the three developmental subsets (Chapter 4).

The findings on the combined data-set suggested that societal and trans-societal variables had the most, and decision-making variables the least, impact on domestic and foreign conflict. The findings on the three developmental stages suggested that the trans-societal level dominated during the early stage, a mixture of levels during the intermediate stage, and the societal level during the late stage. Specifically, as societal actors in the PDS moved across developmental stages, they were characterized less by environmental- and more by *self-stimulation* of conflict, thereby reinforcing Most and Starr's (1989) claim that different theories and models might apply to phenomena occurring under different conditions (e.g. stages of development) and at different levels of analysis, and that a focus on *process* might be more useful than one on *static* events, attributes, and structures.

Sixth, we subjected the multivariate PDS findings to a comprehensive validation assessment through comparisons with findings from other studies (e.g. Vasquez, 1976) in terms of: (a) direction of relationship; (b) magnitude of relationship; (c) ranking of dependent variables by proportion of variation explained; and (d) ranking of independent variables by proportion of variation explained. Across comparisons, the level of agreement between PDS and corresponding (again, mostly real-world) findings was not only relatively high but also consistent, basically falling within the range of the *75 percent norm* established during the bivariate assessment (Chapter 5).

Seventh, on the basis of the results of the multivariate validation assessment, we combined these with the pretheory of Chapter 2 and a revisiting of the conflict/conflict resolution literature to develop a generic theory of violent conflict and war that goes beyond the *concatenated* theory of Chapter 2, reflecting elements of *hierarchical* (including *axiomatic*) theory as well (see Kaplan, 1964, pp. 298–9; Frankfort-Nachmias and Nachmias, 1996, pp. 37–43) (Chapter 6).

Eighth, we then employed the generic reconstruction as a basis for understanding and dealing with the violent ethnic conflict of post-Cold War Europe, especially the wars in former Yugoslavia (Chapter 7).

Since this study is about war "writ large" as well as war "writ small," it is also a response to Christopher Mitchell's (1981, pp. 4, 315–16) challenge to develop, but then to move beyond, "multi-disciplinary, multi-level" *pretheory*, "to advance [the] field . . . towards the development of genuine, empirically based *conflict theory*" (emphasis added):

> to think about . . . wars, urban riots, confrontations, damaging strikes, interpersonal friction, and inter-ethnic struggles in new ways, and to adopt fresh perspectives on the nature of their circumstances, and their options for future relationships and inter-actions.

The question now is, what are the implications of this study for further developments in theory, research, and practice?

Some Further Implications for Theory and Research

The theory developed in Chapter 6 and applied in Chapter 7 assumes that *all* conflicts – whether interpersonal, intergroup, interorganizational, international, or other – are impacted, to varying degrees, by factors operative at the individual, societal, international, and global levels; hence, attempts to deal with conflict at any level must take these four explanatory levels into account as well.

There are, however, other ways to map and develop theory on the causes and conditions of violent conflict and war besides that offered by the four-level, Waltz/North framework. One such way is suggested by my *Four-worlds' Model of the Perceptual and Behavioral Process* (Sandole, 1984, 1987), which assumes that all actors operate in a dynamic space comprised of two external and two internal "worlds" or "fields." Borrowing from and building upon Sir Karl Popper's (1972b) three-worlds' work in this regard, the two external worlds are the world of nature (world 1) and the human-made world (world 3). Both of these "worlds" are sources of stimuli that can impact actors at any time and can be processed by their two internal worlds – their mental worlds (world 2) and biological/physiological worlds (world 4) – leading to "definitions of the situation," corresponding behaviors, and consequences of behaviors.

In any given conflict analysis, therefore, we can map, model, and monitor the situation in terms of the *world of nature* (resource scarcities), the *human-made world* (structural violence; role scarcities), the *mental world* (paradigms, *Weltanschauungen*, beliefs and values), and the *biological/physiological world* (emotions), with the possibility of interactions, not just between the external and internal fields, but between all fields as well as within each of them.

For instance, (a) potential conflicts-as-startup conditions in actors' natural and human-made worlds can interact with (b) actors' modes of processing these in their biological/physiological and mental worlds, and (c) their modes of viscerally responding to these in their biological/physiological worlds, leading to definitions of the situation, corresponding behaviors and perhaps conflicts-as-process in the human-made world, possibly with implications for the world of nature (with, in turn, implications for the human-made world), as well as for the actors themselves.

The four-worlds' model, perhaps more so than the four-level, Waltz/North framework, lends itself to use as something similar to the "unified field theory" that Albert Einstein pursued for years, and that other physicists are still pursuing (see Weinberg, 1992), but, in our case, without the assumption of "finality" sometimes associated with such efforts. A *unified field theory of violent conflict and war* – or what Vasquez (1993, p. 306) calls a "unified theory of conflict and violence"[1] – reflects Kurt Lewin's (1951) argument that "the determinants of human behavior should be treated in a *single unified field* rather than separated into traditional disciplines" (Dougherty and Pfaltzgraff, 1990, p. 51; emphasis added). The unified field theory reformulation is also a further step in the direction of "grand theory" (see Most and Starr, 1989, p. 118).[2]

A unified field theory based on the four-worlds' model also highlights the biological/physiological world (world 4): "human nature" and its contentious role in the etiology of violent conflict and war. Countless debates have occurred over the issue of "nature" versus "nurture," often accompanied by a degree of emotional intensity not unlike that associated with the abortion issue. However, it is no longer necessary (apparently) to walk the fine line between leaving oneself open to accusations of purveying fascistic bio-ideologies on the one hand and being seen as a free-wheeling, *tabula rasa* advocate of environmental determinism on the other: it is *not* "nature" (genetic determinism) *or* "nurture" (environmental determinism), or in a simple additive sense, "nurture" *and* "nature," but the *interaction* between them – with "cause and effect" possible in *both* directions (from "nature" to "nurture" and vice versa) – that appears to play a role in the etiology of violent conflict and war (see Shaw and Wong, 1989; McDonald, 1994; Begley, 1995; Cowley, 1995; Goleman, 1995; Wright, 1995).

The complex relationship between social environment, status, self-esteem, serotonin, and violence is a case in point (Wright, 1995). Serotonin, a neurotransmitter "which plays a role in restraining aggressive impulses" (Goleman, 1995, p. C10), can be affected by one's self-worth (esteem), which can itself be influenced by one's status and social environment. Hence, a brutal social environment, reflective of physical as well as structural violence, with limited, if any, opportunities for personal growth and "social elevation" (world 3), can correlate with low status (worlds 3 and 2), low self-esteem (world 4), low serotonin levels (world 4), "attendant states of mind" (world 2), and an increase in the probability of violent behavior (including internalized violence in the form of depression and suicide). A social environment rich with resources available to an individual, on the other hand, can correlate with positive status, and "the sort of feedback that raises self-esteem and serotonin" and a low probability of "impulsive risk-taking" and violent behavior (Wright, 1995, p. 75).

Accordingly, serotonin levels ("nature"), which can be affected by genes, can clearly affect behavior and environment; but environment ("nurture") can also *negatively* affect serotonin levels – in which case, serotonin level as "a '*biological*' marker may be an '*environmental*' marker, not a '*genetic*' one" (*ibid.*, p. 70; emphasis added). The implications here for social change are profound: whatever our "human nature" is, it can be affected by environment, which can also be changed to *positively* affect serotonin, behavior, and, of course, environment itself.[3]

Clearly, the linkages here are complex, capable even of facilitating the development of *self-stimulating/self-perpetuating conflict-prone* individuals:

> data from several long-range studies of large groups of children show that those who were childhood victims of abuse or neglect were the most violent as teenagers ... or adults. And ... some of the data implicated changes in *serotonin* or related neurotransmitter systems. ... [But, according to Dr Craig Ferris,] "The brain circuits that regulate aggression in humans are *malleable through childhood*, so there may be some corrective experiences that reverse or otherwise improve any adverse impact from early abuse." (Goleman, 1995, pp. C1 and C10; emphasis added)

Gender plays a role here as well. In addition to the observed differences between the sexes in brain function, cognition, and perception (see Begley, 1995), men *are* the culprits in acts of violence: "From an evolutionary point of view, the leading cause of violence is *maleness*" (Wright, 1995, p. 72; emphasis added; also see Galtung, 1993; Wrangham and Peterson, 1996; Fried, 1997).[4] Moreover, according to evolutionary psychologists Martin Daly and Margo Wilson (1988; cited in Wright, 1995), male violence is a "natural" (and *not* a "pathological") response to certain environmental conditions (e.g. life in the inner city):

> the dismay often inspired by reports that a black teenager killed because he had been "dissed" is naive. Nothing was more vital to the reproductive success of our male ancestors than *respect*, so there is nothing that the male mind will more feverishly seek to neutralize than disrespect. All men spend much of their lives doing exactly this; most are just lucky enough to live in a place where guns won't help them do it. ... inner-city thugs may be functioning as "designed": their minds absorb environmental input reflecting their low socioeconomic standing and the absence of "legitimate" routes to self elevation, and incline their behavior in the appropriately criminal direction. ... as Daly and Wilson note by quoting Bob Dylan, "When you ain't got nothin', you got nothin' to lose." (Wright, 1995, pp. 73, 75; emphasis added)[5]

The hypothesized relationship between *basic human needs* (e.g. self-esteem), environments that violate or otherwise frustrate those needs, and violence/violent conflict has been noted by others as well, and at various levels, suggesting that it may truly be "generic" (as well as "real"). For example, in addition to James Chowning Davies's (1962, 1973, 1986) and John Burton's (1972, 1979, 1990a) hypotheses in this regard (as noted in Chapter 6), Francis Fukuyama (1992), building upon Plato and Hegel, has observed:

> The struggle for recognition provides us with insight into the nature of international politics. The desire for recognition that led to the original bloody battle for prestige between two individual combatants leads logically to imperialism and world empire. The relationship of lordship and bondage on a domestic level is naturally replicated on the level of states, where nations as a whole seek recognition and enter into bloody battles for supremacy. Nationalism, a modern yet not-fully-rational form of recognition, has been the vehicle for the struggle for recognition over the past hundred years, and the source of this century's most intense conflicts. This is the world of "power politics," described by such foreign policy "realists" as Henry Kissinger. . . . if war is fundamentally driven by the desire for recognition, it stands to reason that . . . [a] world made up of liberal democracies . . . should have much less incentive for war, since all nations would reciprocally recognize one another's legitimacy. And indeed, there is substantial empirical evidence from the past couple of hundred years that liberal democracies do not behave imperialistically toward one another.

Here, I am reminded of a conversation I had with a colleague who was informing me about a successful prison mediation program. When I asked her why she thought the program was a success, she said that one reason was that the "hardest-core" prisoners were in charge of the program. When I inquired what it was about those particular fellows that made the program so successful, she said, "because they were affirmed, they were affirmed in their worth. I tell them, 'I don't care if you are a rapist, you still have worth for me!' "

Apparently, Burton has a point: if we modify institutions and other aspects of actors' external environments to be more in line with actors' needs, then we may be able to help them shift their behavior. We are clearly not stuck with *Realpolitik Man*. A critical amount of "liberal democracy" could make a difference in the inner city, prison, society, and international system.

But with "needs" we may have to be a bit careful, for in addition to needs for recognition, esteem, and security, there also seems to be a need for, among others, stimulation, which, depending upon prior learning and environmental contingencies, could be expressed as a "longing for war," and therefore as Vamik Volkan's (1985, 1988) "need for enemies." In a review of Martin Gilbert's *The First World War: A Complete History* (1994), for instance, Michael Kernan (1995) writes:

> the British . . . insisted on treating the war as some sort of game . . . apparently in a spirit of sporting machismo, [they] continued to dig their trenches literally under the noses of the Germans, who invariably built with military good sense on the ridges and high ground. British officers continued to lead charges with swords(!), which meant that many never got over the parapet alive, which meant that the men who did reach the objective often just milled around for lack of leadership. As late as the

Somme [a catastrophe that cost Britain 60,000 casualties in a single day], men went over the top dribbling soccer balls.

And then, echoing William James (1910/1985), there is combat veteran Martin van Creveld's (1991) explanation: men fight because of war's "excitement, exhilaration, ecstasy, and delirium" (p. 162). "War is or can be supremely enjoyable" (p. 163): "In the whole of human experience the only thing that even comes close [to war] is the act of sex. . . . However, the thrills of war and fighting are probably more intense than those of the boudoir" (p. 165).[6] But war does more than titillate: "So elemental is the *human need* to endow the shedding of blood with some great and even sublime significance that it renders the intellect almost entirely helpless" (*ibid.*, p. 166; emphasis added). Hence, we saw the fiftieth anniversary celebrations during 1994–5 of D-Day, the Battle of the Bulge, Iwo Jima, Okinawa, and VE Day, when combat veterans assembled on battlefields and at war monuments around the world to honor their fallen comrades and to commemorate their own participation in those great historical events.

War seems to provide defining experiences – *meaning* – for civilians as well. In his review of Philip Ziegler's book, *London at War, 1939–1945*, Jonathan Yardley (1995) tells us:

> Writing of the blitz specifically, Ziegler characterizes London throughout the war: "It never occurred to Londoners that they were being particularly brave; they just got on with it as their friends and neighbors were doing." Their quiet courage was tempered upon occasion by fear or doubt or, most pervasive of all, sheer boredom, but at every crisis it bordered on the heroic. Now, from the vantage point of half a century, we look back on London during the war just as we do at America during the war. We lament the lost unity and sense of purpose, and wonder why these cannot be summoned again to help us meet crises of different but very real urgency. The answer of course is that a state of siege is not the natural human condition, and that once it passes we revert to the normal, which is to say the human, which is to say the fractious, disputatious and the self-interested as well as other, more attractive qualities. Even if inadvertently, Philip Ziegler offers us the useful reminder that war is a terribly high price to pay for a sense of community.

A "sense of community" (Simmel, Coser) seems to correlate with a sense of danger as well as meaning. According to van Creveld (1991, p. 164):

> Danger is much more than simply the medium in which war takes place; from the point of view of all participants and spectators alike, it is among the principal attractions, one would almost say its *raison d'être*. . . . Coping with danger calls forth qualities such as boldness, pride, loyalty, and determination. It is thus able to cause people to transcend themselves, becoming more than they are. . . . danger is what makes war go round. . . . As in any *sport*, the greater the danger the greater both the challenge of braving it and the honor associated with doing so. (Emphasis added)

Or as William James (1910/1985) put it, "The horrors make the fascination. . . .

The horror makes the thrill; and when the question is of getting the extremest and supremest out of human nature, talk of expense sounds ignominious" (*ibid.*, pp. 306, 310).

It is interesting to consider that U.S. Army recruiting literature tells potential recruits that they "can be all that they can be" in the U.S. Army, a claim supported by action-filled photographs and films. This is clearly an appeal to a need for meaning associated with heroic deeds in pursuit of defense of one's identity group: a need to transcend the mediocrity of the everyday Self and to feel good about oneself in the process, thereby fulfilling needs for recognition and esteem as well as meaning and security.

Shaw and Wong (1989) would argue that the motivations that predispose us toward dangerous pursuits, often in defense of our identity groups, are part of our nature. The "seeds of warfare," they argue, lie in *ultimate* (in contrast to *proximate*) causes – *inclusive fitness* and *kin selection*:[7] "Providing an ultimate, evolutionary rationale for cooperation and sociality among genetically related individuals also provides an ultimate rationale for anticipating origins of reduced cooperation among less related individuals[:] a '*sociobiology of ethnocentrism*' " (*ibid.*, pp. 41, 44–5; emphasis added). Not suprisingly, this predisposition toward danger has itself become dangerous. As perhaps the ultimate example of "complex nonlinearity" in human affairs,

> Humans have outfoxed themselves. They have learned to maximize inclusive fitness – through ethnocentrism, out-group enmity, nationalism and patriotism – to the extent that they have created the means to destroy the very inclusive fitness they seek to foster and protect. . . . unless some kind of action is forthcoming along the lines proposed, there is no reason to believe that *Homo sapiens* will escape nuclear devastation, if not extinction. (*Ibid.*, p. 197)

In the meantime, violent conflict and war are ways to increase the danger, to enable the "warrior-hero" to fulfill needs for recognition, esteem, meaning, and security.[8] To eliminate war, therefore, is to eliminate major opportunities for fulfilling these needs: a reason, perhaps, why some have implied or otherwise indicated that they lament the passing of the Cold War (e.g. see Fukuyama, 1989, p. 18). Or as David Hackworth (1995, p. 27), in his attempt to make sense of Oklahoma City bombing suspect Timothy McVeigh, put it: "I've seen countless veterans, including myself, stumble home after the high-noon *excitement* of the killing fields, missing their battle buddies and the *unique dangers and sense of purpose*. Many lose themselves forever" (emphasis added).

Hence, future research and theory-building in violent conflict and war should include biological/physiological factors – which, again, may not be the same as *genetic* factors (see Wright, 1995) – inclusive of gender, as well as other aspects of our generic (or unified field) theory and the interactions between them. Interactions and their effects, perhaps more so than the impact of additive combinations of variables, may provide the most significant answers to questions concerning causes and conditions of violent conflict and war (see Most and Starr, 1989, pp. 172, 186; Shaw and Wong, 1989, pp. 11–12, 193–4; North, 1990, p. 39; Vasquez, 1993, pp. 175, 177; Levy, 1996).

Some Specific "Next Steps" for Empirical Research

As indicated above, and as Dean Pruitt and Richard Snyder (1969, p. 2) remind us, "a sophisticated treatment of war should trace it to a variety of antecedent variables, some operating independently of one another and others operating in a *complex* way" (emphasis added). Clearly, one implication here for further research concerns that "complex way": the *interaction-effects* of combinations of independent variables on conflict. John Vasquez (1993, p. 175) has said in this regard that, for instance, "alliances must be seen as part of a dynamic in which crises, alliance making and military buildups *interact* and reinforce each other" (emphasis added). Although this is interesting *conceptually*, how is one to deal with interaction-effects *operationally*? Vasquez (*ibid.*, p. 177) continues:

> Wayman [1984] ... combines the 1970–74 friendship–hostility judgements and the WEIS [World Event Interaction Survey] conflict and cooperation events to "predict" the WEIS events of 1976–78. He finds that an *interaction model*, initially developed by Mansbach and Vasquez (1981, Ch. 7) and which he *operationalizes* by *multiplying* prior cooperation–conflict *times* the friendship–hostility judgements, accounts for 88 percent of the variance. (Emphasis added)

Among possible "next steps," therefore, we could combine independent variables *multiplicatively* as well as *additively*, and then compare the explanatory potential of both types of models. But what combinations of variables (other than those mentioned above by Vasquez) might be worth looking at? This is one area where theory is clearly deficient (along with how to combine, time-lag, etc.). One tentative answer to this question in terms of the PDS component of the present study might be to look at the interaction between needs (e.g. ACH, POW, AFF) and an assumed assault to needs, such as Attack Victim (VICT), and the effect of these combinations on conflict.

Apropos incorporating *gender* into our future research designs, we could, in terms of the PDS, create a "male" independent variable by computing the proportion of males in each "nation-group" as a proportion of total members, and then explore the extent to which this – in additive versus multiplicative models (see the discussion below on SEC-stimulated "territoriality") – correlates with certain conflict behaviors. We could also compare the behavior of exclusively male versus exclusively female groups.

A related "next step" would be to incorporate, better than we have thus far, other aspects of the individual. We could, for instance, map the belief-value systems and perceptions of particular decision-makers, and assign different weights to them depending upon their location in decision-making groups (see Greenstein, 1969, p. 137). We would, however, still face the problem – and its implications – of how to *operationally* combine the measures of the belief-value systems and perceptions of *differently weighted* individuals:

> Theories of foreign policy and international conflict that recognize the importance of *individual* beliefs must incorporate not only the beliefs themselves, but also an explanation of how the policy preferences of *different* individuals in *different* roles and positions of power get *aggregated*

> into foreign policy decisions for the state. This facilitates the construction of richer and more descriptively accurate theories of international conflict, but these theories are more *complex*, less elegant or *parsimonious*, more demanding in terms of the types of data that are necessary to test them, and less powerful in terms of their generalizability across *different* states in *different* situations at *different* times. (Levy, 1996, p. 16; emphasis added)

We might also face the problem of how "person" and "situational variables" combine to affect behavior. As Druckman (1993, pp. 32–3) puts it:

> The research on [person by situation interactions] has yet to produce clear results on the way that these factors interact. . . . some situations moderate the impact of ["person"] variables, [while] other situations . . . can enhance their impact. Or [person variables] may appear as influences on behavior in subtle, non-obvious ways.

Accordingly, for a variety of reasons, we might want to ensure that our future research projects focus on actors whose behaviors can be examined across successive stages of development, such as the "early," "intermediate," and "late" stages in the PDS. Recalling our earlier reference to Burrowes and Spector (1973, p. 317), "If relationships exist between [certain variables, or certain combinations of variables], they probably do so only for *certain* types of [actors], at *certain* times, and under *certain* circumstances" (emphasis added). In any case, as Most and Starr (1989, p. 100) remind us, "Decision makers, the goals that motivate them, and the choices that they make – whether or not they are value-maximizing selections – must be considered at some point."

Given that Waltz's hypothesis of the primacy of the international level in international conflict was confirmed for the four foreign conflict models for the early stage, the Alliances (ALL) models for all three stages and the Manifest Distrust (MD) model for PDS 1–5 combined, another next step would be to incorporate something like Systemic Environmental Complexity (SEC) – the operative variable in all cases but one in the tests of Waltz – into research designs concerned with real-world conflict processes.

There are other reasons for incorporating SEC into future research designs. For instance, as indicated in Table 5.6, which compared rankings of best-predicting independent variables in the PDS with rankings of corresponding variables in Vasquez's (1976) study, had SEC been included in the rankings, it would have ranked second for the PDS 1–5 combined models, fourth for the intermediate models, and second for the late models, as well as first for the early models. In any case, SEC should continue to be monitored as a source of "complexity, incalculability, and uncertainty" linked to increases in international conflict (Waltz, 1964, 1967 and Rosecrance, 1966), especially given the post-Cold War increase in SEC and ethnic conflict.[9]

Implicit here is yet another reason for including SEC in future research endeavors: SEC seems to "arouse" a major element of ethnic conflict, *territoriality*. In this regard, we noted in Chapter 6 Vasquez's (1993) arguments that "concerns over territory, not power, have been the underlying and fundamental source of conflict that ends in war"; that "issues involving territorial contiguity are indeed the most war prone"; that, therefore, "states with more borders should experience more wars," and, consequently, "the more states in the system" (SEC), the more wars (ATT) can be expected (*ibid.*, pp. 124–5, 142, 145). Vasquez has also argued that territoriality "is deeply ingrained and is part of humanity's collective *genetic* inheritance" (*ibid.*, pp. 139–40; emphasis added).

Vasquez's territoriality thesis coheres with Pfeiffer's (1984, p. 92) speculation that the tendency to bifurcate people into "them" and "us" and to reserve most of our wrath for them may "have been inherited from times past and wired in from birth." It is also compatible with Wilson's (1979, pp. 122–3) observation that "Our brains do appear to be programmed to the . . . extent [that] we are inclined to partition other people into friends and aliens [and] to fear deeply the actions of strangers and to solve conflict by aggression." Hence, the tendency to distinguish *our* land from *their* land and to protect (or retake) *our* land from *them*. And as Terrell Northrup (1989, pp. 68–9) aptly reminds us, "Loss of [one's] land . . . means more than . . . the loss of territory; it implies the loss of self [identity], psychic annihilation in a sense." Suddenly, the otherwise inexplicable "ethnic cleansing" practiced in former Yugoslavia and elsewhere becomes more explicable: territoriality (i.e. the need for a stable, safe environment) is relevant to maximizing inclusive fitness and kin selection.

Assuming that men are more "programmed" in this regard than are women, one next step for research would be to multiply SEC by the number of male decision-makers as a proportion of total decision-makers per group, to explore the interaction effects of (apparent) systemic environment-stimulated territoriality and male gender on conflict behavior.

We should also continue to incorporate something like Systemic Attack Contagion (SAC) in our designs even though, in the present study, it achieved primacy only for the ALL model for the intermediate stage and appeared in only one other model, that for BEL for PDS 1–5 combined, as the least dominant variable. SAC would allow us to explore to what extent, if any, *multiplier-effect systemic contagion* was operative. The more actors in the system (SEC), the more conflicts, and the more conflicts in any part of the system (SAC), the more there may be elsewhere later on; as Griffiths (1993, p. 124) reminds us with regard to the former Soviet Union, where the possibility of "some kind of post-Cold War 'domino-effect' of conflict and societal collapse from region to region and level to level . . . is most credible." In short, SAC would allow us to explore the validity of Robert Kaplan's "The Coming Anarchy" (1994, 1996).

Given the role and record of simulation in this study, i.e. in generating some interesting findings which held up rather well in a comprehensive validation assessment, the technique should continue to be utilized in appropriate research endeavors. One idea that comes to mind is a *gaming simulation/computer simulation/real-world* research design model that fits neatly into Most and Starr's (1989, p. 9) *theory–research design–findings–theory* model, associated with *integrative cumulation*.

In the first phase of such a research paradigm (*context of discovery A*), gaming simulation (e.g. the PDS or INS) could be used, in part, to explore the role of gender and personality in conflict and, assuming an operation involving, for instance, "real" Croats, Serbs, and Muslims, the role of culture as well. In the second phase (*context of discovery B*), computer simulation could be used to explore further the implications of "first-phase" findings, such as the tendency in the PDS for environmentally stimulated conflict processes to be replaced by self-stimulating/self-perpetuating conflict processes. Computer simulation could also be used to experiment with interactions between gender, personality, culture and situational variables and their effects on conflict, and with various time-lags.[10] And then, in the third phase (*context of justification*), the results generated by computer simulation could be tested or otherwise further explored in the real world, either *indirectly*, through *secondary* analyses of existing corresponding data and/or, similar to the validation assessments conducted here, by comparison with findings of corresponding real-world studies; or *directly*, through *primary* analyses of data generated by appropriately designed surveys, field studies or field experiments.

Needless to say, variations on the research paradigm can occur, such that – as in this study – one can go directly from gaming simulation to real-world exploration of findings, or begin with computer simulation, and then go on to the real world. In either case, the objective is, through feedback, to enrich the theory with which one begins, or otherwise develops in, the process.

As will be discussed below, simulation in general can be used to organize bits and pieces of real-world knowledge into coherent descriptive and explanatory systems (see Guetzkow, 1969). Such coherence – especially of knowledge systems tending toward *integrative cumulation* – would facilitate the use of "generic theory" of complex conflict systems as a basis for preventing or otherwise dealing with violent conflict and war. This takes us into practice.

Some Further Implications for Practice

If our findings, including our generic theory, are to be used as a basis for practice, then we have to have something *coherent* to say to policy-makers and, as indicated in Chapter 6, we believe that we do. We then have to communicate that knowledge, in as effective a manner as possible, to appropriate policy-makers at the national and international levels (NGOs as well as IGOs) (see Leatherman and Väyrynen, 1995). And, finally, policy-makers must be able to act upon that knowledge.

Impediments to the Effective Use of Knowledge as a Basis for Practice

All of this may be easier said than done, however, as throughout the processes of knowledge creation, transference and use, there are problems which can impede the effective use of knowledge as a basis for practice. Implicit here is *complexity*, not only of violent conflict and war as *research* and *practical problems*, but also in the communication between conflict researchers and policy-makers that can connect research to practice.

First of all, the PDS findings suggest that conflict behavior, as a practical problem, can become *self-stimulating/self-perpetuating*, perhaps without much thought on the part of the actors involved, except within the context of a *Realpolitik* framework. Or more generally, as Robert North (1975, p. 4), referencing John Platt (1971, p. 33), puts it, "At any given moment, a society, like a vehicle, is 'at a particular place with a particular direction of motion determined by its *previous history*'" (emphasis added). Hence, Sherif's (1967, Ch. 2) thesis of the "heavy hand of the past" and the role it appears to play in apparently self-stimulating/self-perpetuating conflict processes such as those in the Balkans (e.g. the "legacy of Kosovo"), Northern Ireland, and elsewhere. In such cases, "we may be understandably pessimistic . . . that [these observations] offer a gloomy picture, indeed. None of [the] variables are truly manipulative in the policy relevant sense that they can be altered easily by the conscious actions of officials" (Starr, 1975, p. 59).

Accordingly, while policy-makers might find the PDS findings and the generic theory influenced by them interesting and decide, as part of an NEPSS-type of strategy, to intervene in an apparently self-stimulating/self-perpetuating "conflict-as-process" to achieve negative peace, they might experience considerable difficulty in moving beyond negative peace, to encourage the parties to deal with their underlying historical grievances: their conflict-as-startup conditions. This is, perhaps, one reason why peace-keeping (negative peace) rarely gives way to peace-building (positive peace): "history" *is* difficult, if not impossible, to undo, its variables not easily responsive to "manipulation."

The complexity of war as a practical problem, however, is preceded and influenced by the complexity of war as a research problem. Just taking into account the measurement of variables and the number of *bivariate* correlations computed for this study (over one thousand), I am compelled to agree with Karl Deutsch (1964, p. xv) that, "once we try to specify quantitative variables within each of [our broad categories], their number soon becomes large and their analysis difficult"; with Trevor Taylor (1978, p. 11) that, "clearly attempts to keep track of and understand so many variables must meet enormous problems"; with Russett *et al.* (1964, p. 1) that this type of research strategy "clearly can lead to inundation by too much data . . . where neither mind nor computer can absorb and sort out the information"; and with Charles McClelland (1972, p. 36) that, by employing such a strategy, "massive frustrations are . . . to be anticipated."

Cognitive overload of this kind could also affect policy-makers attempting to make sense of the findings of this study, including exploring their relevance as a basis for policy later on. And, whether overloaded or not, policy-makers might still miss the complexity of conflict processes:

> There are real and specific reasons why politicians, planners, managers, and statesmen, *as well as* scholars and the public at large, tend to misjudge the behavior of large and *complex* social systems. . . . "It is my basic

theme," wrote Jay W. Forrester a number of years back [1971], "*that the human mind is not adapted to interpreting how social systems behave. Our social systems belong to the class called multi-loop, non-linear feedback systems.* . . . [Consequently] a society may suffer a "growing sense of futility" as it repeatedly attacks deficiencies while the "symptoms continue to worsen." (North, 1975, p. 6; emphasis added; also see Frei and Ruloff, 1989, pp. 3–4)

Hence, not only policy-makers, but the rest of us as well, tend toward *cognitive simplicity*: to act on the basis of simplistic and often fallacious views about complex systems and as a result, to generate counterproductive and dysfunctional outcomes – a basic point of departure for the present study – without appreciating the role that we ourselves have played in the process.

In between the complexity of violent conflict and war as a research problem and as a practical problem lies the complexity of "intercultural" communication: scholars and policy-makers tend not to communicate too effectively with each other (see O'Leary *et al.*, 1974). Leatherman and Väyrynen (1995, p. 54) indicate that there is a gap, not only "between academics and national foreign policy-makers, but also between academics and international civil servants, diplomats and other international policy-makers involved in multilateral decision-making." Even if communication were more effective on all fronts, however, policy-makers might still not be much better off than they are now in terms of dealing effectively with complex conflict processes:

> It is indeed unfortunate that most political scientists, sociologists, and psychologists tend to be most familiar with *proximate factors* (causes and functions) involving cognitive, social, physical, and neurophysiological stimulus events which surround and mediate conflict. Why is this so? One reason is that the study of proximate factors allows more control, involves less time, and is more convenient and inexpensive than the comparative, longitudinal, and genetic approaches required to shed light on *ultimate factors*. Second, analysis of different *kinds* of proximate causes is the *raison d'être* for the different academic disciplines themselves. An interdisciplinary approach, on the other hand, attempts to decode *complex*, ultimate structures involving the *interaction* of many different kinds of variables. (Shaw and Wong, 1989, pp. 11–12; emphasis added)

Although the findings reported here are more reflective of "proximate" than of "ultimate" causes, they are nevertheless a move in the right direction: an interdisciplinary approach that generates insights into complex conflict processes. Hence, even allowing for cognitive overload, cognitive simplicity, and ineffective communication between conflict researchers and policy-makers, attempts should still be made to make policy-makers aware of what may lead to and perpetuate conflictful and self-defeating relationships. Perhaps then, "controlling" as much as possible for the "heavy hand of the past," "They can . . . take extra care in relations with others so as not to exacerbate the factors of belligerency which could, if unattended, truly make them '*prisoners of the situations* in which they find themselves'" (Starr, 1975, p. 60; emphasis added).

Making policy-makers alone aware of certain knowledge, however, may not be sufficient to encourage them to take care. Conflict researchers must also attempt to make aware those upon whom policy-makers ultimately base their support, the public at large:

> a truly monumental effort involving educational processes and teaching methods, professionals of all fields, minorities, women, and youth must be actively used to stem aggression and eliminate all practices of colonialism, racism, hostility, hatred, prejudice and warfare. Such efforts must, however, be preceded by objective knowledge as to how these behaviors have come about and are perpetuated [i.e. knowledge about violent conflict and war as research problems]. (Shaw and Wong, 1989, p. 208)

The self-stimulating/self-perpetuating conflict processes revealed by the PDS are part of that knowledge. As discussed in Chapter 7, such processes could have led, and as of this writing have led, via various forms of spillover, to further warfare in former Yugoslavia. "Complexity," however, might still inhibit policy-makers from acting.

Managing Complexity in Conflict Systems: Toward a Theory–Research–Practice Synergy

In an article which should be better known than it is, Harold Guetzkow (1969, p. 286) argued persuasively in favor of the use of simulation to achieve three goals relevant to the "consolidation and utilization of knowledge about international relations":

> (1) simulations may be used as techniques for increasing the coherence within and among models, enabling scholars to assess gaps and closure in our theories; (2) simulations may be used as constructions in terms of which empirical research may be organized so that the validity of our assertions may be appraised; [and] (3) simulations may be used by [decisionmakers] in the development of policy, both as devices for making systemic critiques ["hits and misses"], and as formats for the exploration of alternative[s].

Simulation and Integrative Cumulation

Our use of the PDS has focused on objectives (1) and (2), to achieve not only the "normal science" type (see Kuhn, 1970) of *additive cumulation*, whereby one refines and expands on what one already knows, but the potentially "extraordinary science" type of *integrative cumulation* (see Zinnes, 1976; Most and Starr, 1989; Bremer and Cusack, 1995), whereby one goes beyond what one already knows, perhaps shifting or combining paradigms in the process.

As indicated in Chapter 5, the overall findings of the PDS have been subjected to comprehensive validation assessment, with rather impressive results, despite the claims by some (e.g. Bull, 1966) that the really important variables cannot be measured, and by others (e.g. Singer, 1965, p. 76; Vital, 1969, pp. 148–9) that simulation cannot tell us anything that we did not already know or that we could not discover from other sources.

Given the vast methodological and epistemological differences between PDS variables and those of comparable real-world and other studies, the fact that the results of most of our various validation assessments were agreement scores of, or approximating, *75 percent* is suggestive of some very interesting implications. The basic tenet of *general systems theory*, for instance – that apparently different systems can be characterized by structural and behavioral similarities (see von Bertalanffy, 1973) – has been rather impressively supported by our validation assessments. This, coupled with Guetzkow's 75 percent norm validation of the INS, plus the experiences of others (e.g. Saperstein, 1995; Beriker and Druckman, 1996) reinforces the view that some simulations, at least, are appropriate for investigating real-world conflict processes.

The validation assessment encouraged a revamping of the pretheory (Chapter 2) into a generic theory of violent conflict and war (Chapter 6), and an application of that theory to the ethnic conflicts and warfare of the post-Cold War world (Chapter 7). Over the course of its existence, the project has moved beyond "additive" and into "integrative cumulation," especially in the applied theory phase, where NEPSS and its integrated systems of conflict resolution networks effectively combine two, normally competing, paradigms: *Realpolitik* (horizontal integration) and *Idealpolitik* (vertical integration). In Most and Starr's (1989, p. 181) words, "Instead of the critical test perspective, which asks, 'which model/theory [*Realpolitik* or *Idealpolitik*] is better?' we want to ask 'under what conditions does each model work?' " NEPSS's integrated systems are about different responses to shifting conditions, but always in the context of an overall *Idealpolitik* framework.

Kuhn (1970, p. 77) tells us that "crisis is a necessary precondition for the emergence of novel theories." NEPSS is an applied-theory response to the crisis posed by the wars in former Yugoslavia. It is also an attempt to respond to Guetzkow's third objective: providing decision-makers with policy-making insights and recommendations. In Yugoslavia-type situations, especially where genocidal policies have come to characterize the behavior of one or more parties, those members of the international community materially and otherwise capable of acting should, according to NEPSS, collaboratively employ an appropriate degree of *Realpolitik* within a basically *Idealpolitik* framework, to achieve negative peace as a necessary (but not sufficient) condition of positive peace. This is a major policy implication of the *Genesis of War* project, which, thus far, remains "theoretical," in part because of the complexity of war "writ small" as a practical problem.

Catastrophe, Chaos, and Complexity: Revolutionary Shifts from Static Conditions to Dynamic Processes

The shift from *static* structures, attributes, and events to *dynamic* processes, recommended by Most and Starr (1989) as part of their reconceptualization of the relationships between logic, theory, and methodology in research on international conflict and war, dovetails with certain developments in how to think about and deal with complex problems in the natural as well as social sciences (see *ibid.*, p. 184). Among these, *catastrophe theory* is concerned with sudden shifts – "jumps" – from one stable state to another in dynamic "systems which for the most part exhibit *continuous*, smoothly moving forms of behaviour" (Nicholson, 1989, p. 167; emphasis added; also see Zeeman, 1977; Woodcock and Davis, 1978, p. 25).

Chaos theory is concerned with the development of order, stability, and predictability in a world governed by the progressive disorder of the Second Law of Thermodynamics (entropy). Important here is the notion of "sensitive dependence on initial conditions," whereby relatively minor changes in "startup conditions" can lead to massive changes later on: "In weather, for example, this translates into . . . the Butterfly Effect – the notion that a butterfly stirring the air today in Peking can transform storm systems next month in New York" (Gleick, 1987, p. 8).

Also important in chaos theory are *strange attractors*: stable regularities toward which irregularity is pulled. "No matter what the starting 'population,' it will bounce steadily in toward the attractor. . . . [Hence,] *different systems . . . behave identically*" (*ibid.*, pp. 175, 180; emphasis added). Or, as the beauty of *fractals* indicates, there is *self-similarity* at different levels (*ibid.*, Chapter 4), which may account, to some extent, for the fairly consistent 75 percent correspondence rate revealed by the comprehensive validation assessment of PDS findings:

> No matter what the medium, the behavior obeys the same newly discovered laws. That realization has begun to change the way business executives make decisions about insurance, the way astronomers look at the solar system, the way that political scientists talk about the stresses leading to armed conflict. (*Ibid.*, p. 5)

Finally, *complexity theory* deals with behavior at the "edge of chaos" – critical regions in systems involving complex balances between order (stability, predictability) and chaos (instability, unpredictability) – where spontaneous organization, life, and consciousness can occur (see Waldrop, 1992).

All three perspectives reflect a general systems type of interdisciplinarity, in that expressions of them can be found in the social as well as natural sciences. The three are clearly linked, in that, for instance, catastrophe can be generated by chaos, while chaos inheres in complexity. Complexity, then, is the overarching framework for theorists and researchers in economics, biology, physics, and other fields using mathematics and computer simulation, emphasizing holistic *synthesis* instead of atomistic *analysis* and focusing on dynamic process instead of static content, in their efforts to deal with "messy" *nonlinear* processes – *discontinuities*.

Complexity Theory and Conflict Studies

Given small differences in the "start-up conditions" of biological, economic, physical, and other systems, therefore, the consequences may be "catastrophically" or otherwise radically different. To paraphrase Heisenberg's *Uncertainty Principle* from quantum mechanics (see Nagel, 1961, pp. 293–305), in such cases, neither analysts nor policy-makers would be able to predict a system's behavior with "unlimited precision." Nevertheless, there would also be discernible patterns underlying chaos, thereby keeping alive the possibility of prediction.

As with many, if not all, innovations in thought, complexity theory had been around for a while before it was conceptualized as such (see Saperstein, 1995). In conflict analysis and resolution, for instance, Kenneth Boulding (1962, p. 24) remarked:

> Human beings are moved not only by immediate pressures but by distant goals that are contemplated in the imagination. These goals are susceptible of change, often of *dramatic change*, as a result of apparently *slight changes* in current information. On the other hand, they also have a good deal of stability, and this gives a stability to the system in the large that it may not have in the small. (Emphasis added)[11]

Lewis F. Richardson's (1939, 1960a) work on arms race dynamics is another source of ideas in conflict studies overlapping those of complexity theory: in a dyadic relationship, depending upon each actor's *sensitivities* to the other's arms levels (mutual fears), plus each's constraints on further arms spending (limiting factors), and underlying grievances, there could be a *stable balance of power* with regard to "rate[s] of rearmament or disarmament"; or an *unstable equilibrium* in which either complete disarmament or a runaway arms race is possible. There could also be *radical shifts*, either between stable and unstable systems (or vice versa), "for relatively modest variations in . . . assumptions" regarding mutual fears, limiting factors, and grievances (Nicholson, 1989, p. 152);[12] or within the unstable condition, from complete disarmament to a runaway arms race (or vice versa), for "small shift[s] in the position of the initial point" of armament expenditures at "time zero" (*ibid.*) (also see Rapoport, 1960, Chapter 1; Boulding, 1962, Chapter 2; Saperstein, 1995).

Complexity Theory and Conflict Resolution: Managing Entropic Conflict Systems in the Post-Cold War World

It is clear that conflict researchers and policy-makers cannot predict with certainty what kinds of conflicts-as-process will develop from various kinds of conflicts-as-startup conditions, or be able to predict the course of any particular conflict-as-process. The danger in this, of course, is that conflict researchers may be paralyzed into recommending nothing and policy-makers paralyzed into doing nothing, or at least nothing of major significance: witness Bosnia-Hercegovina, at least up to Dayton.

But we should be fair: the danger of paralysis derives from the possibility that conflicts-as-process could, unpredictably, and because of very small shifts in existing conditions, escalate out of control. In other words, beyond some threshold, conflicts-as-process could escalate into self-stimulating/self-perpetuating spirals, where attempts to deal with them could backfire, leading to destruction of the conflict systems themselves. In such cases, we can talk of *entropic conflicts*: conflicts which approach entropy, or progressive disorder.

The danger that, unpredictably, conflicts can assume an entropic character – what Gregory Bateson (1973, p. 98) refers to as a *schismogenic* "regenerative causal circuit or vicious circle" – is implicit in the horizontal dimension of integrated systems of conflict resolution networks. The use of a "measured" amount of *Realpolitik*, even as part of an *Idealpolitik* strategy to achieve negative peace as a necessary (but not sufficient) condition of positive peace, could backfire, making matters worse. This may explain why, with the exception of the NATO bombing campaign, which, in part, led to the Dayton Peace Agreement, Robert Axelrod's (1984) *Theory of Cooperation* has not been applied to Bosnia.

Axelrod has argued that in all situations involving the Prisoners' Dilemma, from the interpersonal to the international levels, the best way to act is in terms of the *TIT FOR TAT* strategy (*ibid.*, p. 176):

> TIT FOR TAT's robust success [in PD situations] is due to being nice, provocable, forgiving, and clear. Its *niceness* means that it is never the first to defect, and this property prevents it from getting into unnecessary trouble. Its *retaliation* discourages the other side from persisting whenever defection is tried. Its *forgiveness* helps restore mutual cooperation. And its *clarity* makes its behavioral pattern easy to recognize; and once recognized, it is easy to perceive that the best way of dealing with TIT FOR TAT is to cooperate with it. (Emphasis added; also see *ibid.*, p. 54)

For TIT FOR TAT to work, however, "the future must have a sufficiently large shadow" (*ibid.*, p. 174):

> the importance of the next encounter between the same two individuals must be great enough to make defection an unprofitable strategy when the other player is provocable. It requires that the players have a large enough chance of meeting again and that they do not discount the significance of their next meeting too greatly.

Extending Axelrod's theory to the wars in former Yugoslavia, leads to the following scenario:

1. Slovenian and especially Croatian declarations of independence from the Yugoslav Federation in June 1991 resurrected Serbian fears (especially among Serbs living in Croatia) of Croatian defection from the stable TIT FOR TAT equilibrium that had existed up to that point.
2. Serbian military successes, plus the "nonprovocability" of the international community, stimulated the development and exacerbation of a violent, asymmetrical conflict-as-process, i.e. "ethnic cleansing," which was prosecuted by the Serbs against the major victims of the wars in former Yugoslavia, Bosnian Slavic Muslims.

3. In the absence of the "provocability" of the Bosnian Slavic Muslims, the international community was effectively shamed into becoming "provocable" and retaliating against the Serbian "defection" from the previously stable TIT FOR TAT equilibrium, although in a very restrained way (as in the "live-and-let-live" system of trench warfare during World War I; see Axelrod, 1984, Chapter 4). Subsequently, the international community has been "forgiving" toward the Serbs to avoid stimulating new or exacerbating ongoing violent conflict spirals.
4. The international community has embarked on a "train-and-equip" program for a joint Bosnian Muslim–Croat army (see Pomfret, 1996a), so that Bosnian Muslims in particular can, in the future, become appropriately "provocable."

In terms of this analysis, the "provocability" of the international community (more so than of the Bosnian Muslims) has been the issue. Until Dayton, the international community had not been sufficiently "provocable" in Bosnia-Hercegovina, perhaps because of paralysis associated with the unpredictability of the consequences of even minor adjustments in complex systems capable of generating entropic conflict processes. As Michael Lund (1996, p. 111) tells us, "From 1990 into 1992, it may be remembered, a major obstacle to European and U.S. involvement in the Yugoslavian imbroglio was considerable *uncertainty* as to the wider ramifications of the gathering storm" (emphasis added). But even with Dayton, the "provocability" of the international community remains an issue:

> The tussle during the last few days between the Bosnian Serb leadership and western leaders was hauntingly familiar.
>
> First came the demand from the international community: Radovan Karadzic must resign. Then came the threat: If Mr. Karadzic does not step down sanctions will be imposed. Then came a vague promise by the Bosnian Serbs to comply, followed by no compliance. And on Monday [July 1, 1996] the [then] chief international mediator, Carl Bildt, who set the whole thing in motion, said that sanctions are probably not such a good idea after all.
>
> The artful dance by the Bosnian Serbs, and less artful retreat by the West, has been polished over the last four years of marathon peace negotiations, broken ceasefires, hostage-taking and military attacks on sanctuaries that were supposed to have been under UN protection.
>
> The Bosnian Serbs have learned that the NATO-led force, just as the UN peacekeeping troops that preceded it, has no stomach for a confrontation. . . .
>
> But the latest round with Mr. Karadzic, a repeat of a similar struggle between Mr. Karadzic and Mr. Bildt in May, is chipping away at the credibility of the NATO-led mission in Bosnia. And the decision by western leaders to back away from the latest demand rather than enforce it, is creating a crisis of confidence that could lead to increasing defiance by the Bosnian Serb leader. . . .
>
> It was, according to many western diplomats, a humiliating retreat and

> one that was greeted with jubilation in the self-styled Republic of Srpska. (Hedges, 1996b)

All this came a week or so before the first "anniversary" of the fall of the UN "protected safe area" of Srebrenica:

> Bosnian Serbs celebrated Thursday [July 11, 1996] the first anniversary of the conquest of Srebrenica while, nearby, war crimes investigators were sorting through bones and fragments of [some 40 corpses believed to be just a fraction of the more than 7000 Muslim] men and boys captured and shot after the Muslim enclave fell. . . .
>
> Serbs marked their victory . . . and reiterated their goal of keeping the territory "*ethnically pure*."
>
> "There is no place for *Turks* [the derogatory term the Serbs use for Bosnian Muslims, whose ancestors adopted the Islamic faith of Turkish invaders] in Republika Srpska," said General Milenko Zivanovic, the regional commander, who led the final assault on Srebrenica. (AP, 1996; emphasis added)

Taking into account the observation that the conditions specified by Dayton for "free and fair elections" in Bosnia – freedom of movement, freedom of expression, freedom of press, and freedom of association – had *not* been met, even though the OSCE declared that national elections could nevertheless take place on September 14, 1996 (see Hedges, 1996a) and municipal elections a year later, it is clear that, as of this writing, with the exception of the NATO bombing campaign leading up to Dayton, Axelrod's theory remains basically untried and untested in former Yugoslavia.

Paul Stern and Daniel Druckman (1994/5, p. 114) view Axelrod's theory as an example of the strongest evidence of the "hegemonic position of realism" in U.S. international relations thinking and practice, because it effectively legitimates cooperation within the *Realpolitik* paradigm.[13] Axelrod's theory is certainly appropriate for *Realpolitik*-defined realities, such as the wars in former Yugoslavia. In Bosnia-Hercegovina, for instance, Anthony Lewis (1996) has concluded that "The only thing that ever moved the Bosnian Serbs to more than empty promises during the war [there] was force." Also, a Bosnian Serb official in the city of Brcko has characterized the Dayton Peace Agreement's call for the return of refugees as "a clear attempt to change the *biological* structure of the city." He went on to assert, with Muslim refugees in mind, that "We will defend our frontiers *biologically*" (Dobbs, 1996a; emphasis added), thereby implying a continuation of the doctrine and practice of "ethnic cleansing."

But of the four elements of TIT FOR TAT, only two – provocability and clarity – reflect *Realpolitik* as such. TIT FOR TAT's other two elements – niceness and forgiveness – locate it in a more "complex" constellation of options, very much like that suggested by Stern and Druckman's own "contours of a new paradigm" (1994/5, pp. 115–17) and by the "4 + 2 framework" mentioned in Chapter 6, which combines *Realpolitik*, *Idealpolitik*, Marxist, and non-Marxist radical definitions of reality, plus cooperative and competitive means for dealing with conflict. This "complex" orientation shares with Fisher and Keashly's (1991) "contingency model" the prescription of using what is necessary under one set of conditions, but of using other tools as well when those conditions have changed (also see Fisher, 1993). It is also compatible with integrated systems of conflict resolution networks, where, if the vertical dimension cannot be implemented because one party is imposing a genocidal "final solution" on another, then the horizontal dimension becomes activated, but only as part of a basically *Idealpolitik* approach. Indeed, TIT FOR TAT, like integrated systems of conflict resolution networks, *is* a response to "complexity": it can encourage, through learning and evolution, the development of cooperation out of the "coevolutionary dance of competition and cooperation" at the "edge of chaos" (see Waldrop, 1992, pp. 259–60, 262–5, 292–4).

But for TIT FOR TAT to be successful, there must be, in addition to a "sufficiently large shadow" of the future (which, admittedly, ethnic cleansing has been eroding), stability in the sense of Richardson's (1939, 1960a) "balance of power" – another *Realpolitik* aspect – between the "coevolving" parties in their respective capabilities to inflict pain on one another. Unless a stable balance exists, the parties may engage in what Lewis Coser (1956, p. 136) calls a "trial by ordeal," in which "conflict may be an important balancing mechanism" designed to achieve the very equilibrium that may be absent to begin with:

> Conflict consists in a test of power between antagonistic parties. Accommodation between them is possible only if each is aware of the relative strength of both parties. However, paradoxical as it may seem, such knowledge can most frequently be attained only through conflict, since other mechanisms for testing the respective strengths of antagonists seem to be unavailable.
>
> Consequently, struggle may be an important way to avoid conditions of disequilibrium by modifying the basis for power relations. (*Ibid.*, p. 137)

Apropos less lethal forms of conflict management (e.g. mediation or arbitration), Coser tells us that such "Efforts . . . encounter the difficulty that the assessment of the actual power relations between the contenders can hardly be made before their relative power has been established through struggle" (*ibid.*, pp. 135–6).

The U.S.-led effort to arm the Bosnian Muslims appears to be designed to "make possible a reassessment of relative power and thus serve as a balancing mechanism which helps to maintain and consolidate societies" (*ibid.*, p. 137). It appears to be designed, therefore, to provide a material basis for increased Muslim "provocability," especially in the relative absence of such on the part of the international community, thereby establishing a stable balance of power and ensuring that TIT FOR TAT succeeds in Bosnia without further international intervention.[14]

There is, however, a problem with "balance of power," as there is with *Realpolitik* in general. As Shaw and Wong (1989, p. 47) imply, "trials by ordeal" to determine "relative strength," as manifested in former Yugoslavia, are associated with "groups as forces of selection [which] represent an emergent, proximate, environmental cause [of war]":

> Since failure to maintain a balance of power could have resulted in extinction, groups and their expansion figure as *forces of selection* in our theory. Motivated by resource competition, conflict, and warfare, struggles to maintain balances of power [have given] rise to more complex societal units which [have] continued the legacy of intergroup warfare. . . . It is by this process that out-group enmity and ethnocentrism have been reinforced and carried over from nucleus ethnic group to band, to tribe, to chiefdom, to nation-state. (*Ibid.*, p. 45)

Complexity theory, therefore, in the full sense of integrated systems of conflict resolution networks, involves more than stable balances associated with negative peace; it also involves building upon and transcending these and, in positive peace fashion, dealing with the deep-rooted causes and conditions that make, in the shorter run, the balances necessary.

The problem with the Dayton Peace Agreement for Bosnia is not only that the physical and emotional reconstruction of the country (positive peace) is lagging behind the enforced prevention of violence (negative peace), but also – with provocability still an issue – that the negative peace is not a stable one. TIT FOR TAT, therefore, and with it complexity theory in general, still remains to be fully applied to Bosnia.[15]

Complexity, Unified Field Theory, and Postmodernism

Complexity theory is associated with the idea that "Everything affects everything else, and [we] have to understand that whole web of connections[:] everything is connected, and often with incredible sensitivity [such that] the slightest uncertainty can grow until the system's future becomes utterly unpredictable – or, in a word chaotic" (Waldrop, 1992, pp. 60–1, 66, and Chapter 2 in general; also see Jervis, 1997). While *complexity* may have generated paralysis over Bosnia, *complexity theory* has given new meaning to a possible antidote: "unified field theory" as a framework that incorporates *all* disciplines in an effort to explain, and to facilitate dealing with, the foci of any one of them:

> Complexity, adaptation, upheavals at the edge of chaos – these common themes are so striking that a growing number of scientists are convinced that there is more here than just a series of nice analogues. . . . they all share the vision of an *underlying unity, a common theoretical framework for complexity* that would illuminate nature *and* humankind alike. (Waldrop, 1992, p. 12; emphasis added)

Heinz Pagels (1988) has also argued in this regard that complexity theory "would produce a dramatic '*new synthesis*' melding computer science, biology, math, anthropology and more [in which] 'the radical distinction between mind *and* nature [would] disappear' " (cited in Suplee, 1992, p. 10; emphasis added). Accordingly, the four-worlds' model offered earlier as a candidate for an embryonic "unified field theory" of violent conflict and war could be seen against the background of this more comprehensive interdisciplinary tendency toward *holism* and, therefore, as a potential contribution to the development of such a synthesis. Together with NEPSS and integrated systems, it could also be used as a basis for capturing the complexity of conflict processes and counteracting the tendency toward paralysis in Bosnia and elsewhere.

The overall sense that traditional disciplinary boundaries are breaking down, together with the emphasis on process and addressing what has traditionally been excluded (e.g. "chaos" and "complexity" themselves), is an idea that complexity theory shares with *postmodernism*: "one of the greatest intellectual challenges to established knowledge of the twentieth century" (Pauline Marie Rosenau, 1992, p. 5 and Chapter 1 in general). Indeed, although differing fundamentally in other ways (e.g. in whether or not there *is* a "reality" which is "knowable"), complexity theory and postmodernism overlap significantly, e.g. complexity theory, as implied above, is itself a postmodern development, while postmodernism is part of the chaos that coexists in complex ways with order (e.g. modernism) at the "edge of chaos." Complexity theory, therefore, remains a significant, overarching framework for future developments in human knowledge, including efforts in conflict analysis and resolution to better understand and deal with "future Yugoslavias."

Conclusion

The PDS has revealed that, over time, conflicts can become self-stimulating/self-perpetuating. If such conflicts-as-process continue, they can, through "positive feedback," overwhelm their original startup conditions and destroy the systems of which they are part. The application of the PDS-influenced generic theory to the apparently self-stimulating/self-perpetuating conflicts in former Yugoslavia facilitated the creation of NEPSS and its integrated systems of conflict resolution networks. Had NEPSS and its corresponding mechanisms been fully in place before 1989, they might have made a difference. In any case, with further appropriate development, as outlined in this volume and elsewhere (Sandole, 1995, 1998), they may help to prevent "future Yugoslavias."

NEPSS is a response to the "common predicament" (Sherif, 1967) embodied in Rousseau's statement that "wars occur because there is nothing to prevent them" (cited in Waltz, 1959, p. 232). NEPSS can attempt to deal with this, and the corresponding superordinate goal of transforming "exogenous" into "endogenous" systems (Rapoport, 1974, p. 175), by, among other things, encouraging international governmental organizations (IGOs) to work together among themselves, and to work with corresponding nongovernmental organizations (NGOs) more synergistically and effectively than they have before, especially in the enhancement of existing, and the creation of new, mechanisms and processes for collaborative problem-solving approaches to conflict resolution:

> [One] challenge of early warning is establishing tighter conceptual and communication linkages between early warning analysts, on the one hand,

> and busy decision makers and practitioners, on the other hand, so that the latter receive analyses in concrete forms that are relevant and usable. . . .
>
> Some early warning data-bases employ complex formats, terminologies, and methodologies that are unfamiliar to policymakers, and ways to encourage use of such systems in the policy and implementation process are needed. (Lund, 1996, pp. 112–13)

Thus far, ideas such as these, while they may have found their way into the thinking, have not appreciably influenced the actions of the peace and security "architects" of post-Cold War Europe (see Sandole, 1994a, 1995a); perhaps, in part, because of paralysis associated with the unpredictability of the consequences of even minor adjustments in complex conflict systems.

The imperative remains, therefore, for conflict researchers and conflict resolution practitioners to continue doing what Samuel Lewis (1992), former president of the U.S. Institute of Peace, has challenged them to do: help policy-makers better understand and deal with the post-Cold War world. For those who are skeptical about the motives of national governments (see Rubenstein, 1992), this is even more reason to respond to the Lewis challenge, to, in effect, invoke John Burton's (1991) *consultative role of the professional in conflict resolution*: to assist policy-makers in identifying, designing, and implementing policies facilitative of conflict resolution, provention (transformation), and positive peace.

Part of this challenge, if Yugoslavia is *not* to become a precedent, model, and metaphor for the future, would be for conflict researchers to continue working on war as a research problem. This means, among other things, *mapping* conceptually and *modelling* empirically, in terms of the four levels of the generic theory or the four worlds of the embryonic "unified field theory," the elements of developing and manifest conflict processes, especially those involving "minorities at risk." It also means *monitoring*, via computer, changes in the primarily "proximate" variables, including SEC and SAC, plus the effects of interaction among the independent variables, keeping in mind that the optimal time to have a positive effect is early in the development of conflict processes, at the preventive diplomacy stage (Boutros-Ghali, 1992; Leatherman and Väyrynen, 1995, p. 63).

There is, of course, the argument that the problem with former Yugoslavia was not one of early warning but one of political will to do something about the situation early on. Perhaps political will would be less of a problem if policy-makers were advised by conflict resolution theorists and practitioners about, among others, Fisher and Keashly's (1991) *contingency model of third party intervention*; Zartman's (1989), Haass's (1990), and Stedman's (1991) work on *ripeness* of conflict for resolution (also see Kleiboer, 1994; Mitchell, 1995); and other work dealing with aspects of conflict termination (e.g. Kriesberg, 1987; Mitchell, 1991); and if diplomats and military personnel were trained in conflict resolution skills, to enhance the probability that knowledge of developing and manifest conflicts could be appropriately and effectively acted on at the preventive diplomacy and other stages.

Needless to say, for such advice and training to be solicited or otherwise welcomed, policy-makers would have to be more receptive to track-2 than they have been in the past. Here, it is encouraging to note that some of the major developers, proponents and users of track-2 processes and mechanisms are former track-1 officials themselves (e.g. Jimmy Carter, John McDonald, Joseph Montville, Harold Saunders). Given their location in (at minimum) a two-dimensional, *Realpolitik–Idealpolitik* space, it should come as no surprise that their approaches capture, to various degrees, the complexity implicit in our generic theory and NEPSS application of it. Saunders (1991, p. 164), for instance, challenges:

> those studying and conducting international relationships to develop a conceptual framework that *integrates* rather than fragments understanding of those relationships. Thinkers and practitioners in many fields [e.g. quantum physics] are well along in articulating different ways of knowing and thinking. . . . The charge is not to scrap present ways of knowing and thinking [but] to build from them a *broader* human understanding. (Emphasis added)[16]

Track-1 itself may even encourage such integration. The enhanced potential emerging from Helsinki '92 for interaction between the OSCE and non-governmental actors (see *CSCE Helsinki Document 1992*, Chapter IV) should make it easier for dialogue to take place between track-1 (e.g. the new and evolving OSCE mechanisms for early warning, conflict prevention, and crisis management) and track-2 (e.g. the centers established in Eastern Europe and the former Soviet Union by Partners for Democratic Change: see Shonholtz and Shapiro, 1997).[17]

We began this study critical of the dominance of political realism (*Realpolitik*) in the study and practice of international conflict and war, primarily because of the significant role it itself plays in the genesis of war. *Realpolitik* sustains, and is an essential ingredient of, the "culture of violence and war" (Vasquez, 1993, pp. 162, 197), encouraging the contagious "steps to war" (*ibid.*, pp. 7–8, 10, 48–9, Chapters 3 and 5, pp. 234, 239–40, 243–4), especially in response to conflicts concerning territorial issues "as the underlying and fundamental source of conflict that ends in war" (*ibid.*, p. 124).

We end, perhaps paradoxically, with a design in which *Realpolitik* plays a role, not as the dominant or only element, but as a significant part of a larger whole which recognizes that, in *complex* conflict situations, negative peace may be a necessary (but not sufficient) condition of positive peace. And negative peace may be, in some cases, attainable only through what we have come to call the horizontal dimension of integrated systems of conflict resolution networks.

If wars occur because there is nothing to prevent them – a "proximate" cause that allows "ultimate" causes and their "proximate" cause manifestations (e.g. ethnocentrism) free reign (Shaw and Wong, 1989, p. 44) – then, with regard to preventing "future Yugoslavias," it might be useful for international relations scholars and conflict and peace researchers to further encourage what Holm and Sorensen (1993, p. 292) see as the developing merger of "modified neorealism and modified neopluralism ... into a single (neo-neorealist/pluralist) paradigm"; in effect, to facilitate the further development of the *Realpolitik–Idealpolitik* synthesis implicit in NEPSS's integrated systems. Then, working together with conflict resolution practitioners and policymakers, they could endeavor to further develop NEPSS, incorporating into its structure mechanisms with accepted rules, norms and procedures which can constitute a "culture of cooperative processes" and a basis for "steps to peace" (see Vasquez, 1993, Chapter 8).

It is appropriately "complex" that we end with a design – NEPSS – in which *Realpolitik* and *Idealpolitik* coexist in a complex interactive relationship whose weights can shift dramatically, chaotically, and catastrophically from one emphasis to the other without warning, in response to otherwise small changes in underlying conditions. As the writing of this volume was coming to an end, this nearly happened in Northern Ireland where events associated with the "marching season" put the peace process there at further risk (see Barbash, 1996a):

> The return of all-out sectarian paramilitary warfare in Northern Ireland has become a distinct possibility following the bombing of a hotel in the province early Sunday morning [July 14, 1996] and a full week of rioting ...
>
> The most recent round of troubles began a week ago, when the British-run police in Northern Ireland – the Royal Ulster Constabulary – banned a march by the Protestant Orange Order through a Catholic neighborhood in the village of Drumcree.
>
> After a four-day standoff, and loyalist violence across Northern Ireland, the police reversed themselves, fearing the ban might produce serious bloodshed in a confrontation with thousands of Orange Order members.
>
> They allowed 1,300 members of the group to march through the neighborhood, using batons and plastic bullets to clear the streets of protesting Catholics. That set off rioting – firebombings, attacks on the police and the torching of cars, trucks, and busses – in a dozen or more largely Catholic areas. *Londonderry was particularly hard hit.* (Emphasis added; also see Barbash, 1996b)

Against the background of Richard Rose's (1971, pp. 354-5) comments, cited in Chapters 6 and 7, about Londonderry on August 12, 1969, nearly 30 years earlier – where "time past and time present ... fuse[d] together in an explosive way" – it is again clear that Northern Ireland, like the Balkans, is a classic case of a self-stimulating/self-perpetuating conflict system where, assuming unresolved conflicts-as-startup conditions, conflicts-as-process are never far from the surface.[18]

This suggests still other "next steps" for practice and research: (a) designing specific conflict resolution systems for Northern Ireland, Chechnya, Nagorno-Karabakh, and elsewhere, as well as for Bosnia-Hercegovina and Croatia, in terms of the vertical and horizontal dimensions of integrated systems of conflict resolution networks; (b) implementing the designs as "*social experiments*" (see Kaplan, 1964, pp. 164–5);[19] and, among other things, (c) monitoring the "*interactive effects* of coercive diplomacy *and* positive inducements . . . of peace enforcement *and* the facilitation of conflict solutions" (Leatherman and Väyrynen, 1995, pp. 69, 72; emphasis added); making "fine-tuning" adjustments or radical changes as necessary in each case. In this way, NEPSS could be evaluated and further developed to include, for instance, elements of non-Marxist radical thought (or what Holm and Sorensen (1993, pp. 295–7) refer to as "global individualism: a new IR paradigm"), "where the individual [and not the state] is the starting-point" (*ibid.*, p. 296). It is the individual, *at all levels*, after all, who is the repository of the basic needs whose violation and frustration seem to figure so prominently in the violent ethnic conflict and war of the post-Cold War era.

But NEPSS should also include elements of Marxism ("globalism": *ibid.*, pp. 292–3), especially in its dealings with developing countries, to contribute to the creation of a "New World Order" that is truly "beyond history", e.g. one that does not threaten the developing world with a new "Fortress Europe" and confirmation of its growing perception, reinforced by the massive Iraqi casualties of the Gulf War and the genocidal slaughter of Muslims in Bosnia-Hercegovina and Chechnya, that the "New World Order" means nothing more than the replacement of East–West by North–South as the dominant axis of international conflict: the filling of the void left by the ending of the Cold War with Huntington's (1993, 1996) "clash of civilizations."

The evaluation and further development of NEPSS should also explore its appropriateness as a regional example of the "integrated approach to human security" associated with *An Agenda for Peace* (Boutros-Ghali, 1995, p. 19); its utility in helping to develop further the OSCE's *Common and Comprehensive Security Model for Europe for the Twenty-first Century* (see *OSCE Review*, 1995a, b); and its relevance to furthering the goals of the *Carnegie Commission on Preventing Deadly Conflict*, whose final report (1997) was issued just as the writing of this volume was coming to an end.[20] Developing these thoughts further is, of course, the subject of another book.

Notes

1. Although, as we noted in Chapter 6, Vasquez (1993) does not believe in the possibility of a generic theory in the special case of war (p. 49), he does accept the possibility of a "unified theory of conflict and violence," with which his findings can be integrated (p. 306): "As they stand, the explanations and propositions are consistent with existing evidence of war. Of no less importance is that by building upon work in the other social sciences and ethology, the explanations are consistent with what is known about violence outside the field of international relations. Despite the limits on the generalizability of some of the propositions, this multidisciplinary perspective makes it possible to integrate this analysis of interstate war within a *unified theory of conflict and violence*" (emphasis added; also see Vasquez, 1992, pp. 165, 169). (For another effort to develop a "unified" view of violent conflict and war, specifically, a "unified model of crisis," see Brecher and Wilkenfeld, 1997.)
2. In contrast to Vasquez and the view expressed here, Stuart Bremer (1995a, pp. 2, 25 fn. 2) is skeptical that a "grand unifying theory" exists or can otherwise be developed and,

in any case, believes that the quest for one represents the "wrong strategy." (For a spirited, eloquent defense of the search for a unified theory linking the natural sciences, social sciences and humanities, see Wilson, 1998a, b.)

3. Serotonin levels and self-esteem can also be positively affected by "Prozac and other serotonin boosters, such as Zoloft" (Wright, 1995, p. 74; also see Cowley *et al.*, 1990; Cowley and Underwood, 1997/8).
4. While men lead in *externalized* aggression, women, according to research conducted by Susan Nolen-Hoeksema, lead in *internalized* aggression; e.g. depression: "Depression . . . is a women's disease: Twice as many women as men experience a major depressive episode, in which . . . suicide seems like a better alternative than unending lethargy and self-loathing. The finding holds true across countries and cultures, even when the definition of depression changes. . . . Overall, . . . , as many as 21 per cent of women, compared with 13 per cent of men, will have at least one major episode" (Shea, 1998). A major reason for this difference, according to Nolen-Hoeksema, is *ruminative coping*: "a tendency to focus inwardly and passively on one's emotions. Women are strikingly more prone to such rumination than men are" (*ibid.*).
5. For another view on the relationship between gender and violence (specifically war), see Shaw and Wong (1989, pp. 179–80).
6. For Barbara Ehrenreich, according to Michael Ignatieff's (1997, pp. 10, 12) review of her *Blood Rites: Origins and History of the Passions of War* (1997), the "ecstasy of war" derives from a very dramatic shift in roles for humans in "survival-of-the-fittest" conflicts with more naturally powerful predators: "When we go to war, [Ehrenreich] argues, the ecstasy we feel is our ancestor's relief that we are going out to eat and not to be eaten. . . . It is only because we once were prey that we fear violence and feel guilty when we commit it ourselves. For even as we turn predator, we may remember what it was to be prey. The ecstasy of war – the feelings of love, solidarity, and comradeship, together with the lust to kill that are part of war – reenacts our primal relief at ceasing to be prey and becoming predators." Building further upon Ehrenreich's provocative thesis, Itzhak Fried (1997, p. 1845) has argued that, "The transformation of groups of previously nonviolent individuals into repetitive killers of defenceless members of society" has been so uniform and regular throughout human history that it "suggests a common syndrome" affecting the individuals doing the killing – what he calls *Syndrome E* – one symptom of which is hyperarousal ("Rausch"), i.e. *elation* which is often invoked by the "repetitive nature of violent acts . . . according to the number of victims and the magnitude of destruction." Could the "slide toward genocide," the motivation to commit unspeakable atrocities, e.g. as Japanese forces did in Nanking during World War II (see Chang, 1997), be explained, in part, by the desire to *maximize* the experience of the "ecstasy of war" as conceptualized by Ehrenreich: the reenactment of "our primal relief [*elation*] at ceasing to be prey and becoming predators"?
7. *Inclusive fitness* is comprised of two components: (a) "increased personal survival and increased personal reproduction (classical Darwinian fitness)" and (b) "the enhanced reproduction and survival of close relatives who share the same genes by common descent (a kinship component)" (Shaw and Wong, 1989, p. 26). "Inclusive fitness thus equals an individual's Darwinian (egoistic) fitness *augmented* by an allowance for the *effect* that the individual can have on the reproductive success of those who share identical genes by common descent" (*ibid.*, pp. 26–7). *Kin selection* "implies that assistance, favors or altruism would be directed at individuals who were genetically related enough to give the common gene pool greater survival advantages. Genetic relatedness would be greatest with members of one's lineage and one's own kin or nucleus ethnic group" (*ibid.*, p. 27).
8. Even *vicariously* experienced war may have utility in this regard. For instance, in addition to military battle re-enactments (see "History as a Hobby," 1992) and "paintball" combat (see Montgomery, 1997) as fairly benign, "safe" ways to identify

with the "warrior-hero" and fulfill these needs, corporate executives have been visiting American Civil War and other battle sites to capture the lessons of leadership learned initially on the battlefield: "By using history as a metaphor, leaders of these trips say they are able to reach executives in new and memorable ways. They say stories of the battlefield, and particularly the *emotional* encounters during the Civil War, stay with managers long after they return to the daily office grind" (Berselli, 1998, p. A1; emphasis added). (For a provocative account of America's post-Vietnam "cult of the warrior," see Gibson, 1994.)

9. According to John Keegan's (1997, p. 115) review of Philippe Delmas's (1997) *The Rosy Future of War*, "The more states there are – [Delmas] points out that the world now has 200 – the weaker they will be and the readier to pursue empowering legitimacy by violent emphasis of their ethnic, religious, or ideological differences from their neighbors."
10. Singer (1982, p. 39) envisaged a similar use for computer simulation in his COW project: "once we better understand which behaviors occur under which systemic, dyadic, and national conditions, we will . . . develop . . . a computer simulation model that can reveal which *combinations* of behavioral and ecological variables best discriminate between the war and no-war outcome during the several historical periods."
11. Hence, "locally unpredictable [systems may nevertheless be] globally stable" (Gleick, 1987, p. 48).
12. See Michael Nicholson's (1989, p. 182) discussion about why movement from the stable to the unstable equilibria, although "discontinuous," is *not* an example of a *catastrophic* "jump": "In the . . . Richardson system we are talking about a change in *pattern*, not a change in *variable*" (emphasis added).
13. For another critique of Axelrod's theory, see Shaw and Wong (1989, pp. 182–5).
14. Indeed, according to James Pardew, the official in charge of the U.S. program, the weapons "would be used for Bosnia's defense and would contribute to *stability* in the region. The purpose of the train-and-equip program [therefore] is to prevent war by creating a military *balance* in Bosnia" (Pomfret, 1996b; emphasis added). (For an assessment of train and equip and its effect on, among other things, the military balance and probability of future armed conflict between the Bosnian Croats, Muslims, and Serbs, see USIP, 1997.)
15. In the sequel to his *The Evolution of Cooperation* (1984), *The Complexity of Cooperation* (1997, p. xiii), Axelrod tells us: "At the height of the fighting [in Bosnia], in the summer of 1995, I was invited by the [UN] to talk about my work on cooperation at a conference designed to bring together nongovernmental representatives of all the warring factions in the former Yugoslavia. The participants had many critical questions about how my Prisoners' Dilemma work applied to the complexity of their conflicts, with its unequal power, with fifteen rather than two sides to the conflicts, and with violations of widely held norms of conduct. Many of the issues raised by the participants did not have simple answers, but they were ones on which I had been actively working. The present volume includes models that deal with unequal power, with multisided as well as two-sided conflict, with misunderstandings and mis-implementations, with the enforcement of norms, with newly emerging political entities, and with the cultural bias for political affiliation and polarization. Although I have no solutions, I believe that analyzing large-scale outcomes in terms of the interactions of actors can enhance our understanding of conflict and cooperation in a complex world."
16. As a further indication that people in different fields and disciplines are arriving at similar conclusions regarding "complexity," compare Saunders' comments with those of entomologist Edward O. Wilson (1998a, p. 62): "Most of the issues that vex humanity daily – *ethnic conflict*, arms escalation, overpopulation, abortion, environmental destruction, and endemic poverty, to cite several of the most persistent – can be solved only by *integrating knowledge* from the natural sciences with that from the social

sciences and the humanities. Only *fluency across the boundaries* will provide a clear view of the world as it really is, not as it appears through the lens of ideology and religious dogma, or as a myopic response solely to immediate need" (emphasis added).

17. One group that has been particularly active in bringing the OSCE – particularly representatives of the office of the High Commissioner on National Minorities – together with track-2 conflict resolution practitioners has been the Conflict Management Group (see Chigas, 1994a, b; Chigas *et al.*, 1996; CMG, 1993, 1994).
18. With the breakthrough in negotiations reached on Good Friday, April 10, 1998, however, perhaps the conflicts-as-startup conditions among the parties to the conflict in Northern Ireland might finally get addressed: "After 21 months of talks and one final marathon 32-hour session, Northern Ireland's political leaders reached a historic agreement here today on a new form of government for the embattled province, holding out the promise of a lasting peace among sectarian groups that have waged terrorist warfare for nearly 30 years. The settlement plan would restore self-rule to Northern Ireland for the first time in 26 years and create new institutions designed to give minority Catholics a greater voice while meeting Protestant demands that the province remain a part of Britain. . . . 'In the past few days, the irresistible force – the political will – has met the immovable object – *the legacy of the past* – and we have moved it,' [British Prime Minister Tony] Blair declared" (Reid, 1998, p. A1; emphasis added). Nevertheless, as with all complex conflicts, there are difficulties ahead for the Northern Irish peace process, including "for police this June to begin the delicate, and potentially dangerous, job of disarming the sectarian street armies that reportedly have accumulated large arsenals of explosives, guns and ammunition" (*ibid.*, p. A12).
19. In this regard, it is encouraging to note two developments that augur well for governmental and intergovernmental support for such social experiments. One is the *National Consortium on Violence Research* (NCOVR), funded by the National Science Foundation in the U.S.A., and based at the H. John Heinz III School of Public Policy and Management at Carnegie-Mellon University in Pittsburgh, Pennsylvania. NCOVR "is developing a major program of [*integrated multilevel*] research and research education on the subject of violence, with a strong objective of using the research to inform policy and practice" (NSF, 1995; ASA, 1996a, b).

    The other is the initiative by the European Union to develop a *European Civilian Peace Corps* (ECPC), which would be a "first step towards a contribution to conflict prevention . . . with training of monitors, mediators and specialists in conflict resolution" (Bourlanges/Martin, 1995). ECPC's "first priority . . . will be conflict transformation of man-made crisis, i.e. the prevention of violent conflict escalation and contributions towards conflict de-escalation [with] special emphasis . . . given to conflict prevention" (Gülcher and Truger, 1996, p. 3).
20. The Commission's *Preventing Deadly Conflict: Final Report* (1997) offers conclusions and recommendations compatible with those reached and made in the present study, including those dealing with NEPSS's integrated systems of conflict resolution networks. (For a review, see Miller, 1998, which fails to capture the final report's overall, comprehensive nature.)

Appendix A
Basic Manual and Related Materials for the Prisoners' Dilemma Simulation

Appendix A.1
Basic Simulation Manual

1. Structure of the Simulation

To begin the simulation the participants will be divided into two groups. Within each group there will be a temporary assignment of participants to a smaller decision-making component and a larger validating component.

The decision-makers, as the name implies, will initiate each stage of the simulation with a choice among alternative decisions. These decisions deal with the regulation of each "nation's" policy toward the other "nation." After a decision has been made, it is communicated to all other players.

The validators play the consumer and citizen counterpart to the decision-makers. After each decision is made, the validators will be asked to register their satisfaction with the decision made by their decision-makers. The basic decisions of both groups of decision-makers will be announced before validator satisfaction is assessed.

Each "nation" will be given a basic gross national product (GNP). Its decision-makers will control the purposes to which this active productive capacity is put. To simplify matters at the beginning, they will be asked only to decide the amount of GNP which will be diverted to the nation's defense from domestic consumption. They will also have the power to decide whether the military force thus produced is to be committed to actual use. In this very simple "world," it will be assumed that any investment force which is meaningful internationally will be incompatible with internation trading at any significant level. Thus, the decision-makers can decide to trade or arm, but not to do both at the same time. This is a clearly somewhat unreal restriction. Generally, lower levels of armaments and trade are not mutually exclusive.

However, at higher levels, the restriction does in most cases seem to be valid, so that this simplification has some justification.

2. The Decisions

There are two basic sets of decision-making alternatives in each play:

A. 1. Do nothing (i.e. choose the status quo).
   2. Arm.
   3. Trade.

B. 1. Declare war.
   2. Not declare war.

3. The Internation Outcomes

A. Taking the first set of choices, there are nine basic outcomes at the initial play as shown by Table A.1.1.

B. A "parity problem" occurs when both nations decide to arm. If they both decide to devote the same amount of GNP to armament production, there is parity. If not, one nation has an advantage over the other, just as when one nation does nothing or decides to trade when the other nation decides to arm. The parity "problem" is whether the edge in military strength is sufficient to guarantee success in war. Initially, we will assume that this is 10 percent.

C. Time lag. From the time economic decisions are announced, there is a time lag before they go into effect. For example, if, after the first decision period, both nations have done nothing, the growth payoff occurs after the validators express themselves. Similarly, if they have both decided to arm, the actual implementation of the decision only occurs after the validation period.

Table A.1.1 The internation outcomes at the first decision period

Nation A's decision	Nation B's decision		
	1. Do nothing	2. Arm	3. Trade
1. Do nothing	Status quo	Nation B*	Status quo
2. Arm	Nation A*	(Parity problem)	Nation A*
3. Trade	Status quo	Nation B*	Both gain from reciprocal trade

* An arms advantage.

Table A.1.2

Nation A's decision	Nation B's decision		
	1. Do nothing	2. Increase trade	3. Arm
1. Do nothing	Status quo	Status quo	Nation B*
2. Increase trade	Status quo	Both gain from reciprocal trade	Nation B*
3. Arm	Nation A*	Nation A*	(Parity problems)

* Arms advantage.

4. The Internation Outcome after the First Decision

A. If first outcome was "status quo," the situation remains exactly as it was before the first decision, except for normal GNP growth.

B. If first outcome was one of reciprocal trade, Table A.1.2 applies.

C. a. For any nation that decided to arm during the first period, there are the following economic alternatives:
   1. Do nothing.
   2. Disarm (and possibly trade, but only if completely disarmed).
   3. Arm.

   b. The armed nation may also decide to declare war.

D. a. For any nation that has not armed at all, the original set of alternatives remain. If the other nation declares war, the unarmed nation has these alternatives:
   1. Resist (the simulation ends).
   2. Sue for peace (ask for terms of surrender).

   b. The armed nation then has these alternatives:
   1. Demand unconditional surrender (the simulation ends).
   2. Offer peace treaty (to which the unarmed nation must agree or the simulation ends).

5. The Calculation of Payoffs, or the Behavior of the Economy

A. At T_0 (time zero, or the beginning) let us say that each nation has a GNP of $500 billion with a stable rate of growth of $20 billion. This means that at the beginning of the next time period, the economy will grow naturally to the GNP of $520 billion. At this zero point, there is no international trade and the economy is devoted entirely to peacetime production.

B. There are three basic types of GNP:

1. GNCP or gross national consumption product.
2. GNTP or gross national trade product.
3. GNAP or gross national armament product.

C. 1. Validator payoff within each nation consists of the GNCP plus the GNTP (not the GNAP). The validator payoff at any point is calculated thus: validator payoff = ΔGNCP + GNTP (the ΔGNCP is the growth rate of $20 billion).
2. Examples: at T_0 what are the ranges of payoff at T_2 that are associated with any decisional outcome at T_1?
   a. Trade/Trade: "Both gain from $500b + $20b + $20b = $540b reciprocal trade"

      Restriction: To simplify matters, the amount by which the GNP can be increased in any decision period by added production for the export trade (GNTP) will be fixed. Initially, it will be assumed that this increase will be the same as that as the growth rate, which in the examples given here is $20 billion.

   b. Status quo: $500b + $20b = $520b
   c. Arm/Do nothing or Trade: Armer = $500b + $20b − GNAP = ? Non-armer = $500b + $20b = $520b

D. Conversion of GNCP to GNAP. The maximum schedule for arms development is $150b, $100b, $50b . . . (until GNCP is reduced to $50 billion, the subsistence level). Other arms rates are allowed. However, no conversion may exceed $150b per period below the $250 billion total GNAP level and $50 billion when that level has been exceeded.

6. Final Payoff

The final payoff for all players is the validator payoff at the end of the simulation run. If war ends the simulation, the losing validators retain only a minimum payoff of $50 billion. The winning validators receive the residual amount of the loser's GNCP (GNCP minus $50 billion) in addition to their own GNCP.

7.A. Validator Responses

After each decision period, the validators will register their satisfaction (by secret ballot) with the outcome situation. Satisfaction or dissatisfaction has a direct effect on the economy. The scale is as follows:

5. Completely satisfied: I am fully in accord with our Nation's decision.
4. Mostly satisfied.
3. Mixed feelings.
2. Mostly dissatisfied.
1. Completely dissatisfied: I disagree entirely.

7.B. Effect of the Validator Satisfaction Level (average satisfaction)

1. 4.0 to 5.0: Decision successfully validated.
2. 3.0 to 4.0: No arms increase greater than $50 billion allowed.
3. 1.5 to 3.0: Decision voided (i.e. "Do nothing").
4. 1.0 to 1.5: Decision-makers removed (a new set will be selected).

7.C. Communication

1. Communications between the decision-making units will be allowed. Messages may be telephoned or sent in writing, and face-to-face conferences can be arranged.
2. Information above and beyond the announcement of decisions can pass freely from decision-makers to validators. Personal appearances are also permitted.
3. Information from decision-makers to validators of the other nation is subject to censorship by the other nation's decision-makers.
4. Questions from validators may be directed to decision-makers, but do not have to be answered.
5. Direct communication among validators within nations can be restricted, and between nations made impossible by either decision-making component.

8. Espionage and Related Tactics

Your choice of tactics is limited only by our physical facilities and the avoidance of violence. Players from other nations who are discovered "in flagrante" must be either permitted to continue their activities or executed. In the latter case, the victim will be removed by the administrators and neutralized.

9. Wars

A. Declarations of war are either unconditional or conditional. They can be delivered at any time; simply hand an appropriately made out form to an administrator. The attacked nation will then be asked whether it resists or surrenders, if that nation possesses arms. If the attacker decides to permit a conditional surrender, the attacked nation will be asked if it will agree to discuss terms. If so, the declaration of war can be nullified. The negotiation and enforcement of treaties is entirely up to the players.
B. Wars declared and effected before the end of a decision period are decided on the basis of the last outcome. Those which occur during a validation period are decided as of the new outcome.

C. A validation less than 3.0 voids any decision, substituting "Do nothing." Of course, after the validation is done, decision-makers are free to make any decision with regard to war and peace. If a decision to attack or retaliate has been voided, the state of war is not lifted unless the other side had refused to participate or withdraws its decision. The administration will not, however, ask this side for a decision – only transmit the validation.

10. The Simulation Administration

The administrators are unbiased. No classified or secret information will be "leaked." Both nations are as closely matched as possible. Whenever imbalances occur, they are solely due to chance. If you have any questions concerning the simulation, please ask them.

11. Participation

You are invited to participate to whatever extent you feel like. No pressure will be applied by the administrators to make you do anything, nor is there any particular way in which you are expected to play. Some participants have found it useful to keep notes on what happens in the simulation, because it helps them afterwards to analyze the action. Whether you take notes or not, one of the most useful aspects of the simulation for the participant lies in its ability to stimulate analytical thinking. Although it is not always possible to tell precisely why one series of outcomes *did* occur, it is usually possible to explain why others *did not* occur. You will find, if you think about it, that your ability to classify some outcomes as impossible or improbable depends upon the assumptions you can make about human behavior, and especially about that troublesome quality "rationality." In this sense, it is not always disadvantageous to be a validator. Although everyone will eventually become a decision-maker (at least formally), it is not true that frantic activity is a prerequisite for the ability to analyze the simulation. Just be yourself, and do what you feel you want to, even if this is mostly passive observation.

12. Addenda

Addenda to the *Basic Simulation Manual* will be given out as the simulation becomes more complex. They will tell you how the rules are being changed or added to.

Appendix A.2
Decision Form

Group:__________ Date:__________ Run:__________

Period: 1 2 3 4 5 6 7 8 9 10

1. Write in the appropriate nation(s):
   Trade Vouchers sent to__________
   Arm against__________
2. Economic decisions:
   Base GNP__________
   Growth__________
   New GNP__________

   Base GNAP__________
   Arm (+)__________
   Disarm (−)__________
   New GNAP__________

   GNP__________
   −GNAP__________
   Net GNCP__________

   From computer:
   Trade/War results:
   GNAP__________
   Loss__________
   Net GNAP__________
   GNCP__________
   +__________
   −__________
   Net GNCP__________
   New GNP__________

Note: After the decisions have been transmitted to the computer, you will be informed of any GNCP increase from trade.

Appendix A.3
War Form

Nation______________

Part A. Declaration of War

1. Immediate attack (retaliation) yes________ no________
2. If not immediate, give exact time for attack:________
   Unless a countermand is received before this time, attack (retaliation) proceeds automatically.

Signed________

Part B. Countermand

Countermand previous declaration of war (retaliation)

Signed________

Part C. Control of GNAP

Decision-maker(s) empowered to control GNAP and to declare war:

1. ______________	6. ______________
2. ______________	7. ______________
3. ______________	8. ______________
4. ______________	9. ______________
5. ______________	

Please note whether *all* the above must sign or if a certain *number* must sign or if *anyone* may sign.

Part D. Deployment

Total GNAP____________

Amount deployed

$______b Against______	$______b Against______
$______b Against______	$______b Against______
$______b Against______	$______b Against______

Appendix A.4
Simulation Manual Addendum Number One

Coups, Revolutions and Counterrevolutions

1. a. If the mean validator satisfaction level falls below 1.5, the government is automatically replaced. If, however, regardless of the mean satisfaction level, some of the validators are completely dissatisfied, these validators may decide to attempt a coup. An immediate validation among the remaining validators is held. If the level is not below 1.5 in satisfaction with the coup, the coup is allowed. The original decision-makers can choose to acquiesce and resign. If they choose to resist, the instigators of the coup must decide either to give up the coup or to start a revolution. Unless the original decision-makers then resign, the nation splits.

   b. Seen schematically: DV = dissident validators; ODM = original decision-makers.

	DV		
t_0	Attempt coup		
t_1	Validation		
> 1.5		1.5 < ______________	coup fails
t_2	ODM		
resist		resign______________	DV takeover
	DV		
t_3			
revolt		give up______________	coup fails
t_4	ODM		
resist		resign______________	DV takeover
nation splits			

2. a. One minute will be allowed for each phase. During the entire uprising, no economic or military decisions can be made. The administrators will not leak the news, but either the ODM or the DV can use the communications system, until one or the other is established as the legitimate decision-makers.

   b. If a nation splits, validators must choose to follow either the ODM or DV. Appropriate changes in room arrangements will be made. The DV will be provided with an inner sanctum. The GNP will be split between the two groups according to their relative numbers (i.e. 12 to 12 means an equal division of GNP).

   c. Clearly, if the large fragment has a 10 percent edge in GNAP, the small fragment can be defeated in war, unless another nation intervenes. If the revolution and secession occur during a validation period (i.e. after a decision by the ODM has been made and before it could be validated), the ODM and DV must make a new decision and have it validated before the next decision period.

Appendix A.5
Simulation Manual Addendum Number Two

1. Growth and Development

a. In a multination situation where sizes of nations vary, some of the smaller nations may be designated as "underdeveloped." Nations designated as underdeveloped may be allowed a choice of development plans:

   1. Fast unbalanced: 100, 100, 50, 20 ...
   2. Fast balanced: 50, 50, 100, 50, 20 ...
   3. Slow balanced: 0, 50, 100, 200, 100, 50, 20 ...

   Taken cumulatively:

   1. Fast unbalanced: 100, 200, 250, 270 ...
   2. Fast balanced: 50, 100, 200, 250, 270 ...
   3. Slow balanced: 0, 50, 150, 350, 450, 500, 520 ...

b. The GNP growth rates of developed nations will usually not vary. Any such variation will be announced to all players.

2. Coalitions, Mergers, Economic Transfers, and Coups

a. A review of the appropriate rules will no doubt be useful, given the multination situation. Coalitions are simple treaties, unless they involve a transfer of GNP or of GNAP control expressed on either a decision form or a war form. Units, whatever their original purpose or composition, to whom such control has been transferred are expected to make out the required forms. Retransfers, returns, or other modifications are decided by this unit itself. Contractual arrangements will not be enforced by the administration, as usual.
b. There will be one minor rule addition in this regard. Internation organizations or decision-making units will not be subject to validation effects or subsistence requirements unless only one or no nation remains associated with them.
c. While individual defections may occur freely, executions, expulsions, and disputes leading to coups and splits must be done according to the specified rules. One-fourth of any nation's membership or fewer may be removed at the loss of a corresponding fraction of GNP. This GNP will simply be erased. In the case of a more even split, a new nation will be formed by an appropriate division of the economy.

d. Remember that a nation may not arm or maintain arms against a trade partner. This means that a nation with GNAP cannot trade with all the other nations at once; the GNAP must be deployed against at least one country.

e. Disarming, incidentally, is considered to be negative arming and must be done within the maximum arming limits. In other words, . . . 50, 100, 150 or . . . 50, 150, 100, where no decrease may exceed 50 above 250 total GNAP and 150 below 250. This holds for all nations, regardless of GNP size.

Appendix A.6
Simulation Manual Addendum Number Three

1. Automatic Validations

For nations without human validating components, validation levels will have to be computed automatically. This computation routine will no doubt seem simple and unrealistic, yet it is the best that can be done without making noncredible assumptions about validator behavior. Satisfaction with decision-making units, as you may have noted, is not related to GNCP reduction, at least not in a direct and simple linear fashion. In other words, there is no gradual curve relating GNCP and satisfaction, but an *abrupt* one. Coups were sudden, even though long-run, phenomena. The following program approximates this function.

2. Schedule of Validation Levels

Find the appropriate GNP level and read off the validation levels.

GNP up to	Validation levels (Size of GNAP)				
	1	2	3	4	5
200	40	80	100	120	140
250	50	100	125	150	175
300	60	120	150	180	210
350	70	140	175	210	245
400	80	160	200	240	280
450	90	180	225	270	315
500	100	200	250	300	350
550	110	220	275	330	385
600	120	240	300	360	420
650	130	260	325	390	455
700	140	280	350	420	490
750	150	300	375	450	525
800	160	320	400	480	560
850	170	340	425	510	595
900	180	360	450	540	630
950	190	380	475	570	665
1000	200	400	500	600	700
1050	210	420	525	630	735
1100	220	440	550	660	770
1150	230	460	575	690	805
1200	240	480	600	720	840
1250	250	500	625	750	875
1300	260	520	650	780	910

Validation effects

0.17 Chance of

Level 1: Arms increase limited to $50b next period.
Level 2: Revolution, coup crushed, lose 50% of GNAP.
Level 3: Revolution, coup crushed, lose 75% of GNAP.
Level 4: Revolution, coup successful, lose 75% of GNAP, plus 50% GNCP.

Level 5: Revolution, coup successful, ODMs reduced to $50b GNCP.

1350	270	540	675	810	945
1400	280	560	700	840	980
1450	290	580	725	870	1015
1500	300	600	750	900	1050
1550	310	620	775	930	1085
1600	320	640	800	960	1120
1650	330	660	825	990	1155
1700	340	680	850	1020	1190
1750	350	700	875	1050	1225
1800	360	720	900	1080	1260
1850	370	740	925	1110	1295
1900	380	760	950	1140	1330
1950	390	780	975	1170	1365
2000	400	800	1000	1200	1400

Validation levels will be repeated during successive periods as long as the GNAP for any nation falls within the specified range.

3. Economic Legerdemain

a. In a multination situation, a nation is allowed to redeploy arms if under attack; however, an attacker is not allowed to change deployment unless another nation enters the war.

b. False coups and other such dealings are allowed within the limitations of the manual. However, any such change in the international situation allows each nation to make an additional decision regarding the development. For example, if Nation A attacks Nation B, and if, after the decisions are in, Nation B "coups" off Nation C in an attempt to avoid destruction, Nation A is allowed to decide whether to attack Nation C as well.

c. In case of multination bloc war, the summed GNAPs deployed by members of bloc A against members of bloc B, and vice versa, are calculated to determine the outcome. Unbalanced deployment schemes are, thus, all to naught.

Appendix A.7
Simulation Manual Addendum Number Four

Trade and Negotiation

1. Trade will be carried out in the international bargaining room. Each nation must send at least one representative to this room if it wishes to carry on trading relationships with other countries. Each representative will be provided with Trade Vouchers. These Trade Vouchers should be filled out with the name of the trade partner and the decision period, and then given to the trade partner. If the trade partner turns in the Voucher, the country of origin will be credited with $20b GNCP. Only ONE Trade Voucher may be sent to any one country per decision period. For example, in a four-nation world, each country has a maximum of $60b of GNCP increase per period resulting from trade.
2. The trade policy of the representative and the overall policy of the nation as expressed on the decision form must be consistent. Whenever there is a contradiction, a "Do nothing" will result. For example, if Nation A's representative trades with B's representative, who actually turns in A's Trade Voucher, and if Nation A elects to arm against Nation B on its decision form, then *both* the trade and the arms increase will be canceled. It will be possible, therefore, to disarm by mistake, and such events will be announced to other nations.
3. Direct face-to-face bargaining will be allowed only at the bargaining room. No meetings between decision-makers will be allowed outside the bargaining room. Those nations with human validators will still be allowed direct decision-maker access to the validating component. Quick "shuffling" of representatives will not be allowed.

Appendix A.8
Simulation Manual Addendum Number Five

Arms increase may not exceed stated level at the specified stage of GNAP conversion.

GNP range	First	Second	Third and all subsequent
200–299	90	60	30
300–399	120	80	40
400–499	150	100	50
500–599	180	120	60
600–699	210	140	70
700–799	240	160	80
800–899	270	180	90
900–999	300	200	100
1000–1099	330	220	110
1100–1199	360	240	120
1200–1299	390	260	130
1300–1399	420	280	140
1400–1499	450	300	150
1500–1599	480	320	160
1600–1699	510	340	170
1700–1799	540	360	180
1800–1899	570	380	190
1900–1999	600	400	200

For GNPs greater or smaller than those listed consult the computer.

Appendix A.9
Simulation Manual Addendum Number Six: Nuclear Weapons

1. A part of GNAP may be invested in research and development (R&D) in order to develop nuclear arms. The level of investment is related to the probability that nuclear capability will be developed:

Level of investment ($ billion)	Probability that nuclear capability is developed
100	1.00
80	0.83
60	0.67
40	0.50
20	0.33

2. When nuclear arms have been developed, R&D is "frozen", i.e. GNAP in R&D cannot be removed, once invested in that sector, nor does it have the status of operational GNAP.
3. Once a nation acquires nuclear arms, it requires a minimum of $100b nuclear GNAP to defend itself against a conventional attack; a minimum of $200b to launch a nuclear attack.
4. Revised war outcomes.

	Outcomes		
Character of War	Win	Lose	Stalemate
a. Conventional war	(Criterion of victory: 10% conventional GNAP advantage) Winner takes all but $50b of loser's GNCP.	All but $50b GNCP	Each side loses 25%
b. Conventional attack on nuclear power with $100b nuclear GNAP	No victor	No loser	Each side loses its GNAP

c. Nuclear power with \$200b nuclear GNAP attacks conventional power	(Criterion of victory: attacker's unique possession of a nuclear strike force). Winner takes 50% of loser's GNCP - \$50b. (The remaining 50% of loser's GNCP will have been destroyed).	All but \$50b GNCP	No stalemate
d. Nuclear war	(Criterion of victory: 50% nuclear GNAP advantage). Winner takes 50% of loser's GNCP - \$50b.	All but \$50b GNCP	Each side loses 50% of GNP

Appendix A.10
Simulation Manual Addendum Number Seven

1. Any two or more nations may integrate formally by notifying the administration of their desire to do so.
2. An integrated nation made up of two or more formerly independent nations acts as a single unit in the international system with one name, one UN representative, one group of decision-makers, etc.
3. The GNP, GNCP, and GNAP of each formerly independent nation is added to that of each nation with which it integrates. Thus, an integrated nation will initially have a comparatively large fund of economic, and perhaps military, resources under the control of a single government.
4. In international trade, an integrated nation receives a multiple of the normal trade increment each time it trades with another nation, and the trade partner also receives a multiple increment. For example, an integrated nation of three formerly independent nations would receive three times the normal trade increment each time it traded with another nation. The trade partner would also receive three times the normal trade increment ($60 billion instead of $20 billion).
5. The growth rate increment of an integrated nation is also a multiple of the normal growth rate increment. The growth rate increment of three formerly independent nations would therefore be three times that of an ordinary nation ($60 billion).
6. In the event that an integrated nation loses a war and becomes "underdeveloped," the normal underdeveloped nation growth rates remain the same as those listed in *Manual Addendum Two* until the nation becomes "developed." At that point, the multiple growth rate increment is resumed. For example, if a three-part integrated nation becomes underdeveloped and chooses the Fast Unbalanced development plan, its growth rate will be $100b, 100b, 50b, 60b, 60b . . . , 60b being its normal growth increment when "developed."
7. In the event that an integrated nation becomes underdeveloped, the multiple trade increment (i.e., ΔGNCP) is not effective until the nation becomes developed. For instance, the trade increment for each exchanged trade voucher, for an undeveloped three-part integrated nation which chooses a Fast Unbalanced development plan, would be 20b, 20b, 20b, 60b, 60b . . .
8. A segment, or segments, of an integrated nation may choose to secede from the integrated nation.
9. In such a case, the administration must be notified.

10. If the decision-makers agree on peaceful secession, the seceding segments become independent nations and receive starting GNP, GNCP, and GNAP in proportion to their numbers. The original, nonseceding segment keeps that part of the GNP, GNCP and GNAP proportional to its numbers.
11. In the event that secession is opposed, civil war results. Two decision periods must elapse between the declaration of civil war and the actual occurrence of the war.
12. In civil war, all resources, including GNAP, are divided proportionally according to the numerical strengths of the factions. The method for determining the outcome of a civil war is the same as that for determining other wars.
13. If the seceding factions win, they become independent nations; if not, they remain within the integrated nation.
14. Outside nations may aid particular factions in civil wars, by declaring war on factions, transfers of GNAP to factions, etc. Thus, a weak faction may win a civil war if it has alliances with outside nations.
15. The World Organization, individual nations, or blocs may take appropriate steps to try to prevent threatening civil wars via, e.g. peace conferences, arbitration, peaceful divisions of nations undergoing civil strife.
16. In the event of a split, trade and growth rate advantages are normally canceled for all factions. If one nation in a split remains predominantly large in numbers, it may retain part of its trade and growth rate advantage.

Appendix A.11
Forms, Part A

1. Validator Form

Name:______________ Group:____________________
Decision period: 1 2 3 4 5 6 7 8 9 10 Date:____________________
Run:____________________

Part A

1. If you were a decision-maker, which alternative would you favor?
    1. Do nothing Against whom?________________
    2. Trade With whom?__________________
    3. Arm Against whom?________________
2. Should the decision-makers try to make an alliance this time?
    ( ) No.
    ( ) Yes. With which nation(s)?
3. In general, do you trust the other nation(s) to keep its (their) word?
    ( ) Yes.
    ( ) No.
4. Do you think you are going to win?
    ( ) Yes.
    ( ) No, stalemate.
    ( ) No, lose.
5. How happy are you with the way things are going?
    ( ) Not very; we are too wishy-washy.
    ( ) Not very; we are being too ruthless and cutthroat.
    ( ) I have mixed feelings.
    ( ) Things are too chaotic to tell.
    ( ) Very happy; our peaceful policy will win in the long run.
    ( ) Very happy; we are going to come out on top.

2. Decision-maker Form

Name:______________ Group:______________
Period:______________ Time:______________
Run:______________

Part A

1. How would you rate this decision?
   ( ) A superb move.
   ( ) Basically sound.
   ( ) It was the best we could do, all things considered.
   ( ) Not so good.
   ( ) Blunder.
2. How much influence do you think you had on the decision?
   ( ) It was my own idea.
   ( ) I had a lot to do with it.
   ( ) I had some influence.
   ( ) I did not have too much to say about it.
   ( ) I think I am being ignored; they'll be sorry.
3. What will be the effect of this decision?
   ( ) We are making ourselves out to be double-crossing cut-throats.
   ( ) I think we have reinforced our strong positive image.
   ( ) I simply don't know.
   ( ) It was a good decision, but it probably won't work.
   ( ) We are just being stupidly foolish and gullible.

Appendix A.12
Forms, Part B

1. Validator Form

Name:______________ Group:______________
Decision period: 1 2 3 4 5 6 7 8 9 10 Date:______________
Run:______________

Part B

1. Was there a part of the decision you think will (or has) turned out to be a blunder? Which part?

2. Do you think that the decision-makers should be replaced?
   ( ) Yes, the sooner the better.
   ( ) Yes, but it would not be wise right now.
   ( ) No, but I may change my mind.
   ( ) No, not all; things are going fine.

Official satisfaction rating

3. How satisfied are you with your decision-makers?
   ( ) Completely dissatisfied.
   ( ) Mostly dissatisfied.
   ( ) Mixed feelings.
   ( ) Mostly satisfied.
   ( ) Completely satisfied.

2. Decision-maker Questionnaire

Name:______________ Group:______________
Period:______________ Time:__________Run:__________

Part B

1. Are you completely surprised by the way things turned out?
   ( ) Completely.
   ( ) Somewhat.
   ( ) Not too much.
   ( ) Not at all.
   ( ) I had no idea what they would do.

2. How does your decision look now?
   ( ) It was a superb move.
   ( ) It was basically sound.
   ( ) It was still the best we could do, all things considered.
   ( ) It was a blunder.
3. Do you think you could have changed the decision?
   ( ) Yes, if I had wanted.
   ( ) Yes, if I had a little support.
   ( ) I could have changed it somewhat.
   ( ) I could not have done too much about it.
   ( ) They wouldn't listen to *me*.

Appendix A.13
Form for Group Administrator

Name of administrator:______________	Group name:__________________
Number of decision period:___________	Actual time:__________________

1. Names of decision-makers in group:

2. Changes in membership and decision period in which change occurred.

3. General observation of harmony or discord at each decision. Names of most dissident or compliant members.

4. Unanimity of the group, whether split internally, etc.

5. Main leaders of group; level of participation of other members in decision-making process.

6. Any other comments.

Appendix B
PDS Participants' Questionnaire

1. Sex:
   1. Male.
   2. Female.
2. Age:
   1. 18–19.
   2. 20–21.
   3. 22–24.
   4. 25–30.
   5. 31 or over.
3. Year in school:
   1. Freshman.
   2. Sophomore.
   3. Junior.
   4. Senior.
   5. Graduate.
4. If student, what major:
   1. Music or fine arts.
   2. Physical education.
   3. Humanities.
   4. Social sciences.
   5. Math.
5. Continuation of question 4: majors
   1. Physical science.
   2. Law (pre-law).
   3. Education.
   4. Journalism.
   5. Business administration.
6. What was your cumulative GPA last year?
   1. 0.0–1.99.
   2. 2.0–2.49.
   3. 2.5–2.99.
   4. 3.0–3.49.
   5. 3.5–4.00.

7. How many credit hours are you taking this term?
    1. 0–6.
    2. 7–11.
    3. 12–15.
    4. 16 or more.
8. If you are a student, do you also hold a job?
    1. Yes.
    2. No.
9. If so, how many hours a week do you spend at your job?
    1. Full-time.
    2. More than half-time, less than full-time.
    3. Half-time.
    4. More than 10 hours, but fewer than 20.
    5. Fewer than 10 hours.
10. Marital status:
    1. Single.
    2. Married.
    3. Divorced.
    4. Widowed.
11. What was the last grade of school your father completed?
    1. Grade school or more, but not high school graduate.
    2. High school graduate.
    3. Some college but not a degree (business college or similar technical training not to be counted as college).
    4. College graduate, BA.
    5. MA degree or more.
12. Please estimate your parents' income last year, including earnings from investments, rental properties, etc., before taxes.
    1. Less than $4000.
    2. $4000–$6999.
    3. $7000–$9999.
    4. $10,000–$14,999.
    5. More than $15,000.
13. How many hours a week do you usually study?
    1. Fewer than 5.
    2. 5–9.
    3. 10–14.
    4. 15–19.
    5. 20 or more.

Notes: The coding on all of the following items runs as follows:
1. Strongly agree.
2. Agree.
3. Mixed feelings.
4. Disagree.
5. Strongly disagree.

14. The work required of a student at my educational level and in my major at Temple University is extremely demanding.
15. The academic pressures to which students are subjected are more constant than professional or career pressures.
16. The academic pressures to which students are subjected are more intense than professional or career pressures.
17. The student, because of academic pressure, has great need to "get away from it all."
18. In a heated discussion I generally become so absorbed in what I am going to say that I forget to listen to what the others are saying.
19. People can be divided into two distinct classes, the weak and the strong.
20. Most of our social problems could be solved if we could somehow get rid of the immoral, feeble-minded and crooked people.
21. What youth needs most is strict discipline, rugged determination, and the will to work and fight for family and country.
22. Voting is the only way that people like me can have any say about how the government runs things.
23. I don't think public officials care much about what the people like me think.
24. People like me don't have any say about what the government does.
25. An insult to our honor should always be punished.
26. Every person should have complete faith in some supernatural power whose decisions he or she obeys without question.
27. Human nature being what it is, there will always be war and conflict.
28. Nowadays more and more people are prying into matters that should remain personal and private.
29. Science has its place, but there are many important things than can never possibly be understood by human beings.
30. Wars and social troubles may someday be ended by earthquake or flood that will destroy the whole world.
31. Most people don't realize how much our lives are controlled by plots hatched in secret places.
32. The concerns of the community are more important than the property rights of individuals.
33. What this country needs is more groups of dedicated people who would vigorously attack the sources of present difficulty.
34. It is important that the government has the right to take over personal property (with payment to the owner) out of consideration for the common welfare.
35. In general, I think it would be better to have close friends who share my political beliefs.
36. The end often justifies the means.
37. A group which tolerates too much difference of opinion among its own members cannot exist for long.
38. One should take into consideration the political implications of every major aspect of day-to-day living.
39. Tampering with society will only lead to a worse state of affairs.

40. In times like these, it is often necessary to be more on guard against ideas put out by people or groups in one's own camp than by those in the opposing camp.
41. People's ideas change so much that I often wonder if we'll ever have anything to depend on.
42. It is often desirable to reserve judgment about what's going on until one has a chance to hear the opinions of those one respects.
43. It is better to adjust to things as they are rather than swim "against the current."
44. The problems of present society are man-made, and man can solve these problems.
45. Everything is relative and there just aren't any definite rules to this life.
46. Too many people just don't care about present political, economic and social issues.
47. In the history of mankind, there have probably been just a handful of really great thinkers.
48. If given a chance, I would do something of great benefit to the world.
49. The future looks very dismal.
50. I look forward with excitement and pleasant anticipation to a vastly different world in the years ahead.
51. All things equal, change is better than stability.
52. The only thing one can be sure of today is that he can be sure of nothing.
53. It is only when a person devotes himself to an ideal or cause that life becomes meaningful.
54. The present is too often full of unhappiness. It is only the future that counts.
55. It is better to be a dead hero than to be a live coward.
56. To compromise with our political opponents is to be guilty of appeasement.
57. There is so much to be done and so little time to do it.
58. In this complicated world of ours, the only way we can know what's going on is to rely on leaders or experts who can be trusted.
59. If a man is to accomplish his mission in life, it is sometimes necessary to gamble "all or nothing at all."
60. Of all the different philosophies which exist in this world, there is probably only one which is correct.
61. Most people just don't know what's good for them.
62. There are two kinds of people in this world: those who are for the truth and those who are against it.
63. Man on his own is a helpless and miserable creature.
64. Fundamentally, the world we live in is a pretty lonesome place.
65. War and social troubles may someday be ended by wisdom and education, not by an earthquake or flood that will destroy the world.
66. People cannot be divided into two distinct classes, the weak and the strong.

67. Human nature being what it is, universal peace will come about eventually.
68. Nowadays, not enough investigation of personal and private matters is done.
69. Most of our social problems would be solved if we could somehow cure or help the immoral, crooked, and feeble-minded people.
70. I can't enjoy relaxation unless I feel I've worked hard enough to deserve it.
71. All in all, it is better to be humble and honest than to be important and dishonest.
72. I set difficult goals for myself which I attempt to reach.
73. I nearly always strive hard for personal achievement.
74. Our lives are not controlled by plots hatched in secret places.
75. I don't blame anyone for trying to grab all he can get in this world.
76. Sometimes politics and government seem so complicated that a person like me can't really understand what is going on.
77. The most important things to me are my duties to my job and to my fellow man.
78. An insult to our honor should be studied, not punished.
79. A person does not need to worry about other people if only he looks after himself.
80. Barnum was wrong when he said that there's a sucker born every minute.
81. Generally speaking, men won't work hard unless they are forced to do so.
82. It is safest to assume that all people have a vicious streak and it will come out when they are given a chance.
83. Because of science, it will be possible for the human mind to understand most important things.
84. The biggest difference between most criminals and other people is that the criminals are stupid enough to get caught.
85. It's too late to try to get back to a simpler way of life.
86. If cities and towns around the country need help to build more schools, the government in Washington ought to give them the money they need.
87. The government ought to see to it that big business corporations don't have much say about how the government is run.
88. The government in Washington ought to see to it that everybody who wants to work can find a job.
89. What a youth needs most is to be free to make up his own mind, to be flexible and to work and fight for what he considers right personally even though it might not be best for his family and country.
90. The government ought to help people get doctors and hospital care at low cost.
91. The government in Washington should stay out of the question of whether white and colored children go to the same school.
92. The government should leave things like electric power and housing for private businessmen to handle.

93. If Negroes are not getting fair treatment in jobs and housing, the government in Washington should see to it that they do.
94. No person should have complete faith in some supernatural power whose decisions he obeys without question.
95. In order to get nominated, most candidates for political office have to make basic compromises and undesirable commitments.
96. Politicians spend most of their time getting re-elected or reappointed.
97. Money is the most important factor influencing public policies.
98. A large number of city and county politicians are political hacks.
99. People are frequently manipulated by politicians.
100. Politicians represent the general interest more frequently than they represent special interests of groups.
101. I would prefer to work on a project that I could see was getting somewhere, even though it was far from where I usually live and work, among people very different from me.
102. I prefer to risk a little to make a lot. That way if you are right one time in five, you are doing all right.
103. An article for sale is worth what people will pay for it.
104. Seniority should be given greater weight than merit in giving promotion.
105. Incentive pay should not be used because workers will overwork and ruin their health or destroy jobs for others.
106. In business, you can only really trust friends and relatives.
107. Workers should not be promoted to managerial jobs even if they are qualified because it would destroy the respect for authority which the workers must have towards management.
108. Those who created the wealth of this country worked for success – not for money – for being able to tell a man to go to hell.
109. Part of the price one pays in joining any organization today is the sacrifice of decision-making, at the individual, personal level, and I, for one, am not willing to pay that price.
110. The amount of education a person has should be a factor in determining his pay scale.
111. There is hardly any such thing as good luck – that is something people have to make for themselves.
112. I approve of a career or job outside the home for married women.
113. Planning only makes a person unhappy because your plans hardly ever work out anyway.
114. If I have to go to a doctor or lawyer, I prefer someone who is not a close personal friend of mine.
115. I feel that I waste time and spend it uselessly.
116. A good son should try to live near his parents even if it means giving up a good job in another part of the country.
117. The most important factor in the success of a firm is the establishment of a reputation for the excellence of its products.
118. A man with money cannot really learn how to behave in polite society if he has not had the proper upbringing.
119. It is remarkable how prayer influences the way things turn out.

120. A corporation does things for one reason – profit.
121. No matter who is "right" and who is "wrong," recourse to war and violence is basically stupid and immoral.

122 to 126.

Please rank the following occupations from 1 to 5 according to their respect and prestige to our society:

122. High school teacher.
123. Cannery worker.
124. Vice-president of a large corporation.
125. Owner of a small retail business.
126. Supreme Court justice.

127. How much would you like to have each of the above occupations someday, especially seeing the hard work involved? Please take them in the order listed above and mark them as follows:

1. Very much.
2. Somewhat.
3. Not so much.
4. Little.
5. Not at all.

Appendix C
Operational Definitions[1]

Decision-making Level

1. *DOGMATISM* (DOG), "an authoritarian outlook, an intolerance of those with opposing beliefs, and a sufferance of those with similar beliefs" (Rokeach, 1960, p. 4), has been measured in this study in terms of eighteen items from Rokeach's 40-item Form-E rendition of his *Dogmatism Scale* (*ibid.*, pp. 73–80). The eighteen items are 18, 37, 40, 42, 47–8, 53–64 of the questionnaire in Appendix B. Each of these items is characterized by "positive wording," i.e. agreement with the statement means possession, to some degree, of the attribute being measured. Each group in the PDS was measured on these items for each two-hour run at time *t* ("present time") by summing and then averaging group members' scores in terms of a 1–5 *Likert scale*,[2] with higher scores indicating possession of the attribute.[3] (This procedure also applies to variables 2–8.)
2. *AUTHORITARIANISM* (AUTH), an anti-democratic syndrome, oftentimes referred to as fascism, has been measured for each group during each run at time *t* in terms of 20 items taken or adopted from the 30-item Forms 45 and 46 of the *Fascism Scale* developed by Adorno *et al.* (1950, pp. 255–7). The 20 items in Appendix B are 19–21, 25–31 (all positively worded) and 65–9, 74, 78, 83, 89, and 94 (all negatively worded).[4]
3. *POLITICAL CYNICISM* (POLC), a contemptuous distrust of politicians and the political process, has been measured for each group during each run at time *t* in terms of the six-item *Political Cynicism Scale* developed by Agger *et al.* (1961, pp. 477, 479). The relevant six items in Appendix B are 95–9 (all positively worded) and 100 (negatively worded).
4. *PERSONAL CYNICISM* (PERC), a contemptuous distrust of people in general, has been measured for each group during each run at time *t* in terms of the four-item *Personal Cynicism Scale* developed by Agger *et al.* (1961, pp. 489, 490). The relevant items in Appendix B are 80 (negatively worded) and 81, 82, and 84 (all positively worded).[5]
5. *POLITICAL EFFICACY* (POLE), the sense that political and social change is possible, and that one can participate in bringing it about, has been measured for each group during each run at time *t* in terms of the four-item *Political Efficacy Scale* developed by Campbell *et al.* (cited in Agger *et al.*, 1961, pp. 492–3). The four items in Appendix B are 22–4 and 76 (all negatively worded).

6. *NEED FOR ACHIEVEMENT* (ACH), a predisposition to strive for satisfaction which derives from pride in accomplishment, from meeting some standard of excellence (McClelland, 1961), has been measured for each group during each run at time *t* in terms of four items which emerged as part of one dimension from a factor analysis of PDS participants' responses to Appendix B. The four items are 101–3 and 111 (all positively worded) in Appendix B.[6]
7. *NEED FOR AFFILIATION* (AFF), a predisposition to strive for satisfaction which derives from establishing and maintaining pleasant relationships with others (McClelland, 1961), has been measured for each group during each run at time *t* in terms of four other items which emerged from the factor analysis of participants' responses to Appendix B. The four items are 71 (positive), 75 (negative), 77 (positive), and 79 (negative).[7]
8. *NEED FOR POWER* (POW), a predisposition to strive for satisfaction which derives from control of the means for influencing others (McClelland, 1961), has been measured for each group during each run at time *t* also in terms of four items which emerged from the factor analysis mentioned above. One of the selected items, 81 (positive), is also a component of the *Personal Cynicism Scale* and, hence, appears in the present study twice. The remaining three items are 107–9 (all positive) in Appendix B.[8]
9. *SUB-SYSTEMIC ENVIRONMENTAL COMPLEXITY* (SSEC), which refers to the size of the decision-making unit, has been measured for each group during each run by number of decision-makers in the group at time *t*.
10. *TEMPORAL OVERLOAD* (TO), which refers to time limits within which decision-makers have to make decisions, has been measured for each group during each run by total number of decision periods experienced by the group at time *t*.

Societal Level

11. *DOMESTIC INSTABILITY* (DI), which refers to internal challenges to incumbent political authority, has been measured for each group during each run in terms of the number of participants who, as a proportion of the total number in a group, staged coups or defected during *crossed intervals*. That is, as a dependent (conflict) variable, DI has been measured across the second half of t ("present time") and the first half of $t + 1$ ("future time") and, as an independent (explanatory) variable, across the second half of $t - 1$ ("single previous time") plus the first half of t.[9]
12. *RELATIVE ECONOMIC STATUS* (RES), a political actor's level of economic development relative to that of other actors, has been measured for each group during each run in terms of the group's average GNP, as a proportion of the sum of all groups' average GNPs, at $t - 1$.
13. *RELATIVE ECONOMIC DEPRIVATION* (RED), the discrepancy between a political actor's preferred and its actual economic status, relative to other actors, has been measured for each group during each run in terms

of the ratio of its (a) frequency of decisions to trade (as a proportion of the sum of all groups' trading decisions) to (b) its average GNP (as a proportion of the sum of all groups' average GNPs), i.e. (a) divided by (b), at $t - 1$.

14. *MANIFEST DISTRUST* (MD), a political actor's location in a conflict–cooperation space, has been measured for each group during each run in terms of the ratio of its arming decisions to its trading decisions. Since MD is both a conflict variable and an explanatory variable, it has been measured at t and $t - 1$.
15. *CHANGE IN MANIFEST DISTRUST* (%MD), the rate of change over time in a political actor's location in a conflict–cooperation space, has been measured for each group during each run by taking the difference between MD at $t - 2$ ("double previous time") and MD at $t - 1$, and then dividing by MD at $t - 2$.
16. *BELLICOSITY* (BEL), a political actor's active capability to wage war, has been measured for each group during each run by calculating its cumulative investment in armaments as a proportion of GNP. Since BEL is both a conflict and an explanatory variable, it has been measured at t and $t - 1$.
17. *CHANGE IN BELLICOSITY* (%BEL), the rate of change over time in a political actor's active capability to wage war, has been measured for each group during each run by taking the difference between BEL at $t - 2$ and BEL at $t - 1$, and then dividing by BEL at $t - 2$.
18. *ALLIANCES* (ALL), a political actor's cooperative associations with other actors for the purpose of common defense, has been measured for each group during each run by the cumulative number of other groups with which it has associated itself, either formally or informally. As both a conflict and an explanatory variable, ALL has been measured at t and $t - 1$.
19. *AGGRESSIVE ATTACKS* (ATT), which refers to the employment by a political actor of its active capability to wage war against one or more other actors for any length of time and for any degree of human and environmental destruction, has been measured for each group during each run by the number of other actors against which it has initiated war. As a conflict as well as an explanatory variable, ATT has been measured at both t and $t - 1$.
20. *CHANGE IN AGGRESSIVE ATTACKS* (%ATT), the rate of change over time in a political actor's actual use of its active capability to wage war, has been measured for each group during each run by taking the difference between ATT at $t - 2$ and ATT at $t - 1$, and then dividing by ATT at $t - 2$.
21. *ATTACK VICTIM* (VICT), the condition of a political actor coming under attack by the armed forces of one or more other actors, has been measured for each group during each run by the total number of wars initiated against it, at $t - 1$.

Trans-societal Level

22. *SYSTEMIC ENVIRONMENTAL COMPLEXITY* (SEC), which refers to a political actor's potential interactions, or interaction opportunities (friendly or otherwise), with other actors, has been measured for each group during each run in terms of the total number of actors in the intergroup system, minus one ($N - 1$), at time t.
23. *SYSTEMIC ATTACK CONTAGION* (SAC), the level of violence in the trans-societal environment, has been measured for each group during each run by the number of wars initiated or joined in by others, against others, in the "international" system, at $t - 1$.

Notes

1. In the operational definitions which follow, the spatial *unit of analysis* is the PDS "nation-group" and the temporal unit is the two-hour weekly PDS operation. Variables have been measured for current runs (at time t, "present time") and, as time-lags, for previous runs (at $t - 1$, "single previous time," or $t - 2$, "double previous time"), or some combination of these.
2. Likert scales are *ordinal scales*. For actors who have been measured on some dimension in terms of such a scale, we can say that one actor has more or less of the dimension than another actor, but we cannot say by how much more or less (see Selltiz *et al.*, 1976, pp. 418–21).
3. Originally, as indicated in Appendix B, 1 = strongly agree, ... , 5 = strongly disagree. This was reversed so that 1 = strongly disagree, 2 = disagree, 3 = undecided, 4 = agree, and 5 = strongly agree. This enabled us to interpret upward movement along the scale as movement from lower to higher degrees of possession of the attribute being measured, in this case, DOG. (This interpretation of the reversed response scheme applies only to positively worded items.)
4. "Negative wording" means that *disagreement* with an item indicates some degree of possession of the attribute being measured. Negatively worded items are used in conjunction with positively worded items to check for *response set*, i.e. the tendency for some to respond to all items in the same mechanical way, which has generated much controversy about the validity of the F-scale as a measure of AUTH (see Greenstein, 1969, pp. 101, 114–15).
5. These items are components of one rendition of the *Machiavellianism Scale* developed by Christie (see Christie and Geis, 1970, pp. 10–34).
6. These items are similar to some of those used by Bernard Rosen (1956, 1964) to measure ACH.
7. These particular items are from one rendition of the *Machiavellianism Scale* (Christie and Geis, 1970). Agger *et al.* (1961, pp. 504–5) used them as a check for response-set.
8. Items 107–9 are similar to those used by Rosen (1956, 1964). Given that POW has been operationalized here in terms of items that are similar to those used by Rosen to operationalize ACH, there may be a link between ACH and POW, i.e. each may somehow entail the other. The framework within which Rosen has operated, which is derived from a scheme developed by Florence Kluckhohn, also suggests that this may be the case. For instance, Kluckhohn's *individualistic, Promethean* actors, who are characterized by "rational mastery over nature," could be reflective of POW as well as ACH (see Kluckhohn, 1950, p. 378).

9. DI was measured *across* temporal units instead of simply at t, $t - 1$, or $t - 2$, because many coups in the PDS occurred during the very first decision period of a simulation run, thereby suggesting that, in those particular cases, some degree of internal conflict, as a *developing process*, occurred during the latter half (at minimum) of the previous run. Operationally, therefore, we were interested in the previous half-interval when DI may have been a developing process and the subsequent half-interval when it could have been expressed as a concrete event.

Appendix D Comparisons Between Relationships in the PDS Models and Corresponding Relationships in Other Studies[1]

DI Relationships

Content	*Sign*	*Location*[2]	*Relationship with other studies' results*
ACH–DI	+	G & I	Although not strictly comparable, Haythorn and Altman (1967) found that subjects matched in ACH got along well when isolated for long periods. (D)
RED–DI	+	G & E	In his study of 114 polities for 1961–5, Gurr (1968) found a positive relationship between economic deprivation and total strife, as well as a positive relationship between economic deprivation and each of the components of total strife: conspiracy, internal war, and turmoil. (A) In their study of 84 nations, the Feierabends (1966) found a positive relationship between systemic frustration for 1948–55 and political instability for 1955–61. (A)
MD–DI	+	G & L	In his study of the People's Republic of China, Onate (1974) found, with a variety of annual and quarterly time-lags, positive relationships between foreign conflict in general and domestic conflict for 1950–70. (A) Copson (1973) found, in his study of 37 African nations, positive relationships between unfriendly (international) interactions for 1964–5 and anti-government

			plotting for 1966–7 and 1968–9. He also found a positive relationship between unfriendly interactions for 1966–7 and anti-government plotting for 1968–9. (A) Wilkenfeld (1973) found, with one-year time-lags, positive relationships between diplomatic foreign conflict and turmoil, and between belligerent foreign conflict and turmoil, for fifteen personalist nations, 26 centrist nations, and 33 polyarchic nations, for 1955–60. (A)
SEC–DI	–	G, E & I	No comparable studies found.
SSEC–DI	+	I	No comparable studies found.

MD Relationships

Content	*Sign*	*Location*	*Relationship with other studies' results*
PERC–MD	+	G	No comparable studies found.
TO–MD	–	G	James Alcock (1974) found, in a study of bargaining behavior among Canadians and among Indians, that Canadian males were the most cooperative when two-minute time limits were applied by the experimenter. (A)
SEC–MD	–	G & E	No comparable studies found.
RES–MD	–	E	The Feierabends (1969), in their study of 84 nations for 1955–61, found a negative relationship between economic development and foreign conflict for mid-modern nations. (A)
RES–MD	+	I	The Feierabends, in the same study, found a positive relationship between economic development and foreign conflict for high-modern nations. (A) Moore (1974) found positive relationships between economic development and foreign conflict for up to 109 nations for 1963, relationships which were stronger for undeveloped than for developed nations. (A)

			East and Hermann (1974), in their study of 33 nations for 1959–68, found a positive relationship between economic development and percentage of foreign conflict events. (A)
MD–MD	+	L	No comparable studies found.

BEL Relationships

Content	*Sign*	*Location*	*Relationship with other studies' results*
BEL–BEL	+	G & L	Lambelet and Luterbacher (1978) found, in their study of American and Soviet defense spending, evidence of self-stimulation (as well as mutual stimulation), for both nations, but especially for the USSR during 1949–75. (A)
VICT–BEL	–	G	No comparable studies found.
SAC–BEL	+	G	No comparable studies found.
ATT–BEL	–	E	No comparable studies found.
SEC–BEL	+	E	No comparable studies found.
DOG–BEL	–	I	Laulicht (1965a, b, c) found, in his sample of 1000 Canadian citizens and 144 Canadian business, trades union, and political elites, that religious DOG was associated with being in favor of conventional and nuclear weapons, and being against peaceful coexistence. (D)
POLC–BEL	–	I	No comparable studies found.
TO–BEL	–	I	The aforementioned study by Alcock (1974), in which Canadian males were the most cooperative when two-minute time limits were imposed by the experimenter, is also relevant here. (A) Charles Hermann (1969) found, in a simulation study, that fifteen-minute decision periods were accompanied by more nonhostile acts than were 50-minute periods. (A)
TO–BEL	+	L	Hermann (1969) also found that fifteen-minute decision periods were accompanied by more hostile acts than were the 50-minute periods. (There were more acts both hostile and nonhostile in the shorter decision period.) (A)

RES–BEL	+	I	Moore (1974) found, in his aforementioned study, positive relationships between economic development and defense expenditures as a percentage of GNP, relationships which were stronger for undeveloped than for developed nations. (A)
SSEC–BEL	–	L	No comparable studies found.
RED–BEL	–	L	No comparable studies found.

ALL Relationships

Content	*Sign*	*Location*	*Relationship with other studies' results*
POLC–ALL	+	G & L	No comparable studies found.
PERC–ALL	–	G & L	No comparable studies found.
TO–ALL	–	G & I	The aforementioned study by Alcock (1974), in which Canadian males were the most cooperative when two-minute time limits were applied by the experimenter, is also relevant here, although perhaps not as directly as in the case of the negative relationships between TO and MD, and TO and BEL. (A)
ALL–ALL	+	G, I & L	No comparable studies found.
%ATT–ALL	–	G	No comparable studies found.
%ATT–ALL	+	E	No comparable studies found.
VICT–ALL	+	G & E	No comparable studies found.
VICT–ALL	–	L	No comparable studies found.
SEC–ALL	+	G, E & L	No comparable studies found.
BEL–ALL	–	I	Using Rummel's DON data and Singer and Small's COW data, Weede (1973) found a positive relationship between power and alliances for 1955–60. (D)
ATT–ALL	–	I	No comparable studies found.
SAC–ALL	+	I	No comparable studies found.
DI–ALL	+	L	No comparable studies found.

ATT Relationships

Content	*Sign*	*Location*	*Relationship with other studies' results*
TO–ATT	+	G & I	Ole Holsti (1972, Chapter 5) found that time pressure seemed to be a central factor in the decisions which led to the outbreak of World War I. (A)

The aforementioned study by Alcock (1974), in which Canadian males were the most cooperative when two-minute time limits were applied by the experimenter, is also relevant here. (D)

The aforementioned study by Hermann (1969), in which both more hostile *and* nonhostile acts were recorded for fifteen-minute decision periods than for 50-minute periods, is relevant too. (A, D)

BEL–ATT + G, E & I

Weede (1970), using Rummel's DON data on 59 nations for 1955–7, found that powerful nations tended to be involved in less violent foreign conflict. (D)

In another study, Weede (1976), using Singer and Small's data and SIPRI data for 82 nations, found both positive and negative relationships between military allocation ratios for 1955 and war for 1956–62 and 1956–69. (A, D)

In this same study, Weede (1976) found, for 82 and 121 nations, positive relationships between military allocation ratios for 1967 and war for 1968–70. (A)

Rummel (1968) found, for 64 nations, a positive relationship between defense expenditure for 1955 and war for 1955–7. (A)

Quincy Wright (1964), in his study of war, found a positive relationship between relative power and warlikeness of states. (A)

Singer (1972) found, in his COW project, that most of the war in the international system between 1816 and 1965 was waged by major powers. He reports, however, that "analysis to date reveals no strong relationship between a given war-proneness and its power rank." (A, D)

In one version of their study of violence between members of the Triple Entente and members of the Triple Alliance during 1870–1914, Choucri and North (1969) found a high positive relationship between defense allocations and international violence. (A)

			In another version of this study, however, Choucri and North (1975) found a negative relationship between military expenditures and violence. (D)
ATT–ATT	+	G, I & L	In his re-examination of Wright's list of wars, Moyal (1949) found, with time-lags of five and fifteen years, relationships between war at one point and war at another point in time. (A) Tanter (1966) found, for 74 nations, a positive relationship between war for 1955–7 and war for 1958–60. (A) Singer *et al.* (1972) found, with five-year lags, a positive relationship between war at one point and war at another point in time for the nineteenth century, and a negative relationship for the twentieth century. (A, D)
SEC–ATT	+	E & I	Haas (1970), using data generated by Wright and Richardson, found that multipolar systems tended to have a larger number of wars and war casualties than did bipolar systems. (A) Midlarsky (1975), using Singer and Small's data, found a positive (nonlinear) relationship between number of poles and frequency of war in the international system for 1822–1945. (A, D)
DOG–ATT	–	I	Driver (1965) found, in a simulation study, that cognitive concreteness, which is related theoretically to DOG, was related to aggressive behavior. (D) Bailes and Guller (1970), in their sample of 150 American undergraduates, found a positive relationship between DOG and attitudes favoring the American use of force in Vietnam. (D)
POLC–ATT	–	I	No comparable study found.
POLC–ATT	+	L	No comparable study found.
AUTH–ATT	+	L	Farris (1960) found a relationship between AUTH and jingoism, and between AUTH and war-expectancy. (A)

			Mackinnon and Centers (1958), in their Los Angeles sample, found that high scorers on AUTH were more likely than low scorers to condone nuclear bombing as a means for preventing propaganda coming into the U.S.A. from Soviet ships at sea. (A)
POLE–ATT	+	L	Kaase and Marsh (1976) found, in a five-nation study of political action, that the more politically activist in orientation respondents were (i.e. the more likely they were to take extralegal as well as legal political action), the more likely they were to be high scorers on POLE – except for the most politically active of all, the protesters. (A, D)

Notes

1. What we were looking at in these particular comparisons was direction or sign of relationship, and not at degree of relationship. Agreement between a PDS finding and a finding from another study, therefore, means that the sign of relationship in both cases is the same (positive or negative).
2. The symbols here refer to the models where the corresponding relationships are located. Hence, G = general (PDS 1–5) model; E = early stage model; I = intermediate stage model; L = late stage model. Also, A = agreement between PDS and other findings, and D = disagreement. When one study seemed to, more or less, equally support *and* challenge a PDS relationship, the results of the comparison were coded as both A and D (see note 1). This also applies throughout this appendix.

References

Abdulai, Napoleon (ed.) (1994). *Genocide in Rwanda: Background and Current Situation.* London: African Research and Information Centre (ARIC), July.

Aberbach, Joel D. (1969). "Alienation and Political Behavior." *American Political Science Review*, **63**(1), 86–99.

Abramowitz, Morton (1998). "Ominous Rumblings from the Balkans." *Washington Post*, February 16, p. A27.

ACDA (1990). "CFE: Treaty on Conventional Forces in Europe – Highlights and Background." Washington, DC: U.S. Arms Control and Disarmament Agency (ACDA), November 16.

Adorno, T. W. (1951). "Freudian Theory and the Pattern of Fascist Propaganda." In *Psychoanalysis and the Social Sciences*, Geza Roheim (ed.). New York: International Universities Press.

Adorno, T. W., E. Frenkel-Brunswik, D. J. Levinson, and R. N. Sanford (1950). *The Authoritarian Personality*. New York: Harper.

AFB-INFO 1/91 (1991). Bonn: Peace Information Unit.

Agger, R. E., M. N. Goldstein, and S. A. Pearl (1961). "Political Cynicism: Measurement and Meaning." *Journal of Politics*, **23**(3), 477–506.

Akashi, Yasushi (1995/6). "The Limits of UN Diplomacy and the Future of Conflict Mediation." *Survival*, **37**(4), 83–98.

Alcock, James E. (1974). "Cooperation, Competition, and the Effects of Time Pressure in Canada and India." *Journal of Conflict Resolution*, **18**(2), 171–97.

Alcock, Norman Z. (1972). *The War Disease*. Oakville, Ontario: Canadian Peace Research Institute (CPRI) Press.

Allison, Graham T. (1971). *Essence of Decision: Explaining the Cuban Missile Crisis*. Boston: Little, Brown.

Allison, Graham T. and Morton H. Halperin (1972). "Bureaucratic Politics: a Paradigm and Some Policy Implications." In *Theory and Policy in International Relations*, Raymond Tanter and Richard H. Ullman (eds). Princeton, NJ: Princeton University Press.

Althauser, Robert P. (1971). "Multicollinearity and Non-additive Regression Models." In *Causal Models in the Social Sciences*, Hubert M. Blalock (ed.). London: Macmillan.

Anderson, Jack and Michael Binstein (1994). "UN Aid: a Boon to the Serbs?" *Washington Post*, January 16, p. C7.

AP (1996). "Serbs Mark a 'Victory,' Victims Are Exhumed." Associated Press. *International Herald Tribune*, July 12, p. 10.

AP (1997). "Ukraine and NATO Set Security Charter." Associated Press. *International Herald Tribune*, May 30, p. 2.

ASA (1996a). "Key NSF Board Approves New Violence Consortium." *Footnotes* (American Sociological Association), **24**(1), 1 and 8.

ASA (1996b). *Employment Bulletin* (American Sociological Association), **21**(3), 7.

Asch, S. E. (1956). "Studies of Independence and Submission to Group Pressure:

1. A Minority of One against a Unanimous Majority." *Psychological Monographs*, **70**(416).
Ashley, Richard K. (1989). "Living on Border Lines: Man, Poststructuralism, and War." In *International/Intertextual Relations: Postmodern Readings of World Politics*, James Der Derian and Michael J. Shapiro (eds). Lexington, MA: Lexington Books.
Ashley, Richard K. and R. B. J. Walker (eds) (1990). *International Studies Quarterly* ("Special Issue on Speaking the Language of Exile: Dissidence in International Studies"), **34**(3).
Atkinson, Rick (1994). "Bosnian Serbs Reject Peace Plan: Big Powers Ponder Punishments." *Washington Post*, July 21, p. A18.
Avruch, Kevin and Peter W. Black (1987). "A Generic Theory of Conflict Resolution: a Critique." *Negotiation Journal*, **3**(1), 87–96.
Avruch, Kevin and Peter W. Black (1993). "Conflict Resolution in Intercultural Settings: Problems and Prospects." In *Conflict Resolution Theory and Practice: Integration and Application*, Dennis J. D. Sandole and Hugo van der Merwe (eds). Manchester: Manchester University Press.
Avruch, K., P. W. Black, and J. A. Scimecca (eds) (1991). *Conflict Resolution: Cross-cultural Perspectives*. Westport, CT: Greenwood Press.
Axelrod, Robert (1984). *The Evolution of Cooperation*. New York: Basic Books.
Axelrod, Robert (1997). *The Complexity of Cooperation: Agent-based Models of Competition and Collaboration*. Princeton, NJ: Princeton, University Press.
Bächler, Günther (ed.) (1997). *Federalism against Ethnicity? Institutional, Legal and Democratic Instruments to Prevent Violent Minority Conflicts*. Zurich: Verlag Ruegger.
Bailes, D. W. and I. B. Guller (1970). "Dogmatism and Attitudes towards the Vietnam War." *Sociometry*, **33**(2), 140–6.
Baker, Peter and Bradley Graham (1996). "Clinton Decides to Keep U.S. Troops in Bosnia: Forces to Stay 18 Months Past First Deadline." *Washington Post*, November 16, pp. A1, A20.
Balanzino, Sergio (1997). "Deepening Partnership: the Key to Long-term Stability in Europe." *NATO Review* ("Summit Edition"), **45**(4), 10–16.
Baldwin, David A. (ed.) (1993a). *Neorealism and Neoliberalism: the Contemporary Debate*. New York: Columbia University Press.
Baldwin, David A. (1993b). "Neoliberalism, Neorealism, and World Politics." In Baldwin (1993a).
Bandura, Albert (1973). *Aggression: a Social Learning Analysis*. Englewood Cliffs, NJ: Prentice Hall.
Bandura, Albert and Richard H. Walters (1970). "Reinforcement Patterns and Social Behavior: Aggression." In *The Dynamics of Aggression: Individual, Group and International Analyses*, Edwin I. Megargee and Jack E. Hokanson (eds). New York and London: Harper and Row.
Banks, Michael (1984). "The Evolution of International Relations Theory." In *Conflict in World Society: a New Perspective on International Relations*, Michael Banks (ed.). New York: St Martin's Press.
Barbash, Fred (1996a). "Renewed Combat Is Feared in Ulster after Hotel Blast: 2-year Truce Is in Jeopardy, Protestant Party Leader Warns." *International Herald Tribune*, July 15, p. 1.
Barbash, Fred (1996b). "Unexpectedly Peaceful Day Eases Fears in Londonderry." *Washington Post*, August 11, p. A24.
Barber, Benjamin R. (1997/8). "Fantasy of Fear: Huntington and the West versus the Rest." *Harvard International Review*, **20**(1), 66–71.

Basic Agreement on Eastern Slavonia, Baranja and Western Sirmium (The "Erdut Agreement") (1995). Erdut ([Occupied] Croatia), November 12.

Bateson, Gregory (1973). *Steps to an Ecology of Mind: Collected Essays in Anthropology, Psychiatry, Evolution, and Epistemology*. St Albans: Paladin.

Battiata, Mary (1992a). "Conference on Balkan Refugee Crisis Pledges Aid but Not Havens." *Washington Post*, July 30, p. A22.

Battiata, Mary (1992b). "New Wave of Terror in Bosnia Described to UN, EC Envoys." *Washington Post*, September 26, p. A16.

Begley, Sharon (1995). "Grey Matters: New Technologies that Catch the Mind in the Very Act of Thinking Show How Men and Women Use Their Brains Differently." *Newsweek*, March 27, pp. 48–54.

Berberoglu, Berch (ed.) (1995). *The National Question: Nationalism, Ethnic Conflict, and Self-determination in the 20th Century*. Philadelphia: Temple University Press.

Beriker, Nimet and Daniel Druckman (1996). "Simulating the Lausanne Peace Negotiations, 1922–1923: Power Asymmetries in Bargaining." *Simulation and Gaming*, **27**(2), 162–83.

Berkowitz, Leonard and Anthony LePage (1967). "Weapons as Aggression-eliciting Stimuli." *Journal of Personality and Social Psychology*, **7**, 202–7. Reprinted in *The Dynamics of Aggression: Individual, Group, and International Analyses*, Edwin I. Megargee and Jack E. Hokanson (eds). New York: Harper and Row (1970).

Berselli, Beth (1998). "Cannons of Management: Executives Flock to Battlefields for Training." *Washington Post*, April 4, pp. A1, A10.

Bertram, Christoph (1995/6). "Multilateral Diplomacy and Conflict Resolution." *Survival*, **37**(4), 65–82.

Biersteker, Thomas J. (1989). "Critical Reflections on Post Positivism in International Relations." *International Studies Quarterly*, **33**(3), 263–7.

Bildt, Carl (1996). "Help the Bosnia Parties to Make Dayton Work." *International Herald Tribune*, April 3, p. 8.

Blalock, Hubert M., Jr (1960). *Social Statistics*. New York: McGraw-Hill.

Blalock, Hubert M., Jr (1961). *Causal Inferences in Nonexperimental Research*. Chapel Hill: University of North Carolina Press.

Blalock, Hubert M., Jr (1969). *Theory Construction: from Verbal to Mathematical Formulations*. Englewood Cliffs, NJ: Prentice Hall.

Blalock, Hubert M., Jr (1971). "Four-variable Causal Models and Partial Correlations." In *Causal Models in the Social Sciences*, Hubert M. Blalock, Jr (ed.). London: Macmillan.

Bloed, Arie (ed.) (1993). *The Conference on Security and Cooperation in Europe: Analysis and Basic Documents, 1972–1993*. Dordrecht: Kluwer Academic Publishers.

Bloomfield, Lincoln and Cornelius J. Gearin (1971). *Games Foreign Policy Experts Play: the Political Exercise Comes of Age* (Arms Control Project C/71-20). Cambridge, MA: MIT Center for International Studies.

Bodin, Jean (1955). *Six Books of the Commonwealth* (translated by M. J. Tooley). Oxford: Basil Blackwell.

Bonham, G. M. (1967). "Aspects of the Validity of Two Simulations of Phenomena in International Relations." Doctoral dissertation. Cambridge, MA: Massachusetts Institute of Technology.

Boocock, Sarane S. and E. O. Schild (eds) (1968). *Simulation Games in Learning*. Beverly Hills, CA: Sage.

Borden, A., B. Cohen, M. Crevatin, and D. Zmiarevic (eds) (1992). *Breakdown: War and Reconstruction in Yugoslavia*. London: Institute for War and Peace Reporting.

Boucher, J., D. Landis, and K. A. Clark (eds) (1987). *Ethnic Conflict: International Perspectives*. Beverly Hills, CA: Sage.

Boulding, Kenneth E. (1956). *The Image: Knowledge in Life and Society*. Ann Arbor: University of Michigan Press.

Boulding, Kenneth E. (1962). *Conflict and Defense: a General Theory*. New York: Harper and Row.

Boulding, Kenneth E. (1965). "The Economics of Human Conflict." In *The Nature of Human Conflict*, Elton B. McNeil (ed.). Englewood Cliffs, NJ: Prentice Hall.

Bourlanges/Martin Report (1995). Strasbourg: European Parliament, May 17.

Boutros-Ghali, Boutros (1992). *An Agenda for Peace: Preventive Diplomacy, Peacemaking and Peace-keeping* (Report of the Secretary-General pursuant to the statement adopted by the Summit Meeting of the Security Council on January 31, 1992). New York: United Nations, Department of Public Information.

Boutros-Ghali, Boutros (1995). "Supplement to an Agenda for Peace: Position Paper of the Secretary-General on the Occasion of the Fiftieth Anniversary of the United Nations" (Fiftieth Session of the General Assembly, Report of the Secretary-General on the Work of the Organization). New York: United Nations.

Bradley, John F. N. (1997). *Post-Communist Czechoslovakia*. Boulder, CO: East European Monographs.

Brady, Linda P. (1997). "On Paradigms and Policy Relevance: Reflections on the Future of Security Studies." *National Security Studies Quarterly*, 3(4), 1–12.

Brandt Commission (1980). *North–South: a Programme for Survival* (Report of the Independent Commission on International Development Issues under the Chairmanship of Willy Brandt). London: Pan.

Brandt, Willy (1980). "A Plea for Change: Peace, Justice, Jobs – an Introduction." In *North–South: a Programme for Survival*, Brandt Commission (1980).

Brecher, Michael and Jonathan Wilkenfeld (1997). *A Study of Crisis*. Ann Arbor: University of Michigan Press.

Bremer, Stuart A. (1977). *Simulated Worlds: a Computer Model of National Decision-making*. Princeton, NJ: Princeton University Press.

Bremer, Stuart A. (1980). "National Capabilities and War Proneness." In *The Correlates of War, Volume 2*, J. David Singer (ed.). New York: Free Press.

Bremer, Stuart A. (ed.) (1987a). *The GLOBUS Model: Computer Simulation of Worldwide Political and Economic Developments* (Report on a Research Project at the Science Center for Social Research, Berlin). Frankfurt: Campus Verlag.

Bremer, Stuart A. (1987b). "Evaluating GLOBUS." In Bremer (1987a).

Bremer, Stuart A. (1995a). "Advancing the Scientific Study of War." In *The Process of War: Advancing the Scientific Study of War*, Stuart A. Bremer and Thomas R. Cusack (eds). Luxembourg: Gordon and Breach.

Bremer, Stuart A. (1995b). "Final Words." In Bremer and Cusack (1995a).

Bremer, Stuart A. and Thomas R. Cusack (eds) (1995). *The Process of War: Advancing the Scientific Study of War*. Luxembourg: Gordon and Breach.

Bromke, Adam (1993). "Post-Communist Countries: Challenges and Problems." In *Central and Eastern Europe: the Challenge of Transition*, Regina Cowen Karp (ed.). Oxford: Oxford University Press.

Brown, Michael E. (ed.) (1993). *Ethnic Conflict and International Security*. Princeton, NJ: Princeton University Press.

Brown, Michael E., Owen R. Coté, Jr, Sean M. Lynn-Jones, and Steven E. Miller (eds)

(1997). *Nationalism and Ethnic Conflict: An International Security Reader*. Cambridge, MA: MIT Press.

Browning, Rufus P. (1968a). "Hypotheses about Political Recruitment: a Partially Data-based Computer Simulation." In *Simulation in the Study of Politics*, William D. Coplin (ed.). Chicago: Markham.

Browning, Rufus P. (1968b). "The Interaction of Personality and Political System in Decisions to Run for Office: Some Data and a Simulation Technique." *Journal of Social Issues*, **24**(3), 93–109.

Buckley, Stephen (1997). "Rwanda's Rising Tide of Violence: Hutu Massacre of Tutsi Refugees Ignites Fears of Return to Widespread Ethnic Terror." *Washington Post*, December 14, pp. A25, A30.

Budiansky, S. (1992). "The Nuclear Epidemic." *Newsweek*, March 16, pp. 40–4.

Bueno de Mesquita, Bruce (1989). "The Contribution of Expected Utility Theory to the Study of International Conflict." In *The Origin and Prevention of Major Wars*, Robert I. Rotberg and Theodore K. Rabb (eds). Cambridge: Cambridge University Press.

Bull, Hedley (1966). "International Theory: the Case for a Classical Approach." *World Politics*, **18**(3), 361–77.

Bulloch, John and Harvey Morris (1989). *The Gulf War: Its Origins, History and Consequences*. London: Methuen.

Burns, Arthur Lee (1957). "From Balance to Deterrence: a Theoretical Analysis." *World Politics*, **9**(4), 494–529.

Burrowes, Robert and Bertram Spector (1973). "The Strength and Direction of Relationships Between Domestic and External Conflict and Cooperation, Syria, 1961–67." In *Conflict Behavior and Linkage Politics*, Jonathan Wilkenfeld (ed.). New York: McKay.

Burton, John W. (1969). *Conflict and Communication: The Use of Controlled Communication in International Relations*. London: Macmillan.

Burton, John W. (1972). *World Society*. Cambridge: Cambridge University Press.

Burton, John W. (1979). *Deviance, Terrorism and War: The Process of Solving Unsolved Social and Political Problems*. New York: St Martin's Press.

Burton, John W. (1984). *Global Conflict: the Domestic Sources of International Crisis*. Brighton: Wheatsheaf Books.

Burton, John W. (1990a). *Conflict: Resolution and Provention*. London: Macmillan.

Burton, John W. (ed.) (1990b). *Conflict: Human Needs Theory*. London: Macmillan.

Burton John W. (1991). "Problems of Leadership." Unpublished manuscript. Fairfax, VA: Institute for Conflict Analysis and Resolution, George Mason University.

Burton, John W. and Frank Dukes (1990). *Conflict: Practices in Management, Settlement and Resolution*. London: Macmillan.

Burton, John W. and Dennis J. D. Sandole (1986). "Generic Theory: the Basis of Conflict Resolution." *Negotiation Journal*, **2**(4), 333–44.

Burton, John W. and Dennis J. D. Sandole (1987). "Expanding the Debate on Generic Theory of Conflict Resolution: a Response to a Critique." *Negotiation Journal*, **3**(1), 97–9.

Buzan, Barry, Charles Jones, and Richard Little (1993). *The Logic of Anarchy: Neorealism to Structural Realism*. New York: Columbia University Press.

Cantril, Hadley (ed.) (1950). *Tensions That Cause Wars*. Urbana: University of Illinois Press.

Carment, David and Patrick James (eds) (1997). *Wars in the Midst of Peace: The International Politics of Ethnic Conflict*. Pittsburgh: University of Pittsburgh Press.

Carnegie Commission on Preventing Deadly Conflict (1997). *Preventing Deadly Conflict: Final Report*. Washington, DC: Carnegie Commission on Preventing Deadly Conflict.

Carr, Edward Hallett (1939). *The Twenty Years Crisis, 1919–1939: an Introduction to the Study of International Relations*. London: Macmillan.

CFR (1993). *The Clash of Civilizations? The Debate: a Foreign Affairs Reader*. New York: Council on Foreign Relations.

Chadwick, Richard W. (1967). "An Empirical Test of Five Assumptions in an Internation Simulation about National Political Systems." *General Systems*, **12**, 177–92.

Chalmers, Malcolm (1993). "Developing a Security Regime for Eastern Europe." *Journal of Peace Research*, **30**(4), 427–44.

Chang, Iris (1997). *The Rape of Nanking: the Forgotten Holocaust of World War II*. New York: Basic Books.

Charter of Paris for a New Europe (1990). Paris, November 21.

Chevrier, Marie Isabelle (1997). "The Threat that Won't Disperse: Why Biological Weapons Have Taken Center Stage." *Washington Post*, December 21, pp. C1–C2.

Chigas, Diana (1994a). "Bridging the Gap between Theory and Practice: the CSCE High Commissioner on National Minorities." *Helsinki Monitor*, **5**(3), 27–41.

Chigas, Diana (1994b). "Building Capacity for Conflict Prevention." *Bulletin* (Warsaw: CSCE Office for Democratic Institutions and Human Rights), **2**(2), 1–6.

Chigas, D., with E. McClintock and C. Kamp (1996). "Preventive Diplomacy and the Organization for Security and Cooperation in Europe: Creating Incentives for Dialogue and Cooperation." In *Preventing Conflict in the Post-Communist World: Mobilizing International and Regional Organizations*, Abram Chayes and Antonia Handler Chayes (eds). Washington, DC: The Brookings Institution.

Choucri, Nazli and Robert C. North (1969). "The Determinants of International Violence." *Peace Research Society (International), Papers*, **12**, 33–63.

Choucri, Nazli and Robert C. North (1975). *Nations in Conflict: National Growth and International Violence*. San Francisco: W. H. Freeman.

Choucri, Nazli and Robert C. North (1990). "Global Environmental Change: toward a Framework for Decision and Policy." Paper presented at the Annual Meeting of the International Studies Association (ISA), Washington, DC, April 10–14.

Christie, Richard and Florence L. Geis (1970). *Studies in Machiavellianism*. New York: Academic Press.

Chufrin, Gennady I. and Harold H. Saunders (1993). "A Public Peace Process." *Negotiation Journal*, **9**(2), 155–77.

Cioffi-Revilla, Claudio (1990). *The Scientific Measurement of International Conflict: Handbook of Datasets on Crises and Wars, 1495–1988 A.D.* Boulder, CO: Lynne Rienner.

Clark, Gregory (1996). "Other Asians Should Have a Word with China and Taiwan." *International Herald Tribune*, February 2, p. 6.

Clark, Mary E. (1989). *Ariadne's Thread: the Search for New Modes of Thinking*. London: Macmillan.

CMG (1993). "Early Warning and Preventive Action in the CSCE: Defining the Role of the High Commissioner on National Minorities." *Working Paper Series* (Project on Preventive Diplomacy and Conflict Management in Europe). Cambridge, MA: Conflict Management Group.

CMG (1994). "Methods and Strategies in Conflict Prevention." *Working Paper Series* (Project on Preventive Diplomacy and Conflict Management in Europe). Cambridge, MA: Conflict Management Group.

Coakley, John (1993). *The Territorial Management of Ethnic Conflict*. Newbury Park, CA: Frank Cass.

Coate, Roger A. and Jerel A. Rosati (eds) (1988). *The Power of Human Needs in World Society*. Boulder, CO: Lynne Rienner.

Cobb, Sara and Janet Rifkin (1991). "Practice and Paradox: Deconstructing Neutrality in Mediation." *Law and Social Inquiry*, **16**, 35–62.

COE (1998). "The 40 Member States of the Council of Europe." COE (http://www.coe.fr/index.htm).

Colosi, Thomas (1987). "A Model for Negotiation and Mediation." In *Conflict Management and Problem Solving: Interpersonal to International Applications*, Dennis J. D. Sandole and Ingrid Sandole-Staroste (eds). London: Frances Pinter.

Conner, Walker (1994). *Ethnonationalism: the Quest for Understanding*. Princeton, NJ: Princeton University Press.

Coplin, William D. (ed.) (1968). *Simulation in the Study of Politics*. Chicago: Markham.

Copson, Raymond W. (1973). "Foreign Policy Conflict among African States, 1964–1969." In *Sage International Yearbook of Foreign Policy Studies*, *Volume I*, Patrick J. McGowan (ed.). Beverly Hills, CA: Sage.

Coser, Lewis A. (1956). *The Functions of Social Conflict*. New York: Free Press.

Cowley, Geoffrey (1995). "It's Time to Rethink Nature and Nurture: Biology and Free Will Aren't at Odds. They're Inseparable." *Newsweek*, March 27, pp. 52–3.

Cowley, G., K. Springen, E. A. Leonard, K. Robins, and J. Gordon (1990). "The Promise of Prozac." *Newsweek*, March 26, pp. 38–41.

Cowley, Geoffrey and Anne Underwood (1997/8). "A Little Help from Serotonin: Could a Single Brain Chemical Hold the Key to Happiness, High Social Status, and a Nice, Flat Stomach." *Newsweek*, December 29, pp. 78, 80–1.

Cox, The Baroness (1991). *Report of an International Delegation from the First International Andrei Sakharov Memorial Congress to Armenia and Azerbaijan*, May 25–31.

Crocker, Chester A. and Fen Osler Hampson with Pamela Aall (eds) (1996). *Managing Global Chaos: Sources of and Responses to International Conflict*. Washington, DC: U.S. Institute of Peace Press.

Crookall, David (1997). "Editorial: Teaching Strategic Management." *Simulation and Gaming*, **28**(4), 357.

Crookall, David and Danny Saunders (eds) (1989). *Communication and Simulation: from Two Fields to One Theme*. Clevedon: Multilingual Matters.

CSBMs Vienna Document (1990). *Vienna Document 1990 of the Vienna Negotiations on Confidence- and Security-Building Measures Convened in Accordance with the Relevant Provisions of the Concluding Document of the CSCE*. Vienna, November 17.

CSBMs Vienna Document (1992). *Vienna Document 1992 of the Negotiations on Confidence- and Security-Building Measures Convened in Accordance with the Relevant Provisions of the Concluding Document of the Vienna Meeting of the CSCE*. Vienna, March 4.

CSBMs Vienna Document (1994). *Vienna Document 1994 of the Negotiations on Confidence- and Security-Building Measures*. Vienna, November 28.

CSCE '94 (1994). "From Process to Organization" (The Finnish National Committee for European Security), no. 4, Helsinki.

CSCE Budapest Document 1994: towards a Genuine Partnership in a New Era (1994). Budapest, December 6.

CSCE Commission (1992). *The Conference on Security and Cooperation in Europe: an Overview of the CSCE Process, Recent Meetings and Institutional Developments*. Washington, DC: Commission on Security and Cooperation in Europe (U.S. Congress), February.

CSCE Commission (1997a). *Treaty on Conventional Armed Forces in Europe (CFE)*. Briefing.

Washington, DC: Commission on Security and Cooperation in Europe (U.S. Congress), February 20.

CSCE Commission (1997b). *The OSCE After the Lisbon Summit*. Washington, DC: Commission on Security and Cooperation in Europe (U.S. Congress), August.

CSCE Digest (1991). "CSCE Parliament Established at Madrid Meeting." *CSCE Digest*, **14**(3), 3.

CSCE Digest (1996). "Partnership for Peace Member Countries." *CSCE Digest*, **19**(6), 8.

CSCE Facts, 1994 (1994). Vienna: The CSCE Secretariat, Department for Chairman-in-Office Support, June 3.

CSCE Helsinki '92 (1992). "European Security and Cooperation" (The Finnish National Committee for European Security), no. 5, Helsinki, July.

CSCE Helsinki Document 1992: the Challenges of Change (1992). Helsinki, July 10.

CSCE Helsinki Final Act (1975). *Conference on Security and Cooperation in Europe*. Helsinki, August 1.

Csepell, Gyorgy (1996). *National Self-identity in Contemporary Hungary*. Boulder, CO: East European Monographs.

CT (1991). "Ethnic Divisions in the Former Soviet Union." *Chicago Tribune*, December 12, Section 1, p. 5.

Curle, Adam (1971). *Making Peace*. London: Tavistock.

Czempiel, Ernst-Otto and James N. Rosenau (eds) (1989). *Global Changes and Theoretical Challenges: Approaches to World Politics for the 1990s*. Lexington, MA: Lexington Books.

Dahrendorf, Ralf (1964). *Class and Class Conflict in Industrial Society*. Stanford, CA: Stanford University Press.

Daly, Martin and Margo Wilson (1988). *Homicide*. New York: Aldine de Gruyter.

Danforth, Loring M. (1997). *The Macedonian Conflict: Ethnic Nationalism in a Transnational World*. Princeton, NJ: Princeton University Press.

Darby, John (1998). "Review of Margareta Sollenberg's *States in Armed Conflict, 1995*." *Ethnic Conflict Research Digest*, **1**, p. 12.

Davidson, William D. and Joseph V. Montville (1981/2). "Foreign Policy According to Freud." *Foreign Policy*, **45**, 145–57.

Davies, James Chowning (1962). "Toward a Theory of Revolution." *American Sociological Review*, **27**, 5–19.

Davies, James Chowning (1973). "Aggression, Violence, Revolution and War." In *Handbook of Political Psychology*, Jeanne N. Knutson (ed.). San Francisco and London: Jossey-Bass.

Davies, James Chowning (1986). "Roots of Political Behavior." In *Political Psychology: Contemporary Problems and Issues*, Margaret G. Hermann (ed.). San Francisco and London: Jossey-Bass.

Deak, Istvan (1990). "Nationalism in the Soviet Bloc: Uncovering Eastern Europe's Dark History." *Orbis*, Winter, 51–65.

Delmas, Philippe (1997). *The Rosy Future of War*. New York: Free Press.

Denitch, Bogdan (1994). *Ethnic Nationalism: the Tragic Death of Yugoslavia*. Minneapolis: University of Minneapolis Press.

Der Derian, James and Michael J. Shapiro (eds) (1989). *International/Intertextual Relations: Postmodern Readings of World Politics*. Lexington, MA: Lexington Books.

Deutsch, Karl W. (1964). "Quincy Wright's Contribution to the Study of War." In *A Study of War*, abridged edition, Quincy Wright. Chicago: University of Chicago Press.

Deutsch, Karl W. (1987a). "Peace, Violence and War: from the Viewpoint of Cybernetics and Computer Modelling." In *The Quest for Peace: Transcending Collective Violence and*

War among Societies, Cultures and States, R. Väyrynen, D. Senghaas, and C. Schmidt (eds). London: Sage.

Deutsch, Karl W. (1987b). "Foreword: GLOBUS – the Rise of a New Field of Political Science." In *The GLOBUS Model: Computer Simulation of Worldwide Political and Economic Developments* (Report on a Research Project at the Science Center for Social Research, Berlin), Stuart A. Bremer (ed.). Frankfurt: Campus Verlag.

Deutsch, Karl W. and Dieter Senghaas (1973). "The Steps to War: a Survey of System Levels, Decision Stages, and Research Results." In *Sage International Yearbook of Foreign Policy*, *Volume I*, Patrick J. McGowan (ed.). Beverly Hills, CA: Sage.

Deutsch, Karl W. and J. David Singer (1964). "Multipolar Power Systems and International Stability." *World Politics*, **16**(3), 390–406. Reprinted in James N. Rosenau (1969).

Deutsch, Morton (1960). "Trust, Trustworthiness, and the F Scale." *Journal of Abnormal and Social Psychology*, **61**(1), 138–40.

Deutsch, Morton (1971). "Conflict and Its Resolution." In *Conflict Resolution: Contributions of the Behavioral Sciences*, Clagett G. Smith (ed.). Notre Dame, IN: University of Notre Dame Press.

Deutsch, Morton (1973). *The Resolution of Conflict: Constructive and Destructive Processes.* New Haven, CT: Yale University Press.

Deutsch, Morton (1982). "Preventing World War III: a Psychological Perspective." Presidential Address, Fifth Annual Scientific Meeting of the International Society of Political Psychology (ISPP), Washington, DC, June 24–27.

Diamond, Louise and John W. McDonald, Jr (1996). *Multi-track Diplomacy: a Systems Approach to Peace*, 3rd edn. West Hartford, CT: Kumarian Press.

Diehl, Jackson (1988). "Yugoslavia Is Lesson in Ethnic Conflicts for Gorbachev." *Washington Post*, March 13, pp. A29, A34.

Dillon, Leo (1990). "Ethnicity and Political Boundaries in the Soviet Union." Washington, DC: Department of State, Office of the Geographer.

Dinmore, Guy (1998). "Simmering Conflict in Kosovo Intensifies: Ethnic Albanian Death Toll Rises as Serbian Authorities Escalate Offensive." *Washington Post*, April 28, p. A11.

Dobbs, Michael (1991a). "Nationalism Eclipsing Communism: across the Former East Bloc, Ethnic Rivalries Erupt." *Washington Post*, 27 October, pp. A1, A32.

Dobbs, Michael (1991b). "Rising Nationalism Hurts East Europe's Economies." *Washington Post*, October 28, pp. A1, A18.

Dobbs, Michael (1991c). "Ethnic Strife Splintering Core of Russian Republic." *Washington Post*, October 29, pp. A1, A19.

Dobbs, Michael (1992). "Kremlin Coup Conspirators Unrepentant." *Washington Post*, August 19, p. A12.

Dobbs, Michael (1993). "Yugoslavia's Inferno Is Russia's Nightmare." *Washington Post*, September 5, p. A40.

Dobbs, Michael (1995). "Serbs Sign Agreement to Return Key Region: Croatia Will Reacquire Eastern Slavonia." *Washington Post*, November 13, pp. A1, A15.

Dobbs, Michael (1996a). "The Story of Brcko Is the Story of Bosnia." *International Herald Tribune*, June 28, p. 2.

Dobbs, Michael (1996b). "U.S. Ready to Participate in New Force in Bosnia: Gore Signals Willingness, NATO Officials Say." *Washington Post*, November 14, p. A25.

Dobbs, Michael and Peter Baker (1996). "U.S. Ready to Extend Bosnia Stay: Perry Confers with Hill on Details of New Force." *Washington Post*, November 15, pp. A1, A26.

Dollard, J., L. W. Doob, N. E. Miller, O. H. Mowrer, and R. R. Sears (1939). *Frustration and Aggression*. New Haven, CT: Yale University Press. Abridged and reprinted in Megargee and Hokanson (1970).

Dougherty, James E. and Robert L. Pfaltzgraff, Jr (1990). *Contending Theories of International Relations: a Comprehensive Survey*, 3rd edn. New York: Harper and Row.

Doyle, Michael W. and G. John Ikenberry (eds) (1997). *New Thinking in International Relations Theory*. Boulder, CO: Westview.

Dragnich, Alex N. (1992). Serbs and Croats: the Struggle in Yugoslavia. New York: Harcourt Brace Jovanovich.

Dragnich, Alex N. (1996). *Yugoslavia's Disintegration and the Struggle for Truth*. Boulder, CO: East European Monographs.

Dragnich, Alex N. and Slavko Todorovich (1984). *The Saga of Kosovo: Focus on Serbian–Albanian Relations*. New York: Columbia University Press.

Draper, Norman and Harry Smith (1966). *Applied Regression Analysis*. New York: John Wiley.

Driver, Michael J. (1965). "A Structural Analysis of Aggression, Stress, and Personality in an Inter-nation Simulation." *Paper No. 97*, Institute for Research in the Behavioral, Economic, and Management Sciences, Purdue University, January.

Drozdiak, William (1991). "Europeans Agree on Trade Pact: Seven Countries Join with EC to Create Huge Economic Bloc." *Washington Post*, October 23, pp. A1, A40.

Drozdiak, William (1996). "Aid Goal for Bosnia is Reached." *International Herald Tribune*, April 15, p. 7.

Drozdiak, William (1997a). "NATO Commander Urges Follow-on-Force in Bosnia: U.S. General Says Mission Needed to Sustain Peace." *Washington Post*, December 3, p. A41.

Drozdiak, William (1997b). "U.S. Pushes NATO on Arms Proliferation: Albright Stresses Threat in Mideast." *Washington Post*, December 17, pp. A1, A32.

Druckman, Daniel (1967). "Dogmatism, Prenegotiation Experience, and Simulated Group Representation as Determinants of Dyadic Behavior in a Bargaining Situation." *Journal of Personality and Social Psychology*, **6**, 279–90.

Druckman, Daniel (1993). "An Analytical Research Agenda for Conflict and Conflict Resolution." In *Conflict Resolution Theory and Practice: Integration and Application*, Dennis J. D. Sandole and Hugo van der Merwe (eds). Manchester: Manchester University Press.

Druckman, Daniel (1994). "Tools for Discovery: Experimenting with Simulations." *Simulation and Gaming*, **25**(4), 446–55.

Duckitt, John (1989). "Authoritarianism and Group Identification: a New View of an Old Construct." *Political Psychology*, **10**(1), 303–8.

Duke, Richard D. (1974). *Gaming: the Future's Language*. New York: Sage.

East, Maurice A. and Charles F. Hermann (1974). "Do Nation-types Account for Foreign Policy Behavior?" In *Comparing Foreign Policies: Theories, Findings, and Methods*, James N. Rosenau (ed.). New York: John Wiley.

Easton, David (1969). "The New Revolution in Political Science." *American Political Science Review*, **63**, 1051–61.

Eberwein, Wolf-Dieter (1982). "The Seduction of Power: Serious International Disputes and the Power Status of Nations, 1900–1976." *International Interactions*, **9**(1), 57–74.

Eckhardt, William (1987). "Preparation of data for 'Wars and Deaths 1700–1987'." In *World Military and Social Expenditures 1987–1988*, Ruth Sivard (ed.). Washington, DC: World Priorities.

Eckhardt, William (1991). "Authoritarianism." *Political Psychology*, **12**(1), 97–124.

Economist (1992). "Bombs for All?" March 14, pp. 15–16, 45–7.

Edwards, David V. (1969). *International Political Analysis*. New York: Holt, Rinehart and Winston.

Ehrenreich, Barbara (1997). *Blood Rites: Origins and History of the Passions of War*. New York: Metropolitan Books/Henry Holt and Company.

Elliott, Michael (1998). "The Lessons of Bosnia's War." *Newsweek*, April 20, p. 35.

Elsie, Robert (1997). *Kosovo. In the Heart of the Powder Keg: a Reader*. Boulder, CO: East European Monographs.

Emmert, Thomas (1993). "Why Serbia Will Fight for 'Holy' Kosovo." *Washington Post*, June 13, pp. C1, C4.

Enloe, Cynthia (1973). *Ethnic Conflict and Political Development*. Boston: Little, Brown.

Erlanger, Steven (1996). "U.S. Condemns Duma Vote Backing a Soviet Revival." *International Herald Tribune*, March 20, p. 10.

Europe in Figures (1995). Fourth edition. Luxembourg: Statistical Office for Official Publications of the European Communities (Eurostat).

Ezekiel, Mordecai and Karl A. Fox (1959). *Methods of Correlation and Regression Analysis*, 3rd edn. New York: John Wiley.

Farris, C. D. (1960). "Selected Attitudes on Foreign Affairs as Correlates of Authoritarianism and Political Anomie." *Journal of Politics*, **22**, 50–67.

Feierabend, Ivo K. and Rosalind L. Feierabend (1966). "Aggressive Behaviors within Polities, 1948–1962: a Cross-national Study." *Journal of Conflict Resolution*, **10**, 249–72. Reprinted in Megargee and Hokanson (1970).

Feierabend, Ivo K. and Rosalind L. Feierabend (1969). "Level of Development and Internation Behavior." In *Foreign Policy and the Developing Nation*, R. Butwell (ed.). Lexington: University of Kentucky Press.

Festinger, Leon (1953). "Laboratory Experiments." In *Research Methods in the Behavioral Sciences*, Leon Festinger and Daniel Katz (eds). New York: Holt, Rinehart and Winston.

Festinger, Leon (1962). *A Theory of Cognitive Dissonance*. Stanford, CA: Stanford University Press.

Fine, John V. A. and Robert W. Donia (1995). *Bosnia and Hercegovina: a Tradition Betrayed*. New York: Columbia University Press.

Fisher, Marc (1993). "Germany: Reunified, but a Nation Without a Dream." *Washington Post*, June 29, pp. 1, 6.

Fisher, Ronald J. (1993). "The Potential for Peacebuilding: Forging a Bridge from Peacekeeping to Peacemaking." *Peace and Change*, **18**(3), 247–66.

Fisher, Ronald J. and Loraleigh Keashly (1991). "The Potential Complementarity of Mediation and Consultation within a Contingency Model of Third Party Intervention." *Journal of Peace Research*, **28**(1), 29–42.

Fitchett, Joseph (1996). "Hurdle for Leaders at Balkans Summit: Healing the Split in Mostar." *International Herald Tribune*, February 17–18, p. 4.

Forbes, H. D. (1997). *Ethnic Conflict: Commerce, Culture, and the Contact Hypothesis*. New Haven, CT: Yale University Press.

Forrester, Jay W. (1971). "Counterintuitive Behavior of Social Systems." *ZPG National Reporter*, **3**(6), pp. 1–6.

Frankfort-Nachmias, Chava and David Nachmias (1996). *Research Methods in the Social Sciences*, 5th edn. New York: St Martin's Press.

Franklin, Mark N. and Thomas T. Mackie (1978). "New Perspectives on the Formation of Governing Coalitions in Parliamentary Situations." Paper presented to the Workshop on

Formal Political Analysis, Joint Sessions of Workshops, European Consortium for Political Research (ECPR), Université des Sciences Sociales de Grenoble, France, April 6–12.

Frei, Daniel (1974). "The Regulation of Warfare: a Paradigm for the Legal Approach to the Control of International Conflict." *Journal of Conflict Resolution*, **18**(4), 620–33.

Frei, Daniel and Dieter Ruloff (1989). *Handbook of Foreign Policy Analysis: Methods for Practical Application in Foreign Policy Planning, Strategic Planning and Business Risk Assessment* (published under the auspices of the United Nations Institute for Training and Research). Dordrecht: Martinus Nijhoff.

French, John R. P., Jr (1953). "Experiments in Field Settings." In *Research Methods in the Behavioral Sciences*, Leon Festinger and Daniel Katz (eds). New York: Holt, Rinehart and Winston.

Freud, Sigmund (1922). *Beyond the Pleasure Principle*. London: Hogarth Press.

Freud, Sigmund (1959). "Why War?" A letter from Sigmund Freud to Albert Einstein written in 1932. In *The Collected Papers of Sigmund Freud, Volume 5*, Ernest Jones (ed.). New York: Basic Books.

Freud, Sigmund (1961). *Civilization and Its Discontents*. New York: W. W. Norton.

Fried, Itzhak (1997). "Syndrome E." *The Lancet*, **350**, 1845–7.

Friedman, Alan (1996). "World Bank Will Call for Bosnia Jobs Plan." *International Herald Tribune*, April 11, pp. 1, 6.

FT (1993). "New World Wars: Conflicts Riddle the Old Soviet Empire." *Financial Times. Reprinted in World Press Review*, **40**(10), p. 8.

Fukuyama, Francis (1989). "The End of History?" *The National Interest*, Summer, 3–18.

Fukuyama, Francis (1992). *The End of History and the Last Man*. New York: Free Press.

Gallagher, Tom (1995). *Romania After Ceausescu*. Edinburgh: Edinburgh University Press.

Galtung, Johan (1964). "A Structural Theory of Aggression." *Journal of Peace Research*, **1**, 95–119.

Galtung, Johan (1969). "Violence, Peace and Peace Research." *Journal of Peace Research*, **6**(3), 167–91.

Galtung, Johan (1993). "Women : Man = Peace: War? Peace Theory, Feminist Theory and Epistemological Adequacy." In *Peace Research for the 1990s*, Judit Balázs and Hakan Wiberg (eds). Budapest: Akadémiai Kiadó.

Gantzel, Klaus Jürgen (1988). "Kriegsursachen: Fakten, Thesen, Probleme," *Arbeitspapiere Nr 19*. Hamburg: Institut für Politische Wissenschaft, Forschungszentrum Kriege, Rüstung und Entwicklung der Universität Hamburg.

Gardner, Richard N. (1992). "Collective Security and the 'New World Order': What Role for the United Nations?" In *Post-Gulf War Challenges to the UN Collective Security System: Two Views on the Issue of Collective Security*. Washington, DC: U.S. Institute of Peace, June.

Geller, Daniel S. (1990). "Capability Concentration, Power Transition, and War." Paper presented at the Annual Meeting of the American Political Science Association (APSA), San Francisco, August 30 to September 2.

General Framework Agreement for Peace in Bosnia and Herzegovina ("The Dayton Peace Accords") (1995). Paris, December 14.

Geneva Report (1991). *Report of the CSCE Meeting of Experts on National Minorities*. Geneva, July 19.

George, Jim (1989). "International Relations and the Search for Thinking Space: Another View of the Third Debate." *International Studies Quarterly*, **33**(3), 269–79.

Geraghty, Tony (1978). "Five Years to Doomsday." *Sunday Times*, November 19, p. 13.

Gibbs, G. I. (ed.) (1974). *Handbook of Games and Simulation Exercises*. Beverly Hills, CA: Sage.

Gibson, James William (1994). *Warrior Dreams: Violence and Manhood in Post-Vietnam America*. New York: Hill and Wang.

Gilbert, Martin (1994). *The First World War: a Complete History*. New York: Henry Holt.

Gleick, James (1987). *Chaos: Making a New Science*. New York: Penguin.

Glenny, Misha (1993). *The Fall of Yugoslavia: The Third Balkan War*, rev. edn. New York: Penguin.

Glenny, Misha (1994). "Hope for Bosnia?" *The New York Review of Books*, April 7, pp. 6–8.

Glenny, Misha (1995). "Heading off War in the Southern Balkans." *Foreign Affairs*, **74**(3), 98–108.

Glynn, Patrick (ed.) (1989). *Unrest in the Soviet Union*. Washington, DC: American Enterprise Institute.

Gochman, Charles S. and Russell J. Leng (1983). "Realpolitik and the Road to War." *International Studies Quarterly*, **27**, 97–120.

Gochman, Charles S. and Zeev Maoz (1984). "Militarized Interstate Disputes, 1816–1976: Procedures, Patterns, and Insights." *Journal of Conflict Resolution*, **28**, 585–616.

Goertz, Gary and Paul F. Diehl (1988). "A Territorial History of the International System." *International Interactions*, **15**(1), 81–93.

Goldman, Minton F. (ed.) (1990). *The Soviet Union and Eastern Europe*, 3rd edn. Guilford, CT: Dushkin.

Goleman, Daniel (1995). "Early Violence Leaves Its Mark on the Brain." *The New York Times*, October 3, pp. C1, C10.

Gompert, David (1994). "How to Defeat Serbia." *Foreign Affairs*, **73**(4), 30–47.

Goodman, Louis W. and Brian S. Mandell (1994). *International Conflict Resolution for the 21st Century: Preparing Tomorrow's Leaders*. Washington, DC: Association of Professional Schools of International Affairs.

Gordon, Michael R. (1997). "Calm on the Black Sea: Moscow and Kiev Resolve Fleet Dispute." *International Herald Tribune*, May 30, p. 2.

Goshko, John M. (1991). "Ethnic Strife Replaces Cold War Rivalries." *Washington Post*, July 14, p. A27.

Greenblatt, Cathy S. and Richard D. Duke (eds) (1975). *Gaming-simulations: Rationale, Design and Applications*. New York: Sage.

Greenstein, Fred I. (1969). *Personality and Politics*. Chicago: Markham.

Greenstein, Fred I. and Sidney G. Tarrow (1969). "The Study of French Political Socialization: toward the Revocation of a Paradox." *World Politics*, **22**(1), 95–137.

Griffiths, Stephen Iwan (1993). *Nationalism and Ethnic Conflict: Threats to European Security* (SIPRI Research Report No. 5, Stockholm International Peace Research Institute). Oxford: Oxford University Press.

Groom, A. J. R. (1986). "Cyprus, Greece, and Turkey: a Treadmill for Diplomacy." In *Cyprus in Transition 1960–1985*, John T. A. Koumoulides (ed.). London: Trigraph.

Guetzkow, Harold (ed.) (1962). *Simulation in Social Science: Readings*. Englewood Cliffs, NJ: Prentice Hall.

Guetzkow, Harold (1966). "Some Correspondences between Simulations and Realities in International Relations." Paper presented during the Norman Wait Harris Conference in Celebration of the 75th Anniversary of the University of Chicago, June.

Guetzkow, Harold (1968a). "Simulations in International Relations." In *Simulation in the Study of Politics*, William D. Coplin (ed.). Chicago: Markham.

Guetzkow, Harold (1968b). "Some Correspondences between Simulations and 'Realities' in International Relations." In *New Approaches to International Relations*, Morton A. Kaplan (ed.). New York: St Martin's Press.

Guetzkow, Harold (1969). "Simulations in the Consolidation and Utilization of Knowledge about International Relations." In *Theory and Research on the Causes of War*, Dean G. Pruitt and Richard C. Snyder (eds). Engelwood Cliffs, NJ: Prentice Hall.

Guetzkow, Harold (1976). "Substantive Developments from the Simulation of International Processes." Paper presented at the Tenth World Congress of the International Political Science Association, Edinburgh, August 16–21.

Guetzkow, H., C. F. Alger, R. A. Brody, R. C. Noel, and R. C. Snyder (1963). *Simulation in International Relations: Developments for Research and Teaching*. Englewood Cliffs, NJ: Prentice Hall.

Guetzkow, Harold and Joseph J. Valadez (eds) (1981a). *Simulated International Processes: Theories and Research in Global Modeling*. Beverly Hills, CA: Sage.

Guetzkow, Harold and Joseph J. Valadez (1981b). "Simulation and Reality: Validity Research." In Guetzkow and Valadez (1981a).

Gülcher, Ernst and Arno Truger (1996). "European Civilian Peace Corps – Taskforce Meeting, 16–18 February in Stadtschlaining, Austria." European Parliament, Brussels, Belgium.

Gürkaynak, Mehmet R. (ed.) (1993). *Who's Who in Europe, in Peacemaking and Conflict Resolution* (European Conference on Peacemaking and Conflict Resolution). Ankara: Middle East Technical University (METU).

Gurr, Ted Robert (1968). "A Causal Model of Civil Strife: a Comparative Analysis Using New Indices." *American Political Science Review*, **62**(4), 1104–24.

Gurr, Ted Robert (1970). *Why Men Rebel*. Princeton, NJ: Princeton University Press.

Gurr, Ted Robert (1972). *Politimetrics: An Introduction to Quantitative Macropolitics*. Englewood Cliffs, NJ: Prentice Hall.

Gurr, Ted Robert (1993). *Minorities at Risk: a Global View of Ethnopolitical Conflicts*. Washington, DC: U.S. Institute of Peace Press.

Gurr, Ted Robert (forthcoming). *Peoples versus States: Ethnopolitical Conflict and Accommodation at the End of the 20th Century*. Washington, DC: U.S. Institute of Peace Press.

Gurr, Ted Robert and Barbara Harff (1994). *Ethnic Conflict and World Politics*. Boulder, CO: Westview Press.

Gurr, Ted Robert and James R. Scarritt (1989). "Minorities Rights at Risk: A Global Survey." *Human Rights Quarterly*, **11**(4), 375–405.

Gutman, Roy (1993). *A Witness to Genocide*. New York: Macmillan.

Gutman, Roy (1995). "Signed Sealed, Undelivered." *War Report: Bulletin of the Institute for War and Peace Reporting*, **38**, 3–9.

Haas, Ernst B. (1953). "The Balance of Power: Prescription, Concept, or Propaganda." *World Politics*, **5**, 442–77. Reprinted in James N. Rosenau (1961).

Haas, Michael (1965). "Societal Approaches to the Study of War." *Journal of Peace Research*, **2**(4), 307–23.

Haas, Michael (1970). "International Subsystems: Stability and Polarity." *American Political Science Review*, **64**, 98–123.

Haass, Richard N. (1990). *Conflicts Unending: the United States and Regional Disputes*. New Haven, CT: Yale University Press.

Haass, Richard N. and Gideon Rose (1997). "Facing the Nuclear Facts in India and Pakistan: It's Time to Refine a Simple-minded U.S. Policy." *Washington Post*, January 5, p. C2.

Hackworth, David H. (1992). "The Wasteland." *Newsweek*, September 14, pp. 42–3.

Hackworth, David H. (1995). "Talking 'Soldier to Soldier' Behind Bars. Impressions: What Tim McVeigh Was Really Like." *Newsweek*, July 3, pp. 27–8.

Harden, Blaine (1992). "Sarajevo's Fortunes This Winter Hinge on Serbs' Mood." *Washington Post*, September 27, pp. A37, A43.

Harff, Barbara and Ted Robert Gurr (1988). "Toward Empirical Theory of Genocides and Politicides: Identification and Measurement of Cases Since 1945." *International Studies Quarterly*, **32**(3), 359–71.

Harris, John F. (1997). "Clinton Says Troops to Stay in Bosnia Indefinitely." *Washington Post*, December 19, pp. A1, A45.

Harwood, Richard (1997). "America's Unchecked Epidemic." *Washington Post*, December 1, p. A25.

Havemann, Judith (1997). "For Children, an Epidemic of Homicide: U.S. Leads Rich Nations in Violence against Youth." *Washington Post*, February 7, pp. A1, A6.

Haythorn, W. and I. Altman (1967). "Together in Isolation." *Transaction*, **4**(3), 18–22.

HCA (1990). *Founding Session, October 19-21, 1990*. Prague: HCA Secretariat.

HCA (1992). *HCA 2nd General Assembly. New Walls in Europe: Nationalism and Racism – Civic Solutions. Bratislava, 26–29 March. Report of Proceedings*. Prague: HCA Secretariat.

Hearst, David (1996). "NATO Rules out Moscow Offer." *Guardian*, April 17, p. 12.

Hedges, Chris (1996a). "Bosnian Vote in the Fall Wins a Wary Approval." *International Herald Tribune*, June 26, p. 6.

Hedges, Chris (1996b). "West's About-face on Karadzic: Familiar and Sad." *International Herald Tribune*, July 2, pp. 1, 10.

Heldt, Birger (ed.) (1992). *States in Armed Conflict 1990–91*. Uppsala: Department of Peace and Conflict Research, Uppsala University.

Helenius, Harry (1995). "More Stability in Europe." *OSCE Review*, **3**(1/95), 8–9.

Heraclides, Alexis (1989). "Conflict Resolution, Ethnonationalism and the Middle East Impasse." *Journal of Peace Research*, **26**(2), 197–212.

Heraclides, Alexis (1991). *The Self-determination of Minorities in International Politics*. London: Frank Cass.

Hermann, Charles F. (1967). "Validation Problems in Games and Simulations with Special Reference to Models of International Politics." *Behavioral Science*, **12**(3), 216–31.

Hermann, Charles F. (1969). *Crises in Foreign Policy: a Simulation Analysis*. Indianapolis: Bobbs-Merrill.

Herz, John H. (1959). *International Politics in the Atomic Age*. New York: Columbia University Press.

Heyns, Roger W. and Alvin F. Zander (1953). "Observation of Group Behavior." In *Research Methods in the Behavioral Sciences*, Leon Festinger and Daniel Katz (eds). New York: Holt, Rinehart and Winston.

Hilgard, E. R., R. L. Atkinson, and R. C. Atkinson (1979). *Introduction to Psychology*, 7th edn. New York: Harcourt Brace Jovanovich.

"History as a Hobby: Civil War" (1992). *The Connection* (Burke, VA), **7**(33), 15–18.

Hoagland, Jim (1997). "A New Look at the 'Indo-Pak' Conflict." *Washington Post*, January 16, p. A21.

Hobson, John A. (1965). *Imperialism: a Study*. Ann Arbor: University of Michigan Press.

Hockstader, Lee (1994). "Yeltsin Swats at a Haiti in His Own Back Yard." *Washington Post*, August 12, p. A33.

Hockstader, Lee (1997a). "Moscow Weighs Costs of War in Chechnya: Toll in Lives, Army's

Prestige and Pride Balanced by Continued Role in World Affairs." *Washington Post*, January 3, pp. A27, A28.

Hockstader, Lee (1997b). "In Bosnia, Peace on Paper but Not in Practice: West Can Enforce Order but Not Impose Unity." *Washington Post*, December 7, pp. A1, A36.

Hockstader, Lee (1997c). "EU Rejection a Blow to Turkey's Pride: Despite Acknowledged Contradictions, 'We Feel Ourselves to Be Children of Europe'." *Washington Post*, December 21, p. A25.

Hockstader, Lee (1998). "Kosovo Rebels Prepare for War with Serbians." *Washington Post*, March 25, pp. A1, A26.

Hockstader, Lee and Kelly Couturier (1997). "Ankara Ready to Sever European Ties: Angered by EU Rejection, Turkish Leader Threatens Cyprus Peace Effort." *Washington Post*, December 15, p. A22.

Hoffman, David (1995). "Yeltsin Links Bigger NATO to New War." *Washington Post*, September 9, pp. A1, A21.

Hoffman, David (1996). "Chechen, Lebed Sign Peace Deal: Decision on Sovereignty for Russian Region Deferred for Five Years." *Washington Post*, August 31, pp. A1, A25.

Hoffman, David (1997). "Russia and Chechnya Sign Peace Pact, without Details." *International Herald Tribune*, May 13, p. 6.

Hoffmann, Stanley (1995/6). "The Politics and Ethics of Military Intervention." *Survival*, **37**(4), 29–51.

Holbrooke, Richard (1998). *To End a War: from Sarajevo to Dayton – and Beyond*. New York: Random House.

Holm, H. H. and G. Sorensen (1993). "A New World Order: the Withering Away of Anarchy and the Triumph of Individualism? Consequences for IR-Theory." *Cooperation and Conflict: Nordic Journal of International Studies*, **28**(3), 265–301.

Holsti, Kalevi J. (1989a). "Ecological and Clausewitzean Approaches to the Study of War: Assessing the Possibilities." Paper presented at the 30th Anniversary Convention of the International Studies Association (ISA), London: March 28 to April 2.

Holsti, Kalevi J. (1989b). "Mirror, Mirror on The Wall, which Are the Fairest Theories of All?" *International Studies Quarterly*, **33**(3), 255–61.

Holsti, Kalevi J. (1991). *Peace and War: Armed Conflicts and International Order 1648–1989* (Cambridge Studies in International Relations 14). Cambridge: Cambridge University Press.

Holsti, Kalevi J. (1996). *The State, War, and the State of War*. Cambridge: Cambridge University Press.

Holsti, Kalevi J. (1998). "The Problem of Change in International Relations Theory." *Working Paper no. 26*, Institute of International Relations, University of British Columbia, Vancouver, December.

Holsti, Ole R. (1969). *Content Analysis for the Social Sciences and Humanities*. Reading, MA: Addison-Wesley.

Holsti, Ole R. (1972). *Crisis, Escalation, War*. Montreal: McGill–Queen's University Press.

Holsti, O. R., R. C. North and R. A. Brody (1968). "Perception and Action in the 1914 Crises." In *Quantitative International Politics: Insights and Evidence*, J. David Singer (ed.). New York: Free Press.

Homer-Dixon, Thomas F. (1991). "On the Threshold: Environmental Changes as Causes of Acute Conflict." *International Security*, **16**(2), 76–116.

Homer-Dixon, T. F., J. H. Boutwell, and G. W. Rathjens (1993). "Environmental Change and Violent Conflict." *Scientific American*, February, pp. 38–44.

Honig, Jan Willem and Norbert Both (1996). *Srebrenica: Record of a War Crime*. London: Penguin.

Horowitz, Donald L. (1985). *Ethnic Groups in Conflict*. Berkeley: University of California Press.

Houweling, Henk W. and Jan G. Siccama (1988). *Studies of War*. Dordrecht: Martinus Nijhoff.

Höynck, Wilhelm (1994a). "CSCE Capabilities for Contributing to Conflict Prevention and Crisis Management." Speech by the Secretary General of the CSCE, at the NATO Seminar in Brussels, March 7.

Höynck, Wilhelm (1994b). "The CSCE in the New Europe." Speech by the Secretary General of the CSCE, at the Royal Institute of International Affairs, London, May 18.

Hunter, Robert (1989). "Political Stability in Europe: the Dynamics of the East–West Relationship." Seminar on Implications of CFE (Conventional Armed Forces in Europe Treaty) for Political and Military Stability in Europe. McLean, VA: Science Applications International Corporation (SAIC), November 9.

Huntington, Samuel P. (1993). "The Clash of Civilizations?" *Foreign Affairs*, **72**(3), 22–49.

Huntington, Samuel P. (1996). *The Clash of Civilizations and the Remaking of World Order*. New York: Simon and Schuster.

IA (1996). *Resolution and Reconciliation: International Alert Annual Report 1996*. London: International Alert.

Ignatieff, Michael (1997). "The Gods of War" (Reviews of Barbara Ehrenreich's *Blood Rites: Origins and History of the Passions of War*; Philippe Delmas's *The Rosy Future of War*; and Chris Hables Gray's *Postmodern War: the New Politics of Conflict*). *New York Review of Books*, **44**(15), October 9, 10, 12–13.

IHT (1995). "Serbs Seize UN Peacekeepers: 3 Observers Left Shackled at Potential NATO Target." *International Herald Tribune*, May 27–28, pp. 1, 4.

IHT (1996). "Greek Vessel Opens Fire on Turkish Fishing Boat," *International Herald Tribune*, April 23, p. 2.

IHT (1997). "Angry Turks Consider an EU Embargo: Ankara May Block Bids by European Firms after Membership Rebuff." *International Herald Tribune*, December 17, p. 6.

Jackson, Jay W. (1991). "Authoritarian Personality Theory of Intergroup Hostility: a Review and Evaluation of the Theoretical and Empirical Literature." *International Journal of Group Tensions*, **21**(4), 383–405.

James, William (1910). "The Moral Equivalent of War." *McClure's Magazine*, August, 463–8. Reprinted in Small and Singer (1985).

Janis, Irving L. (1972). *Victims of Groupthink*. Boston: Houghton Mifflin.

Jervis, Robert (1976). *Perception and Misperception in International Politics*. Princeton, NJ: Princeton University Press.

Jervis, Robert (1997). *System Effects: Complexity in Political and Social Life*. Princeton, NJ: Princeton University Press.

Job, Cvijeto (1992). "Requiem for a Nation: Can My Yugoslavia Find a Rational Peace?" *Washington Post*, March 15, pp. C1, C4.

Johnston, J. (1963). *Econometric Methods*. New York: McGraw-Hill.

Joint Declaration (1990). Paris, November 19.

Judah, Timothy (1997). *The Serbs: History, Myth, and the Destruction of Yugoslavia*. New Haven, CT: Yale University Press.

Kaase, Max and Alan Marsh (1976). "The Matrix of Political Action: Protest and Participation in Five Nations." Paper presented at Special Meeting no. 22 on "Dissatisfaction,

Protest and Change in Advanced Industrial Societies," Tenth World Congress of the International Society of Political Psychology (IPSA), Edinburgh, August 16–21.
Kaplan, Abraham (1964). *The Conduct of Inquiry: Methodology for Behavioral Science*. Scranton, PA: Chandler.
Kaplan, Morton A. (1957). *System and Process in International Politics*. New York: John Wiley.
Kaplan, Robert D. (1993). *Balkan Ghosts: a Journey through History*. New York: St Martin's Press.
Kaplan, Robert D. (1994). "The Coming Anarchy: How Scarcity, Crime, Overpopulation, Tribalism, and Disease Are Rapidly Destroying the Social Fabric of Our Planet." *Atlantic Monthly*, **273**(2), 44–6, 48–9, 52, 54, 58–60, 62–3, 66, 68–70, 72–6.
Kaplan, Robert D. (1996). *The Ends of the Earth: a Journey at the Dawn of the 21st Century*. New York: Random House.
Karklins, Rasma (1986). *Ethnic Relations in the USSR: the Perspective from Below*. Boston and London: Unwin Hyman.
Katz, Daniel (1953). "Field Studies." In *Research Methods in the Behavioral Sciences*, Leon Festinger and Daniel Katz (eds). New York: Holt, Rinehart and Winston.
Kean, James G. and Patrick J. McGowan (1973). "National Attributes and Foreign Policy Participation: a Path Analysis." In *Sage International Yearbook of Foreign Policy Studies, Volume I*, Patrick J. McGowan (ed.). Beverly Hills, CA: Sage.
Keane, Fergal (1996). *Season of Blood: A Rwandan Journey*. London: Penguin.
Keegan, John (1997). "War ça Change: The End of Great Power Conflict" (Review of Philippe Delmas's *The Rosy Future of War*). *Foreign Affairs*, **76**(3), 113–16.
Kegley, Charles W., Jr and Margaret G. Hermann (1995). "The Political Psychology of 'Peace through Democratization.'" *Cooperation and Conflict: Nordic Journal of International Studies*, **30**(1), 5–30.
Kelman, Herbert C. (1965). "Social-psychological Approaches to the Study of International Relations: Definition of Scope." In *International Behavior: a Social-psychological Analysis*, Herbert C. Kelman (ed.). New York: Holt, Rinehart and Winston.
Kelman, Herbert C. (1986). "Interactive Problem Solving: a Social Psychological Approach to Conflict Resolution." In *Dialogue toward Inter-faith Understanding*, William Klassen (ed.). Jerusalem: Tantur Ecumenical Institute for Theological Research.
Kelman, Herbert C. (1991). "Interactive Problem Solving: the Uses and Limits of a Therapeutic Model for the Resolution of International Conflicts." In *The Psychodynamics of International Relationships, Volume 2*, Vamik D. Volkan, Joseph V. Montville, and Demetrios A. Julius (eds). Lexington, MA: Lexington Books.
Kelman, Herbert C. (1993). Seminar on the Integration Between Theory, Research, and Practice in Conflict Resolution. Fairfax, VA: Institute for Conflict Analysis and Resolution, George Mason University, April 5.
Kemp, Walter A. (1996). "The OSCE in a New Context: European Security towards the Twenty-first Century." *Discussion Paper 64*. London: The Royal Institute of International Affairs.
Keohane, Robert O. (ed.) (1986a). *Neorealism and Its Critics*. New York: Columbia University Press.
Keohane, Robert O. (1986b). "Realism, Neorealism and the Study of World Politics." In Keohane (1986a).
Kerlinger, Fred and Milton Rokeach (1966). "The Factorial Nature of the F and D Scales." *Journal of Personality and Social Psychology*, **4**(4), 391–9.

Kernan, Michael (1995). "Playing the Deadliest Game" (Reviews of Martin Gilbert's *The First World War: a Complete History and Lyn MacDonald's 1915: the Death of Innocence*). *Washington Post Book World*, **25**(4), 5.

Kitschelt, Herbert with Anthony J. McGann (1995). *The Radical Right in Western Europe: a Comparative Analysis*. Ann Arbor: University of Michigan Press.

Klarevas, Louis J. (1998). "If This Alliance Is to Survive: Greece and Turkey Have Been Arming and Practicing for a Military Showdown Since 1974." *Washington Post*, January 2, p. A23.

Kleiboer, Marieke (1994). "Ripeness of Conflict: a Fruitful Notion." *Journal of Peace Research*, **31**(1), 109–16.

Kluckhohn, Florence R. (1950). "Dominant and Substitute Profiles of Cultural Orientation: Their Significance for an Analysis of Social Stratifications." *Social Forces*, **28**, 376–93.

Knorr, Klaus and James N. Rosenau (eds) (1969). *Contending Approaches to International Politics*. Princeton, NJ: Princeton University Press.

Koestler, Arthur (1967). *The Ghost in the Machine*. New York: Macmillan.

Koestler, Arthur (1978). "The Brain Explosion." *Observer* (London), January 15, p. 25.

Kornhauser, William (1959). *The Politics of Mass Society*. New York: Free Press.

Kriesberg, Louis (1987). "Timing and the Initiation of De-escalation Moves." *Negotiation Journal*, **3**(5), 375–84.

Kuhn, Thomas S. (1970). *The Structure of Scientific Revolutions*, 2nd edn. Chicago: University of Chicago Press.

Kuzmanic, Tonci and Arno Truger (eds) (1992). *Yugoslavia War*. Stadtschlaining: Austrian Study Center for Peace and Conflict Resolution (ASPR).

Lambelet, J. and U. Luterbacher, with P. Allen (1978). "Dynamics of Arms Races: Mutual Stimulation vs. Self-stimulation." Paper presented at the 15th European Conference of the Peace Science Society (International), Geneva: September 3–5.

Lampe, John R. (1996). *Yugoslavia as History: Twice There Was a Country*. Cambridge: Cambridge University Press.

Lapid, Yosef (1989). "The Third Debate: on the Prospects of International Theory in a Post-positivist Era." *International Studies Quarterly*, **33**(3), 235–54.

Lapid, Yosef and Friedrich Kratochwil (eds) (1995). *The Return of Culture and Identity in International Relations Theory*. Boulder, CO: Lynne Rienner.

Lapidoth, Ruth (1997). *Autonomy: Flexible Solutions to Ethnic Conflicts*. Washington, DC: U.S. Institute of Peace Press.

Laue, James H. (1992). "A Conversation on Peacemaking With Jimmy Carter." Washington, DC: The National Institute for Dispute Resolution (NIDR).

Laue, James H. and Gerald Cormick (1978). "The Ethics of Intervention in Community Disputes." In *The Ethics of Social Intervention*, G. Bermant, H. C. Kelman, and D. Warwick (eds). New York: Halsted Press.

Laulicht, Jerome (1965a). "An Analysis of Canadian Foreign Policy Attitudes." *Peace Research Society (International), Papers*, **3**, 121–36.

Laulicht, Jerome (1965b). "Canadian Foreign Policy Attitudes: Some Major Conclusions." *International Social Science Journal*, **17**, 472–86.

Laulicht, Jerome (1965c). "Public Opinion and Foreign Policy Decisions." *Journal of Peace Research*, **2**(1), 147–69.

Lawler, Peter (1995). *A Question of Values: Johan Galtung's Peace Research*. Boulder, CO: Lynne Rienner.

Leatherman, Janie and Raimo Väyrynen (1995). "Conflict Theory and Conflict Resolution:

Directions for Collaborative Research Policy." *Cooperation and Conflict: Nordic Journal of International Studies*, **30**(1), 53–82.

Lebed, Alexander (1996). "The Chechen War Is over for Russia." *Washington Post*, October 9, p. A19.

Lemonick, Michael D. (1993). "Secrets of the Maya." *Time*, August 9, pp. 44–50.

Leng, Russell J. (1982). "Realpolitik and Interstate Behavior in Successive Disputes." Paper presented at the Annual Convention of the International Studies Association (ISA), Cincinnati, March 24–27.

Leng, Russell J. (1983). "When Will They Ever Learn? Coercive Bargaining in Recurrent Crises." *Journal of Conflict Resolution*, **27**, 379–419.

Leng, Russell J. (1986). "Realism and Crisis Bargaining: a Report on Five Empirical Studies." In *Evaluating U.S. Foreign Policy*, John A. Vasquez (ed.). New York: Praeger.

Leng, Russell J. with Robert A. Goodsell (1974). "Behavioral Indicators of War Proneness in Bilateral Conflicts." In *Sage International Yearbook of Foreign Policy Studies, Volume 2*, Patrick J. McGowan (ed.). Beverly Hills, CA: Sage.

Lenin, Vladimir I. (1939). *Imperialism: the Highest Stage of Capitalism*. New York: International Publishers.

Leopold, George (1990). "CFE Ends Fear of Sudden Strike by Soviet Force." *Defense News*, November 19.

Lerner, Daniel (1958). *The Passing of Traditional Society*. New York: Free Press.

Levi, Werner (1960). "On the Causes of War and the Conditions of Peace." *Journal of Conflict Resolution*, **4**, 411–20. Reprinted in Clagett G. Smith (1971).

LeVine, Robert A. and Donald T. Campbell (1972). *Ethnocentrism: Theories of Conflict, Ethnic Attitudes and Group Behavior*. New York and London: John Wiley.

LeVine, Steve (1994). "Yeltsin Moves to Reverse Gun-happy Chechenia's Secession." *Washington Post*, September 5, p. A15.

Levinson, M. with K. Breslau, R. Marshall, D. Pedersen, and N. Vivarelli (1992). "Europe in Pieces." *Newsweek*, September 28, pp. 24–6.

Levy, Jack S. (1989a). "The Causes of War: a Review of Theories and Evidence." In *Behavior, Society, and Nuclear War, Volume 1*, P. E. Tetlock, J. L. Husbands, R. Jervis, and P. S. Stern (eds). New York and London: Oxford University Press.

Levy, Jack S. (1989b). "The Diversionary Theory of War: a Critique." In *Handbook of War Studies*, Manus I. Midlarsky (ed.). Ann Arbor: University of Michigan Press.

Levy, Jack S. (1996). "Contending Theories of International Conflict: a Levels-of-analysis Approach." In *Managing Global Chaos: Sources of and Responses to International Conflict*, Chester A. Crocker and Fen Osler Hampson, with Pamela Aall (eds). Washington, DC: U.S. Institute of Peace Press.

Lewin, Kurt (1951). *Field Theory in Social Science*. New York: Harper and Row.

Lewis, Anthony (1996). "Karadzic and Co. Have to Be Tried," *International Herald Tribune*, July 9, p. 11.

Lewis, Flora (1991). "How to Stop a Civil War: Europe's Own Peacekeeping Force Can Save Yugoslavia." *New York Times*, May 31, p. A31.

Lewis, Paul (1992). "U.N. Council Votes for Use of Force for Bosnia Relief." *New York Times*, August 14, pp. A1, A6.

Lewis, Samuel W. (1992). "Creative Peacemaking: Perspectives from a Policy Participant." Keynote Address at the Fifteenth Annual Scientific Meeting of the International Society of Political Psychology (ISPP), San Francisco, July 4.

Lindgren, K. (ed.) (1991). *States in Armed Conflict 1989*. Uppsala: Department of Peace and Conflict Research, Uppsala University.

Lindgren, K., G. K. Wilson, P. Wallensteen, and K. A. Nordquist (1990). "Major Armed Conflicts in 1989." In *SIPRI Yearbook 1990: World Armaments and Disarmament*. Oxford: Oxford University Press.

Lippman, Thomas W. (1996). "Clinton Cautious on Aegean Islets." *International Herald Tribune*, April 11, p. 5.

Loeb, Vernon (1998) "End of fighting in Kosovo May Be 'Within Sight,' Holbrooke Says." *Washington Post*, October 29, pp. A38–9.

Lorenz, Joseph P. (1992). "The Case for Collective Security." In *Post-Gulf War Challenges to the UN Collective Security System: Two Views on the Issue of Collective Security*. Washington, DC: U.S. Institute of Peace, June.

Lorenz, Konrad (1967). *On Aggression*. New York: Bantam Books.

Luard, Evan (1986). *War in International Society: a Study in International Sociology*. London: I. B. Tauris.

Lucas, Michael R. (1990). "The Conference on Security and Cooperation in Europe and the Post-Cold War Era." *Hamburger Beiträge zur Friedensforschung und Sicherheitspolitik*. Hamburg: Institut für Friedensforschung und Sicherheitspolitik an der Universität Hamburg.

Lucas, Michael R. (ed.) (1993). *The CSCE in the 1990s: Constructing European Security and Cooperation*. Baden-Baden: Nomos Verlagsgesellschaft.

Luce, R. D. and H. Raiffa (1957). *Games and Decisions*. New York: John Wiley.

Lukic, Reneo and Allen Lynch (1996). *Europe from the Balkans to the Urals: The Disintegration of Yugoslavia and the Soviet Union*. Stockholm International Peace Research Institute. Oxford: Oxford University Press.

Lund, Michael S. (1996). *Preventing Violent Conflicts: a Strategy for Preventive Diplomacy*. Washington, DC: U.S. Institute of Peace Press.

Lyotard, Jean-François (1984). *The Postmodern Condition: A Report on Knowledge*. Minneapolis: University of Minnesota Press.

Maass, Peter (1992). "Region 'Liberated' by Serbs Isolated, Desolate." *Washington Post*, August 3, p. A14.

McBride, William Leon (1977). *The Philosophy of Marx*. London: Hutchinson.

McClelland, Charles (1972). "On the Fourth Wave: Past and Future in the Study of International Systems." In *The Analysis of International Politics*, J. N. Rosenau, V. Davis, and M. A. East (eds). New York: Free Press.

McClelland, David C. (1961). *The Achieving Society*. Princeton, NJ: D. van Nostrand.

McClosky, Herbert (1956). "Concerning Strategies for a Science of International Politics." *World Politics*, **8**(2), 281–95.

McDonald, John W., Jr and Diane B. Bendahmane (eds) (1987). *Conflict Resolution: Track Two Diplomacy*. Washington, DC: U.S. Department of State, Foreign Service Institute, Center for the Study of Foreign Affairs.

McDonald, Kim A. (1994). "An Anthropologist's Risk: Rutger's Scholar Backs up Her Theories that There Are Evolutionary and Genetic Bases for Human Behavior." *Chronicle of Higher Education*, **41**(3), A12, A20–1.

Macedonian Embassy (1996). Washington, DC. Personal communication, December 11.

McGowan, Patrick J. and Howard B. Shapiro (1973). *The Comparative Study of Foreign Policy: a Survey of Scientific Findings*. Beverly Hills, CA: Sage.

Mack, Raymond W. and Richard C. Snyder (1957). "The Analysis of Social Conflict – toward an Overview and Synthesis." *Journal of Conflict Resolution*, **1**(2), 212–248.

MacKinnon, W. J. and R. Centers (1958). "Social-psychological Factors in Public Orientation toward an Outgroup." *American Journal of Sociology*, **63**, 415–19.

MacLean, Paul (1975). "On the Evolution of Three Mentalities." In *New Dimensions in Psychiatry: A World View, Volume 2*, S. Arieti and G. Chrzanowski (eds). New York: John Wiley.

MacLean, Paul (1978). "A Mind of Three Minds: Educating the Triune Brain." In *Education and the Brain* (77th Yearbook of the National Society for the Study of Education, Part 2). Chicago: University of Chicago Press.

McNamara, Ron (1995). "Implementation Problems Persist as CFE Deadline Passes." *CSCE Digest*, **18**(11), 3–4.

Magas, Branka (1993). *The Destruction of Yugoslavia: Tracking the Break-up 1980–92*. London: Verso.

Maghroori, Ray and Bennett Ramberg (eds) (1982). *Globalism Versus Realism: International Relations' Third Debate*. Boulder, CO: Westview Press.

Mansbach, Richard W. and John A. Vasquez (1981). *In Search of Theory: a New Paradigm for Global Politics*. New York: Columbia University Press.

Maoz, Zeev (1983). "Resolve, Capabilities, and the Outcomes of Interstate Disputes, 1816–1976." *Journal of Conflict Resolution*, **27**, 195–229.

Maoz, Zeev (1989). "Joining the Club of Nations: Political Development and International Conflict, 1816–1976." *International Studies Quarterly*, **33**(2), 199–231.

Maresca, John J. (1985). *To Helsinki: the Conference on Security and Cooperation in Europe, 1973–1975*. Durham, NC: Duke University Press.

Marshall, Rick (1997). "NATO–Ukraine Charter, EAPC Meeting Top Second Day at Summit." *Wireless File*, U.S. Information Service, Embassy of the USA, Vienna, no. 133, July 10, pp. 10–11.

Maslow, Abraham H. (1987). *Motivation and Personality*, 3rd edn. New York: Harper and Row.

Mathews, Jessica (1992). "The Greater Threat to Democracy." *Washington Post*, March 13, p. A25.

Mathias, Barbara (1994). "High Anxiety: Antidotes for Phobias and Panic Attacks." *Washington Post*, June 30, p. C5.

Mearsheimer, John J. (1990a). "Back to the Future: Instability in Europe after the Cold War." *International Security*, **15**(1), 5–56.

Mearsheimer, John J. (1990b). "Why We Will Soon Miss the Cold War." *Atlantic Monthly*, August, 35–50.

Megargee, Edwin I. and Jack E. Hokanson (eds) (1970). *The Dynamics of Aggression: Individual, Group, and International Analyses*. New York: Harper and Row.

Meloen, J. D., L. Hagendoorn, Q. Raaijmakers, and L. Visser (1988). "Authoritarianism and the Revival of Political Racism: Reassessments in The Netherlands of the Reliability and Validity of the Concept of Authoritarianism by Adorno et al." *Political Psychology*, **9**(3), 413–29.

Merkl, Peter H. and Leonard Weinberg (eds) (1997). *The Revival of Right-wing Extremism in the Nineties*. Newbury Park, CA: Frank Cass.

Midlarsky, Manus I. (1975). *On War: Political Violence in the International System*. New York: Free Press.

Midlarsky, Manus I. (ed.) (1989). *Handbook of War Studies*. London: Unwin Hyman.

Miller, Alden Dykstra (1971). "Logic of Causal Analysis: from Experimental to Non-experimental Designs." In *Causal Models in the Social Sciences*, Hubert M. Blalock, Jr (ed.). London: Macmillan.

Miller, Delbert C. (1970). *Handbook of Research Design and Social Measurement*, 2nd edn. New York: McKay.

Miller, Judith (1998). "Preaching to the Converted." (Review of the Carnegie Commission on Preventing Deadly Conflict's *Preventing Deadly Conflict: Final Report.*) *New York Times Book Review*, February 15, p. 39.

Miller, Neal E. (1941). "The Frustration–Aggression Hypothesis." *Psychological Review*, **48**, 337–42.

Milstein, Jeffrey S. (1972). "American and Soviet Influence, Balance of Power, and Arab–Israeli Violence." In *Peace, War, and Numbers*, Bruce M. Russett (ed.). Beverly Hills, CA: Sage.

Mitchell, Christopher R. (1981). *The Structure of International Conflict*. London: Macmillan.

Mitchell, Christopher R. (1991). "A Willingness to Talk: Conciliatory Gestures and De-escalation." *Negotiation Journal*, 7(4), 405–30.

Mitchell, Christopher R. (1995) "The Right Moment: Notes on Four Models of 'Ripeness'." *Paradigms: The Kent Journal of International Relations*, 9(2), 38–52.

Mitchell, Christopher R. and Michael Banks (1996). *Handbook of Conflict Resolution: The Analytical Problem-solving Approach*. London: Pinter.

Modelski, George (1972). *Principles of World Politics*. New York: Free Press.

Montgomery, David (1997). "Paint It Green: Endorsement Deals, TV Coverage, Even a World Cup. Paintball Isn't Just a Weekend in the Woods Anymore." *Washington Post*, November 9, pp. F1, F4–5.

Montville, Joseph V. (1988). "Foreword" to Vamik Volkan's *The Need to Have Enemies and Allies: From Clinical Practice to International Relationships*. Northvale, NJ: Jason Aronson.

Montville, Joseph V. (ed.) (1990a). *Conflict and Peacemaking in Multiethnic Societies*. Lexington, MA: Lexington Books.

Montville, Joseph V. (1990b). "Epilogue: the Human Factor Revisited." In Joseph V. Montville (1990a).

Montville, Joseph V. (1993). "The Healing Function in Political Conflict Resolution." In *Conflict Resolution Theory and Practice: Integration and Application*, Dennis J. D. Sandole and Hugo van der Merwe (eds). Manchester: Manchester University Press.

Moore, Christopher W. (1986). *The Mediation Process: Practical Strategies for Resolving Conflict*. San Francisco: Jossey-Bass.

Moore, Davis W. (1974). "National Attributes and Nation Typologies." In *Comparing Foreign Policies: Theories, Findings and Methods*, James N. Rosenau (ed.). New York: John Wiley.

Morgenthau, Hans J. (1946). *Scientific Man vs. Power Politics*. Chicago: University of Chicago Press.

Morgenthau, Hans J. (1973). *Politics among Nations: the Struggle for Power and Peace*, 5th edn. New York: Alfred Knopf.

Most, Benjamin A. and Randolph Siverson (1987). "Substituting Arms and Alliances, 1870–1914: an Exploration in Comparative Foreign Policy." In *New Directions in the Study of Foreign Policy*, C. F. Hermann, C. W. Kegley, Jr, and J. N. Rosenau (eds). Boston: Allen and Unwin.

Most, Benjamin A. and Harvey Starr (1989). *Inquiry, Logic and International Politics*. Columbia: University of South Carolina Press.

Motyl, Alexander J. (1995a). *The Post-Soviet Nations: Perspectives on the Demise of the USSR*. New York: Columbia University Press.

Motyl, Alexander J. (1995b). *Thinking Theoretically about Soviet Nationalities: History and Comparison in the Study of the USSR*. New York: Columbia University Press.

Moyal, J. E. (1949). "The Distribution of Wars in Time." *Journal of the Royal Statistical Society*, **112**, 446–58.

Mueller, John (1989). *Retreat from Doomsday: the Obsolescence of Major War*. New York: Basic Books.

Nagel, Ernest (1961). *The Structure of Science: Problems in the Logic of Scientific Explanation*. London: Routledge and Kegan Paul.

Nahaylo, Bohdan and Victor Swoboda (1990). *Soviet Disunion: a History of the Nationalities Problem in the USSR*. New York: Free Press.

NATO Basic Fact Sheet No. 2 (1997). "The North Atlantic Cooperation Council (NACC)." NATO, March.

NATO Brussels Summit (1994). "Partnership for Peace: Invitation." NATO, January 10.

NATO Fact Sheet No. 9 (1997). "The Enhanced Partnership For Peace Programme (PfP)." NATO, July.

NATO Rome Summit (1991). "Rome Declaration on Peace and Cooperation." NATO, November 8.

Nelson, Stephen D. (1974). "Nature/Nurture Revisited I: a Review of the Biological Bases of Conflict." *Journal of Conflict Resolution*, **18**(2), 285–335.

Neufeld, Mark A. (1995). *The Restructuring of International Relations Theory* (Cambridge Studies in International Relations: 43). Cambridge: Cambridge University Press.

Nicholson, Michael (1975). "Fantasy – a Tool for Research?" *Conflict Research Society Bulletin*, May/June. London: Richardson Institute for Conflict and Peace Research.

Nicholson, Michael (1989). *Formal Theories in International Relations* (Cambridge Studies in International Relations: 3). Cambridge: Cambridge University Press.

Nicholson, Michael (1996). *Causes and Consequences in International Relations: a Conceptual Study*. London: Pinter.

Niebuhr, Reinhold (1940). *Christianity and Power Politics*. New York: Charles Scribner's Sons.

Niebuhr, Reinhold (1953). *Christian Realism and Political Problems*. New York: Charles Scribner's Sons.

Nordland, Rod and Russell Watson (1998). "Yugoslavia: More 'Ethnic Cleansing'? The Serbs Attack Kosovo, Threatening a Wider War." *Newsweek*, March 16, p. 39.

North, Robert C. (1975). "Some Paradoxes of War and Peace." *Peace Science Society (International), Papers*, **25**, 1–14.

North, Robert C. (1990). *War, Peace, Survival: Global Politics and Conceptual Synthesis*. Boulder, CO: Westview Press.

Northrup, Terrell A. (1989). "The Dynamic of Identity in Personal and Social Conflict." In *Intractable Conflicts and Their Transformation*, L. Kriesberg, T. A. Northrup, and S. J. Thorson (eds). Syracuse: Syracuse University Press.

NPF (1997). *National Peace Foundation 1997 Year-end Report*. Washington, DC: National Peace Foundation.

NSF (1995). "National Consortium for Research on Violence." Program Solicitation, NSF 95-54 (new). Arlington, VA: National Science Foundation (NSF), Directorate for Social, Behavioral and Economics Sciences.

Nullis, Clare (1994). "U.N. Resolution to Toughen Sanctions on Serbs Planned." *Philadelphia Inquirer*, July 31, p. A8.

NYT (1993). "Europeans Fear 'Many Yugoslavias' Unless 'Overburdened System' Changes." *New York Times*, August 8, p. 17.

O'Leary, M. K., W. D. Coplin, H. B. Shapiro, and D. Dean (1974). "The Quest for

Relevance: Quantitative International Relations Research and Government Foreign Affairs Analysis." *International Studies Quarterly*, **18**(2), 211–37.

Ollman, Bertell (1971). *Alienation: Marx's Conception of Man in Capitalist Society*. London: Cambridge University Press.

Onate, Andres D. (1974). "The Conflict Interactions of the People's Republic of China, 1950–1970." *Journal of Conflict Resolution*, **18**(4), 578–94.

O'Neill, Robert (1996). "Possible Threats to the West: Russia, China, Militant Islam." *International Herald Tribune*, May 10, p. 6.

Organski, A. F. K. (1968) *World Politics*, 2nd edn. New York: Knopf.

OSCE Lisbon Document 1996: Lisbon Summit (1996). Lisbon, December 3.

OSCE Newsletter (1995). **2**(5).

OSCE Newsletter (1996). "Peace Agreement for Bosnia and Herzegovina Calls for Important OSCE Role"; "Confidence Building and Arms Control Talks Begin under OSCE Auspices"; and "OSCE Mission to Bosnia and Herzegovina Begins Work toward Election Goals," **3**(1), 1, 8; 1, 10; 3, 8.

OSCE Newsletter (1997). "NATO–Russia Charter Underlines Importance of the OSCE," **4**(5), 3.

OSCE Review (1995a). "Security Model Choices under Scrutiny" (Finnish Committee for European Security), **3**(3/95), 4.

OSCE Review (1995b). "Defining the 21st Century Security Model," **3**(4/95), 4.

OSCE Review (1995c). "Herculean Task for OSCE" and "Ministerial Council Launches Bosnia Mission," **3**(4/95), 1, 9; 8–9.

OSCE Review (1997). "Mission to NATO," **5**(4/97), 6.

Ostrom, Charles W., Jr and John H. Aldrich (1978). "The Relationship Between Size and Stability in the Major Power International System." *American Journal of Political Science*, **22**(4), 743–71.

Pagels, Heinz R. (1988). *The Dreams of Reason: the Computer and the Rise of the Sciences and Complexity*. New York: Simon and Schuster.

Paige, Glenn D. (1968). *The Korean Decision: June 24–30, 1950*. New York: Free Press.

Patchen, Martin (1970). "Models of Cooperation and Conflict: a Critical Review." *Journal of Conflict Resolution*, **14**, 389–408.

Patrick, James (1973). *A Glasgow Gang Observed*. London: Eyre Methuen.

PDC (1992). *Partners for Democratic Change Brochure*. San Francisco: Partners for Democratic Change.

Pfaff, William (1996). "It's Time for Europe to Settle on a Balkan Policy." *International Herald Tribune*, March 20, p. 8.

Pfeiffer, John (1984). "Human Nature: the Universe Inside Your Skull." *Science Digest*, **92**, 92.

PfP (1998). "Partnership for Peace, Euro-Atlantic Partnership Council Member Countries." NATO, February 13 (http://www.nato.int/pfp/partners.htm).

Pilisuk, M., P. Potter, A. Rapoport, and J. A. Winter (1965). "War Hawks and Peace Doves: Alternative Resolutions of Experimental Conflicts." *Journal of Conflict Resolution*, **9**, 491–508.

Platt, John (1971). "How Men Can Shape Their Future." *Futures*, **3**(1).

Podestra, Don (1987). "The Terrible Toll of Human Hatred: Wars May Come and Go, but Ethnic Rivalries Are Forever." *Washington Post National Weekly Edition*, June 8, pp. 9–10.

Pomfret, John (1994a). "U.N. Tells Troops from Turkey to Keep Low Profile in Bosnia." *Washington Post*, July 16, p. A15.

Pomfret, John (1994b). "Bosnian Serbs Sound More Like Victims: Ally's Border Closing Is Psychological Blow." *Washington Post*, August 12, p. A33.

Pomfret, John (1995). "Balkans Must Confront a History of Hatred." *Washington Post*, December 17, pp. A1, A34–5.

Pomfret, John (1996a). "Croats and Muslims Edge toward a Joint Army." *International Herald Tribune*, July 8, p. 5.

Pomfret, John (1996b). "U.S. Starts Delivery of Heavy Weapons to Bosnia's Muslim–Croat Forces." *Washington Post*, November 22, p. A44.

Pondy, L. R. (1967). "Organizational Conflict: Concepts and Models." *Administrative Science Quarterly*, **12**(2), 296–320. Abridged and reprinted in Thomas and Bennis (1972).

Popper, Karl R. (1959). *The Logic of Scientific Discovery*. London: Hutchinson.

Popper, Karl R. (1961). *The Poverty of Historicism*, 2nd edn. London: Routledge and Kegan Paul.

Popper, Karl R. (1972a). *Conjectures and Refutations: the Growth of Scientific Knowledge*, 4th edn. London: Routledge and Kegan Paul.

Popper, Karl R. (1972b). *Objective Knowledge: An Evolutionary Approach*. London: Oxford University Press.

Posen, Barry (1993). "The Security Dilemma and Ethnic Conflict." *Survival*, **35**(1), 27–47.

Post, T., with M. Liu, T. Sonenshine, B. Turgue, S. Sullivan, and R. Nordland (1995). "Make War, Make Peace." *Newsweek*, September 11, pp. 37–40.

Powell, Charles A. (1969a). "Simulating International Politics: a Reconstruction." Unpublished manuscript, Department of Politics, University of Strathclyde, Glasgow.

Powell, Charles A. (1969b). "Simulation: the Anatomy of a Fad." *ACTA Politica*, April, 299–330.

Prague CSCE (1992). *Prague Meeting of the CSCE Council*, January 30–31.

Preston, Julia (1993). "Boutros-Ghali: 'Ethnic Conflict' Imperils Security." *Washington Post*, November 9, p. A13.

Pruitt, Dean G. and Richard C. Snyder (1969). "The Study of War: Theory and Method." In *Theory and Research on the Causes of War*, Dean G. Pruitt and Richard C. Snyder (eds). Englewood Cliffs, NJ: Prentice Hall.

Rapoport, Anatol (1960). *Fights, Games, and Debates*. Ann Arbor: University of Michigan Press.

Rapoport, Anatol (1964). *Strategy and Conscience*. New York: Harper and Row.

Rapoport, Anatol (1965). "Game Theory and Human Conflict." In *The Nature of Human Conflict*, Elton B. McNeil (ed.). Englewood Cliffs, NJ: Prentice Hall.

Rapoport, Anatol (1972). "The Application of Game Theory to Peace Research." In *Disarmament and Arms Control*, Carlo Schaerf and Frank Barnaby (eds). New York: Gordon and Breach.

Rapoport, Anatol (1974). *Conflict in Man-made Environment*. Harmondsworth: Penguin.

Rapoport, Anatol and Albert M. Chammah (1965). *Prisoner's Dilemma: a Study in Conflict and Cooperation*. Ann Arbor: University of Michigan Press.

Raser, John R. (1966). "Personal Characteristics of Political Decision-makers: a Literature Review." *Peace Research Society (International), Papers*, **5**, 161–81.

Raser, John R. (1969). *Simulation and Society: an Exploration of Scientific Gaming*. Boston: Allyn and Bacon.

Ray, John J. (1988a). "Cognitive Style as a Predictor of Authoritarianism, Conservatism, and Racism: a Fantasy in Many Movements." *Political Psychology*, **9**(2), 303–8.

Ray, John J. (1988b). "Authoritarianism, Racism, and Anarchocapitalism: a Rejoinder to Eckhardt." *Political Psychology*, **9**(4), 693–9.

Ray, John J. (1990). "The Old Fashioned Personality." *Human Relations*, **43**(10), 997–1013.

Reid, T. R. (1998). "Historic Promise of Peace for N. Ireland: Accord Reached on Good Friday Offers a Return to Self-rule after 26 Years." *Washington Post*, April 11, pp. A1, A12.

Reiss, Albert J., Jr and Jeffrey A. Roth (eds) (1993). *Understanding and Preventing Violence* (Panel on the Understanding and Control of Violent Behavior, National Research Council). Washington, DC: National Academy Press.

Restak, Richard M. (1979). *The Brain: the Last Frontier*. Garden City, NY: Doubleday.

Richardson, Lewis F. (1939). "Generalized Foreign Politics: a Study in Group Psychology." *British Journal of Psychology, Monograph Supplements*, **23**(7), 1–91.

Richardson, Lewis F. (1960a). *Arms and Insecurity*. Chicago: Quadrangle Books.

Richardson, Lewis F. (1960b). *Statistics of Deadly Quarrels*. Chicago: Quadrangle Books.

Richburg, Keith B. (1994). "Somalia Slips Back to Bloodshed: Anarchy, Death Toll Grow as U.N. Mission Winds Down." *Washington Post*, September 4, pp. A1, A43.

Rieff, David (1994). "Accomplice to Genocide." *Balkan War Report: Bulletin of the Institute for War and Peace Reporting*, **28**, 35–40.

Rieff, David (1995). *Slaughterhouse: Bosnia and the Failure of the West*. New York: Simon and Schuster.

Rikhye, Indar Jit (1992). *Strengthening UN Peacekeeping: New Challenges and Proposals*. Washington, DC: U.S. Institute of Peace, May.

Robbins, C. A. (1992). "The X Factor in the Proliferation Game: the Former Soviet Union's Explosive Potential." *Newsweek*, March 16, pp. 44–51.

Roberts, Adam (1995/6). "From San Francisco to Sarajevo: the UN and the Use of Force." *Survival*, **37**(4), 7–28.

Robinson, William S. (1950). "Ecological Correlations and the Behavior of Individuals." *American Sociological Review*, **15**, 351–7.

Rokeach, Milton (1954). "The Nature and Meaning of Dogmatism." *Psychological Review*, **61**, 194–204.

Rokeach, Milton (1960). *The Open and Closed Mind: Investigations into the Nature of Belief Systems and Personality Systems*. New York: Basic Books.

Rokeach, Milton and Benjamin Fruchter (1956). "A Factorial Study of Dogmatism and Related Concepts." *Journal of Abnormal and Social Psychology*, **53**(4), 356–60.

Ronen, Dov (1997). *The Challenge of Ethnic Conflict, Democracy and Self-determination in Central Europe*. Newbury Park, CA: Frank Cass Publishers.

Ropers, Norbert (1993). "CSCE Foundation for Peace-building: a Contribution for Mobilizing Social Agents (NGOs) for the Peaceful Resolution of Conflict in Europe." Unpublished paper.

Ropers, Norbert (1995). "Peaceful Intervention: Structures, Processes, and Strategies for the Constructive Regulation of Ethnopolitical Conflicts." *Berghof Report No. 1*. Berlin: Berghof Research Center for Constructive Conflict Management.

Ropers, Norbert and Peter Schlotter (1993). "The CSCE: Multilateral Conflict Management in a Transforming World Order – Future Perspectives and New Impulses for Regional Peace Strategies." *Interdependence*, no. 14 (Stiftung Entwicklung und Frieden, Bonn).

Rose, Richard (1971). *Governing without Consensus: an Irish Perspective*. London: Faber and Faber.

Rosecrance, Richard N. (1966). "Bipolarity, Multipolarity, and the Future." *Journal of Conflict Resolution*, **10**, 314–27. Reprinted in James N. Rosenau (1969).

Rosen, Bernard C. (1956). "The Achievement Syndrome: a Psycho-cultural Dimension of Social Stratification." *American Sociological Review*, **21**(2), 203–11.

Rosen, Bernard C. (1964). "The ACH Syndrome and Economic Growth in Brazil." *Social Forces*, **42**(3), 341–54.

Rosenau, James N. (ed.) (1961). *International Politics and Foreign Policy: A Reader in Research and Theory*. New York: Free Press.

Rosenau, James N. (1966). "Pre-theories and Theories of Foreign Policy." In *Approaches to Comparative and International Politics*, R. Barry Farrel (ed.). Evanston, IL: Northwestern University Press.

Rosenau, James N. (ed.) (1969). *International Politics and Foreign Policy: a Reader in Research and Theory*, rev. edn. New York: Free Press.

Rosenau, James N. (1973). *International Studies and the Social Sciences: Problems, Priorities and Prospects in the United States*. Beverly Hills, CA: Sage.

Rosenau, James N. (1974). "Assessment in International Studies: Ego Trip or Feedback?" *International Studies Quarterly*, **18**(3), 339–67.

Rosenau, James N. (1990). *Turbulence in World Politics: a Theory of Change and Continuity*. Princeton, NJ: Princeton University Press.

Rosenau, Pauline Marie (1992). *Post-modernism and the Social Sciences: Insights, Inroads, and Intrusions*. Princeton, NJ: Princeton University Press.

Rosenberg, Tina (1993). "Centuries of Hatred and Strife" (Review of Robert D. Kaplan's *Balkan Ghosts*). *Washington Post Book World*, **23**(13), 1.

Rotfeld, Adam Daniel (1993). "The CSCE: towards a Security Organization." In *SIPRI Yearbook 1993: Armaments and Disarmaments* (Stockholm International Peace Research Institute). Oxford: Oxford University Press.

Rotfeld, Adam Daniel (1997). *From Helsinki to Lisbon and Beyond: Analysis and Documents of the OSCE, 1973–96* (Stockholm International Peace Research Institute). Oxford: Oxford University Press.

Rubenstein, Richard E. (1992). "Dispute Resolution on the Eastern Frontier: Some Questions for Modern Missionaries." *Negotiation Journal*, **8**(3), 205–13.

Rudner, Richard S. (1966). *Philosophy of Social Science*. Englewood Cliffs, NJ: Prentice Hall.

Rummel, Rudolph J. (1963). "Dimensions of Conflict Behavior Within and Between Nations." *General Systems Yearbook*, **8**, 1–50.

Rummel, Rudolph J. (1964). "Testing Some Possible Predictors of Conflict Behavior Within and Between Nations." *Peace Research Society (International), Papers*, **1**, 79–111.

Rummel, Rudolph J. (1968). "The Relationship between National Attributes and Foreign Conflict Behavior." In *Quantitative International Politics: Insights and Evidence*, J. David Singer (ed.). New York: Free Press.

Rummel, Rudolph J. (1979). *War, Power, Peace: Understanding Conflict and War, Volume 4*. Beverly Hills, CA: Sage.

Rummel, Rudolph J. (1987). "Deadlier than War." *Institute of Public Affairs Review*, **41**(2), 24–30.

Rupert, James (1993). "World's Welcome Strained by 20 Million Refugees: Xenophobia Surging, U.N. Commissioner Says." *Washington Post*, November 10, p. A32.

Russett, B. M., H. R. Alker, K. W. Deutsch, and H. D. Lasswell (1964). *World Handbook of Political and Social Indicators*. New Haven, CT: Yale University Press.

Russian Embassy (1995). Washington, DC. Personal communication, September 7.

Ryan, Alan (1970). *The Philosophy of the Social Sciences*. London: Macmillan.

Ryan, Randolph (1997). "The Long Haul. Exit, the Exit Strategy: Why Preventing War in Bosnia Remains America's Job." *Washington Post*, December 28, pp. C1, C2.

St Augustine (1948). *The City of God* (translated by Marcus Dods). New York: Hafner.

Sandole, Dennis J. D. (1978a). "Mapping and Modelling of Complex Conflict Processes: a Report of Research in Progress." Paper presented at the Workshop on Formal Political Analysis, the European Consortium for Political Research (ECPR), Grenoble, France, April 6–12.

Sandole, Dennis J. D. (1978b). "A Mega-concatenated Theory of Complex Conflict Processes." Paper presented at the Fifteenth European Conference of the Peace and Science Society (International), Geneva, Switzerland, September 3–5.

Sandole, Dennis J. D. (1979a). *The Genesis of War: Mapping and Modelling of Complex Conflict Processes*. Unpublished doctoral dissertation, Department of Politics, University of Strathclyde, Glasgow, July.

Sandole, Dennis J. D. (1979b). "Political Realism and International Conflict: Assessment of a Paradigm." Paper presented at the Sixteenth European Conference of the Peace Science Society (International), Berlin, September 2–4.

Sandole, Dennis J. D. (1980a). "Changing Perceptions: an Approach to Teaching International Relations and Its Impact on the Attitudes of Mid-career Students." In *The Study and Teaching of International Relations: a Perspective on Mid-career Education*, Randolph C. Kent and Gunnar P. Nielsson (eds). London: Frances Pinter.

Sandole, Dennis J. D. (1980b). "Economic Conditions and Conflict Processes." In *Models of Political Economy*, Paul Whiteley (ed.). Beverly Hills, CA: Sage.

Sandole, Dennis J. D. (1984). "The Subjectivity of Theories and Actions in World Society." In *Conflict in World Society: A New Perspective on International Relations*, Michael Banks (ed.). New York: St Martin's Press.

Sandole, Dennis J. D. (1986). "Traditional Approaches to Conflict Management: Short-term Gains vs. Long-term Costs." *Current Research on Peace and Violence*, **9**(3), 119–24.

Sandole, Dennis J. D. (1987). "Conflict Management: Elements of Generic Theory and Practice." In *Conflict Management and Problem Solving: Interpersonal to International Applications*, Dennis J. D. Sandole and Ingrid Sandole-Staroste (eds). London: Frances Pinter.

Sandole, Dennis J. D. (1988). "Paradigms, Movements, and Shifts: Indicators of a Social Invention." In *New Approaches to International Mediation*, Christopher R. Mitchell and Keith Webb (eds). Westport, CT: Greenwood Press.

Sandole, Dennis J. D. (1990). "The Biological Basis of Needs in World Society: the Ultimate Micro–Macro Nexus." In *Conflict: Human Needs Theory*, John W. Burton (ed.). New York: St Martin's Press.

Sandole, Dennis J. D. (1991). "The Conflict Prevention Centre and Cooperative Conflict Resolution in Europe." *Peace and the Sciences* (International Institute for Peace, Vienna), June, pp. 9–18.

Sandole, Dennis J. D. (1992a). "Conflict Resolution in the Post- Cold War Era: Dealing with Ethnic Violence in the New Europe." *Working Paper no. 6*, Institute for Conflict Analysis and Resolution, George Mason University, Fairfax, VA, October.

Sandole, Dennis J. D. (1992b). "Ethnic Conflict and Conflict Resolution in the New Europe: the Fly in the Ointment," *Wiener Blätter zur Friedensforschung* (Vienna Journal in Peace Research), **71**, 26–37.

Sandole, Dennis J. D. (1993a). "Paradigms, Theories, and Metaphors in Conflict and Conflict Resolution: Coherence or Confusion?" In *Conflict Resolution Theory and Practice:*

Integration and Application, Dennis J. D. Sandole and Hugo van der Merwe (eds). Manchester: Manchester University Press.

Sandole, Dennis J. D. (1993b). "Epilogue: Future Directions in Theory and Research." In Sandole and van der Merwe (1993).

Sandole, Dennis J. D. (1993c). "Ethnic Conflict Resolution in the New Europe: a Case for an Integrated Systems Approach." In *Peace Research for the 1990s*, Judit Balázs and Hakan Wiberg (eds). Budapest: Akadémiai Kiadó.

Sandole, Dennis J. D. (1993d). "Post-Cold War Peace and Security Systems in Europe: Prospects and Prescriptions." *Peace and the Sciences* (International Institute for Peace, Vienna), March, pp. 5–12.

Sandole, Dennis J. D. (1994a). "The New European Peace and Security System (NEPSS): Preliminary Analysis of a CSCE Elite Survey." *Final Report for NATO Research Fellowship*, February.

Sandole, Dennis J. D. (1994b). "Ethnic Conflict in the New World Disorder: Dilemmas for the International Conflict Resolution Community." *Newsletter of the Centre for Conflict Resolution* (Macquarie University, Sydney, Australia), **9**, 9–10.

Sandole, Dennis J. D. (1995a). "Changing Ideologies in the Conference on Security and Cooperation in Europe." In "Flexibility in International Negotiation and Mediation," Special Issue of *The Annals* of The American Academy of Political and Social Science, Daniel Druckman and Christopher R. Mitchell (eds), **542**, 131–47.

Sandole, Dennis J. D. (1995b). "Ethnic Conflict as Low Intensity Conflict in Post-Cold War Europe: Causes, Conditions, Prevention." In *The First International Workshop on Low Intensity Conflict (ILIC '95)*, Alexander E. R. Woodcock, S. Anders Christensson, Henrik Friman, and Magnus Gustafsson (eds). Stockholm: Royal Swedish Society of Naval Sciences, March 29–31.

Sandole, Dennis J. D. (1997a). "Developing Conflict Resolution in Transcaucasia: a University-based Approach." In "Strengthening Transitional Democracies Through Conflict Resolution," Special issue of *The Annals* of the American Academy of Political and Social Science, Raymond Shonholtz and Ilana Shapiro (eds), **552**, 125–38.

Sandole, Dennis J. D. (1997b). "Institutionalizing Conflict Resolution in Transcaucasia: a Progress Report." In "Conflict Management within Transitioning Societies," Special issue of *NIDR News* (National Institute for Dispute Resolution, Washington, DC), Raymond Shonholtz and Juliette Linzer (eds), **IV**(4), 7, 11–12.

Sandole, Dennis J. D. (1998). "A Peace and Security System for Post-Cold War Europe: Preventing Future Yugoslavias." In *Encyclopedia of the European Union*, Desmond Dinan (ed.). Boulder, CO: Lynne Rienner.

Sandole, Dennis J. D. and Ingrid Sandole-Staroste (eds) (1987). *Conflict Management and Problem Solving: Interpersonal to International Applications*. London: Frances Pinter.

Sandole, Dennis J. D. and Hugo van der Merwe (eds) (1993). *Conflict Resolution Theory and Practice: Integration and Application*. Manchester: Manchester University Press.

Saperstein, Alvin M. (1995). "War and Chaos." *American Scientist*, **83**(6), 548–57.

Saunders, Harold H. (1991). *The Other Walls: the Arab–Israeli Peace Process in a Global Perspective*, rev. edn. Princeton, NJ: Princeton University Press.

Schaerf, Carlo and Frank Barnaby (eds) (1972). *Disarmament and Arms Control*. New York: Gordon and Breach.

Schelling, Thomas C. (1967). "What Is Game Theory?" In *Contemporary Political Analysis*, James C. Charlesworth (ed.). New York: Free Press.

Scott, Andrew M. (1967). *The Functioning of the International Political System*. New York: Macmillan.

Scott, John Paul (1958). *Aggression*. Chicago: University of Chicago Press.

Seeman, Melvin (1959). "On the Meaning of Alienation." *American Sociological Review*, **24**(6), pp. 783–91.

Selltiz, C., L. S. Wrightsman, and S. W. Cook (1976). *Research Methods in Social Relations*. 3rd edn. New York: Holt, Rinehart and Winston.

SFCG (1997). *Search for Common Ground and European Centre for Common Ground: Report*. Washington, DC: Search for Common Ground.

Shapiro, Margaret (1992). "In Armenia and Azerbaijan, Old Enemies at War Anew." *Washington Post*, June 10, p. A25.

Sharp, Jane M. O. (1993). "Conventional Arms Control in Europe." In *SIPRI Yearbook 1993: World Armaments and Disarmaments* (Stockholm International Peace Research Institute). Oxford: Oxford University Press.

Shaw, R. Paul and Yuwa Wong (1989). *Genetic Seeds of Warfare: Evolution, Nationalism, and Patriotism*. Boston: Unwin Hyman.

Shea, Christopher (1998). "Why Depression Strikes More Women than Men: 'Ruminative Coping' May Provide Answers." *Chronicle of Higher Education*, **44**(21), A14.

Shenon, Philip (1996). "Pentagon Expects Trouble in Bosnia When NATO Pulls Out." *International Herald Tribune*, March 21, pp. 1, 6.

Sherif, Muzafer (1967). *Group Conflict and Cooperation: Their Social Psychology*. London: Routledge and Kegan Paul.

Sherif, Muzafer and Carolyn W. Sherif (1953). *Groups in Harmony and Tension*. New York: Harper and Row.

Shonholtz, Raymond and Juliette Linzer (eds) (1997). "Conflict Management within Transitioning Societies." Special issue of *NIDR News* (National Institute for Dispute Resolution), **4**(4).

Shonholtz, Raymond and Ilana Shapiro (eds) (1997). "Strengthening Transitional Democracies through Conflict Resolution." Special issue of *The Annals* of the American Academy of Political and Social Science, **552**, July.

Shubik, Martin (1967). "The Uses of Game Theory." In *Contemporary Political Analysis*, James C. Charlesworth (ed.). New York: Free Press.

Sidanius, Jim (1988). "Intolerance of Ambiguity, Conservatism, and Racism – Whose Fantasy, Whose Reality? A Reply to Ray." *Political Psychology*, **9**(2), 309–16.

Silber, Laura and Allan Little (1997). *Yugoslavia: Death of a Nation*, rev. edn. London: Penguin.

Simmel, Georg (1955). *Conflict and the Web of Group-affiliations* (translated by Kurt H. Wolff and Reinhard Bendix). New York: Free Press.

Singer, J. David (1961). "The Level-of-analysis Problem in International Relations." In *The International System: Theoretical Essays*, Klaus Knorr and Sidney Verba (eds). Princeton, NJ: Princeton University Press.

Singer, J. David (1965). "Data-making in International Relations." *Behavioral Science*, **10**(1), 68–80.

Singer, J. David (1969). "The Global System and its Sub-systems: a Developmental View." In *Linkage Politics*, James N. Rosenau (ed.). New York: Free Press.

Singer, J. David (1972). "The 'Correlates of War' Project: Interim Report and Rationale." *World Politics*, **24**(2), 243–70.

Singer, J. David (1976). "Environmental Ambiguity and the War Proneness of Major Powers, 1816–1965: an Historical Experiment." Paper presented at the Tenth World Congress of the International Political Science Association, Edinburgh, August 16–21.

Singer, J. David (ed.) (1979a). *Explaining War: Selected Papers from the Correlates of War Project*. Beverly Hills, CA: Sage.

Singer, J. David (1979b). *The Correlates of War: 1. Research Origins and Rationale*. New York: Free Press.

Singer, J. David (1980). *The Correlates of War: 2. Testing Some Realpolitik Models*. New York: Free Press.

Singer, J. David (1981). "Accounting for International War: The State of the Discipline." *Journal of Peace Research*, **18**(1), 1–18.

Singer, J. David (1982). "Confrontational Behavior and Escalation to War, 1816–1980: a Research Plan." *Journal of Peace Research*, **19**(1), 37–48.

Singer, J. David (1989). "System Structure, Decision Processes, and the Incidence of International War." In *Handbook of War Studies*, Manus I. Midlarsky (ed.). Boston: Unwin Hyman.

Singer, J. David (1995). "Metaphors and Models in the Explanation of War." In *The Process of War: Advancing the Scientific Study of War*, Stuart A. Bremer and Thomas R. Cusack (eds). Luxembourg: Gordon and Breach Science Publishers.

Singer, J. David and Melvin Small (1966). "National Alliance Commitments and War Involvement, 1818–1945." *Peace Research Society (International) Papers*, **5**. Reprinted in James N. Rosenau (1969).

Singer, J. David and Melvin Small (1968). "Alliance Aggregation and the Onset of War, 1815–1945." In *Quantitative International Politics: Insights and Evidence*, J. David Singer (ed.). New York: Free Press.

Singer, J. David, S. Bremer, and J. Stuckey (1972). "Capability Distribution, Uncertainty, and Major Power War, 1820–1965." In *Peace, War, and Numbers*, Bruce M. Russett (ed.). Beverly Hills, CA: Sage.

Singer, J. David and Melvin Small (1972). *The Wages of War, 1816–1965: A Statistical Handbook*. New York: John Wiley.

Singer, Max (1993). "The Two-world Order: the Planet Realigns into Zones of Peace and Turmoil." *Washington Post*, August 29, p. C5.

Singer, Max and Aaron Wildavsky (1993). *The Real World Order: Zones of Peace, Zones of Turmoil*. Chatham, NJ: Chatham House.

Sisk, Timothy D. (1996). *Power Sharing and International Mediation in Ethnic Conflicts*. Washington, DC: U.S. Institute of Peace Press.

Sivard, Ruth Leger (1987). *World Military and Social Expenditures 1987–88*, 12th edn. Washington, DC: World Priorities.

Sivard, Ruth Leger (1991). *World Military and Social Expenditures 1991*, 14th edn. Washington, DC: World Priorities.

Sivard, Ruth Leger (1993). *World Military and Social Expenditures 1993*, 15th edn. Washington, DC: World Priorities.

Small, Melvin and J. David Singer (1982). *Resort to Arms: International and Civil Wars, 1816–1980*. Beverly Hills, CA: Sage.

Small, Melvin and J. David Singer (eds.) (1985). *International War: An Anthology and Study Guide*. Homewood, IL: Dorsey.

Smith, Clagett G. (ed.) (1971). *Conflict Resolution: Contributions of the Behavioral Sciences*. Notre Dame, IN: University of Notre Dame Press.

Smith, Steve, Ken Booth, and Marysia Zalewski (eds) (1996). *International Theory: Positivism and Beyond*. Cambridge: Cambridge University Press.

Smither, Robert (1993). "Authoritarianism, Dominance, and Social Behavior: a Perspective from Evolutionary Personality Psychology." *Human Relations*, **46**(1), 23–43.

Smoker, Paul (1970). "International Relations Simulations: a Summary." Paper presented at the Eighth World Congress of the International Political Science Association, Munich, August 31 to September 5.

Smoker, Paul (1976). "Some Problems for Next Generation Global Models and Realities." Paper presented at the Tenth World Congress of the International Political Science Association, Edinburgh, August 16–21.

Snyder, R. C., H. W. Bruck, and B. Sapin (eds) (1962). *Foreign Policy Decision Making: An Approach to the Study of International Politics*. New York: Free Press.

Sollenberg, Margareta (ed.) (1996). *States in Armed Conflict, 1995*. Uppsala: Department of Peace and Conflict Research, Uppsala University.

Soloway, Colin and Chris Stephen (1998). "Kosovo Under 2nd Day of Heavy Serb Assault: Forces Claim to Have Killed Key Albanian Rebel." *Washington Post*, March 7, pp. Al, A14.

Sørbø, Gunnar M., Joanna Macrae, and Lennart Wohlgemuth (1997). *NGOs in Conflict – an Evaluation of International Alert* (CMI Report Series, R 1997: 6). Bergen: Chr. Michelsen Institute.

Sorokin, Pitirim A. (1937). *Social and Cultural Dynamics, Volume 3: Fluctuation of Social Relationships, War, and Revolution*. New York: American Book Company.

Spector, Leonard S. (1987). *Going Nuclear*. Cambridge, MA: Ballinger.

Spinoza, Benedict de (1951). *The Chief Works of Benedict de Spinoza* (translated by R. H. M. Elwes), two volumes. New York: Dover.

Spolar, Christine (1998a). "Last Serb-held Enclave Nervously Nears Return to Croatia's Control." *Washington Post*, January 11, p. A25.

Spolar, Christine (1998b). "U.N. Returns E. Slavonia to Croatia: Serbs Captured Corridor at Outset of War in 1991." *Washington Post*, January 16, p. A15.

Spolar, Christine (1998c). "Albania: Ethnic Brethren Express Concern. Neighbors Can Offer Only Moral Support." *Washington Post*, March 10, p. A13.

Stanhope, Henry (1978). "How the West Won in 1985." *The Times*, June 29, p. 18.

Starovoitova, Galina (1997). "Sovereignty after Empire: Self-determination Movements in the Former Soviet Union." *Peaceworks No. 19*. Washington, DC: U.S. Institute of Peace, November.

Starr, Harvey (1975). "Coalitions and Future War: a Dyadic Study of Cooperation and Conflict." *Sage Professional Papers in International Studies Volume 3* (Series No. 02-034). Beverly Hills, CA: Sage.

State of World Conflict Report 1991–1992. Atlanta, GA: The International Negotiation Network, The Carter Center of Emory University.

State of World Conflict Report 1995–1996. Atlanta, GA: The International Negotiation Network, The Carter Center of Emory University.

Stavanhagen, Rodolfo (1996). *Ethnic Conflicts and the Nation-state*. London: Macmillan.

Stedman, Stephen J. (1991). *Peacemaking in Civil War: International Mediation in Zimbabwe, 1974–1980*. Boulder, CO: Lynne Rienner.

Stein, Eric (1997). *Czecho/Slovakia: Ethnic Conflict–Constitutional Fissure–Negotiated Breakup*. Ann Arbor: University of Michigan Press.

Stern, Paul C. and Daniel Druckman (1994/5). "Has the 'Earthquake' of 1989 Toppled International Relations Theory?" *Peace Psychology Review*, **1**(2), 109–22.

Stockholm Document (1986). *Document of the Stockholm Conference on Confidence- and Security-building Measures and Disarmament in Europe Convened in Accordance with the Relevant Provisions of the Concluding Document of the Madrid Meeting of the [CSCE]*. Stockholm, September 19.

Strickland, D. A., L. L. Wade, and R. E. Johnston (1968). *A Primer of Political Analysis*. Chicago: Markham.

Sullivan, John D. (1972). "Cooperation to Conflict: Sources of Informal Alignments." In *Peace, War, and Numbers*, Bruce M. Russett (ed.). Beverly Hills, CA: Sage.

Sullivan, Michael P. (1976). *International Relations: Theories and Evidence*. Englewood Cliffs, NJ: Prentice Hall.

Sumner, William Graham (1906). *Folkways*. New York: Ginn.

Suny, Ronald Grigor (ed.) (1996). *Transcaucasia, Nationalism, and Social Change: Essays in the History of Armenia, Azerbaijan, and Georgia*, rev. edn. Ann Arbor: University of Michigan Press.

Suplee, Curt (1992). "The Order of Things" (Review of Roger Lewin's *Complexity: Life at the Edge of Chaos*, and M. Mitchell Waldrop's *Complexity: the Emerging Science at the Edge of Order and Chaos*). *Washington Post Book World*, **22**(51), 1, 10.

Suro, Roberto (1997). "Drop in Murder Rate Accelerates in Cities: District, P. G. County among Leaders in Trend." *Washington Post*, December 31, pp. A1, A6.

Swardson, Anne (1993). "Ruling on Doctor-assisted Suicide." *Washington Post*, October 1, p. A40.

Sylvester, Christine (1994). *Feminist Theory and International Relations in a Postmodern Era* (Cambridge Studies in International Relations: 32). Cambridge: Cambridge University Press.

Tanner, Marcus (1997). *Croatia: a Nation Forged in War*. New Haven, CT: Yale University Press.

Tanter, Raymond (1966). "Dimensions of Conflict Behavior within and between Nations, 1958–60." *Journal of Conflict Resolution*, **10**, 41–64.

Tarnoff, Peter (1989). "A Bizarre Nostalgia for the Cold War." *New York Times*, September 19, p. A25.

Taylor, John L. and Rex Walford (1972). *Simulation in the Classroom*. Harmondsworth: Penguin.

Taylor, Trevor (1978). "Introduction: the Nature of International Relations." In *Approaches and Theory in International Relations*, Trevor Taylor (ed.). London: Longman.

Terhune, Kenneth W. (1968). "Studies of Motives, Cooperation and Conflict within Laboratory Microcosms." *Buffalo Studies*, **4**(1), pp. 29–56.

Terhune, Kenneth W. (1970). "The Effects of Personality in Cooperation and Conflict." In *The Structure of Conflict*, Paul Swingle (ed.). New York and London: Academic Press.

Tharoor, Shashi (1995/6). "Should UN Peacekeeping Go 'Back to Basics'?" *Survival*, **37**(4), 52–64.

Thomas, John M. and Warren G. Bennis (eds.) (1972). *The Management of Change and Conflict: Selected Readings*. Harmondsworth: Penguin.

Thompson, J. L. P. (1989). "Deprivation and Political Violence in Northern Ireland, 1922–1985." *Journal of Conflict Resolution*, **33**(4), 676–99.

Thompson, William R. (1983). "The World Economy, the Long Cycle, and the Question of World-system Time." In *Foreign Policy and the Modern World System*, Patrick J. McGowan and Charles W. Kegley, Jr (eds). Beverly Hills, CA: Sage.

Thornberry, Terence P., Alan J. Lizotte, Marvin D. Krohn, Margaret Farnworth, and Sung Joon Jang (1991). "Testing Interactional Theory: an Examination of Reciprocal Causal Relationships among Family, School, and Delinquency." Rochester Youth Development Study. *Journal of Criminal Law and Criminology*, **82**(1), 3–35.

Tickner, J. Ann (1992). *Gender in International Relations: Feminist Perspectives on a Changing Global Society*. New York: Columbia University Press.

Tishkov, Valery (1997). *Ethnicity, Nationalism and Conflict in and after the Soviet Union: the Mind Aflame*. Thousand Oaks, CA: Sage.

Trueheart, Charles (1994). "Right-to-die Crusader Ends Her Life by Choice." *Washington Post*, February 15, p. A12.

Truger, Arno (1993/4). "The IPT (International Civilian Peace Keeping and Peace-building) Program." *Pax Schlaining*, Winter, p. 13.

Tutuncu, Mehmet (ed.) (1998). *Caucasus: War and Peace. New World Disorder in Caucasia*. Haarlem: Stichting Onderzoek Turkestan.

Ullman, Richard H. (1991). *Securing Europe* (A Twentieth Century Fund Book). Princeton, NJ: Princeton University Press.

UN (1995). *Information Notes: United Nations Peacekeeping*. New York: United Nations, Peace and Security Programmes Section, Department of Public Information, February.

Urquhart, Brian (1991a). "Sovereignty vs. Suffering: Obsolete Values Victimize the Kurds." *New York Times*, April 17, p. A23.

Urquhart, Brian (1991b). "Who Can Stop the Civil Wars?" *New York Times*, December 29, p. E9.

USIP (1990). *Prospects for Conflict or Peace in Central and Eastern Europe*. Washington, DC: U.S. Institute of Peace, May.

USIP (1992a). "Lessons from Central Asia – Nagorno-Karabakh and Afghanistan Considered." *United States Institute of Peace Journal*, **5**(3), 1–3.

USIP (1992b). "Peace and Conflict in Nagorno-Karabakh: a Preliminary Report." Washington DC: U.S. Institute of Peace, July 13.

USIP (1997). "Dayton Implementation: the Train and Equip Program." *Special Report* of the Dayton Implementation Working Group. Washington, DC: U.S. Institute of Peace, September.

USIP (1997/8). *Guide to Specialists '97–98*. Washington, DC: U.S. Institute of Peace.

Valletta Report (1991). *Report of the CSCE Meeting of Experts on Peaceful Settlement of Disputes*. Valletta, February 8.

van Creveld, Martin (1991). *The Transformation of War*. New York: Free Press.

Vasquez, John A. (1976). "Statistical Findings in International Politics: a Data-based Assessment." *International Studies Quarterly*, **20**(2), 171–218.

Vasquez, John A. (1983). *The Power of Power Politics: a Critique*. New Brunswick, NJ: Rutgers University Press.

Vasquez, John A. (1987). "The Steps to War: toward a Scientific Explanation of Correlates of War Findings." *World Politics*, **40**, 108–45.

Vasquez, John A. (1992). "Factors Related to the Contagion and Diffusion of International Violence." In *The Internationalization of Communal Strife*, Manus I. Midlarsky (ed.). London: Routledge.

Vasquez, John A. (1993). *The War Puzzle* (Cambridge Studies in International Relations: 27). Cambridge: Cambridge University Press.

Vassall-Adams, Guy (1994). *Rwanda: an Agenda for International Action*. Oxford: Oxfam Publications.

Verba, Sidney (1961). "Assumptions of Rationality and Non-rationality in Models of the International System." In *The International System: Theoretical Essays*, Klaus Knorr and Sidney Verba (eds). Princeton, NJ: Princeton University Press.

Vital, David (1969). "Back to Machiavelli." In *Contending Approaches to International Politics*, Klaus Knorr and James N. Rosenau (eds). Princeton, NJ: Princeton University Press.

Vobejda, Barbara (1997). "Love Conquers What Ails Teens, Study Finds." *Washington Post*, September 10, pp. A1, A10.

Volkan, Vamik D. (1985). "The Need to Have Enemies and Allies: a Developmental Approach." *Political Psychology*, **6**(2), 219–45.

Volkan, Vamik D. (1988). *The Need to Have Enemies and Allies: from Clinical Practice to International Relationships*. Northvale, NJ: Jason Aronson.

Volkan, Vamik D. (1991). "On Chosen Traumas." *Mind and Human Interaction*, **3**(1), p. 13.

Volkan, Vamik D. (1992). "Ethnonationalistic Rituals: an Introduction." *Mind and Human Interaction*, **4**(1), 3–19.

Volkan, Vamik D. and Norman Itzkowitz (1993). "Istanbul, not Constantinople: the Western World's View of 'the Turk'." *Mind and Human Interaction*, **4**(3), 129–34.

Volkan, Vamik D., Joseph V. Montville, and Demetrious A. Julius (eds) (1991a). *The Psychodynamics of International Relationships, Volume 1. Concepts and Theories*. Lexington, MA: Lexington Books.

Volkan, Vamik D., Joseph V. Montville, and Demetrious A. Julius (eds) (1991b). *The Psychodynamics of International Relationships, Volume 2. Unofficial Diplomacy at Work*. Lexington, MA: Lexington Books.

von Bertalanffy, Ludwig (1973). *General System Theory*. Harmondsworth: Penguin.

von Neumann, John and Oscar Morgenstern (1944). *Theory of Games and Economic Behavior*. Princeton, NJ: Princeton University Press.

Waldrop, M. Mitchell (1992). *Complexity: the Emerging Science at the Edge of Order and Chaos*. New York: Simon and Schuster.

Walker, Christopher J. (ed.) (1991). *Armenia and Karabagh: The Struggle for Unity*. London: Minority Rights Group.

Walker, Jennone (1993a). "European Regional Organizations and Ethnic Conflict." In *Central and Eastern Europe: The Challenge of Transition*, Regina Cowen Karp (ed.) (Stockholm International Peace Research Institute). Oxford: Oxford University Press.

Walker, Jenonne (1993b). "International Mediation of Ethnic Conflicts." *Survival*, **35**(1), 102–17.

Walker, Jenonne (1994). *Security and Arms Control in Post-confrontation Europe* (Stockholm International Peace Research Institute). Oxford: Oxford University Press.

Wallace, Michael D. (1972). "Status, Formal Organization, and Arms Levels as Factors Leading to the Onset of War, 1820–1964." In *Peace, War, and Numbers*, Bruce M. Russett (ed.). Beverly Hills, CA: Sage.

Wallace, Michael D. (1979). "Arms Races and Escalation: Some New Evidence." *Journal of Conflict Resolution*, **23**, 3–16.

Wallensteen, Peter and Karin Axell (1993). "Armed Conflicts at the End of the Cold War." *Journal of Peace Research*, **30**(3), 331–46.

Waltz, Kenneth N. (1959). *Man, the State, and War: a Theoretical Analysis*. New York: Columbia University Press.

Waltz, Kenneth N. (1964). "The Stability of a Bipolar World." *Daedalus*, **93**, 881–909.

Waltz, Kenneth N. (1967). "International Structure, National Force, and the Balance of World Power." *Journal of International Affairs*, **21**(2), 215–31.

Waltz, Kenneth N. (1979). *Theory of International Politics*. Reading, MA: Addison-Wesley.

Waltz, Kenneth N. (1989). "The Origins of War in Neorealist Theory." In *The Origin and Prevention of Major Wars*, Robert I. Rotberg and Theodore K. Rabb (eds). Cambridge: Cambridge University Press.

Wayman, Frank Whelon (1984). "Voices Prophesying War: Events and Perceptions as Indicators of Conflict Potential in the Middle East." In *Quantitative Indicators in World*

Politics: Timely Assistance and Early Warning, J. David Singer and Richard J. Stoll (eds). New York: Praeger.

Wedge, Bryant and Dennis J. D. Sandole (1982). "Conflict Management: a New Venture into Professionalization." *Peace and Change* (Special Issue on Conflict Resolution, ed. by Maire A. Dugan), **8**(2/3), 129–38.

Weede, Erich (1970). "Conflict Behavior among Nation-states." *Journal of Peace Research*, **7**, 229–35.

Weede, Erich (1973). "Nation–Environment Relations as Determinants of Hostilities Among Nations." *Peace Science Society (International), Papers*, **20**, 67–90.

Weede, Erich (1976). "National Position in World Politics and Military Allocation Ratios in the 1950s and 1960s: Assertions, Evidence, and Problems." Paper presented at the Tenth World Congress of the International Political Science Association, Edinburgh, August 16–21.

Week in Germany (1996). "German and Russian Politicians Welcome European Council's Vote to Accept Russia as a Member" (German Information Center, New York), February 2, p. 1.

Week in Germany (1997). "European Union Approves Plans for Expansion and 'Euro Club' at Luxembourg Summit" (German Information Center, New York), December 19, pp. 1, 2.

Weinberg, Steven (1992). *Dreams of a Final Theory*. New York: Pantheon Books.

White, John P. (1997). "Transforming the NATO Alliance for the 21st Century." *Wireless File*, U.S. Information Service, Embassy of the U.S.A., Vienna, no. 123, June 25, pp. 13–15.

Whitney, Craig R. (1996). "Bildt Full of Doubt on Bosnia's Future." *International Herald Tribune*, March 27, p. 2.

Wilkenfeld, Jonathan (1973). "Domestic and Foreign Conflict." In *Conflict Behavior and Linkage Politics*, Jonathan Wilkenfeld (ed.). New York: McKay.

Willetts, Peter (1978). *The Non-aligned Movement*. London: Frances Pinter.

Williams, Daniel (1994). "Russia Signs on with NATO in Peace Alliance." *International Herald Tribune*, June 23, pp. 1, 4.

Williams, Daniel (1996). "For 6 Bosnians, an 11-Month Ordeal of Terror and Survival: Fugitives from the Fall of Srebrenica." *International Herald Tribune*, April 10, p. 7.

Wilson, Edward O. (1979). *On Human Nature*. New York: Bantam Books.

Wilson, Edward O. (1998a). "Back from Chaos." *Atlantic Monthly*, **281**(3), 41–4, 46–9, 52, 54–6, 58–9, 62.

Wilson, Edward O. (1998b). *Consilience: the Unity of Knowledge*. New York: Knopf.

Winch, Peter (1958). *The Idea of a Social Science and Its Relation to Philosophy*. London: Routledge and Keegan Paul.

Winter, David G. (1976). "What Makes the Candidate Run?" *Psychology Today*, **10**(2), 32–9.

Wold, Herman and Lars Jureen (1953). *Demand Analysis*. New York: John Wiley.

Woodcock, Alexander and Monte Davis (1978). *Catastrophe Theory*. New York: E. P. Dutton.

Woodward, Susan L. (1995). *Balkan Tragedy: Chaos and Dissolution after the Cold War*. Washington, DC: The Brookings Institution.

WP (1993). "U.N. Troops in Former Yugoslavia." *Washington Post*, November 24, p. A14.

WP (1994). "Chechen Troops Seize Base of Kremlin-backed Opposition." *Washington Post*, September 6, p. A11.

WP (1998a). "NATO to Extend Bosnia Force's Stay Past June." *Washington Post*, February 19, p. A24.

WP (1998b). "Non-NATO Nations Approve Bosnia Extension." *Washington Post*, February 21, p. A13.

WP (1998c). "Serb Police, Ethnic Albanians in Deadly Clash." *Washington Post*, March 2, p. A12.

WP (1998d). "Background: the Kosovo Crisis." *Washington Post*, October 11, p. A39.

WP (1999). "Mr Milosevic's Massacre." *Washington Post*, January 18, p. A22.

Wrangham, Richard W. and Dale Peterson (1996). *Demonic Males: Apes and the Origins of Human Violence*. Boston: Houghton Mifflin.

Wright, John F. R., Suzanne Goldenberg, and Richard Schofield (eds) (1996). *Transcaucasian Boundaries*. London: UCL Press.

Wright, Quincy (1964). *A Study of War*, abridged edn. Chicago: University of Chicago Press (originally published as two volumes in 1942).

Wright, Robert (1995). "The Biology of Violence." *New Yorker*, March 13, pp. 68–77.

Yardley, Jonathan (1995). "Their Finest Hours" (Review of Philip Ziegler's *London at War*). *Washington Post Book World*, **25**(21), 3.

YIO (1997/8). *Yearbook of International Organizations 1997/98. Volume 1: Organization Descriptions*, 34th edn. Union of International Associations, Brussels (eds). Munich: K. G. Saur Verlag.

Zaagman, Rob and Joanne Thorburn (1997). *The Role of the High Commissioner on National Minorities in OSCE Conflict Prevention: an Introduction*. The Hague: The Foundation on Inter-ethnic Relations, June.

Zartman, I. William (1989). *Ripe for Resolution: Conflict and Intervention in Africa*, 2nd edn. New York: Oxford University Press.

Zeeman, E. C. (1977). *Catastrophe Theory: Selected Papers, 1972–1977*. Reading, MA: Addison-Wesley.

Ziegler, Philip (1995). *London at War, 1939–1945*. New York: Knopf.

Zinnes, Dina A. (1976). "The Problem of Cumulation." In *In Search of Global Patterns*, James N. Rosenau (ed.). New York: Free Press.

Zinnes, D. A., R. C. North and H. E. Koch, Jr. (1961). "Capability, Threat, and the Outbreak of War." In *International Politics and Foreign Policy: a Reader in Research and Theory*, James N. Rosenau (ed.). New York: Free Press.

Zucchino, David (1995). "Terror Rides Coattails of Chechyna War." *Philadelphia Inquirer*, August 4, pp. A1, A14.

Author Index

Subject Index